Celebrating Our Lord and Christ

Celebrating Our Lord and Christ

A Biblical Theology of Tongues

BRIAN W. LIDBECK

WIPF & STOCK · Eugene, Oregon

CELEBRATING OUR LORD AND CHRIST
A Biblical Theology of Tongues

Wipf & Stock
An Imprint of Wipf and Stock Publishers
199 W. 8th Ave., Suite 3
Eugene, OR 97401

www.wipfandstock.com

PAPERBACK ISBN: 979-8-3852-6706-4
HARDCOVER ISBN: 979-8-3852-6707-1
EBOOK ISBN: 979-8-3852-6708-8

VERSION NUMBER 04/09/26

To my students,
May your lives be a celebration of our Lord and Christ.

Contents

Acknowledgements

The initial work on this book began during my doctoral studies at the Assemblies of God Theological Seminary. Under the supervision of Dr. Douglas Oss, I began the research for a biblical theology of tongues in Acts. Dr. James Railey graciously allowed me to expand this work and write on tongues in the ending of Mark. Their guidance and enthusiasm during my initial work in 2013 to 2014 provided the encouragement to keep working and finally bring this project to completion.

Larry Brooks spent many hours pouring over the manuscript, checking Scripture references, correcting errors, and recommending improvements. The final product is in much better shape than it was because of his hard work.

Over the course of many years of teaching, my students have asked difficult and insightful questions about the Spirit and speaking in tongues. Their questions have motivated me to continue my research and find biblical answers to their questions. It is my sincere hope that my dear students will rejoice in the Christ-centered answers to their questions found in the pages of this book.

My wife, Diane, is the equal partner in bringing this work to fruition. Her sacrifices, constant encouragement, and daily prayers enable me to continue researching and writing. Anyone who comes to a greater appreciation of the christocentric nature of tongues will benefit from her prayers as much as my words.

Abbreviations

AB	Anchor Bible
AJPS	*Asian Journal of Pentecostal Studies*
ANF	*Ante-Nicene Fathers*. Edited by Alexander Roberts and James Donaldson. 1885–1887. 10 vols. Reprint, Peabody, MA: Hendrickson, 1994.
ASV	American Standard Version
AYB	Anchor Yale Bible
BBR	*Bulletin for Biblical Research*
BDAG	Bauer, Walter, Frederick W. Danker, W. F. Arndt, and F. W. Gingrich. *A Greek-English Lexicon of the New Testament and Other Early Christian Literature*. 3rd ed. University of Chicago Press, 2000.
BDF	Blass, Friedrich, and Albert Debrunner. *A Greek Grammar of the New Testament and Other Early Christian Literature*. Translated and revised by Robert. W. Funk. University of Chicago Press, 1961.
BECNT	Baker Exegetical Commentary on the New Testament
BHGNT	Baylor Handbook on the Greek New Testament
BNTC	Black's New Testament Commentaries
BQ	*The Baptist Quarterly*
BSac	*Bibliotheca Sacra*
BTNT	Biblical Theology of the New Testament
BZ	*Biblische Zeitschrift*

BZNW	Beihefte zur Zeitschrift für die neutestamentliche Wissenchaft
CCSS	Catholic Commentary on Sacred Scripture
CSB	Christian Standard Bible
CBC	*Catholic Biblical Quarterly*
CFTL	Clark's Foreign Theological Library
COQG	Christian Origins and the Question of God
EDNT	Balz, Horst, and Gerhard Schneider, eds. *Exegetical Dictionary of the New Testament*. 3 vols. Grand Rapids: Eerdmans, 1990–93.
EKKNT	Evangelisch-katholischer Kommentar zum Neuen Testament
ETL	*Ephemerides Theologicae Lovanienses*
ESV	English Standard Version
ET	English Text
HNTC	Harper's New Testament Commentaries
HThKNT	Herders Theologischer Kommentar zum Neuen Testament
HTS	Harvard Theological Studies
IBC	Interpretation: A Bible Commentary for Teaching and Preaching
ICC	The International Critical Commentary
IVPNTC	The IVP New Testament Commentary Series
JBL	*Journal of Biblical Literature*
JETS	*Journal of Evangelical Theological Society*
JPT	*Journal of Pentecostal Theology*
JPTSup	Journal of Pentecostal Theology Supplement Series
JSNT	*Journal for the Study of the New Testament*
JSNTSup	Journal for the Study of the New Testament Supplement Series
JTS	*The Journal of Theological Studies*

L&N	Louw, Johannes P. and Eugene A. Nida, eds. *Greek-English Lexicon of the New Testament Based on Semantic Domains*. 2 vols. New York: United Bible Societies, 1988.
LNTS	The Library of New Testament Studies
LSJ	Liddell, Henry George, and Robert Scott. *A Greek-English Lexicon*. Revised and edited by Henry Stuart Jones and Roderick McKenzie. Reprint, Oxford: Clarendon Press, 1985.
LXX	Septuagint
MT	Masoretic Text
NA28	*Novum Testamentum Graece*. Nestle-Aland 28th ed. Edited by Barbara Aland, Kurt Aland, Johannes Karavidopoulos, Carlo M. Martini, and Bruce Metzger. Stuttgart: Deutsche Bibelgesellschaft, 2012.
NAC	The New American Commentary
NASB	New American Standard Bible
NCBC	New Cambridge Bible Commentary
NCCS	New Covenant Commentary Series
NET	The New English Translation
NETS	A New English Translation of the Septuagint
NFTL	New Foundations Theological Library
NIBCNT	New International Biblical Commentary on the New Testament
NICNT	New International Commentary on the New Testament
NICOT	New International Commentary on the Old Testament
NIGTC	New International Greek Testament Commentary
NIV	New International Version
NJB	New Jerusalem Bible
NovT	*Novum Testamentum*

NPNF1	*Nicene and Post-Nicene Fathers*. First Series. Edited by Philip Schaff. 1886–1889. 14 vols. Reprint, Peabody, MA: Hendrickson, 1994.
NPNF2	*Nicene and Post-Nicene Fathers*. Second Series. Edited by Philip Schaff and Henry Wace. 1890–1900. 14 vols. Reprint, Peabody, MA: Hendrickson, 1994.
NRSV	New Revised Standard Version
NSBT	New Studies in Biblical Theology
NTC	New Testament Commentary
NTL	New Testament Library
NTS	*New Testaments Studies*
OTP	*The Old Testament Pseudepigrapha*. Edited by James H. Charlesworth. 2 vols. Peabody, MA: Hendrickson, 2011.
PBM	Paternoster Biblical Monographs
PCNT	Paideia Commentaries on the New Testament
PNTC	The Pillar New Testament Commentary
RSV	Revised Standard Version
RTR	*Reformed Theological Review*
SJT	*Scottish Journal of Theology*
SP	Sacra Pagina
SPCI	Studies in Pentecostal and Charismatic Issues
TDNT	*Theological Dictionary of the New Testament*. 10 vols. Edited by Gerhard Kittel and Gerhard Friedrich. Translated by G. W. Bromiley. Grand Rapids: Eerdmans, 1964–76.
TNTC	Tyndale New Testament Commentaries
TZ	*Theologische Zeitschrift*
UBC	Understanding the Bible Commentary
UBS5	*The Greek New Testament*. United Bible Societies 5th rev. ed. Edited by Barbara Aland, Kurt Aland,

	Johannes Karavidopoulos, Carlo M. Martini, and Bruce M. Metzger. Stuttgart: Deutsche Bibelgesellschaft, 2014.
WBC	Word Biblical Commentary
WTJ	*Westminister Theological Journal*
WUNT	Wissenchaftliche Untersuchungen zum Neuen Testament
ZAW	*Zeitschrift für die alttestamentliche Wissenschaft*
ZECNT	Zondervan Exegetical Commentary on the New Testament
ZNW	*Zeitschrift für die neutestamentliche Wissenschaft und die Kunde der älteren Kirche*

Introduction

One might justifiably ask whether or not the world needs another book that addresses the subject of speaking in tongues (also known as "glossolalia"), as the literature on this subject is already quite extensive.[1] Scholars have examined the subject from a variety of perspectives and covering various disciplines including exegesis, systematic theology,[2] practical theology, historical theology,[3] philosophy,[4] psychology,[5] and sociology.[6] Biblical studies have also tackled numerous thorny exegetical issues such as the relation of tongues to the story of Babel, the function of tongues in Acts compared to 1 Corinthians, the human or heavenly nature of tongues, and the connection between tongues and baptism in the Spirit. While this study addresses many of the difficult issues that have arisen, the primary purpose of this work is to examine the biblical passages on tongues in relation to Christology. The central thesis of this work is that the biblical texts containing a reference to glossolalia exhibit a strong connection between Christ's exaltation as Lord and the manifestation of this charism. It is hoped that this christological perspective will shed new light on several difficult exegetical issues and bring a more christocentric focus to the theology and practice of speaking in tongues.

1. Even as early as 1985 Watson Mills had included 1158 entries in his bibliography of works on tongues, and numerous publications have followed in the intervening years. Mills, *Glossolalia*, 23–121.

2. Grudem, *Systematic Theology*; Williams, *Renewal Theology*.

3. See Ackland, *Toward a Pentecostal Theology*; Burgess, *Christian Peoples of the Spirit*; Kelsey, *Tongue Speaking*, 32–68.

4. See Del Colle, "Postmodernism," 97–116; Smith, *Thinking in Tongues*.

5. See Kelsey, *Tongue Speaking*; Mills, *Speaking in Tongues*, 264–69; Mills, *A Theological/Exegetical Approach*, 88–94.

6. Watson Mills highlights some various approaches in his research guide. Mills, *Speaking in Tongues*.

Methodology

As the title of this work indicates, this is a biblical theology of tongues or glossolalia (I use the terms interchangeably).[7] As such, the study examines a variety of passages from both testaments, and while there are no occurrences of speaking in tongues in the Hebrew Scriptures, there are theological threads that have their origin there and come to a new stage of development in the New Testament. Each text that clearly refers to tongues receives in-depth, exegetical treatment, but this is accomplished with an eye on the broader biblical threads that are shared with other authors of the sacred text. This approach assumes that the biblical text has an underlying unity to it and that Christology is an essential element of that unity.

Many of the older studies on glossolalia expended considerable energy employing grammatical-historical methods to investigate the reliability of Lukan historiography,[8] to contrast the kinds of tongues in Paul's and Luke's writings, and to explain the supposed cessation of tongues. In more recent decades, Luke has benefited from studies demonstrating the theological nature of Acts as well as from those incorporating literary criticism as a means of grasping Luke's theology.[9] This work does not engage in criticizing Luke as a mere inventor of stories, but attempts to understand his theological intent in shaping his records of events in the early church. Consequently, this biblical-theological approach accepts the biblical books in their canonical form[10] and incorporates grammatical, historical, theological, and literary insights. Chapter three, in particular, uses the tools of literary criticism to understand the constellation of themes converging at Pentecost.

While this project benefits from the many significant works from other disciplines, this monograph does not attempt to delve into the

7. The term "glossolalia" does not actually occur in the biblical text but is a combination of the Greek terms γλῶσσα ("tongue") and λαλιά ("speech").

8. I agree with the general consensus that a single author wrote both the Gospel of Luke and Acts. I also believe that the author is most likely Luke the physician (Col 4:14).

9. Ju Hur emphasizes the necessity of incorporating literary criticism into Lukan studies: "In other words, this paradigm shift of biblical interpretation from 'historical' and 'theological' to 'literary' means that the author of Luke-Acts can be conceived not only as a 'historian' and 'theologian', but also as a (biblical literary) 'artist'." Hur, *A Dynamic Reading*, 29.

10. The textual issues regarding the longer ending of Mark will receive attention in Part 2.

areas of psychology or to provide an ecclesiastical history of speaking in tongues. However, the results of this study could have important implications for systematic and practical theology.

All biblical translations in this work are my own unless otherwise noted. When an English text is employed, it is often the English Standard Version or the New International Version.

Summary

This work contains three units of material consisting of a Lukan, Markan, and Pauline perspective on tongues. The Lukan unit has five chapters, and the first chapter introduces the kingdom context of Acts and suggests that tongues must be understood within the boundaries of Luke's emphasis on the kingdom and his intention to identify Jesus as the Lord and Christ.

The second chapter focuses on the occurrence of speaking in tongues in Acts 2. It emphasizes the importance of Acts 2:36 as the pinnacle of Peter's speech and examines the occurrence of tongues in light of the declaration of Jesus as Lord and Christ. The symbolism, nature, content, and orientation of tongues are highlighted in the discussion.

The third chapter approaches Acts 2 from a literary perspective. The discussion examines Luke's identification of certain themes related to the arrival of the Spirit in the Hebrew Scriptures. The argument proposes that Luke tailors his account of Pentecost to include a number of ancient themes, develops them in terms of the new era, and establishes a Pentecostal type-scene that serves as a lens for the arrival of the Spirit throughout Acts.

The fourth chapter considers the "gentile Pentecost" of Acts 10, compares it with Acts 2, and highlights the christological elements of the outpouring of the Spirit at Caesarea. The difficult grammar of Acts 10:36 and questions about the continuation and normativity of tongues receive attention.

The fifth chapter reviews the "Ephesian Pentecost" of Acts 19 in order to determine whether or not the occurrence of tongues in this passage shares the same christological emphasis as the tongues in Acts 2 and 10. The discussion addresses the issue of the spiritual condition of the Ephesian disciples and examines the lordship of Jesus in the land of Artemis.

The second unit covering the Markan perspective on tongues has two chapters. The textual issue in Mark 16:9–20 presents a considerable challenge to the exegete working through the charismatic signs in verses 17–18. Chapter six summarizes some of the recent scholarship on the Markan ending and then analyzes the arguments in light of contemporary findings. Chapter seven traces the charismatic elements of Mark's Gospel and finds some theological consistency between the body of the Gospel and the longer ending. The investigation looks at the christological elements in the longer ending and the possible background of the charismatic signs in the exodus narrative.

The third unit covers the Pauline perspective on tongues. A handful of Pauline passages that may point to the use of tongues receive some attention,[11] but the discussion primarily focuses on tongues in 1 Cor 12–14.[12] Chapter eight draws attention to the christological elements of Paul's argument and the confession that "Jesus is Lord" in 12:3. Chapter nine examines Paul's discussion of tongues in light of the christological analogy of the church as Christ's body (12:4—13:13). Chapter ten continues emphasizing the body of Christ in 1 Cor 14. It examines the corporate use of tongues in relation to prophecy, Paul's instruction on order and intelligibility, and the private use of tongues. Paul's reference to the lordship of Jesus in v. 37 is highlighted. Because of the alleged similarities between the tongues of 1 Cor 14 and the "groans" of Rom 8:26, the issue of a possible glossolalic understanding of the latter passage receives treatment here. I offer an interpretation but especially emphasize the christocentric context of the passage.

In the final chapter I present a synthesis of my findings from the three units and comment on the practical implications of this study. While some scholars have entirely dismissed the account in Mark 16 or have viewed the occurrences of tongues in Acts and 1 Corinthians as rather disparate accounts, I explore some common theological threads that unify the perspectives of Mark, Luke, and Paul. Chief among these threads is the lordship of Jesus Christ, which forms the context in which

11. For example, see Rom 8:26–27 (cf. 2 Cor 5:4); Eph 5:19; 6:18; Col 3:16; 1 Thess 5:19–21. Although not Pauline, Jude 20 is sometimes thought to refer to speaking in tongues as well. Menzies, *Speaking in Tongues*, 16n1. Morton Kelsey, a non practitioner, also sees allusions to tongues in Acts 4:23–32, Gal 4:6, and Rom 8:14–15. Kelsey, *Tongue Speaking*, 30–31.

12. Gordon Fee leans toward viewing Rom 8:26–27 as a reference to tongues. See Fee, *Listening to the Spirit*, 46–47. Douglas Moo thinks this identification is unlikely. See Moo, *Romans*, 524–26.

tongues function in Mark 16:17; Acts 2:4; 10:46; 19:6; and 1 Cor 12–14. It is my profound hope that readers will not simply view tongues in the New Testament as merely a matter of theological interest or controversy, but as a means of celebrating Jesus as Lord and Christ.

Part One

A Lukan Perspective on Tongues

1

The Kingdom Context of Pentecostal Tongues

THE SPEAKING IN TONGUES arrested the attention of many Jews in Jerusalem on the Day of Pentecost, and Luke's story continues to do so today, but the following discussion proposes that Pentecost is not primarily about the phenomenon of speaking in tongues; it is about the lordship of Jesus over every tongue. In this chapter I attempt to place the tongues of Pentecost in their broader christological context by highlighting the pinnacle of Peter's Pentecostal sermon (Jesus as Lord and Christ) and examining Luke's overall emphasis on the kingdom. Luke's kingdom language, his threefold designation of Jesus, and some of his key themes related to the kingdom and kingship of Jesus receive attention. Neglect of this kingdom context and the centrality of Jesus as Lord and Christ seriously impairs the study of tongues in Acts.

PENTECOST AS A KINGDOM EVENT

Most scholars see the commencement of Peter's sermon in Acts 2:14 as providing a natural break in the narrative after the Pentecostal outpouring. While Peter's address does mark a new stage in the development of the story, the reader should not forget that the sermon serves as an explanation to the question, "What does this mean?" (v. 12b).[1] In other words, the reader expects that the content of Peter's sermon will provide some explanation for this miraculous language event. All too often interpreters

1. Translations are my own unless otherwise noted.

seem to lose sight of the miracle that spawned the sermon, resulting in a treatment of Acts 2:1–13, with its other tongues, as if it were a separate story with little relationship to the themes that follow.[2]

Peter's sermon contains several elements that alert the reader that he or she has been drawn into a story about the advancing of God's kingdom. The outpouring of the Spirit, and even just the mention of the Spirit, induces one to consider that God's kingdom is in view (Acts 2:4, 17, 18, 33, 38, 39).[3] Jesus has already taught the disciples to pray, "Let your kingdom come," (Luke 11:2b) and then identified the central focus of prayer in the same passage: "How much more will the Father from heaven give the Holy Spirit to those who ask him" (v. 13b). Peter quotes Joel's prediction of an outpouring of the Spirit, and Luke records enough of the citation to include the "day of the Lord" reference and an invitation to call on "the name of the Lord" (Acts 2:17–21). It is very likely that Luke intends the latter mention of "Lord" to refer to Jesus, and this royal attribution along with the heavy eschatological language of the "last days" (v. 17), the outpouring of the Spirit, the miraculous and apocalyptic signs, and the provision of salvation conveys a strong sense that the atmosphere of Pentecost was infused with the reality of the kingdom.

This kingdom context is made even more obvious in Peter's mention of David three times (Acts 2:25, 29, 34) and in quotations from the Psalms that use royal language. Peter paraphrases Ps 131:11 (LXX) and refers to a Davidic descendent who would sit on the throne (v. 30). Peter also refers to Jesus as "being exalted to the right hand of God" (v. 33a) as the "Lord" who would sit at God's right hand (v. 34) and reign over his enemies (v. 35; cf. Ps 110:1). The resurrection features prominently in this kingdom sermon, as the resurrection is viewed not merely as a

2. Dale Bruner rightly recognizes the christocentric nature of Pentecost when he comments, "In the center of Luke's attention at Pentecost—even quantitatively—is not what we usually think when we say 'Pentecost,' i.e., the Spirit, it is Jesus Christ; not spiritual ecstasy, but a Christian sermon." Bruner highlights the christocentric nature of Pentecost in order to refute Pentecostal teaching, but, ironically, he repeats the common error of bifurcating Pentecost into a tongues text and then a christological text. However, I argue throughout this work that a christocentric understanding of the entire Pentecostal event does not help a cessationistic perspective but properly contextualizes Pentecost and reinforces a continuationist position. Bruner, *A Theology of the Holy Spirit*, 165. David Peterson takes a more balanced position than Bruner and recognizes that Peter's sermon interprets the events of Acts 2:1–11 and explains the significance of Christ. Peterson, *Acts*, 138–39.

3. Several Old Testament passages contributed to the expectation of an outpouring of the Spirit in an eschatological kingdom (e.g., Num 11:29; Isa 44:3; 59:21; 61:1–2).

resuscitation, but as an act of enthronement (Acts 2:24–33).[4] All this royal language comes to a climax in the final sentence of Peter's speech before he is interrupted by the narrator's comments and the audience's response: "Therefore let all the house of Israel know for certain that God made him both Lord and Christ [κύριον αὐτὸν καὶ χριστὸν], this Jesus whom you crucified" (v. 36). In the Greek text, "Lord and Christ" precedes the clause's subject and verb for added emphasis. In this manner the identification of Jesus as Lord and Christ serves as the primary point of the sermon upon which the response of salvation depends. Therefore, one cannot fully comprehend the significance of speaking in tongues without also contemplating the kingdom and the identity of Jesus as the King. Acts 2 will receive more detailed attention later, but first it is necessary to demonstrate how this kingdom focus is consistent throughout Luke's two volumes and provides the context for speaking in tongues.

Luke's Kingdom Focus

The kingdom concept in Luke's two volumes is ubiquitous and encompasses virtually every theme and aspect of his writing.[5] The following discussion reviews Luke's kingdom language, literary features, and themes that draw the reader's attention to the kingdom and its King.

Luke's Kingdom Language

Royal terms alone do not capture the breadth of Luke's emphasis on the kingdom, but he often refers to the kingdom with the usual terms. He employs "kingdom" (βασιλεία) forty-six times in his Gospel and eight times in Acts.[6] Luke never uses the phrase "kingdom of heaven" as Matthew often does, but he mentions the "kingdom of God" thirty-two times in Luke and six times in Acts. Luke employs the verb "to reign" (βασιλεύω) in reference to Jesus (Luke 1:33; 19:14, 27), and none of the other gospel writers use it except for in one allusion to Archelaus (Matt 2:22). Luke also refers to Jesus as the "king" (βασιλεύς) five times (Luke

4. For resurrection as an act of enthronement, see Lidbeck, *Resurrection and Spirit*, 108–16; and Brueggemann, "From Dust to Kingship," 1–18.

5. A. R. C. Leaney heavily emphasizes the reign of Christ in his commentary. Leaney, *Gospel According to St. Luke*, 34–37.

6. Matthew has the most references to βασιλεία with fifty-five; twelve of those occur in the parables in chapter 13. Mark uses the term twenty times and John five times.

19:38; 23:2, 37, 38; Acts 17:7) and to David as "king" on one occasion (Acts 13:22). The mention of David also has obvious royal significance in Luke's writings (cf. 2 Sam 7:12–16), and Luke names him thirteen times in the Gospel and eleven times in Acts.[7] David is only mentioned once in the body of Luke's Gospel (6:3), but the clustering of the Davidic references around Jesus' birth and his approach to Jerusalem have strong christological implications. The christological element is also significant in Acts, where the majority of occurrences appear around Pentecost or in Paul's sermon at Pisidian Antioch (Acts 13), which intentionally mirrors the themes addressed in Peter's Pentecostal sermon.

Luke expends considerable energy demonstrating the royal status of Jesus in this new stage of the kingdom. In doing so, he applies several exalted titles to Jesus, but the central focus in Acts 2 is his identification of Jesus as Lord and Christ.[8] The "Christ" (Χριστός) term appears a dozen times in Luke's Gospel, especially in relation to the Passion and resurrection narratives and focusing on Jesus' identity (22:67; 23:2, 35, 39; 24:26, 46). It appears another twenty-five times in Acts. The royal connotations of the term are evident in Luke's narrative, as he connects the title with "kingdom" (Acts 8:12; 28:31), Jesus' identity as "king" (Luke 23:2), and David (2:11; 20:41). In Luke 20:41, Jesus asks, "How can they say that the Christ is David's son?" He then quotes Ps 110:1, which refers to David's son, with the term "Lord" and shows that there was a long tradition of expecting a royal "messiah" or "anointed one" (מָשִׁיחַ; cf. Ps 2:2; Dan 9:25). Some strands of intertestamental literature also evince such an expectation (Pss. Sol. 17–18; 1 En. 48.10; 52.4; 55.4; 4Q521 2 II, 1–12).

By far the most common designation for Jesus in Luke-Acts is "Lord" (κύριος). Of the 211 occurrences of the term, only a few do not refer to divinity,[9] and about two thirds of the rest refer to Jesus (approximately 135x). A precise count is difficult due to textual variants, challenges ascertaining the identity of characters in parables, and ambiguity

7. Luke 1:27, 32, 69; 2:4 (2x), 11; 3:31; 6:3; 18:38, 39; 20:41, 42, 44; Acts 1:16; 2:25, 29, 34; 4:25; 7:45; 13:22 (2x), 34, 36; 15:16.

8. Other christological titles such as "Son of God" (Luke 1:35; 4:41; 22:70), "Son of man" (6:5; 9:22, 26; 22:69), and "Chosen One" (9:35; 23:35) are related to the kingdom. The latter expression also has ties to David, as Jesus' mockers echo the words of Ps 22:8 at the crucifixion. In addition, the expression is reminiscent of God's choice of David in 1 Sam 16:6–13. For an overview of various perspectives on the nature of Luke's Christology, see Buckwalter, *Character and Purpose*, 3–31.

9. These are best translated as "sir" or "master." E.g., Luke 19:33; Acts 10:4; 16:16, 19, 30; 25:26.

between the Lord Jesus and Lord God.[10] However, Luke's lack of clarity on the latter issue at several points strengthens the case for the divine identity of Jesus.[11] The ease with which he applies "Lord" to both and often without distinction suggests that this is done intentionally to draw attention to the divine status of Jesus. The preferred term for translating the Tetragrammaton in the Septuagint was "Lord" (κύριος), and the term had royal connotations there (e.g., Deut 9:26; 1 Sam 8:6–7; Ps 5:1–4; 23:7–10; Isa 6:5). The Roman rulers of the New Testament period were also often referred to as "Lord."[12]

Luke uses the birth narratives in his Gospel to immediately focus the reader's attention on his key interests.[13] Luke employs a great deal of kingdom language and emphasizes the Davidic descent of Jesus in order to identify Jesus as the long-awaited King. Joseph is from the "house of David" (Luke 1:27), God will give Mary's infant the "throne of David" (v. 32), God has "raised up a horn of salvation in the house of his servant David" (v. 69), Bethlehem is "the city of David" (2:4), Joseph is from "the house and family of David" (v. 4), and "a Savior who is Christ the Lord" is born in the "city of David" (v. 11).

The final chapters of Luke's Gospel also incorporate numerous royal terms, as Luke explains to Theophilus the messianic identity of Jesus and prepares for the kingdom's advance in Acts. Luke highlights Jesus as the Davidic Lord (20:41–4), the risen Lord (24:3, 34), the eschatological banquet host (22:16, 18) and kingdom proprietor (22:29, 30; 23:42), "the Son of Man" (21:27, 36; 22:22, 48, 69; 24:7), "Son of God" (22:70), the "Christ" (22:67; 23:2, 35, 39; 24:26, 46), and the king of the Jews (23:2, 3, 37, 38). Karl Kuhn sees a strong conceptual link between Luke 1–2 and Luke 24: "All the dimensions of the worldview that Luke presents in his opening chapters are recapitulated here in Luke 24."[14] He sees these

10. Consider the following examples where identification of the "Lord" in mind is not entirely certain: Luke 1:76; 3:4; Acts 1:24; 2:20, 47; 5:9; 8:22, 24, 39; 9:31; 10:14, 33; 11:8; 12:7, 11, 17, 23; 13:2, 10, 11, 12, 44, 47, 48, 49; 15:35, 36, 40; 16:14, 15; 19:10, 20; 20:19.

11. Buckwalter, *Character and Purpose*, 186; Kuhn, *Kingdom*, 175. On the divinity of Jesus in Luke-Acts, see Henrichs-Tarasenkova, *Luke's Christology*; and Witherington, *Acts*, 147–53.

12. Examples include Augustus, Tiberius, Nero, and Vespasion. Foerster, "κύριος," 1054–57, especially 1055n70.

13. Tannehill, *Narrative Unity*, 1:20–21.

14. Kuhn, *Kingdom*, 147.

chapters as forming an "interpretive frame" for Luke's Gospel.[15] It is certainly no accident that the kingdom is prominent in the opening and closing chapters of the Gospel of Luke.

Various scholars have also noted a kingdom frame around Acts, with "kingdom" occurring twice in the opening verses (1:3, 6) and twice in the closing chapter (28:23, 31).[16] The frame, along with the Davidic emphasis in Acts 2, proclamation of the kingdom of God in Acts,[17] and the content of Jesus' teaching for forty days as "concerning the kingdom of God" (1:3),[18] suggests that the entire narrative of Acts concerns the kingdom and the royal Christ—even when overt kingdom language is not apparent.[19] The kingdom phrase in 1:3 also summarizes Jesus' pre-ascension instruction to his disciples in Luke 24. The christocentric nature of that discussion ties the kingdom concept directly to Jesus and his resurrection. Robert Tannehill well summarizes the significance of this in relation to Pentecost: "Having been instructed in 'the things concerning the kingdom of God,' Peter proclaims Jesus as the Messiah seated on David's throne and the Lord seated at God's right hand in fulfillment of Scripture (Acts 2:30–36). The Davidic Messianism of the Lukan birth story, which carries with it the imagery of Jesus as King and Lord (Luke 1:32–33; 2:11), reappears in the Pentecost speech. Thus the 'reign of God' includes the reign of Jesus as Messiah in Acts."[20] One might say that the kingdom of God in Luke–Acts is also the kingdom "of our Lord and of his Christ" (Rev 11:15).

15. Kuhn, *Kingdom*, 148.

16. E.g., Fitzmyer, *Acts*, 203n3; Keener, *Acts: Exegetical*, 1:670; Polhill, *Acts*, 82; Thompson, *Acts of the Risen Lord*, 44.

17. The phrase "the kingdom of God" (ἡ βασιλεία τοῦ θεοῦ) in Acts relates to its proclamation. See variations of the phrase in Acts 1:3, 8:12; 14:22; 19:8; 20:25; 28:23, 31.

18. See the more detailed discussion of how Luke connects Acts 1 and Luke 24 to emphasize the christocentric nature of the kingdom proclamation in Lidbeck, *Resurrection and Spirit*, 131–35.

19. Robert O'Toole observes, "Luke speaks of Jesus and the kingdom of God together (Acts 8:12; 28:23, 31); he probably does not intend two different realities, but is rather using one of his favorite literary devices, a double expression, and is simply repeating the one idea in the other." O'Toole, "The Kingdom of God," 151.

20. Tannehill, *Narrative Unity*, 2:13.

Luke's Threefold Designation of Jesus

Luke's interest in demonstrating the messianic and royal identity of Jesus is evident throughout Luke-Acts, but Luke applies a threefold identification of Jesus on six occasions that highlights the saving, royal, and pneumatic aspects of his identity.[21] In Luke 2:11 the angel announces that the newborn babe is "a Savior who is Christ the Lord." At Pentecost Peter declares that "God made him both Lord and Christ, this Jesus whom you crucified" (Acts 2:36). Peter commences his sermon at Cornelius's home by asserting that the good news of peace comes "through Jesus Christ—he is Lord of all" (Acts 10:36). Peter defends his actions at Cornelius's home by claiming that the same baptism with the Holy Spirit applied to the gentiles was first experienced by those at Pentecost "who believed on the Lord Jesus Christ" (Acts 11:17). At the Jerusalem council Paul and Barnabas were commended as men who had risked their lives "for the name of our Lord Jesus Christ" (Acts 15:26). Luke closes Acts with Paul continuing to teach "the things concerning the Lord Jesus Christ" (Acts 28:31). The strategic location of these six triads at the most crucial turning points in Luke-Acts suggests that the full identification of Jesus has both structural and theological significance for Luke.

In the crucial birth narrative, Luke emphasizes the importance of this royal figure proclaimed by the angel in several ways. First, the piling up of the terms "Savior," "Christ," and "Lord" is, in itself, an emphatic statement about Jesus' identity (Luke 2:11). In addition, several other terms that have considerable theological significance surround the announcement. Luke specifies the location as the city of "David" and the timing of the birth as "today"—a term that often has saving significance in Luke-Acts (Luke 4:21; 19:5, 9; 23:42–43; Acts 13:33).[22] He uses his favorite expression for the Jewish "people" (λαός) while hinting at the universal scope of the message in "all the people" (Luke 2:10). The proclamation of the "good news" (εὐαγγελίζομαι) is one of "joy" (v. 10) and the angelic chorus proclaims "peace [εἰρήνη] among men of God's pleasure" (v. 14).[23]

21. For more on the threefold designation of Jesus in Luke-Acts, see Lidbeck, *Resurrection and Spirit*, 82–83, 120–23.

22. Bock notes that the term relates to "special acts of God" in the Lukan plan of salvation. Bock, *Theology of Luke and Acts*, 135.

23. For a discussion of Luke's use of "peace" (εἰρήνη), see Mittelstadt, "Spirit and Peace."

Second, the location of the "Savior who is Christ the Lord" in the birth narratives and toward the beginning of Luke's two volumes heightens the prominence of this declaration. Third, the magnitude of the announcement is accentuated by the employment of an angelic messenger. Along with the previous angelic appearances to Elizabeth and Zechariah, the narrative capitalizes on an ancient tradition of drawing attention to significant moments and personages in history by incorporating an announcement from an angelic being (e.g., Gen 18:1–15; 32:22–32; Judg 13). Fourth, not only does an angel announce the identity of the newborn babe, but an angelic host praises God because of the event (Luke 2:13–14). The titles of Jesus rest comfortably between the angelic appearances. Finally, the "glory of the Lord" (δόξα κυρίου; v. 9) and "glory [δόξα] to God in the highest" (v. 14) phrases surround the christological titles and inspire a sense of awe. The adjective "great" (μέγας) adds to the grandeur of the announcement, as the "great fear" (v. 9) of the shepherds turns to good news of "great joy" (v. 10).

The christological thrust of the birth announcement looms large over the entire narrative of Luke-Acts, and the threefold identification of the Savior in Peter's sermon at Pentecost serves to reassert what Luke has already established. The strategic placement of "Lord and Christ, this Jesus" (Acts 2:36) at the pinnacle of the sermon alerts the reader that the focal point of Pentecost is the royal identity of Jesus and not the various manifestations of his presence. In short, this christological focus helps the reader see that the miraculous languages glorify Jesus, not that Jesus glorifies the miraculous languages. Consequently, when Peter begins to preach at Cornelius's home, he starts with the messianic identification: "Jesus Christ: this one is Lord of all" (Acts 10:36; cf. 11:17). The designation occurs at an event of enormous significance, and the miraculous tongues break forth under the banner of Jesus' lordship over the gentiles. The charismatic manifestation occurs in the context of Christ. The triad occurs again at the Jerusalem Council because of the similar issues raised regarding the status of gentiles. Thus, the triad of terms is preceded by the plural "our," and both gentiles and Jews are included in "our Lord Jesus Christ" (15:26).

Just as the initial triad in Luke 2:11 is highly significant, so Luke's ending in Acts 28 confirms the importance of this phrase and caps Luke's two volumes with a christocentric conclusion. Paul received visitors while in custody in Rome, and he continued "preaching the kingdom of God and teaching the things concerning [περὶ] the Lord Jesus Christ with all boldness, unhindered" (v. 31). The ending is revealing for several reasons. This conclusion repeats the phrase "kingdom of God" (v. 23) and makes it the object of the proclamation in both cases. In the earlier passage Paul entertains Jewish guests, explaining to them and "solemnly testifying [διαμαρτυρόμενος] about the kingdom of God and persuading them concerning [περὶ] Jesus from both the Law of Moses and the prophets" (v. 23). The double reference to the kingdom of God combines with the christological triad to emphasize the kingdom metanarrative of Luke-Acts and the centrality of Jesus as the King. Both passages show the strong affinity between the kingdom message and the person of Jesus by using parallelism. In verse 23, to testify about the kingdom is to persuade the auditors about Jesus. In verse 31, to preach the kingdom is to teach about the Lord Jesus Christ.

Luke's employment of the compound verb διαμαρτύρομαι ("to solemnly testify") draws attention to the urgency of the proclamation about Jesus. Luke can claim ten of the fifteen occurrences of the verb in the New Testament,[24] and some of those relate directly to earnest testimony about the identity of Jesus. The term is used in summary fashion at Pentecost (Acts 2:40) and by Peter at Cornelius's home: "And he commanded us to preach to the people [τῷ λαῷ] and to solemnly testify [διαμαρτύρασθαι] that he is the one who has been appointed by God as judge of the living and the dead" (10:42).[25] These passages highlight Jesus' exalted identity, and this trend continues at Corinth, where "Paul was utterly consumed with the word, solemnly testifying [διαμαρτυρόμενος] to the Jews that Jesus is the Christ" (18:5).

Although the context of the birth narrative in Luke 2:11 differs from the conclusion of Acts, some important commonalities between the texts point to an intentional structure. The angel's announcement of joy "for all the people" (παντὶ τῷ λαῷ) points first to the Jewish people and then hints at a universal gospel (v. 10; cf. 2:32). Likewise, the ending of Acts pictures Paul pleading with the Jewish people but quoting Isaiah regarding the hardness of heart "of this people [τοῦ λαοῦ τούτου]" (Acts 28:27; Isa 6:10 LXX).[26] However, the gentiles will hear the message of

24. Luke 16:28; Acts 2:40; 8:25; 10:42; 18:5; 20:21, 23, 24; 23:11; 28:23.

25. Keener rightly observes that λαός is a term for the people of Israel in Luke-Acts. Keener, *Acts*, NCBC, 304. Perhaps this slight hesitation of Peter to include all people partially explains the outpouring of the Spirit apart from human agency.

26. The quotation also begins with a command to "go to this people" (Isa 6:9; Acts 28:26).

"salvation" (σωτήριον; Acts 28:28), in keeping with the arrival of a "Savior" (σωτὴρ) in Luke 2:11. In addition, the arrival of the kingdom in Jesus is anticipated by the Law of Moses and the Prophets (Acts 28:23), just as Luke demonstrates on numerous occasions and records in detail in the birth narratives.

The overall effect of Luke's strategic placement of the threefold designation at the beginning of the Gospel, the end of Acts, and at key turning points in the discussion is to focus the reader's attention on the identity of Jesus as the King of this new phase of God's kingdom. Jew and gentile alike must acknowledge who he is and respond to him in faith. This larger issue of Jesus' identity is a central element in the sermons of Peter at Pentecost and at Caesarea. Consequently, any understanding of the tongues in those passages that does not consider this context will be significantly impaired.

The Kingdom, the King, and Lukan Themes

In order to confirm that the manifestion of tongues in Acts occurs within a broader context of the kingdom and the identification of its King, the following discussion reviews the relationship between the kingdom and some prominent themes in Luke-Acts. While a detailed discussion of each theme exceeds the scope of this work, I offer examples of how the themes connect to the kingdom theme and how they center on the Lord Jesus. The discussion highlights the kingdom and the Scriptures, the kingdom's progress, the kingdom and salvation, and the kingdom's ethics and praxis.

Luke refers to a variety of Hebrew Scriptures, both presupposing their christocentric nature and demonstrating their fulfillment in Jesus (e.g., Luke 24:25–27, 44–49). On thirty-four occasions Luke uses γραφή ("writing," "Scripture") or its cognate verb in reference to all or a portion of the Old Testament or in a formula introducing a quotation. Sometimes the phrase ἐν βίβλῳ ("in the book of") accompanies a citation (Luke 3:4; 20:42; Acts 1:20; 7:42);[27] other times the νόμος ("law") occurs in combination with the γραφή word group (Luke 2:23; 10:26). Luke refers to

27. In Luke 20:42 there is no mention of "Scripture," but Luke introduces his reference with "in the book of Psalms." Conzelmann is right to point out that the use of this phrase as an introductory formula is particular to Luke. However, the same phrase with an additional article is not unknown in the New Testament (Mark 12:26) and in the Septuagint (Tob(S) 7:13). Conzelmann, *Theology of St. Luke*, 158.

the Law alone as a category of Scripture about seventeen times, three of them adding the qualifier "of Moses" (Luke 2:22; Acts 13:38; 15:5). He also refers to "the Law and the Prophets" (Luke 16:16; Acts 13:15; 24:14; 28:23)[28] and "the Law of Moses, and the Prophets and Psalms" (Luke 24:44). In addition, Luke uses προφήτης ("prophet") and its cognates about thirty times in reference to Old Testament prophets as authors of Scripture.[29] Luke also refers to the Scriptures in a general manner on several occasions.[30]

Luke and Acts incorporate numerous references to Isaiah[31] and portray both Moses and Elijah as pattern characters fulfilled in Jesus, although David remains the primary model for Luke's Christology in the crucial birth narratives.[32] Even the programmatic text of Luke 4:18–19, which is drawn from Isaiah (58:6; 61:1–2), builds on the identification of Jesus as the Davidic Messiah (Luke 2:11, 26) when Jesus claims to be anointed by the Spirit: "The Spirit of the Lord is upon me, because he anointed me [οὗ εἵνεκεν ἔχρισέν με]" (4:18a). This Davidic pattern is part of the biblical metanarrative of the promise of a seed (Gen 3:15; 17:6; 35:11; 49:8–12; 2 Sam 7:12; cf. Ps 132:11–12) that Luke highlights especially in the lives of Abraham and David (Luke 1:54–55; 68–73).[33]

It is important to emphasize that Luke views the concept of the kingdom as a continuation of the Hebrew Scriptures and not as a novelty. The phrase "kingdom of God" has its closest counterpart in 1 Chr 28:5, where David reviews Solomon's accession "to sit on the throne of the kingdom of Yahweh [מַלְכוּת יְהוָה] over Israel." Similar references to Yahweh's kingdom occur in Pss 103:19; 145:11, 12, 13; and 1 Chr 17:14, where personal pronouns are used to describe his kingdom.[34] Balaam

28. Luke also substitutes "Moses" for "Law" and speaks of "Moses and the Prophets" (Luke 16:29, 31; Acts 26:22).

29. Luke 1:70; 3:4; 4:17; 16:16, 29, 31; 18:31; 24:25, 27, 44; Acts 2:16; 3:18, 21, 24, 25; 7:42, 48; 8:28, 30, 34; 10:43; 13:15, 27, 40; 15:15; 24:14; 26:22, 27; 28:23, 25.

30. Luke 16:16–17, 29–31; 18:31–33; 21:22; 24:25–27, 32, 44–48; Acts 3:18, 24; 8:35; 10:43; 13:15, 29; 17:2–3, 11; 18:24, 28; 24:14; 26:22–23; 28:23.

31. See Pao, *Acts*.

32. Neither Moses nor the giving of the law at Sinai serve as the main models for Luke's saving message in the birth narratives. Luke does not mention Moses or the law except to establish the obedient character of Joseph and Mary (2:21–24, 27, 39) and Zechariah and Elizabeth (1:5–6). See O'Toole, "Acts 2:30," 250.

33. See the more detailed discussion in Lidbeck, *Resurrection and Spirit*, 123–27.

34. Patrick also notices these and points out some similar constructions in 1 Chr 29:11, Ps 22:28, and Obad 21. Patrick, "Kingdom of God," 72.

prophesies a future time when Israel's "king shall be higher than Agag, and his kingdom shall be exalted" (Num 24:7b ESV). Yahweh has a kingdom, and so will his Messiah. The kingdom (מַלְכוּת) of a Davidic son is anticipated in 1 Chr 17:11 and 22:10. Although the "kingdom of God" phraseology is not common in the Hebrew Scriptures, the concept of God as sovereign King who has dominion over all (Ps 47:7; 95:3; Jer 10:7; Dan 4:34, 37; Mal 1:14),[35] including his own people (Isa 43:15; 44:6; Zeph 3:15), is not uncommon.[36] He is "Yahweh the King" in Ps 98:6 and "the King, Lord of Hosts" (אֶת־הַמֶּלֶךְ יְהוָה צְבָאוֹת) in Isa 6:5 (cf. Jer 46:18; 48:15; 51:57). In the future the Messiah will also be a King (Ps 2:6, 9; Ezek 37:24; Hos 3:5; Zech 9:9–10) who will reign (Ps 110; Isa 9:7; Ezek 34:24; Dan 7:13–14; Zech 6:12–13) in the line of David (Ps 16:8–11; 89:3–4, 29, 35–37; Isa 11:1).

Judaism also embraces the notion of God as King, as is evident in the Sibylline Oracles,[37] 1 Enoch,[38] 2 Maccabees (1:24; 7:9), 3 Maccabees (2:2, 9, 13), and Sirach (51:1), as well as in other places. The War Scroll of Qumran also evinces the Jewish familiarity with the notion of God as King and as having a kingdom (1QM XII, 6–7; cf. 4Q246).[39] First Enoch also anticipates the coming of a Davidic Messiah (48.10; 52.4) who will be empowered by the Spirit (49.2–3) and have a glorious reign (55.4).[40] The psalmist in the Psalms of Solomon bemoans the ungodliness of Israel and reminds God of his promises to David of an eternal kingdom (17.4–6). He prays that the Lord will "raise up for them their king, the son of David, to rule over your servant Israel" (17.21). He confidently affirms, "And he will be a righteous king over them, taught by God. There will be no unrighteousness among them in his days, for all shall be holy, and their king shall be the Lord Messiah [χριστὸς κύριος]" (17.32).[41] The

35. See the celebration of God's reign in Pss 96–99.

36. Ridderbos speaks of God's "general and particular" kingship in the Old Testament. Ridderbos, *Coming of the Kingdom*, 4.

37. E.g., Sib. Or. 1.8, 73; 2.347; 3.56, 499, 616, 717, 808. See the discussion of the kingdom of God in the Sybilline Oracles in Collins, "Kingdom of God," 84–87.

38. 1 En. 9.4; 12.3; 25.3, 5, 7; 27.3; 97.5.

39. Viviano, "Kingdom of God," 101.

40. The allusion to Isa 11:2 in 1 En. 49.2–3 suggests that the writer was very familiar with the expectation of a Spirit-filled, Davidic Messiah. See the discussion in Lidbeck, *Resurrection and Spirit*, 147–149.

41. Translation by R. B. Wright, who points out that "there is no textual evidence" for emending κύριος to a genitive case. Wright, "Psalms of Solomon," 667nz.

latter expression is identical to Luke's "Christ the Lord" (χριστὸς κύριος) who would be born in the city of David (Luke 2:11).

The expectation of a royal, Davidic messiah is evident in the Dead Sea Scrolls. The Genesis Commentary on 49:10 refers to the Davidic ruler mentioned in Jer 33:17 and then continues, "For the ruler's staff (xlix, 10) is the Covenant of kingship, [and the clans] of Israel are the divisions, until the Messiah of Righteousness comes, the Branch of David. For to him and his seed is granted the Covenant of kingship over his people for everlasting generations which he is to keep" (4Q252 V, 1–6).[42] Another Qumran manuscript gives instruction on blessing the messiah. The scroll anticipates "the Prince of the Congregation" who will establish an eternal kingdom (line 20), and this messiah is described in terminology reflecting Isa 11:1–5 (1QSb V, 20–29). Another fragment from Qumran describes a "Messiah" (line 1); an "eternal Kingdom" (line 6); healing and resurrection (line 11); and "good news" (line 11; 4Q521 Fr. 2, II, 1–12). As Geza Vermes notes, "As in the Gospels, healing and resurrection are linked to the idea of the Kingdom of God."[43] Other passages from the Dead Sea Scrolls anticipate a messiah, but the picture gets more complex when the Scrolls envision two future messiahs.[44]

When one looks at the hope of a Davidic king in the Hebrew Scriptures and in intertestamental Judaism, it becomes evident that Luke taps into an expectation that is both ancient and current among the Jewish people. The new element in the proclamation of the kingdom in Luke-Acts is not the concept of a Davidic king or primarily even the kingdom language. The new revelation is the inauguration of the anticipated kingdom in Jesus and the identity of Jesus as its King.[45]

The progress of the gospel in Luke-Acts is manifestly the progress of the kingdom. The "kingdom of God" is the object of proclamation or teaching seven times in the Gospel of Luke (4:43; 8:1; 9:2, 11, 60; 10:9; 16:16) and five times in Acts (1:3; 8:12; 19:8; 28:23, 31).[46] The first reference is important because Jesus summarizes his ministry of preaching the

42. Quotation is from Vermes, *Complete Dead Sea Scrolls*, 494.

43. Vermes, *Complete Dead Sea Scrolls*, 412.

44 I agree with Van Henten that 11Q13 (concerning Melchizedek) refers to the Messiah of Dan 9:25. Van Henten, "The Hasmonean Period," 23. The following passages may have two messiahs in view: CD VII, 19–20; CD B II, 1; CD XII, 22; CD XIII, 20; CD XIV 19; 1QS IX, 10; 1QSa II, 11–22; 4Q174, 10–13; 4Q175.See the discussion in Van Henten, 21–28.

45. See a similar observation in Ridderbos, *Coming of the Kingdom*, 3.

46. The shorter "kingdom" is preached in Acts 20:25.

good news of the kingdom of God as the reason he was sent. This passage links to the programmatic passage of Luke 4:18–19, and the frame essentially identifies Jesus' entire charismatic ministry as one of spreading the kingdom. Luke even places "the kingdom of God" and "the name of Jesus Christ" as parallel objects of the gospel proclamation in Acts 8:12. In Acts, to preach the kingdom is to preach Jesus.[47] In Acts 1:6 the disciples enquire about the timing of the restoration of the kingdom "to Israel," but Jesus refocuses their attention from limitation to expansion and their assignment to testify about him to the "end of the earth" (v. 8). Luke has a habit of recording the numerical expansion of the church,[48] and in Thessalonica he reports the addition of significant numbers of God fearers and several leading women (Acts 17:4). After Paul successfully persuades some that the Scriptures teach that the Messiah must rise from the dead and that Jesus is this Messiah (v. 3), some troublemakers accuse the believers of claiming that there is another king than Caesar—Jesus. The accusation of treason, although offered by a malicious or at least confused mob, is a serious one. Nevertheless, Luke apparently intends his readers to see the irony in it—Jesus is another King, even though he is not the kind of king the rioters envision.[49] The Messiah and King Jesus takes center stage as the kingdom spreads to Thessalonica.

Luke has pointed to the superiority of Jesus' kingdom over that of the empire throughout his two volumes. Various scholars have pointed out how Luke presents the good news of the birth of the Savior and the peace that ensues in contrast to the accomplishments of Caesar Augustus. Augustus was recognized as a Savior, and the Priene calendar inscription written in 9 BC in celebration of his birthday reads, "The birth date of our God has signaled the beginning of good news for the world."[50] But Luke ascribes the good news of great joy for all people (Luke 2:10) to

47. For a more detailed discussion of the kingdom proclamation in Luke-Acts, see Lidbeck, *Resurrection and Spirit*, 128–35.

48. Acts 1:15; 2:41, 47; 4:4; 5:14; 6:1, 7; 8:25, 40; 9:31, 35, 42; 11:21, 24, 26; 12:24; 13:44, 49; 14:1, 21; 16:5; 17:4, 12, 34; 18:8; 19:7, 20, 26; 21:20.

49. Keener, *Acts: Exegetical*, 3:2555. Kuhn emphasizes the "subversive" nature of the gospel: "For a time, it was common for scholars to argue that one of Luke's main objectives in writing his narrative was to demonstrate to Roman leaders that Christianity was politically and socially benign, posing no threat to the current world order, . . . He [Luke] considered the reign of God to be not a benign reality but a deeply subversive and disturbing force that was already undermining the foundations of Rome and all earthly claims to power." Kuhn, *Kingdom*, xvii.

50. Danker, *Benefactor*, 217. Also quoted in Danker, *Jesus and the New Age*, 54. See also Brown, *Birth of the Messiah*, 416.

Jesus and piles on the divine titles at his birth: "a Savior who is Christ the Lord" (v. 11). Augustus was celebrated for ushering in the age of peace,[51] but Luke points to Jesus as the source of peace (v. 14). Zechariah's prophecy climaxes with "the way of peace" (1:79) before introducing the decree from Caesar Augustus (2:1).[52] The "in darkness" (ἐν σκότει) and "shadow of death" (σκιᾷ θανάτου) where the people dwell (1:79) directly reflects the influence of Isa 9:2 (NIV 1984): "The people walking in darkness [ἐν σκότει] have seen a great light; on those living in the land of the shadow of death [σκιᾷ θανάτου] a light has dawned." Isaiah continues, "For to us a child is born, to us a son is given, and the government will be on his shoulders. And he will be called Wonderful Counselor, Mighty God, Everlasting Father, Prince of Peace. Of the increase of his government and peace there will be no end. He will reign on David's throne and over his kingdom, establishing and upholding it with justice and righteousness from that time on and forever. The zeal of the LORD Almighty will accomplish this" (Isa 9:6–7 NIV 1984). The pointer to this larger Isaian context not only provides a foundation for Luke's Christology but also sets forth a clear line of demarcation between the true author of peace and the vastly inferior Roman emperor. The kingdom that will stretch far beyond the Roman Empire, touching "all people" (Luke 2:10) and every tongue, is the kingdom of Christ.

The extensive manner in which the kingdom is integrated into Luke's volumes is also evident in the varying responses to the kingdom message as the kingdom progresses. The demons fear Jesus, but, ironically, they recognize his divine and royal status (Luke 4:34, 41; 8:28). Luke lists several women who respond appropriately to the kingdom message and join Jesus' entourage (8:1–3), but excuse-makers refuse to follow Jesus and are neither proclaimers of the kingdom nor fit for the kingdom (9:57–62). Jesus issues severe warnings to those who resist the disciples' kingdom proclamation (10:9–16). Some people fail to recognize the arrival of the kingdom and attribute Jesus' ministry of exorcism to Beelzeboul (11:14–23). The religious leaders are often the epitome of opposition to the kingdom (e.g., 13:14), but the kingdom will progress despite this (vv. 18–20). Luke places a great deal of emphasis on how people respond to the kingdom message and the King himself, and Acts

51. Brown, *Birth of the Messiah*, 415; Bock, *Luke*, 1:203.

52. Mittelstadt, "Spirit and Peace," 7.

chronicles in detail the opposition to and acceptance of the kingdom proclamation (e.g., 2:36–37; 7:54–60).

Luke also moves beyond merely recording the responses to the message to the consequences in the eternal kingdom. One way he accomplishes this is through his accounts of feasts and table fellowship. Jesus affirms the concept of an eschatological feast in the kingdom of God, but he warns that the guest list will look very different than anticipated (13:22–30; 14:15–24). The traitorous act of Judas is magnified by the fact that he was with Jesus "at the table" (22:21)—in violation of every decent social expectation. In light of this, the disciples must act honorably and with humility, as they will eat at Jesus' eschatological table and will exercise royal prerogatives (24–30).[53]

Just as Isaiah connects the gospel proclamation with the reign of God and salvation (52:7), so Luke connects the gospel with the arrival of the royal Lord and Savior (Luke 2:10–11, 30; cf. 1:69; 23:35–43). Luke equates salvation with entrance into the kingdom in his pericope about the narrow door (13:22–30) and in the narrative of the rich ruler (18:18–30). When Jesus responds to the thief's request for entrance into the kingdom, he replies, "Today [σήμερον] you will be with me in paradise" (23:43). "Today" is a term often used by Luke to indicate the day of salvation,[54] and here the term directly associates the kingdom with salvation in Jesus. Salvation is not limited to eternal life in Luke-Acts, but it includes physical healing and deliverance from Satan's oppression (Acts 10:38). The programmatic passage of Luke 4:18–19 includes these concepts, and after Luke describes Jesus' healing and delivering activity, he frames the narrative with a conclusion that summarizes the reason Jesus was sent and describes his ministry as preaching the good news of "the kingdom of God" (v. 43). Luke 9:1–2 clearly ties the ministry of healing and deliverance to the proclamation of the kingdom of God in the sending of the Twelve.

Jesus was sent "to preach the acceptable year of the Lord" (κηρύξαι ἐνιαυτὸν κυρίου δεκτόν; Luke 4:19), a reference to Isa 61:1 and to the Jubilee (Lev 25:10), but the language also reflects that of Isa 49:8, which directly connects the acceptable time to salvation: "In the acceptable time I heard you, and in the day of salvation I helped you" (Καιρῶι δεκτῶι

53. Kuhn notes that "the practice of table fellowship with Jesus is itself a manifestation of God's new age." *Kingdom*, 145. On table fellowship, see Capper, "Reciprocity and the Ethic," 512–18; Neyrey, "Ceremonies in Luke-Acts," 361–87.

54. Bock, *Theology of Luke and Acts*, 135.

ἐπήκουσά σου καὶ ἐν ἡμέραι σωτηρίας ἐβοήθησά σοι; LXX). The verse continues and employs the infinitive of the verb καθίστημι ("to restore") to describe God's intention to restore the land. The language is important because Luke uses the cognate verb ἀποκαθίστημι ("to restore") in connection with the disciples' query about the timing of the restoration of the kingdom (Acts 1:6) and the cognate noun ἀποκατάστασις ("restoration") in reference to the eschaton (3:21). These various but connected concepts come together in Luke 6:1–11, where Jesus refers to David as setting a precedent for bypassing a Sabbath regulation and then refers to himself as the "Lord of the Sabbath" (v. 5). This leads to the story of Jesus healing a man with a withered hand on the Sabbath, when Jesus questions the Pharisees about whether it is legal "to save [σῶσαι] a life or to destroy a life" on the Sabbath. Luke records the restoration of the man's hand with the verb ἀποκαθίστημι ("to restore"; v. 10). The Pharisees should have understood that the Sabbath is the most appropriate day for healing, as the Sabbath is an eschatological concept that represents ultimate salvation and restoration. All this is related to a greater David who reigns over an everlasting kingdom. The story of the man with the withered hand provides a good example of how the kingdom is related to a variety of salvific images in Luke-Acts.[55]

The close connection between ethics and the kingdom is apparent in Luke-Acts. Luke advocates an ethic of humility and receptivity of the kingdom as illustrated in children (Luke 18:9–17) but that excludes hypocrisy (12:1), judgmentalism (6:37–42), legalism (11:46), self-aggrandizement (9:46–48), and pride (11:43; 14:7–11). Similarly, greed and the pride and prestige that often accompany wealth are uncharacteristic of the kingdom and bar entrance into it (18:18–30). Luke repeatedly warns his readers of the danger of reliance on wealth and possessions (Luke 6:24; 11:39; 12:13–21; 16:19–31; 20:47; Acts 5:1–11; 8:20) and affirms the kingdom principle of generosity (Luke 10:35; 19:1–10; 21:1–4; Acts 2:44–45; 4:32–37; 10:2, 31). Luke's kingdom ethics spill over into daily practice, and one of his primary kingdom practices includes the discipline of prayer. Luke establishes the appropriate posture toward Jesus in the story of Mary and Martha (10:38–42); this leads naturally into a discussion of prayer and Jesus' directive to pray, "Let your kingdom come" (11:2). Instruction to ask for the Holy Spirit soon follows (v. 13), and further discussion about the source of Jesus' power and the arrival

55. The future resurrection is also related to ultimate salvation and is connected to the eschatological feast (Luke 14:15; cf. 22:16, 18).

of the kingdom continues in verses 14–23. Prayer is one of several characteristics of church praxis included in Luke's summary after Pentecost (Acts 2:42–47), implying that such practices are the natural consequence of Jesus' exaltation as the Davidic Lord and his pouring out of the Spirit.[56]

Pentecost, Kingdom, and Covenant Renewal

In preparation for the discussion of Pentecost in the next chapter, it is necessary to lay some groundwork regarding the nature of the Spirit's outpouring. The kingdom context of Luke-Acts and the emphasis on the identity of Jesus naturally lends to an understanding of Pentecost in royal and Davidic terms, but there has been much discussion about Moses' giving of the law at Sinai as a potential backdrop to Pentecost.[57] Some argue that Pentecost is heavily laden with new exodus and Sinaitic images in order to present it in covenantal terms and therefore, so it is thought, as necessarily an insufflation of the Spirit in conversion-initiation, regeneration, or salvation. Others object to this reading, viewing Pentecost's baptism in the Spirit as a work of prophetic empowerment. Some seek a mediating position, suggesting that the outpouring is an event of both conversion and prophetic empowerment for mission.[58] How one approaches this issue will also have a bearing on how one interprets the symbolism and significance of tongues. In the discussion to follow, I will review the main arguments for a covenantal or Sinaitic backdrop to Pentecost and propose a reading that considers Luke's terminology and his primary interests.

Pentecost was known as the Feast of Weeks (Exod 23:16; 34:22; Deut 16:9–12) or Firstfruits (Num 28:26) in the Hebrew Scriptures, and it marked the fiftieth day from the beginning of the barley harvest, which was also the first Sunday after Passover.[59] No scholarly consensus

56. Tannehill, *Narrative Unity*, 2:44–45.

57. There is also much discussion about the extent to which Luke incorporates cultic images related to the temple and Jesus as priest into the story of Pentecost. For a discussion of these issues, see Lidbeck, *Resurrection and Spirit*, 188–99.

58. Some charismatic scholars find this position appealing. In recent decades some revisionist Pentecostal scholars have gravitated toward a broader version of this position by redefining baptism in the Spirit as an all-inclusive, eschatological, new creation concept. For examples of the latter position, see Macchia, *Baptized in the Spirit*; Studebaker, "Pentecostal Soteriology," 248–70; Yong, *Spirit Poured Out*, 101.

59. Bruce, *Book of the Acts*, 49–50. The Greek term πεντηκοστός is twice used in reference to the Feast of Weeks in the Septuagint (Tob 2:1; 2 Macc 12:32).

exists in regard to how the festival of Pentecost (Acts 2:1) relates to the events which transpired on that day,[60] but the opposing views of James Dunn and Robert Menzies indicate the degree of importance some have attributed to finding an appropriate backdrop to the event. Dunn sees Pentecost as the beginning of the new covenant and claims, "Pentecost was more and more coming to be regarded as the feast which commemorated the lawgiving at Sinai."[61] Dunn cites passages from *Jubilees* (6.17–21; 15.1–24) and Qumran (1QS 2) in support of his position. But Menzies hesitates to connect the practices of the Qumran community with Pentecost and demurs from associating the giving of the law at Sinai with Pentecost.[62] Dunn presses the extra-biblical materials into the service of his conversion-initiation thesis, and Menzies reacts against this application of the literature.

Jubilees emphasizes a renewal of covenant at the Feast of Weeks (6.17) and supports the notion that the Feast of Weeks (Shavuot) was associated with more than a harvest celebration. But although *Jubilees* mentions the Mosaic law (1.1–4), the primary covenant envisioned in Jub. 6.18 is the Noahic covenant. Some of the dates offered in *Jubilees* seem contrived, and the extra-biblical material often seems fanciful, so one wonders how much credibility Luke would have attributed to such writings. Nonetheless, the concept of a covenant renewal is present, and the Essenes of Qumran followed the calendar in *Jubilees* (6.32; cf. 4Q394 I, 15; 4Q394, 20) and probably celebrated their annual covenant renewal at the time of the Feast of Weeks (4Q266, 11).[63] The covenant played a vital role in the life of the Essenes, and this is evident throughout the Damascus Document, in the Community Rule, in the Thanksgiving Hymns (1QH VI, 22), and in the Liturgical Prayer (1Q34 II, 5–7). But even though the Essenes based their covenant emphasis squarely on the Hebrew Scriptures, they also added to the laws and transformed the Mosaic covenant into a new sectarian covenant. It is doubtful that Luke would care to draw from this altered version of a covenant with its hierarchical structure (1QS II, 19–23) and severe curses (1QS I, 5–10). For

60. Keener, *Acts: Exegetical*, 1:784.

61. Dunn, *Baptism*, 48.

62. Menzies, *Empowered for Witness*, 191–92. In the debate over the nature of Spirit baptism, Dunn argues that Pentecostal Spirit baptism constitutes a conversion-initiation event while Menzies argues that Spirit baptism is an experience of prophetic empowerment logically distinct from conversion.

63. So Turner, *Power from on High*, 281.

this reason, it is best to acknowledge these sources as part of the milieu Luke drew from but also to note that he neither explicates their merits nor embraces them indiscriminately.

Eventually Rabbinical Judaism celebrated the Feast of Weeks in association with the giving of the law at Sinai. Rabbi Eleazer b. Pedath (c. AD 270) apparently identifies the festival of Pentecost with the giving of the law when he claims, "It is the day on which the Torah was given" (b. Pesaḥ 68b).[64] Menzies dismisses such evidence as late and "given impetus through the destruction of the temple,"[65] but the value of later sources amounts to a judgment call, and such texts could represent an older tradition and imply that their concepts were already in the air at Pentecost. However, even if the sights and sounds of Pentecost find their roots in the theophany of Sinai (Exod 19:16–19), and if the association of Pentecost with the giving of the law was so widely established that the Jews of Acts 2 would connect them, this still does not identify Luke's primary interest. In Acts 2 he focuses on the Spirit's prophetic empowerment (vv. 17–18; cf. 1:8) and the Davidic reign of Christ, but makes no explicit mention of Moses or the giving of the law.[66] Turner has argued that Luke's record of Jesus' exaltation, reception of the Spirit, and pouring out of the Spirit in Acts 2:33 reflect Ps 68:18 (67:19 LXX) and Moses' ascent of Sinai and subsequent dissemination of the law. If this is the case, "then this whole part of the story is not essentially Davidic in character at all. Indeed, Luke's tradition is specific on that point; David did not ascend to God (2.34a)."[67] Turner suggests there is a "gap . . . at the theological crux of Peter's argument" that is best understood to be filled by a reference to Moses.[68] It is by no means certain that Acts 2:33 depends on Ps 68:18, but

64. It is difficult to ascertain whether R. Eleazer or a later redactor made this statement, as a later compiler says a few lines later that Pentecost "is the day on which the Torah was given" in connection with a certain Mar son of Rabina who would not fast on the Feast of Weeks. In any event, R. Eleazer is credited with holding this belief. R. Jose b. Chalaphta (c. AD 150) also identifies Pentecost with the giving of the law (S. 'Olam Rab. 5). Quotations are from Epstein, *The Babylonian Talmud*.

65. Menzies, *Empowered for Witness*, 191. Roger Stronstad's position is similar to Menzies'. Stronstad, *Charismatic Theology: Trajectories*, 65. Bruce offers the opposite opinion of Menzies. Bruce, *Book of Acts*, 49–50.

66. Bock, *Acts*, 96. Also Polhill, *Acts*, 105. Talbert lists various "echoes" of Sinai that he sees in the narrative of Pentecost. Talbert, *Reading Acts*, 24–25.

67. Turner, *Power from on High*, 286.

68. Turner, *Power from on High*, 286. The structure of Peter's speech depends heavily on Davidic quotations and does not exhibit any signs of a gap that requires a Mosaic insertion into his argument. See the structural discussion in chapter two.

to suggest that the limitations of David as a model of the superior Messiah somehow opens the door for a Mosaic figure defeats Luke's point: there is no human figure that fully prefigures the Messiah in his exalted, royal, and divine status.[69]

Turner is right to argue that there are reflections of the Mosaic history in the Pentecostal story. Certainly the Joel citation does ultimately refer to Num 11, and the mention of signs and wonders is reminiscent of the exodus,[70] but his eagerness to show that "Pentecost is viewed as part of the fulfilment and *renewal* of Israel's covenant" makes it necessary for him to establish a Mosaic connection at Pentecost, even though Luke clearly quotes David's messianic psalms and refers to David as a royal type of Christ (Acts 2:24–36).[71] The theophany of Sinai probably does lie in the background of Pentecost, but the numerous references to David indicate that the primary covenant Luke has in mind is Davidic.[72] It seems unwise to impose a Mosaic covenant theme on the events of Pentecost without a clear call for it. Even Dunn is hesitant to make too strong of affirmations about the influence of the law and new covenant in shaping the story of the Spirit's coming at Pentecost, and Turner is cautious about how to apply the law as a parallel to Pentecost.[73] If this kind of Mosaic influence were of major importance to Luke in Acts 2, the reader would expect to find a clear reference to it on the lips of Peter in his Pentecostal sermon.

However, Luke's incorporation of various theophanic elements from the Hebrew Scriptures and Jewish tradition is not determinative for resolving the debate over the definition and timing of Spirit baptism.

69. Fitzmyer comments on the notion that Acts 2:33 refers to Ps 68:18: "This suggestion . . . is eisegetical." Fitzmyer, *Acts*, 259. O'Toole also rejects identification with Ps 68. O'Toole, "Acts 2:30," 248. Williams also doubts that Acts 2 contains a Moses/Jesus analogy. Williams, *Acts of the Apostles*, 69.

70. Turner, *Power from on High*, 285. Not all of Turner's suggestions are such evident allusions to the period of Moses, as Bock has noted. Bock, *Acts*, 131. Wenk follows Turner's general line of thinking regarding Pentecost and Sinai. Wenk, *Community-Forming Power*, 246–51.

71. Turner, *Power from on High*, 289. Emphasis original.

72. John Levison concludes, "If the story of Sinai lies in the background of Pentecost, it does so quiescently, by way of subtle allusion rather than the shout of clear correspondence." Levison, *Filled with the Spirit*, 325. Keener notes, "Luke provides few clear indications linking the day of Pentecost with Sinai, fewer than one would expect if Luke recognized and hence wished to make use of such connections." Keener, *Acts: Exegetical*, 1:787.

73. Dunn, *Baptism*, 49. Turner, *Power from on High*, 289.

Luke draws on a rich heritage of theophanic material to emphasize the eschatological significance of the event and to indicate that a new phase of God's redemptive plan has come to fruition. This is indicated by the prominent position of "to be fulfilled" (συμπληροῦσθαι; Acts 2:1), which occurs prior to the mention of Pentecost in the Greek text: Καὶ ἐν τῷ συμπληροῦσθαι τὴν ἡμέραν τῆς πεντηκοστῆς ("And when was fulfilled the day of Pentecost"). In addition, it should come as no surprise that such a major event incorporates multiple biblical images and turns the attention of all the onlookers to Christ. Jesus himself asserted such a christocentric view of Scripture: "These are my words that I spoke to you while I was still with you, that everything written about me in the Law of Moses and the Prophets and the Psalms must be fulfilled" (Luke 24:44b).

It should be remembered that the day of Pentecost involved two distinct groups of people—the disciples and the Diaspora Jews. The disciples were present because of their prior faith and experience with the risen Lord, whose ascension to the Father's right hand they had personally witnessed. They needed the outpouring of the Spirit for empowered witness to the nations but not to realize for themselves the identity of Jesus as the exalted Messiah. However, the outpouring of the Spirit on the disciples served an identifying purpose for the Diaspora Jews gathered at Pentecost. For those Jews, the outpouring served to identify Jesus as the Lord and Christ (Acts 2:32–36). They needed this identification in order to come to faith in Jesus, enter into the new covenant, and receive the benefits of the covenant dispensed by the Lord Jesus (vv. 38–39). Consequently, it is not surprising if there is some covenantal language at Pentecost, since the disciples received the charismatic benefits of it and 3,000 in the crowd entered into it.

Luke seldom uses the actual term "covenant" (διαθήκη), and when he does, he usually refers to the Abrahamic covenant (Luke 1:72; Acts 3:25; 7:8).[74] However, the institution of the "new covenant" (ἡ καινὴ διαθήκη) in Jesus' "blood" (Luke 22:20; cf. Jer 31:31) clearly points to the Mosaic covenant (Exod 24:8). It appears that Luke views Jesus' death as the ratification of the new covenant,[75] much as the shedding of blood of sacrificial animals ratified the Mosaic covenant. Luke's emphatic assertion that the day of Unleavened Bread was the one "on which the Passover lamb [τὸ πάσχα] had [ἔδει] to be sacrificed" (Luke 22:7 ESV) points

74. No New Testament authors use the term a great deal except for the author of Hebrews, who uses the noun seventeen times.

75. Williams, *Renewal Theology*, 1:301.

directly to Christ as the Passover lamb. The six occurrences of "Passover" (πάσχα) in Luke 22 (vv. 1, 7, 8, 11, 13, 15) reinforce the importance of this identification of Christ with the Passover lamb. Luke has repeatedly connected this divine necessity with the necessity of the resurrection (9:22; 18:31–33; 24:7), and ascension and enthronement are integral to resurrection, as the goal of resurrection is not merely resuscitation but restoration to and manifestation of Christ's royal position.[76] The resurrection is essential to Luke because the full, present benefits of the atoning work of Christ are only realized from Christ and by faith in Christ in his resurrected and exalted position.

One can see an allusion to covenantal terminology when Peter exhorts the crowd to repent and informs them that "the gift," that is, "the promise" of the Spirit is for them and "their children" (Acts 2:38–39). The promise to the descendants apparently echoes Isa 59:20–21, where Yahweh makes a covenant with Israel and promises to grant them and their children the presence of the prophetic Spirit.[77] The order of repentance and then the Spirit occurs in both passages, suggesting that the Spirit comes as a benefit of entrance into a covenant relationship. In Isaiah's text, the benefit is the Spirit's presence directly in connection with Yahweh placing his words in the mouths of his people. The passage fits very well with the occurrence of tongues at Pentecost.

For the disciples, Pentecost does not initiate them into the new covenant in the sense of defining the moment of faith. For Luke, empowerment by the Spirit is a new-covenant experience in line with the Old Testament but not necessarily equivalent to the experience of the new birth as described by Paul (Rom 8), for this reason Luke can record several receptions of the Spirit where the moment of faith is either distinct from Spirit reception or not immediately apparent in the text (Acts 4:31; 8:15; 9:17; 10:44; 19:6). The emphasis in Acts 2 is on the identity of Jesus as Lord and Christ and his role as dispenser of the blessings of the new covenant, including both salvation and reception of the Spirit. The Davidic covenant is central to this, and it is natural to expect some covenantal connections at Pentecost, but the presence of covenantal allusions does not imply that the outpouring of the Spirit at Pentecost is a conversion-initiation experience. Attempts to make Pentecost a Mosaic renewal of the covenant not only miss the royal reason for Luke's use of

76. See the discussion of this in Lidbeck, *Resurrection and Spirit*, 53–85.

77. Ruthven, *On the Cessation*, 221–25.

Davidic material, but they wrongly conclude that references to Moses or Sinai infer that the bestowal of the Spirit at Pentecost is necessarily a conversion-initiation event.

In keeping with the fulfillment theme mentioned above, the theophanic signs of Pentecost primarily serve an eschatological purpose—God is present and acting in a powerful way in history,[78] and Pentecost is a climactic event introducing a new phase of God's working. Any Sinai or covenant renewal allusions could easily suggest this notion without defining the precise nature of the new divine activity. Luke defines that for us. With the Davidic King's pouring out of the Spirit comes a climactic and unique sign in salvation history—speaking in other tongues. The sound of a violent wind and the appearance of fiery tongues indicate the divine presence and heavenly source of the speaking in tongues. The language miracle receives the focus of attention in Acts 2:4–21, and Peter specifically connects the tongues to prophetic speech and eschatological signs (vv. 17–22). Thus, the allusions in Acts 2 ultimately function to indicate the divine presence and place tongues in an eschatological context where Christ is enthroned as the Davidic King.

Summary

There is an abundance of evidence that Luke's key themes relate directly to Luke's emphasis on the kingdom and Christ's central role as the Lord of this kingdom. Luke taps into the kingdom theme and royal expectations in the Hebrew Scriptures and among the Jewish people of the intertestamental period. He presents the gospel's progress as the kingdom's progress, and the divine, royal status of Jesus far exceeds that of Roman emperors. Luke uses multiple images to convey the concept of salvation, and these images relate directly to the kingdom; the arrival of salvation is the arrival of the kingdom. Luke's kingdom ethics and praxes require an appropriate heart of humility in response to Christ, an eschewing of greed, and a prayerful life.

The language of Luke-Acts and framing techniques employed reflect a strong concern with the kingdom, and there is a stress on Jesus as the fulfillment of the Davidic promises. The threefold designation applied to him as the Lord, Jesus/Savior, and Christ/Messiah identifies

78. Keener suggests eschatological associations with the signs of Acts 2. *Acts: Exegetical*, 1:787.

Jesus as the anticipated Davidic King and gives a christological weight to those passages. The triad of Jesus Christ as Lord occurs at both Pentecost and Cornelius's household, and the emphasis on this identification of the Messiah where tongues occur suggests that speaking in tongues should be understood as a christological event.

There are some Sinaitic and covenantal allusions in Acts 2, and these images serve Luke's purposes in describing Pentecost as a significant eschatological event and the fulfillment of many Scriptures. However, Luke's primary focus on the exaltation of Jesus as the fulfillment of Davidic expectations takes center stage. Christ is the King of the kingdom who dispenses the Spirit to the faithful to enable them to proclaim his kingship, and this distribution of the Spirit testifies to his kingship and identifies him as Lord and Christ to the very people who sought his death. This King exercises the divine prerogative to grant salvation to those who repent and the gift of the charismatic Spirit as a benefit of the new covenant. It is within this sphere of the kingdom that one interprets the tongues of Pentecost and discovers their essence, symbolism, nature, content, and orientation.

2

Jesus—The Lord of Pentecost

With the centrality of the kingdom and Christ as the Davidic King firmly in place in Luke-Acts, I now turn to the discussion of how Acts 2 fits into this program. Acts 1 emphasizes the kingdom (vv. 3, 6), records the ascension of Jesus, and details the replacement of Judas with Matthias. Although the first occurrence of the phrase "Lord Jesus" comes from the mouth of the narrator in the resurrection narrative (Luke 24:3), the first character to use the phrase is Peter (Acts 1:21), when he elucidates the requirements for joining the Twelve and specifies that the job description entails being a witness of the resurrection (v. 22). The new member must have first-hand knowledge of Jesus' life right up until Jesus' ascension (v. 22). Consequently, the reader is primed for another kingdom event rooted in the resurrection and ascension of Jesus.

The start of a new story is signaled by the new setting on Pentecost in Acts 2:1, when "they were all together [ἦσαν πάντες ὁμοῦ] in one place."[1] After the outpouring of the Spirit in 2:1–4, a new segment of the story is introduced in a similar manner with the phrase, "And there were in Jerusalem" (Ἦσαν δὲ εἰς Ἰερουσαλὴμ; v. 5). Luke details the international origins of the Jews present at Pentecost (vv. 5–13) and then focuses the attention back on Peter and the eleven disciples for Peter's sermon explaining the christological significance of the outpouring of the Spirit and accompanying languages (vv. 14–36). Peter's sermon

1. Although Luke was certainly concerned to show that the disciples once again numbered twelve, the choosing of Matthias took place among the 120 (Acts 1:15), and the emphasis on the size of the whole group and their prayerfulness suggests that all participated in Pentecost. See Marshall, *Acts*, 68.

begins in response to the crowd's enquiry (v. 12), and at the climax of the speech, the crowd interrupts with another question (v. 37), and Peter responds with instructions regarding salvation and the gift of the Spirit (vv. 38–39). The narrator then summarizes Peter's sermon and records that 3,000 were saved. The following discussion highlights this progression in Acts 2 and shows the relationship between speaking in tongues and the pinnacle of Peter's speech in Acts 2:36.

Filled with the Holy Spirit (Acts 2:1–4)

Eschatological overtones abound in the Pentecostal narrative. Acts 2:1 opens with an indicator that another phase of God's kingdom has come to fulfillment: "When the day of Pentecost arrived [Καὶ ἐν τῷ συμπληροῦσθαι τὴν ἡμέραν τῆς πεντηκοστῆς]" (ESV).[2] English translations have difficulty conveying the eschatological significance of συμπληροῦσθαι ("to be fulfilled"), but Luke employs the identical phrase ἐν τῷ συμπληροῦσθαι in Luke 9:51: "When the days were nearing fulfillment [ἐν τῷ συμπληροῦσθαι] for his ascension, he set his face to go to Jerusalem." The close association of Pentecost with Jesus' ascension and Luke's preoccupation with fulfillment make it highly unlikely that this fulfillment terminology indicates only the arrival of a particular day on the calendar. R. C. H. Lenski's sentiments are correct: "The phrase is too weighty for that."[3] The record of the fulfilling of God's promises immediately follows in verse 2. The eschatological event unfolding on Pentecost is also a christological event.

The eschatological allusions continue as Luke twice mentions the Spirit as the cause of the speaking in other tongues (Acts 2:4). The mention of Jerusalem (2:5, 14), the beginning point of the mission (Luke 24:47; cf. v. 52) and the place Jesus identified as the site of the impending outpouring of the Spirit (Acts 1:4, 8; cf. v. 12), adds to the climate of eschatological expectation.[4] But any remaining doubt as to the es-

2. Kurz believes these passages speak of the time of fulfillment. He believes this is a reference to the prophecy of Jeremiah (25:11–12 LXX) regarding the 70 years of captivity, although Jeremiah uses the simple verb πληρόω (25:12) while Luke uses the compound συμπληρόω (Acts 2:1) to indicate fulfillment. Because Luke 9:51 starts a new epoch, he believes Acts 2:1 terminology signals a new epoch of God's salvation. See also the Septuagint of 2 Chr 36:21; 1 Esd 1:58; Dan 9:2 (Th). Kurz, *Reading Luke-Acts*, 77–78.

3. Lenski, *Acts*, 56; cf. Peterson, *Acts*, 131.

4. Jerusalem is also prominent in the birth narratives as part of Luke's eschatological

chatological nature of the Spirit's outpouring is completely removed by Peter's interpretation of Joel's "after these things" (μετὰ ταῦτα; Joel 3:1 LXX) as "in the last days" (ἐν ταῖς ἐσχάταις ἡμέραις; Acts 2:17).[5] The repeated Scripture citations in Peter's sermon lead to the conclusion that Jesus' identity is that of "Lord and Christ" (2:36), so that the reader must conclude that the signs of Pentecost (including the speaking tongues) originate from the Lord and Christ. Tongues have their origin in the enthroned Christ and, as an eschatological sign, testify that the eschatological reign of Messiah has begun.

Luke uses repetition and wordplays to paint the Pentecostal picture and draw attention to some of his important interests. He uses the compound form (συμπληροῦσθαι) of the verb πληρόω ("I fill") to record the fulfillment of the day of Pentecost (Acts 2:1). He uses the basic form of the verb to describe how the sound "filled the whole house" (v. 2) and then a related verb (πίμπλημι) to report how the disciples "were all filled with the Holy Spirit" (v. 4). Luke employs a cognate noun to emphasize the size of the crowd (πλῆθος) witnessing the language miracle (v. 6).[6] The four terms together accentuate the eschatological significance of the day and the progress of God's plans coming to fulfillment.

Luke fills his narrative with action and gives the first four verses of Acts 2 a sense of cohesiveness by beginning a series of phrases with a verb and joining them with the conjunction καί ("and").[7] The first of these phrases, "And came suddenly from heaven a sound" (v. 2) draws attention to the source of the sights and sounds (cf. Luke 2:15; 3:21–22). Once again, Luke is using repetition to highlight the significance of the

---

scheme. The association of various personages with this city and temple also lends credibility to their character and prophetic pronunciations (Luke 1:9; 2:22, 25, 38, 41, 43).

5. Robert Menzies believes that James Dunn and Ernst Haenchen have exaggerated the eschatological import of Luke's alteration of Joel. Menzies emphasizes that Pentecost is one event in several, beginning with Jesus' birth, and Pentecost "does not mark the beginning of the 'the last days.'" Menzies, *Empowered for Witness*, 180. Keener attributes greater significance to the alteration than Menzies does: "But the Davidic kingdom announced at the beginning of the Gospel (Luke 1:32, 69) enters a new phase with Jesus' exaltation (Acts 2:33–36), and the issue of eschatology suffuses the context (1:6–7)." Keener, *Acts: Exegetical*, 1:878. While I appreciate Menzies's caution, I agree with Keener that underemphasizing the eschatological significance of this text may undermine Luke's attempt to portray the exaltation of Christ and outpouring of the Spirit as a climactic event.

6. MacDonald, "Glossolalia," 129.

7. The phrases are: "and came" (v. 2), "and filled" (v. 2), "and appeared" (v. 3), "and it sat" (v. 3), "and they were all filled" (v. 4), and "and they began" (v. 4).

event. He has already used the phrase "into heaven" four times in Acts 1:10–11. The signs of Pentecost come "from heaven" and seize the attention of devout men from every nation "under heaven" (v. 5), pointing to the enthroned Christ as the source of the Pentecostal outpouring (cf. Luke 9:51; 24:50–51; Acts 2:33–36). Peter confirms this when he demonstrates that Jesus is the Davidic King who is also superior to David, as David did not ascend "into heaven" as Jesus did (v. 34). Not only Peter's speech, but the whole of Acts 2 is christologically oriented.

It appears that Luke may be using a play on words when he records that the sound of a powerful wind "filled the whole house where they were sitting [καθήμενοι]" and that cloven tongues like fire "sat [ἐκάθισεν] on each one of them" (Acts 2:2–3). The disciples sat and waited just as Jesus had instructed them to sit (καθίσατε) in Luke 24:49. Peter explains that God had promised David that one of his descendants would sit (καθίσαι) on his throne (Acts 2:30), and based on Ps 110:1, Jesus is the Lord who sits (κάθου) at God's right hand (Acts 2:34).[8] The picture is that of the reigning Lord Jesus, sitting on his throne, sending his presence to sit on the disciples who sat waiting. The wordplay points to Christology again.

C. K. Barrett notes that it seems odd that "sat" is a singular verb in Acts 2:3 despite the plural "tongues" like fire. He gives a reasonable resolution to the tension: "Luke probably means that one tongue-like flame rested upon each person."[9] Perhaps something like a mass of fire appeared over the entire group and was "distributed" (διαμεριζόμεναι) as a single flame over each believer.[10] Luke seems intent on stressing the scale of the event when he comments on how the sound "filled the *whole* house where they were sitting," how the divided tongues like fire "sat on *each one* of them," and how "*all* were filled with the Holy Spirit" (vv. 2–4). This is consistent with Peter's remarks on the scope of the Spirit's availability (vv. 17–18, 39), and the "filled" terminology is consistent with the language of abundance employed in the "outpouring" expression (vv. 17–18, 33). Divine beneficence is also evident in that every time Luke

8. Luke is using two similar verbs for "sit" in these texts. He uses καθίζω in Luke 24:49, Acts 2:3, and 30, and κάθημαι in Acts 2:2 and 34. For a discussion of the christological significance of κάθημαι in relation to Ps 110, see Bühner, "κάθημαι," 222–24.

9. Barrett, *Acts*, 1:114.

10. Horton views the distribution of the tongues of fire as a symbol of God's acceptance of his people as a new temple and each person as an individual temple. According to Horton, the fire descending on the initial sacrifice in the tabernacle and temple in the Old Testament provides the backdrop. Horton, *What the Bible Says*, 140–42.

gives a detailed description of a reception of the Spirit it is a corporate event (Acts 4:31; 10:44; 19:6).[11] A significant point to note is that the aorist verb ἐπλήσθησαν ("they were filled") in 2:4 is in the passive voice. The divine passive indicates the activity of God, but this time the divine being in view is Jesus.[12] This is another way Luke makes Pentecost a christological event.

Given Luke's careful use of his vocabulary, it is probably not a coincidence that he uses the term γλῶσσαι ("tongues") in his "tongues like fire" phrase (Acts 2:3) shortly before recording how the disciples "began to speak in other tongues [γλώσσαις] as the Spirit was giving them utterance" (v. 4). The fiery tongues anticipate the disciples' speaking in other tongues by the Spirit.[13] Many scholars see the language of theophany in the sound of the wind and the appearance of tongues like fire.[14] Fire often appears in theophanies in the Hebrew Scriptures,[15] and it is often understood as indicative of the divine presence.[16] The fire as divine presence in Acts 2 appears primarily as a sign of divine favor, inspiring exalted speech, and not as a mark of judgment or cleansing from sin.[17] The prediction of Jesus' baptizing work by John (Luke 3:16–17) stresses the superiority of the one Baptizer who has the power to exercise the divine prerogatives of dispensing a baptism in the Spirit (Acts 2:4) and a baptism in (judgment) fire (10:42). Jesus emphasizes how the disciples will experience a baptism superior to that of John's when he predicts, "In not many days you will be baptized with the Holy Spirit" (1:5; cf. 11:16). The promise uses the divine passive and omits the "and fire," as the disciples will not be recipients

11. Luke alludes to Saul's individual filling with the Spirit, but he does not describe the event (Acts 9:17–19). Apparently, Luke wants to emphasize that the charismatic filling of the Spirit is available to all believers in Jesus everywhere.

12. Lenski, *Acts*, 60.

13. Fitzmyer relates the tongues of fire to the empowered speech that the disciples experience. Fitzmyer, *Acts*, 238. Schnabel follows this line of reasoning. Schnabel, *Acts*, 114.

14. E.g., Barrett, *Acts*, 1:113; Conzelmann, *Acts*, 13; Fitzmyer, *Acts*, 238; Johnson, *Acts*, 42; Marshall, *Acts*, 68. Witherington, *Acts*, 132.

15. E.g., Gen 15:17; Exod 3:2–4; 13:21–22; 14:24; 19:18; 24:17; 40:38; Num 14:14; Deut 4:12, 24, 33, 36; 5:4; 10:4; 1 Kgs 19:12; 2 Kgs 2:11; 2 Chr 7:1–3; Ps 18:8; 29:7; Job 37:2–5; Ezek 1:25–28; Dan 7:9–10.

16. E.g., Bruce, *Book of Acts*, 50; Peterson, *Acts*, 133; Schnabel, *Acts*, 114.

17. One might argue that any manifestation of God's presence automatically involves a warning about sin and rebellion, and the disciples will certainly preach such warnings, but Luke does not emphasize a judgment or purification theme in regard to the disciples' own reception of the Spirit.

of the eschatological wrath of Jesus referenced in John's prophecy.[18] The "tongues like fire" (2:3) are related to the "other tongues" (v. 4) in that the former indicate that the divine presence has come to touch the tongues of the disciples with prophetic power. An historical glimpse at the idea of "tongues of fire" helps clarify the symbolism of fire as indicative of the divine presence but not necessarily the divine presence as judgment. "Fire" has various nuances in Scripture and Judaism, and John's judgment fire is a separate function of Christ from the blessing of his divine presence symbolized in the tongues of fire.

Tongues of Fire

In this section I will investigate the Jewish origins of the phrase "tongues of fire" (γλῶσσαι ὡσεὶ πυρὸς) found in Acts 2:3 in order to shed light on the nature of this fire. The similar phrase "a tongue of flame" is found in Gen. Rab. 59:4. This phrase occurs as part of a digression in a teaching about righteousness, and it records the story of how R. Samuel b. R. Isaac was vindicated by a miraculous sign after his death when "a tongue of flame descended, assumed the shape of a myrtle branch, and interposed between his bier and the people."[19] The flaming tongue conveys the idea of the divine presence.

18. This omission has been noted by many scholars. For example, Peterson opines, "But it is doubtful that the tongues 'like fire' (*hōsei pyros*) in Acts 2:2 [sic] are to be related to John's prophecy, especially since the element of fire was excluded from Jesus's report of John's words in 1:5." Peterson, *Acts*, 133. Along with others, Marshall sees a cleansing and judgment symbolism in the fire (Luke 3:16). Marshall, *Acts*, 69. Charette argues that the tongues of Pentecost are also a sign of judgment, but he has trouble accounting for the absence of "fire" in Acts 1:5. No adequate explanation is given for the appearance of judgment fire over the blessed, and his attempt to harmonize Acts 2 with Paul's judgment theme in 1 Cor 14:20–22 is interesting but unconvincing. The harmonization relies too heavily on Luke's use of "other" in "other tongues" as a supposed reference to Isa 28:11. Charette, "'Tongues as of Fire': Judgement," 177, 184. Turner is forced to differentiate between John the Baptist's understanding of his own prediction in Luke 3:16–17 and the understanding of Jesus or Luke of what baptism in the Spirit entails. He attributes the lack of "and fire" in Acts 1:5 to an adjustment made in order to fit the immediate context of the disciples as recipients of the Spirit, but the omission "is perhaps of little significance." Turner, *Power from on High*, 187, 298, 299n87. Turner's explanation is driven by his argument that John's "Holy Spirit and fire" is a single baptism of restoration and cleansing in Israel. The omission does not help Turner's argument that the fire of Luke 3 refers to Israel's cleansing. I find the omission to be quite significant and indicative of a different kind of baptism intended for the disciples.

19. Freedman and Simon, *Midrash Rabbah*, 2:517. Strack and Stemberger date the final redaction of this midrash to the early half of the fifth century, but one must ask

The Babylonian Talmud records a traditional language miracle in Šabb. 88b (cf. Tanḥ. 26c on Exod 20:18). Rabbi Jochanan (d. AD 279) explains Ps 68:12 this way: "Every single word that went forth from the Omnipotent was split up into seventy languages."[20] Similarly, the midrash refers to Sinai and cites Rabbi Jochanan as saying "that God's voice, as it was uttered, split up into seventy voices, in seventy languages, so that all the nations should understand. When each nation heard the Voice in their own vernacular their soul departed, save Israel who heard but who were not hurt" (Exod. Rab. 5:9; cf. 28:6).[21] And the school of R. Ishmael (d. AD 135) is credited with the following comment (Šabb. 88b): "And like a hammer that breaketh the rock in pieces: just as a hammer is divided into many sparks, so every single word that went forth from the Holy One, blessed be He, split up into seventy languages."[22] These texts are often associated with the Sinai tradition. Although the similarities with Acts 2:5–12 are not particularly impressive, these texts do inform us that Rabbinic Judaism did associate God's voice at Sinai with a language miracle, and this may have a bearing on Acts 2.

Although Philo connects the giving of the law with the Feast of Trumpets rather than Pentecost (*Spec.* 2:188–89), his first-century voice adds to the tradition of a language miracle at Sinai. He records that God "wrought a most conspicuous and evidently holy miracle, commanding an invisible sound [ἦχον ἀόρατον] to be created in the air." He further describes it as "a rational soul . . . which fashioned the air and stretched it out and changed it into a kind of flaming fire [πῦρ φλογοειδὲς]." This voice was like a "breath [πνεῦμα] passing through a trumpet" (*Decal.* 1:33).[23] Philo also associates God's breath with his "power" (δύναμις; *Decal.* 1:35; cf. Acts 1:8). God's voice rang out of the midst of "a fire from heaven" (ἀπ᾽ οὐρανοῦ πυρὸς) and the flame was "endowed with articulate speech in a language [διάλεκτον] familiar to the hearers" (*Decal.* 1:46). Philo's description of the Sinai theophany shares several similar terms

if the content reflects an older tradition. There does seem to be a traceable tradition if one either follows the phrase "tongue of flame" or either of the key words in the phrase. Strack and Stemberger, *Introduction to the Talmud*, 279.

20. Epstein, *Babylonian Talmud*, 420.

21. Freedman and Simon, *Midrash Rabbah*, 3:86.

22. Epstein, *Babylonian Talmud*, 420.

23. Philo, *The Works of Philo*, 520.

and concepts with Acts 2:1–6, which records a "sound from heaven" (ἐκ τοῦ οὐρανοῦ ἦχος), fire, and a familiar language (διαλέκτῳ).[24]

A text that offers a verbal parallel closer to Gen. Rab. 59:4 and Acts 2:3 occurs in the Qumran literature (1Q29; partially overlapping with 4Q376). This document, called the *Liturgy of Three Tongues of Fire*, is based on Exod 28:9–12 and describes the use of the gemstones set on the shoulders of the high priest's ephod in a ritual for testing prophets.[25] "And he shall go out with it with tongues of fire. The left-hand stone on his left side will show itself to the eyes of all the assembly until the priest has completed his speech."[26] Fragments 2–7 of 1Q29 contain the unusual phrase "three tongues of fire," which apparently "come to rest on the high priest."[27] What is significant in this study is that the tongues of fire here represent the divine presence and that they are associated with the high priest's prophetic activity.

First Enoch 14:8–25 (apparently pre-Maccabean; cf. 71:5) offers an early point of comparison for examining tongues of fire. Here the phrase "tongues of fire" occurs three times in Enoch's heavenly vision, and the tongues seem "to delimit spheres of holiness as one approaches closer and closer to the presence of God."[28] The vision incorporates images from Ezekiel's vision of the *merkabah* (Ezek 1) and phraseology from Isaiah: "Therefore, as tongues of fire lick up straw and as dry grass sinks down in the flames, so their roots will decay and their flowers blow away like dust" (Isa 5:24 NIV 1984). Isaiah provides the earliest biblical occurrence of "tongues of fire," and here it is a figure of judgment. A similar judgment passage, not unlike the theophany at Sinai, occurs at 30:27–28, where the Lord comes "with burning anger and dense clouds of smoke; his lips are full of wrath, and his tongue is a consuming fire. His breath is like a rushing torrent, rising up the neck. He shakes the nations in the sieve of destruction" (NIV 1984). This vision of God as a consuming fire

24. See also Tg. Ps.-J. on Exod 20:2 for a description of the theophany at Sinai somewhat similar to Philo's.

25. Glen Menzies, "Pre-Lucan Occurrences," 58. For a description of how the stones function, see Josephus, *Ant.* 3.214–18.

26. 4Q376 Fr. 1 II, 1–3. English translation from Vermes, *Complete Dead Sea Scrolls*, 578.

27. Glen Menzies, "Pre-Lucan Occurrences," 55.

28. Glen Menzies, "Pre-Lucan Occurrences," 41.

is often repeated in Jewish literature (Deut 4:24; 9:3; Heb 12:29; Exod. Rab. 30:19; Pesiq. Rab. 11:7).[29]

While the passages cited above come from a wide variety of literary genres and contexts, there is a generally discernible development of themes based largely on the Sinai event of Exod 19, Isaiah's use of "tongues of fire" in 5:24, and Ezekiel's vision in chapter 1. Throughout the intertestamental period various authors expanded on the language and fire themes, embellished them, and combined them in new ways, resulting even in a "tongue of flame" assuming the shape of an olive branch in Gen. Rab. 59:4. But the one overarching theme that ties together the various language miracles and fiery visions is the divine presence.[30] Thus, Gen. Rab. 59:4 and Acts 2:3 share a common tradition but exercise individual authorial license. Given that the events of Acts 2 describe the arrival of a new stage in redemptive history, one should expect (1) Luke to record them using terminology from this Jewish tradition; (2) there to be unique features that have no direct parallel in other accounts; and (3) his readers to understand the symbolism of divine presence.

Although the "tongues like fire" (γλῶσσαι ὡσεὶ πυρὸς; Acts 2:3) are not identical to the "other tongues" (ἑτέραις γλώσσαις) in verse 4, their close association and the theophanic context suggest that the reader should connect the act of speaking in tongues with the divine presence. What is equally as stunning as the unusual miracle of speaking in previously unknown languages is the christocentric nature of the event, for the "Lord and Christ" (2:33, 36) is the one who pours out the Spirit. Thus, the theophany of Pentecost is more than a traditional theophany (Exod 3:2–6; 19:18; 24:17; 2 Chr 7:1–3; Isa 6:1–5; cf. Matt 3:6; 17:5); it is, in a sense, a christophany designed to invoke a sense of awe over the greatness of Christ and a momentous occasion in history.[31] Consequently, Pentecost contains both continuity with historical manifestations of God's presence and progress in centering the new divine experiences on Christ's glorification.

29. Psalm 28:7 (LXX) records, "A voice of the Lord divides a flame of fire." This is another example of theophanic language celebrating the glory of God in terms of fire, but this Psalm emphasizes God's majesty and does not focus on his wrath.

30. Glen Menzies, "Pre-Lucan Occurrences," 58.

31. Thus, the symbol of fire as a theophanic sign that induced awe in the Hebrew people now induces awe in the reader as the reader contemplates the glory of Christ manifest at Pentecost.

Inspired Utterance

Luke accentuates inspired speech in Acts 2, as is evident from the vocabulary he employs. In Acts 2:1–18 "tongues" (γλῶσσαι) occurs three times (vv. 3, 4, 11), "to speak" (λαλέω) four times (vv. 4, 6, 7, 11), "language" (διάλεκτος) twice (vv. 6, 8), "voice" (φωνή) twice (vv. 6, 14), "word" (ῥῆμα) once (v. 14), "to say" (λέγω) two times (vv. 16, 17),[32] "prophet" (προφήτης) once (v. 16; cf. v. 30), "to prophesy" (προφητεύω) twice (vv. 17, 18), and "to speak under inspiration" (ἀποφθέγγομαι) twice (vv. 4, 14). Each of these is used in reference to an inspired utterance of some kind, and the repetition of the latter, rare verb[33] looks like a deliberate attempt to point to the supernatural nature of both the speaking in tongues and Peter's sermon. In this way, Luke highlights the divine source of both the tongues speech and the gospel preaching of those filled with the Spirit. In addition, the phrase "filled with the Holy Spirit" (v. 4) carries a prophetic connotation with it in Luke's writings (Luke 1:15, 41, 67; Acts 4:8, 31; 13:9).[34]

Given Luke's extensive use of vocabulary related to inspired speech, it seems highly unlikely that the real miracle of Pentecost was not one of speech but one of hearing.[35] Gregory of Nazienzen rejected the notion of a miracle of hearing because it would require the miracle to take place in the unbelieving hearers rather than the Spirit-filled disciples in whom the crowd recognized some kind of miracle and whom they wrongly accused of drunkenness.[36] Neither does the hearing theory fit well with the

32. The verb λέγω is used of more mundane utterances also in Acts 2:7, 12, and 13.

33. The verb is used only in Acts 2:4, 14 and 26:25 in the New Testament.

34. Stronstad develops this thesis; see *Spirit, Scripture and Theology*, 79–98. In addition to the prophetic element, I also see room for a charismatic templing theme in the expression. Lidbeck, *Resurrection and Spirit*, 23–39.

35. Powers, in an attempt to avoid concluding that the tongues of Pentecost were human languages, suggests that Pentecost involved a miracle of both speaking and hearing. She believes this approach opens the door for non-human ecstatic language in both Acts and 1 Corinthians. However, this approach seems strained, and it is not necessary to conclude that the "other tongues" of Acts 2:4, as human languages (xenolalia), necessitates that tongues (without the "other") in Acts 10:46 and 19:6 are also human languages. Powers, "Missionary Tongues?" 46–50.

36. Gregory of Nazianzen, "Oration XLI: On Pentecost," 41.15 (*NPNF2* 7:384). See Mills, *A Theological/Exegetical Approach*, 60–62. Turner articulates a modern-day version of Gregory's point: "We may not seriously doubt that Luke attributed the fundamental charism in this process to the activity of God in the one hundred and twenty *believers*. He would not wish to suggest that the apostolic band merely prattled incomprehensibly, while God worked the yet greater miracle of interpretation of tongues in

combination of λαλέω ("to speak") and γλῶσσα ("tongue") found nineteen times in the New Testament in reference to speaking in tongues and consistently highlighting inspired speech.[37] There is no hint of a hearing miracle in Acts 10 and 19,[38] and the three references to hearing (ἀκούω) in Acts 2:6, 8, and 11 provide essential vocabulary for the narrative.[39] In other words, the reason for mentioning the hearing is that the story is narrated from the perspective of the crowd at that point and not for the purpose of shifting the emphasis away from inspired speech. Without the crowd hearing, there simply is no miracle story of speaking.

In Acts 2:2–4 a series of five main verbs describe each new major event in the action,[40] but the relationship between the last two ("they were all filled" and "began to speak") is particularly tight. The full verse reads, "And they were all filled with the Holy Spirit and began to speak in other tongues as the Spirit was giving them utterance" (καὶ ἐπλήσθησαν πάντες πνεύματος ἁγίου καὶ ἤρξαντο λαλεῖν ἑτέραις γλώσσαις καθὼς τὸ πνεῦμα ἐδίδου ἀποφθέγγεσθαι αὐτοῖς; v. 4). Several items are noteworthy. First, the parallelism between the two independent clauses separated by "and" highlights the close association between Spirit-filling and speaking in other tongues. Second, the dependent clause following "as" (καθὼς) repeats the mention of the Spirit, creating a pneumatic frame around the speaking in tongues, and draws a distinction between the speakers themselves and the Spirit as the source of their speech. Third, the choice of the infinitive ἀποφθέγγεσθαι ("to utter") along with ἐδίδου ("was giving") emphasizes the inspired nature of the utterance (cf. 1 Chr 25:1 LXX).[41] Finally, the Spirit is not the subject of the main verbs in this section.

---

the *un*believers." Turner, *The Holy Spirit*, 218. Emphasis original.

37. This is according to the count by Harrisville. Sometimes one of the words is supplied by the context so that the exact pair does not occur nineteen times (e.g., 1 Cor 14:2). He counts thirty-five total references to speaking in tongues. Harrisville, "Speaking in Tongues," 36. Hovenden finds no parallel use of the word pair outside the New Testament. Hovenden, *Speaking in Tongues*, 59–60. See his discussion of a possible hearing miracle. *Speaking in Tongues*, 64–72.

38. Turner, "Early Christian Experience," 7.

39. Contra Johnson, *Religious Experience*, 111; Everts suggests both a speaking and hearing miracle. Jenny Everts, "Tongues or Languages?" 74–75. Montague suggests a hearing miracle or possibly interpretation of tongues. Montague, *First Corinthians*, 281.

40. These five phrases dominate the narrative at this point: "a sound came," "it filled the house," "divided tongues were seen," "all were filled," and "they began to speak." Other verbs are present, but these five appear to capture the main thoughts.

41. Bruce, *Acts of the Apostles*, 82. In 1 Chr 25:1, ἀποφθέγγομαι is used in reference to prophesying with the harp.

Only when the source of inspired utterance is mentioned does the Spirit become the subject, which helps define the Spirit's distinctive role in inspiring speech. The structure and vocabulary of this section reinforce the Spirit's role in inspiring speech (especially tongues), but Luke does not credit the Spirit with any miracle of hearing in this narrative.

The Tongues of Nations (Acts 2:5–13)

An Overview of Acts 2:5–13

Luke's repetition of "And there were" in Acts 2:5 (cf. v. 1) along with an update on the setting that includes the presence of many devout Jews in Jerusalem signals to the reader that the next phase of the story has begun. The origin of the festival's participants "from every nation under heaven" provides a transition into the list of nations, anticipates the universal scope of the gospel, emphasizes the invitation to "the whole house of Israel" addressed at the pinnacle of Peter's speech (2:36),[42] and reminds the reader of the Christ who entered into heaven. The sound that caught the attention of the crowd could be a reference to the tongues only, but perhaps the similarity of the phrases "And suddenly a sound came from heaven" (καὶ ἐγένετο ἄφνω ἐκ τοῦ οὐρανοῦ ἦχος; v. 2) and "and when this sound came" (γενομένης δὲ τῆς φωνῆς ταύτης; v. 6) indicates that the sound like a forceful wind and the sound of other tongues both capture the audience's attention.

Upon his stating that the crowd gathered, Luke follows with five verbs that describe the emotional state of the observers (a typical Lukan feature). They were "bewildered" because each person heard the disciples speaking in his own native language (v. 6). They were also "amazed" (ἐξίσταντο) and were "marveling" because of the Galilean identity of the speakers (v. 7). With this third verb the crowd speaks in the first person as a character in the story, and the reader views the event through its eyes.[43] The lengthy list of nations is framed with two similar statements emphasizing the intelligibility of the language miracle: "How is it that we each hear in our own language in which we were born?" (v. 8) and "We hear them speaking in our own tongues the great things of God" (v. 11). One senses the immanence of God in revealing himself to humanity

42. Fitzmyer, *Acts*, 239.

43. Tannehill, *The Narrative Unity*, 2:28–29.

in all its diversity of geography and language. The list of nations is also framed by the resumption of emotional verbs, as the fourth verb expresses the amazement of all from the perspective of the narrator and with an identical term to that in verse 7: "And they were all amazed" (ἐξίσταντο δὲ πάντες; v. 12). They were also "perplexed," (v. 12) which has its counterpart in "bewildered" (v. 6) and which leads to the question: "What does this mean?" (v. 12). The ridiculous suggestion that the disciples have had too much to drink is countered by the adversative δὲ ("but") when Peter stands to speak under the inspiration of the Spirit (vv. 13–14).

This portion of the narrative provides the bridge between the outpouring of the Spirit and Peter's sermon, which explains the event and expounds on the christological implications of it. Although there are several thorny interpretive issues in this middle section of the story, the record is essential for establishing the symbolic significance of tongues and their doxological content. The discussion below addresses these issues.

The Symbolism of Tongues: The International Reign of Christ

Two related issues confront interpreters of Acts 2:5–13. The first concerns the origin of the list of nations (vv. 9–11), and the second concerns the possible relationship between Pentecost and Babel. The former issue is not essential to the interpretation of the passage, but if Luke intends his list of nations to echo the Table of Nations (Gen 10), then Luke likely intends his readers to view Babel as somehow related to Pentecost. The search for a backdrop to Luke's list of nations has engendered a considerable amount of controversy among interpreters. "The four most commonly suggested sources are ancient astrological lists, lists of the Jewish Diaspora, Gen 10 and the Table of Nations, and biblical prophecies such as Isa 11:11 that speak of the eschatological ingathering of Jews from the Diaspora."[44] Among the least likely explanations for Luke's list is the notion that Luke borrows from an astrological chart.[45] While Luke takes

44. Gilbert, "List of Nations," 500–1. Not all of these views are entirely mutually exclusive, especially if later biblical texts or lists of Diaspora Jews reflect the Table of Nations.

45. Not only is the evidence for this view lacking, but it seems highly unlikely that an author who expends considerable energy refuting witchcraft and related practices would seek to introduce something connected to superstition into his narrative. Beare is representative of those who view the list as "drawn from an astrological grouping of nations and countries according to the sign of the Zodiac." Beare, "Speaking with Tongues," 116. See also Williams, *Acts of the Apostles*, 64. Metzger dispels the notion

an interest in the Jewish Diaspora, it is unlikely that Luke incorporates an ancient list of the Diaspora, as areas of significant Jewish populations such as Greece and Syria are absent from Luke's list.

The view that Luke is drawing from biblical lists of nations that will partake of Israel's national restoration also runs into problems. Isaiah 11:11–12 is relevant to this discussion: "In that day the Lord will extend his hand yet a second time to recover the remnant that remains of his people, from Assyria, from Egypt, from Pathros, from Cush, from Elam, from Shinar, from Hamath, and from the coastlands of the sea. He will raise a signal for the nations and will assemble the banished of Israel, and gather the dispersed of Judah from the four corners of the earth" (ESV). Apart from the obvious problem that Luke's list does not match very well with this list is the further problem that Luke does not envision a soon return of Jews to Jerusalem but a departure from Jerusalem (Acts 1:8; 8:1) and the destruction of the city (Luke 21:20–24). While Israel's restoration awaits the *eschaton* (Acts 3:21), Luke's universal theme receives the accent. In addition, Luke gives no hint in the narrative that the Jews gathered at Pentecost had gathered in expectation of an eschatological fulfillment of the sort pictured in the above passage.[46]

Many scholars associate Luke's list with the Table of Nations in Gen 10, some of them also envisioning Pentecost as "nothing less than a reversal of the curse of Babel."[47] Others, such as Ben Witherington, register an opposing opinion: "There is no hard evidence that Luke intended Theophilus to think of Pentecost as the Tower of Babel in reverse, not least because the Spirit does not eliminate the difference in languages, but rather allows each to hear in those different languages."[48] Scott argues that the list of nations in Acts 2:9–11 is a partial list of the Table of Nations similar to Philo's list in *Legat.* 281–83.[49] Keener also believes Luke "provides samples" of the seventy nations from Gen 10, and therefore Luke likely alludes to the tower of Babel. "This suggestion becomes more likely when we consider that Babel represents the only scattering of languages in the OT and hence the only potential background for Luke's

---

that Luke depended on a non-extant, early version of Paulus of Alexandria's *Rudiments of Astrology* (A. D. fourth century). Metzger, "Ancient Astrological Geography," 123–33. See the discussion in Gilbert, "List of Nations," 501–2; Polhill, *Acts*, 103.

46. Gilbert, "List of Nations," 507.

47. Bruce, *Book of Acts*, 59.

48. Witherington, *Acts*, 131.

49. Scott, "Luke's Geographical Horizon," 528.

story shared by all his ideal audience."[50] The obvious commonality of a language miracle in Acts 2 and Gen 11 often causes scholars to assume some level of theological connection between the two.

Gilbert makes one of the more compelling cases for the backdrop of Acts 2:9–11, arguing that Christ's reign over the nations challenges Rome's claim to universal authority. He cites Tertullian (*Against the Jews* 7) as an early interpreter who held this position and backs his thesis with an impressive array of Roman propaganda lists of nations.[51] The disadvantage of Gilbert's position is that he must appeal to extra-biblical sources to establish his argument, but the advantage is that his thesis fits quite well with Luke's emphasis on Christ's Davidic reign. Ultimately, and Gilbert acknowledges this,[52] one could dismiss the notion that Luke fashions his list of nations after Roman lists and still embrace Luke's emphasis on the universal reach of the gospel, because Peter interprets the events in such a manner (Acts 2:14–36, 38–39, especially v. 17). The views represented by Keener and Gilbert are the most attractive, but perhaps it is simplest to say that Luke employed a familiar style to record an event that involved Diaspora Jews from all over the known world and that he was well aware that readers would reflect on the Genesis narrative. The discussion to follow suggests some verbal and theological parallels between Luke's narratives and the Genesis story that point to an intentional echo of Babel.

Luke's use of the Septuagint makes it the natural place to begin the search for verbal parallels. Many students of Acts point to the use of the aorist passive verb συνεχύθη from συγχέω ("bewildered" ESV, NASB, NLT; "confounded" KJV; "confused" NAB) in Acts 2:6 as an allusion to the Babel narrative, as this verb occurs in Gen 11:7, 9.[53] The verb συγχέω occurs only ten times in the Old Testament (LXX), and the noun σύγχυσις ("confusion") occurs only four times.[54] Neither the verb nor the noun ever occurs in the New Testament except for in Acts.[55] Because Luke

50. Keener, *Acts: Exegetical*, 1:841–42.

51. Gilbert, "List of Nations," 508–18.

52. Gilbert, "List of Nations," 521–22.

53. E.g., Keener, *Acts: Exegetical*, 1:843–44. Bock cautions against pressing the analogy with Babel too far. *Acts*, 101. The cognate noun σύγχυσις also occurs in Gen 11:9.

54. The verb: Gen 11:7, 9; 1 Sam 7:10; 1 Kings 21:43; Amos 3:15; Mic 7:17; Joel 2:1, 10; Jon 4:1; Nah 2:5. The noun: Gen 11:9; 1 Sam 5:6, 11; 14:20.

55. The verb: Acts 2:6; 9:22; 19:32; 21:27, 31. The noun: 19:29. It is also important to note that Luke uses the terms in the riot at Ephesus (19:29, 32) as part of a constellation of terms intentionally alluding to Pentecost yet contrasting with it. See the discussion in chapter 5.

commonly records people's reaction to events, the use of such expressive terms is not surprising. However, it is a bit surprising that Luke reserves the use of the term until Acts 2. In Acts the four other occurrences of the verb and one occurrence of the noun all occur in reference to unbelievers who are thrown into confusion as a result of the proclamation of Christ (9:22) or who are reacting in opposition to the message (21:27, 31). Of particular interest is the episode in Ephesus, where the verb (19:32) and the noun (v. 29) occur in reference to the riot instigated by the craftsmen opposing Paul. Echoes of Babel resound when the Ephesians are united (vv. 29, 34) in their idolatry and in defense of the greatness of Artemis, who is purportedly worshipped in all of Asia and in the entire inhabited world (v. 27; see chapter 5 below). "The city was filled with confusion [συγχύσεως]" (v. 29). It would be much easier to dismiss the possible association between Ephesus, Pentecost, and Babel if it were not for the fact that one of the key purposes of the Genesis account was to explain the origin of that name: "On account of this the name of it was called Confusion [Σύγχυσις]" (Gen 11:9).[56] Therefore, it is likely that Luke intends an echo of Babel in his employment of this term and its cognates.

Some other verbal parallels between Pentecost and Babel exist. Genesis 11:7 not only has the "confusion" but also τὴν γλῶσσαν ("the tongue"), the similar phrase μὴ ἀκούσωσιν ἕκαστος ("each may not hear"; cf. ἡμεῖς ἀκούομεν ἕκαστος, "we each hear"; Acts 2:8), and τὴν φωνὴν ("the voice;" cf. τῆς φωνῆς; Acts 2:6).[57] It is also ironic that Luke emphasizes how Jesus went "into heaven" and how the sound came "from heaven" (Acts 2:2) to Jews from every nation "under heaven," while those at Babel aspire to build a tower "unto heaven" (Gen 11:4). In addition, Luke not only lists the nations in Acts 2 but also mentions "the nations" (τὰ ἔθνη) in Luke 24:47 and Acts 2:5. This may reflect the repeated reference to nations in Gen 10:5, 20, 31, 32 (cf. 12:2).[58]

The story of Babel may have been on Luke's mind when he penned the account of the irrational devotion to Artemis in Acts 19, but there is also substantial reason to believe that Babel was directly in Luke's purview

56. Wenham comments, "The whole story is built up to explain the word 'Babel' and to characterize it as under divine judgment." Wenham, *Genesis 1–15*, 241.

57. Davies has also noticed some verbal parallels. Davies, "Pentecost and Glossolalia," 228–29.

58. Scott also points to Luke's references to the whole "inhabited world" and the "earth" as indicative of Luke's cognizance of the Table of Nations. Scott, "Luke's Geographical Horizon," 524n159.

in the story of Paul's witness in Athens (Acts 17:16–34). Paul alludes to the creation story (17:24–25) as a refutation of idolatry and rehearses the origin of the nations: "And he made from one man every nation of mankind to live on all the face of the earth, having determined allotted periods and the boundaries of their dwelling place, that they should seek God, and perhaps feel their way toward him and find him" (vv. 26–27a ESV; cf. Deut 32:8).[59] Frank Macchia notes the connection between Acts 17:24–27 and Gen 10 and how Paul's sermon implies "a positive reading of the Babel narrative, or at least its message."[60] Macchia sees tongues as not only a reversal of the judgment of Babel but also as symbolizing the fulfillment of its promise, as is illustrated in Acts 17.[61] Further evidence that Luke was cognizant of the account of Babel is supplied by a portion of his genealogy (Luke 3:35), which contains several names from Gen 11.[62] Given the apparent verbal and theological allusions to the account of Babel and Luke's integration of numerous Scripture references in his writings, it seems reasonable to conclude that Luke intended his audience to hear an echo of Babel in the Pentecostal story.

More pointers to an intentional allusion to Babel will be highlighted below, but the larger question concerns Luke's purpose in stirring memories of Babel in his readers. Pentecost is technically not a reversal of Babel, as Witherington notes, but this is not the end of the story,[63] as a more nuanced perspective allows for an allusion to Babel without demanding that Pentecost be, strictly speaking, a reversal of the event. A good place to begin in determining Luke's possible interest in the story is with an understanding of Babel as not only an act of judgment but also one of grace.

The events of Babel only make sense within the larger primeval history of Genesis and the account of Adam and Eve. The first couple are

59. Mathews sees this passage as reflecting the words of Moses' song in Deut 32:8. Mathews, *Genesis 1—11:26*, 430.

60. Macchia, "Babel," 43.

61. Macchia, "Babel," 45. For a detailed comparison of Paul's speech at Athens and the Table of Nations, see Scott, *Paul and the Nations*, 176–79.

62. Bock, *Luke*, 1:358. The names also appear in 1 Chr 1.

63. Kurz sees Babel as a reversal, but the reversal he envisions involves God's healing of division in humanity. "The unifying power of the Spirit will be frequently demonstrated throughout Acts as people who would never before have associated with one another—Jews and Gentiles, slaves and prominent people, the upright and the formerly impious—share a common life of brotherhood and sisterhood in the Church." Kurz, *Acts of the Apostles*, 45.

made in the image of God (1:27), blessed (v. 28), commanded to "be fruitful and multiply and fill the earth" (v. 28 ESV), and instructed to exercise royal authority in subduing and ruling over the earth (v. 28; cf. 2:15). Humanity's call to cover the earth and act as God's royal vassals in making the earth a place of praise and a sanctuary of God's presence preceded the fall, but this divine intention was not nullified by human sin. After Adam's arrogant attempt to become like God, the narrative affirms the image of God in humanity but also points to a new kind of human solidarity with Adam, who has a son in his own likeness and image (5:1–3). This new solidarity involves death, as the refrain "and then he died" reminds the reader (vv. 5, 8, 11, 14, 17, 20, 27, 31). Yet even the escalation of sin resulting in the flood judgment does not entirely remove all grace (6:8) and blessing (9:1) nor abolish the original command, "Be fruitful and multiply and fill the earth" (9:1, 7 ESV). The Septuagint even suggests the concept of "ruling over" (κατακυριεύσατε) after the flood in 9:1. Immediately after the record of God's covenant with Noah and every living thing, the reader discovers that, from Noah's three sons, people have scattered over "the whole earth" (כָל־הָאָרֶץ; πᾶσαν τὴν γῆν LXX; v. 19). The report seems encouraging, as God's plan moves in the right direction, but hints of what lay ahead come in the form of a curse on Canaan (9:25) and the completion of the account of Adam (5:1) with a final "and then he died" in reference to Noah (9:29).

Still, the new division starting in Gen 10:1 gives hope for the fulfillment of the divine directive, with the table of seventy nations symbolizing the fullness of humanity.[64] In addition, the genealogies of Noah's sons form three divisions in the Table of Nations, each ending with a summary of the dispersal of the nations into their own territories by clan and language (10:5, 20, 31). The Table of Nations concludes with a summary of how the nations spread out "over the earth" (בָּאָרֶץ; ἐπὶ τῆς γῆς LXX; v. 32). At this point it appears that God's purposes are being realized, but the explanation of how the scattering transpired reinforces the notion that God's purposes advance with a mixture of judgment and grace, and largely despite the fallenness of humanity. Hamilton points out how the Table of Nations precedes the Babel narrative as a means of connecting the nations to God's blessing of fruitfulness in 9:1 and not only to his judgment in 11:1–9.[65]

64. Wenham also notices several multiples of seven within the genealogies. Wenham, *Genesis 1–15*, 209. Also see Sailhamer, "Genesis," 99–100.

65. Hamilton, *Genesis: Chapters 1–17*, 347.

The account of Babel commences immediately after the language and territorial summary related to Shem's line (10:31) and the overall genealogical summary of Noah's sons spreading out over the earth (v. 32). The beginning of the Babel account reflects these summaries and especially 9:19 when it commences, "Now the whole earth [כָל־הָאָרֶץ; πᾶσα ἡ γῆ] had one language and the same words" (11:1 MT, LXX). Various scholars have noticed the chiastic arrangement of the episode,[66] which ends with the explanation of the name "Babel" and the Lord confusing the language of "the whole earth" (כָּל־הָאָרֶץ; πάσης τῆς γῆς) and scattering the people "over the face of all the earth" (כָּל־הָאָרֶץ; πάσης τῆς γῆς; v. 9 MT, LXX). The irony in the story is that humans in their Adamic arrogance rebelled against the divine blessing and sought to "make a name" for themselves and avoid scattering "over the face of all the earth" (כָל־הָאָרֶץ; πάσης τῆς γῆς; v. 4 MT, LXX) but experienced precisely what they intended to avoid. The name "Babel" is not what they had in mind, and "Yahweh scattered them from there over the face of all the earth" (כָל־הָאָרֶץ; πάσης τῆς γῆς; v. 8 MT, LXX).

The Table of Nations emphasizes the solidarity of humanity in sharing the same father but also humanity as invested with a great deal of diversity. However, God's original plan for humanity to cover the earth and express the image of God through praise of its creator with creativity, artistry, diversity, and even a complexity of language development has been nearly thwarted. Man is not only in the image of God, but in a negative way, also in the image of Adam. The people of Babel mirror Adam in his fall, refuse to fill the earth with the glory of God, and pervert the sacredness of human solidarity by using it for idolatrous ends. But the judgment of Babel is laced with grace, for God intervenes in order to prevent humanity's self-destruction and to reorient the people toward the divine purpose. In addition, the location of the episode of Babel between God's blessing of fruitfulness and the story of Abraham accentuates God's redemptive plan for a pathetic people and fallen nations who cannot save themselves.[67]

66. Mathews, *Genesis 1—11:26*, 468; Wenham, *Genesis 1–15*, 235.

67. Mathews notes the arrangement of material: "This interspersal of narrative (11:1–9) separates the two genealogies of Shem (10:21–31; 11:10–26), paving the way for the particular linkage between the Terah (Abraham) clan and the Shemite lineage (11:27). The story of the tower also looks ahead by anticipating the role that Abram (12:1–3) will play in restoring the blessing to the dispersed nations." Mathews, *Genesis 1—11:26*, 428.

The lineage of Shem (11:10–26) forms a bridge to the account of Terah,[68] Abraham's father (v. 27), and to the story the author is most eager to tell, but even Abraham's story begins with the smell of death. There is a death sandwich in 11:27–32, for between the deaths of Haran (v. 28) and Terah (v. 32), the problem of death confronts Abram in the form of Sarai's barrenness (v. 30). From this environment of death, the Lord over the nations of chapters 10–11 demonstrates his mastery over death and raises up a line that will bring blessing to the nations. Consequently, the call of Abraham echoes the language of the previous narrative when God instructs him: "Go out from your land [τῆς γῆς σου] and go to the land which I will show you [τὴν γῆν ἣν ἄν σοι δείξω]" (Gen 12:1 LXX). In Abraham will be blessed "all the families of the earth" (כֹּל מִשְׁפְּחֹת הָאֲדָמָה; πᾶσαι αἱ φυλαὶ τῆς γῆς; v. 3 MT, LXX).[69] In the particularity of Abraham's call, the universal picture remains in view. God's intention to bless continues (vv. 2–3), and, in contrast to the attempt of the people of Babel to make a name for themselves (11:4), God will make Abraham's "name great" (12:2).[70] In contrast to the crowd at Babel, Abraham is a man who calls on "the name of the Lord" (12:8; 13:4; 21:33) and receives a new name (17:5).

The discussion above highlights the repeated references to "the earth," and especially the various versions of "all the earth" in Gen 9:19; 11:4, 8, 9 (2x); and 12:3.[71] This is only the beginning of the universal concern for the nations expressed in the Scriptures. God speaks to Isaiah and promises, "It is too light a thing that you should be my servant to raise up the tribes of Jacob and to bring back the preserved of Israel; I

68. Sailhamer articulates how the genealogies accentuate the role of Abraham as God's central agent in his gracious response to the nations of Babel: "The genealogy of Shem in 10:21–31 is traced from Shem to the sons of Joktan, the brother of Peleg. After the account of the building of the city of Babylon, the genealogy of Shem is taken up again and traced through Peleg to Abraham (11:10–26). Thus the one line of Shem ends in Babylon and thither in the land with Abraham." Sailhamer, "Genesis," 102n25.

69. Mathews highlights the verbal connections between the Table of Nations and the call of Abraham: "The table's common use of 'lands' (*ʾarṣîm*), 'families' (*mišpĕḥōt*), and 'nations' (*gôyim*) in its structural refrain (vv. 5, 20, 31–32) is heard again in the call to Abraham (12:1–3)." Mathews, *Genesis 1–11:26*, 430.

70. Hamilton, *Genesis: Chapters 1–17*, 372.

71. The "earth" or "land" is mentioned 358 times in Genesis, but the scattering over all the earth is primarily mentioned in the pericopes under discussion.

will make you as a light for the nations, that my salvation may reach to the end of the earth [ἕως ἐσχάτου τῆς γῆς]" (Isa 49:6 ESV). In Acts 1:8 the disciples will be empowered with the Spirit to be witnesses "unto the end of the earth" (ἕως ἐσχάτου τῆς γῆς). Thus it comes as no surprise when Peter preaches this message: "You are the sons of the prophets and of the covenant that God made with your fathers, saying to Abraham, 'And in your offspring shall all the families of the earth be blessed'" (Acts 3:25 ESV; cf. Gen 12:3; 22:18; 26:4).[72] Luke points to the Hebrew Scriptures (via the LXX) not to show a reversal of Babel, but to point to the covenant with Abraham as an explanation of the events of Pentecost. The Davidic reign of Christ has its roots in the covenant with Abraham (Luke 1:69–73), and Luke depicts Pentecost as the event that commences the expansion of Christ's rule over all the nations of the earth. Luke depicts Pentecost as a major update of the progress of redemption since Babel.

Luke develops the theme of the universal reach of the gospel in fulfillment of the Abrahamic and Davidic promises all throughout Luke-Acts. The good news and joy is for all people (Luke 2:10), salvation is for both gentiles and Jews (vv. 30–32; cf. Isa 42:6; 49:6), "All flesh will see God's salvation" (Luke 3:6), Luke's genealogy includes Adam and embraces all of humanity (3:38), Elisha and Elijah minister outside of Israel (4:26–27), the Roman Centurion is a man of faith (7:9), a Samaritan acts with love (10:33), another Samaritan is the only thankful person among ten (17:15–19), people from all directions will eat at the eschatological banquet (13:29), the outcasts also attend this banquet (14:23), and Jesus promises that the gospel will be preached "to all nations" (εἰς πάντα τὰ ἔθνη; 24:47; cf. Gen 12:3). From Acts 1:8 forward the entire book of Acts catalogs the spread of Christ's kingdom to the nations.

Comparing Pentecost with Babel is a bit complex and requires more nuance than to just say that Pentecost is a reversal of Babel. On the surface, the stories share a language miracle, a sense of human solidarity, a concern for the global praise of God, and a clear path to the accomplishment of that concern. But diversity in language is not inherently bad, and Pentecost does not reverse the multiple languages. The process of diversification was accelerated at Babel, and the diverse tongues at Pentecost represent God's interest in the diversity of people scattered over the globe. The solidarity of Babel was wicked and idolatrous and wielded against God, but the unity of the believers at Pentecost came in direct

72. Although the Septuagint of these texts does not provide a verbatim match with Acts 3:25, the quotation obviously has its roots in these texts.

obedience to the command of Christ (Luke 24:49; Acts 1:4) and was endorsed and energized by the Spirit. The spreading of the nations over the earth from Babel was forced because of the indifference to God's command and to his plan to make the whole earth a sanctuary of his presence and praise. Pentecost marks the beginning of the universal praise of God. After Babel the reorientation of humanity back to fulfilling God's purpose proceeds through the line of Abraham. At Pentecost, the same is true, only a new level of fulfillment in the historical-redemptive plan has come to pass in the Lord Jesus Christ.

The story of Pentecost almost inevitably brings to mind the story of Babel, but this is not to present a reversal of the tongues of Babel or to strictly identify Luke's list of nations with those in Genesis;[73] the purpose is to point to God's redemptive plan in reaching all nations through Abraham. Luke embraces the larger theological purpose of Gen 10–12, and even though the people gathered at Pentecost are Jewish, the "devout men from every nation under heaven" (Acts 2:5) proleptically signify the spread of the gospel to the gentiles (ch. 10). Christology and missiology are inseparable, for the exalted Christ is Lord of the nations. Tongues are therefore the perfect symbol of the Spirit's empowerment to witness to Christ among the nations. This is also why the tongues are known languages in Acts 2, for the first occurrence establishes their symbolic significance in relation to the nations.[74] Keener notes, "Luke does not present tongues as a sign of Spirit baptism merely arbitrarily, but because it is logically connected to the purpose of baptism in the Spirit. Luke emphasizes baptism in the Spirit as power to testify for Christ cross-culturally."[75] Keener and others see in the sign of tongues and Peter's sermon a basis for ethnic reconciliation and "the church's multiethnic mission to bring all humanity to recognize its rightful Lord, Jesus Christ."[76] Tongues, then, are the perfect symbol connecting the blessing of the nations through Abraham with the reign of Jesus Christ and mission of the church. Luke's

73. That is, Luke's list of nations may be reminiscent of Gen 10–11, but he does not intend to copy the list.

74. Hovenden correctly points out that other occurrences of tongues in Acts do not include the element of intelligibility; consequently, tongues must have some other purpose for Luke than to reverse unintelligibility in language. That is, the symbolic element must be central to the phenomenon. Hovenden, *Speaking in Tongues*, 87.

75. Keener, "Why Does Luke Use Tongues?" 178.

76. Keener, "Why Does Luke Use Tongues?" 182. See Dempster, "The Church's Moral Witness," 1–7; Macchia, "Baptized in the Spirit," 10; Amos Yong, *Spirit Poured Out*, 171–76.

allusions to redemptive history connect the tongues of Pentecost with missiology and Christology.

The Content and Orientation of Tongues: Praise to the King

The nature of Pentecostal tongues is a matter of debate among interpreters, but most view the tongues of Pentecost as a form of praise. The text in question is Acts 2:11b: "We hear them speaking in our own tongues the mighty deeds of God" (ἀκούομεν λαλούντων αὐτῶν ταῖς ἡμετέραις γλώσσαις τὰ μεγαλεῖα τοῦ θεοῦ). Menzies opts for the minority position: "The product of this divine gift should not be understood simply as praise directed to God. It is, above all, proclamation. This is suggested by the language miracle and confirmed by the content of the inspired speech, τὰ μεγαλεῖα τοῦ θεοῦ (Acts 2:11). In the LXX τὰ μεγαλεῖα is usually connected with verbs of proclamation and, as such, is addressed to people."[77] Turner alludes to the birth narratives as a backdrop of "invasive charismatic praise" and concludes that Pentecostal tongues are "a special form of doxological prophetic speech" (cf. Acts 10:46; 19:6).[78] The adjective μεγαλεῖος ("greatness") seldom occurs in the Old Testament but occurs more frequently in the Apocrypha, especially in Sirach.[79] In Deut 11:2 it refers to God's miracles during the exodus, and in Ps 70:19 (LXX; 71:19 ET) the psalmist addresses God in the second person and praises him for his greatness.

In Sirach the poet tells of God's greatness rather than addressing him directly, but this is not proclamation in the evangelistic sense; it is praising God by reviewing his mighty acts. In Sir 17:10 (LXX), praising God's holy name is in parallel with relating his mighty works. At Sinai "their eyes saw the greatness [μεγαλεῖον] of his glory and their ears heard the glory of his voice" (Sir 17:13; cf. Acts 2:11, 33). In Sir 42:21 and 43:15 the poet describes the greatness of God in a manner not unlike the biblical wisdom literature, but the genre would not likely preclude anyone from classifying such extolling of God's works as praise.[80] That the priestly blessing of Jesus in Luke 24:50–51 seems to reflect the blessing

77. Menzies, *Empowered for Witness*, 177.

78. Turner, *Power from on High*, 271.

79. Sir 17:8, 10, 13; 18:4; 36:10; 42:21; 43:15; 45:24; cf. Tob 11:15; 2 Macc 3:34; 7:17; 3 Macc 7:22. The T. Job 51.4 has the identical phrase τὰ μεγαλεῖα τοῦ θεοῦ, but this may reflect Christian influence.

80. So Turner, *Power from on High*, 272.

of the high priest Simon II in Sir 50:20–21 might suggest that Luke was familiar with that work.[81]

Since the adjective is a *hapax legomenon* in the New Testament, there is no reason to believe Luke intends a technical definition for the adjective μεγαλεῖος; however, this word and its cognates play a significant role in Luke's emphasis on praise, in the tongues passages in Acts, and in contrasting the greatness of God and Christ with the imposters mentioned in Acts. Simon's magic (Acts 8:9–10) and the idolatrous allegiance to Artemis (19:23–41) illustrate the latter point (see chapter 5).[82] In reference to tongues, Luke uses the verbal form to describe a similar outpouring in Acts 10:46: "For they were hearing them speaking in tongues and magnifying [μεγαλυνόντων] God." The outcome of Paul's christocentric and Spirit-empowered ministry in Ephesus was that "the name of the Lord Jesus was magnified [ἐμεγαλύνετο]" (Acts 19:17; cf. Phil 1:20; 2 Pet 1:16).

It is well known that Luke focuses on prayer and praise,[83] and sometimes the two seem to merge into one prayer/praise prophetic pronouncement (Luke 1:46–55, 67–79; 10:21), much as in the Psalms. The *Magnificat* is a mix of prayer and praise reflecting Hannah's song (1 Sam 2:1–10), and Mary's song begins with "My soul magnifies [μεγαλύνει] the Lord" (Luke 1:46; cf. v. 58). Both songs also have a prophetic element focused on a coming king (1 Sam 2:10; Luke 1:32–33, 43, 46–55), and Mary's song follows a reference to her experiencing the power of the Spirit (v. 35). In 1 Chr 25 David, Israel's great psalmist, organizes prophetic worship in preparation for temple service. Prophetic prayer and praise were not uncommon in Israel's history (1 Sam 10:5; 2 Sam 23:2–4; 2 Kings 3:15), so it is quite in keeping with tradition for Luke to narrate the Spirit's filling with a convergence of praise and prophecy. Luke cradles the Pentecostal outpouring in prayer (Acts 1:14; 2:42) and associates the Spirit with prayer on various occasions (Luke 3:21–22; 4:1–2; 11:13; Acts 4:31). Seeing as Peter explains the tongues of Pentecost as prophetic in nature (Acts 2:17–18), it is reasonable to view the disciples'

81. See the discussion in Lidbeck, *Resurrection and Spirit*, 188–92.

82. There appears to be a play on words in Acts 8:9, as Simon the "magician" (μαγεύων) thinks he is someone "great" (μέγαν). The adjective "great" (μέγας) is used two more times in verse 10. At Ephesus the adjective is used four times of Artemis (19:27, 28, 34, 35), and the noun "magnificence" (μεγαλειότης) is used of her once (v. 27). This is in contrast to the greatness of the Lord Jesus, whose name is "magnified" (ἐμεγαλύνετο) in 19:17.

83. E.g., see the discussion in Shelton, *Mighty in Word*, 85–92.

declaration of the "the great deeds" (τὰ μεγαλεῖα) of God in Acts 2:11 as a form of prophetic praise in keeping with Israel's psalmists and prophets.[84] Such prayer and praise often includes a rehearsal of God's mighty deeds, but it does not quite qualify as preaching per se.[85] Peter follows the tongues speech with preaching in a familiar language, and, as D. A. Carson observes, the speaking in tongues "generates questions . . . not conversions."[86] The tongues of Pentecost are a form of prophetic praise.

What are the "mighty deeds," "wonders" (NIV 2011), or "great things" (τὰ μεγαλεῖα) for which the disciples offer praise (Acts 2:11)? Luke 9:43 offers an interesting parallel for comparison with Pentecost. After Jesus' transfiguration he performs an exorcism on a boy, and the crowd reacts, "And they were all amazed at the greatness [μεγαλειότητι] of God." The praise to God and the miracles of Jesus are not far apart, even though the audience is still in the dark about Jesus' identity. The close proximity between the praise of God and the awe of Jesus occurs again at Pentecost when Peter implies that the Day of the Lord is the Day of the Lord Jesus and the name of the Lord is the name of the Lord Jesus (Acts 2:20–21). The miracle in Luke 9 points the way to a greater expression of worship in Acts 2, where the betrayed Jesus has risen from the dead and become "both Lord and Christ" (v. 36). Thus, even though the praise concerns the great deeds "of God" (Acts 2:11), "the reference is probably to the mighty acts of God which are contained in His epiphany in Christ."[87] Given the christocentric sermon of Peter in Acts 2 and the entire resurrection and ascension context of Acts 1–2, the only reasonable answer to the question is that the "great deeds" directly concern the miraculous and salvific work of God in Christ. More specifically, given the emphasis on the Spirit's outpouring as a direct consequence of Jesus' resurrection and enthronement, it is safe to conclude that the praise is both theocentric and christocentric, in honor of the God who exalted

84. Zechariah's restoration of speech and prophetic utterance (Luke 1:64) shares with Acts 2:4 the verb λαλέω ("to speak") and the noun γλῶσσα ("tongue"). The result of the loosing of Zechariah's tongue was that "he was speaking, blessing God" (ἐλάλει εὐλογῶν τὸν θεόν). The content of the inspired speech was praise to God.

85. Peterson arrives at a similar conclusion: "From Peter's sermon in vv. 16–36 we may judge that this included affirmations about Jesus and his exaltation, as well as thanksgiving for the gift of his Spirit, but such speech cannot simply be identified as missiological proclamation. Clearly there was a missiological implication of their praise, but this was not its primary function and purpose." Peterson, *Acts*, 137–38.

86. Carson, *Showing the Spirit*, 143.

87. Grundmann, "μέγας, μεγαλεῖον, κτλ.," 541.

Jesus as Lord and Christ and of the Davidic King who is Lord and Christ (2:36). The content of tongues in Acts 2 is praise, and its orientation is toward God and Christ.

Jesus, the Davidic Lord and Christ (Acts 2:14–36)

After the crowd at Pentecost remarks about hearing the great things of God in their own tongues, Luke adds his fourth and fifth expressions of their amazement (Acts 2:12; cf. vv. 6–7) and uses two additional comments from them to transition into Peter's speech (vv. 14–36). First they ask, "What does this mean?" (v. 12). The question not only indicates the crowd's confusion, "but also marks an appropriate reader response to the story and an effective bridge to Peter's explanatory speech in the next scene."[88] The previous episode of tongues speech cannot be disconnected from Peter's speech. The second response of others in the crowd is a dismissive mocking of the disciples for supposedly having had too much new wine (v. 13).[89] The adversative δὲ ("but") in verse 14 contrasts Peter, supported by the Eleven, with the confused crowd. Luke employs the same term he previously used to describe the inspired nature of tongues to describe Peter's inspired speech (ἀποφθέγγομαι; vv. 4, 14). The effect is to present Peter as having divine revelation, acting as an inspired hermeneut, and explaining the day's events under the Spirit's inspiration in contrast to the ridiculous accusations and spiritual obtuseness of the crowd. With the filling of the Spirit, Peter acts as a prophet who declares the message of Christ.[90] Peter's argument is examined below.

Acts 2:14–36 contains several structural elements indicating that this passage should be understood as a unit and that the declaration of Jesus as "Lord and Christ" in verse 36 serves as the main theological point of Peter's sermon. The record of Peter's speech itself makes this passage a natural unit, but the phrases "let this be known to you" (v. 14) and "let all the house of Israel know" (v. 36) seem to form an inclusio.[91] Both verses address the Jewish people. Peter's direct address to the Jewish men (v. 14)

88. Spencer, *Journeying through Acts*, 44.

89. The Spirit and wine are also differentiated in Luke 1:15 (cf. Eph 5:18).

90. Spencer notes how Luke "stresses the importance of Peter's speech through a string of redundant introductory comments in 2.14–15 linked by 'and.'" Spencer, *Journeying through Acts*, 45. Dibelius highlights how ancient authors incorporated speeches into their writings with a specific agenda in mind. Dibelius, *Studies in Acts*, 145–55.

91. Tannehill, *Narrative Unity*, 2:35.

followed by his quotation of Joel 2:28–32 forms the first of three such divisions in Peter's speech (Acts 2:14–21). Peter appeals to the Israelite men in verse 22 and quotes Ps 15:8–11 (LXX), forming a second division (Acts 2:22–28). A third unit follows (vv. 29–36) when he addresses the Jewish men as "brothers" (v. 29) and quotes Ps 109:1 (LXX).[92] The quotation of Joel (Acts 2:17–21) demonstrates that the outpouring of the Spirit and speaking in tongues is a fulfillment of biblical prophecy, that Pentecost is an eschatological event (Peter interprets Joel's "afterward" as "in the last days" [Joel 3:1 LXX; Acts 2:17]), and that the ultimate goal of all this is salvation (2:21, 38). The Joel quotation also helps the speech transition into its primary focus on the story and identity of Jesus (vv. 20–21) in the speech's second and third segments. Regarding the biblical precedent for Pentecost, Peter explains that Joel's prophecy of the outpouring of the Spirit issuing forth in prophetic speech is fulfilled at Pentecost; that is, tongues are a form of prophetic utterance.

The Nature of Tongues: Prophetic Speech

Many Lukan scholars now acknowledge the prophetic nature of tongues in Acts 2, and several authors have addressed this.[93] Peter responds to the crowd's question, "What does this mean?" (v. 12b), with a pesher style reference to Joel ("this is that"; v. 16).[94] Although Peter will not elucidate the full meaning of the day's events until the end of the speech, the quotation of Joel provides an immediate insight into the prophetic nature of the speaking in tongues: "And it shall come to pass afterward, that I will pour out my Spirit on all flesh; your sons and your daughters shall prophesy, your old men shall dream dreams, and your young men shall see visions. Even on the male and female servants in those days I will pour out my Spirit" (Joel 2:28–29 ESV). For emphasis Peter makes some alterations to Joel's text, and he adds "and they will prophesy" at the end of this quotation. Thus, ἐκχεῶ ἀπὸ τοῦ πνεύματός μου ("I will pour out of my Spirit") with καὶ προφητεύσουσιν ("and they will prophecy") frame the quotation in Acts 2:17–18, suggest that dreams and visions

92. Moessner, "*Two* Lords 'at the Right Hand'?" 216–17.

93. E.g., Stronstad, *Charismatic Theology: Trajectories*; Stronstad, *Prophethood of All Believers*; Menzies, *Empowered for Witness*; Oss, "A Pentecostal/Charismatic View," 254; Peterson, *Acts*, 134; Polhill, *Acts*, 109; Turner, *Power from on High*.

94. See the discussion of the pesher style of interpretation of events in Keener, *Acts: Exegetical*, 1:873–74.

are prophetic, emphasize the prophetic nature of the outpouring of the Spirit, and define speaking in tongues as a form of prophetic utterance.

The diversity of people represented in Joel's prophecy fits well with the variety of people at Pentecost and elaborates on the barrier-breaking nature of the event. The Spirit not only crosses national, racial, and ethnic lines, but the scope of his acceptance includes both genders and all ages without regard to status in society. The presence of women at Pentecost, including Jesus' mother (Acts 1:14), illustrates the realization of Joel's prophecy and expands the symbolic breadth of speaking in tongues.[95] God's prophets will span the globe and will be identified by relationship with and testimony to Christ rather than by geography, physical description, and status position.[96] Lenski notices how the phrase "and even on my male slaves and on my female slaves" includes a "climacteric or ascensive" *καί γε* ("and even" or "indeed") in 2:18,[97] stressing that no child of God (δούλους μου; "my male slaves") of any social status is beyond the Spirit's scope of blessing.[98] The addition of γε and μου (neither are found in the Septuagint) in Luke's account emphasizes not only the crossing of status boundaries but the identity of these diverse prophets as God's own, personal servants.[99] The God to whom death poses no barrier to his relationship with his people (Luke 20:34–38) is the God who generously blesses (he "pour[s] out" his Spirit) his people, turning their humble positions into exalted ones and making them his prophets to the nations.

Luke emphasizes the prophetic nature of the Spirit's work throughout his narrative. The early chapters of his Gospel are virtually a compendium of inspired utterances (1:41–55, 67–79; 2:25–38; 3:1–18; 4:18–19). Jesus is a prophet like Moses (Acts 3:22–23; 7:37; cf. Deut 18:15, 18–19; cf. 4Q175 5–8).[100] The Spirit is especially associated with empowering speech, and in Acts this empowerment is particularly associated with

95. Although some scholars limit the outpouring of the Spirit to the reconstituted Twelve at Pentecost, it seems likely that the entire 120 were present and that the specific mention of the women in Acts 1:14 intentionally points to diversity among the recipients of the Spirit (cf. Acts 21:9).

96. For an expectation that all Israelites would one day be prophets, see Num Rab 15:25.

97. Lenski, *Acts*, 75.

98. Menzies suggests that the alteration of the Septuagint from "the" to "my" (μου) in Acts 2:18 indicates that those who receive the Spirit are already believing members of the community. Menzies, *Empowered for Witness*, 182–84.

99. See the discussion in Keener, *Acts: Exegetical*, 2:882–86.

100. See the discussion of this in Johnson, *Prophetic Jesus*, 29–35.

the witnesses to Christ's resurrection (e.g., 1:8; 3:15; 4:31–33; 5:32).[101] In the tradition of the Old Testament prophets, the disciples preach "the word of the Lord,"[102] but in Luke's narrative "the word" has become the kerygma, with its center the resurrection of Jesus (e.g., Acts 4:4; 8:14, 25; 10:36, 44; 13:49).

As Peter points out, there exists in the Old Testament an eschatological expectation of an outpouring of the Spirit characterized by prophetic speech. The Hebrew Scriptures mention the divine Spirit over 100 times. The Spirit plays a role in creation (Gen 1:2; Job 33:4; cf. Luke 1:35) and in giving and sustaining life (Job 34:14; Ezek 37:14). He is also associated with purity (Gen 6:3; 1 Sam 16:14; Ps 51:11; 143:10; Isa 63:10–11; Ezek 8:3; 11:1, 5; 36:27), judgment (Isa 4:4), and revelation (1 Chr 28:12). The Spirit is associated with God's presence and is often seen empowering the movement of God's plan toward divine goals. Thus, a major role of the Spirit is to grant divine enablement to Israel's leaders. He empowers Israel's craftsmen (Exod 31:3; 35:31) and the nation's deliverers and warriors, including Moses (Num 11:17), Joshua (27:18), Othniel (Judg 3:10), Gideon (6:34), Jephthah (11:29), and Samson (13:25). He empowers King Saul (1 Sam 10:1, 6, 10; 11:6) and King David (16:13). The prophets Elijah and Elisha owe their miraculous ministries to the Spirit (1 Kings 18:12; 2 Kings 2:9, 16), and Micah owes his boldness to the Spirit (Mic 3:8). The post-exilic leaders also function under the Spirit's enablement (Zech 4:6), and Isaiah envisions the Messiah as anointed with the Spirit for service (11:2; 61:1). Douglas Oss notes that the Old Testament held a two-fold expectation regarding the Spirit's work in the latter days. The first expectation was of the Spirit's work in performing an inner transformation of the heart (Jer 31:31–34; Ezek 11:19–20; 36:26–27; 37:14), but the second, the empowering work of the Spirit, "is much more evident than the inner-transforming" work.[103] It is this empowering work that Luke integrates into his story.

101. The Holy Spirit, witness/testimony, and resurrection are prominent themes in Luke-Acts. Reference to the divine Spirit (πνεῦμα) occurs 17 times in Luke's Gospel and 57 times in Acts. Eight different words for "witness," all sharing the same root, occur in Luke-Acts: μάρτυς (Luke 2x, Acts 13x), μαρτυρέω (Luke 1x, Acts 11x), διαμαρτύρομαι (Luke 1x, Acts 9x), μαρτύριον (Luke 3x, Acts 2x), μαρτυρία (Luke 1x, Acts 1x), μαρτύρομαι (Acts 2x), ἀμάρτυρος (Acts 1x), and ψευδομαρτυρέω (Luke 1x). A variety of words are used to describe the resurrection, but of the approximately 62 resurrection texts, 37 refer to Jesus' resurrection.

102. Keener, *Acts: Exegetical*, 1:881.

103. Oss, "A Pentecostal/Charismatic View," 245. See especially 245–49.

The author of Genesis depicts the activity of the hovering Spirit (1:2) in relation to the prophetic, creative pronouncements of Elohim (vv. 3–27),[104] so it is no surprise when prophetic activity is attributed to the Spirit throughout biblical literature. David (2 Sam 23:2), Amasai (1 Chr 12:18), and the Messiah (Isa 61:1) all speak under the Spirit's influence. The Spirit's prophetic enabling is evident in the seventy elders (Num 11:25), Saul (1 Sam 10:6), Azariah (2 Chr 15:1), Jahaziel (20:14), Zechariah (24:20), Isaiah (Isa 48:16), Ezekiel (Ezek 2:2), and all the prophets of Israel (Zech 7:12; Neh 9:30; cf. Num 24:2; 1 Sam 19:20, 23). I have listed many of the clearest references to the Spirit in the Old Testament, and it should be apparent how dominant is the emphasis on divine enablement (or the "vocational motif," to borrow a phrase from Stronstad) and prophetic speech throughout Israel's history.[105]

Luke clearly focuses on this vocational/prophetic role of the Spirit in Luke-Acts, although other roles are not entirely absent (Luke 1:35; Acts 9:31). But aside from Joel 2:28–29, the passage that most clearly expresses the eschatological hope for the democratization of the prophetic Spirit is Numbers 11:16–30. Moses, frustrated by the people's complaints, takes his own complaint to the Lord. In order to provide help with the task of leadership, the Lord transfers the Spirit to seventy elders, which is immediately evidenced by prophetic speech (v. 25). However, two of the men who had remained in the camp continued to prophesy after the others had ceased, and Joshua, anxious to protect Moses' unique status as God's prophet, appeals to Moses to stop them (v. 28). Moses replies, "Are you jealous for my sake? Would that all the LORD's people were prophets, that the LORD would put his Spirit on them!" (v. 29 ESV). Moses' holy wish and Joel's prophecy are fulfilled at Pentecost in the transfer of the Spirit from the exalted Christ to the disciples, in the prophetic sign of tongues, in the empowerment to serve, and in the democratization of the charismatic Spirit.[106]

104. Hildebrandt, *Old Testament Theology*, 35.

105. Stronstad, *Charismatic Theology: Trajectories*, 26. For a discussion of how Luke uses the Hebrew Scripture to advance his prophetic agenda, see Johnson, *Prophetic Jesus*, 23–38.

106. See Stronstad, *Charismatic Theology* and also *Prophethood of All Believers* for a discussion of these emphases.

Jesus, the Risen and Ascended Davidite

Peter's quotation of Joel began with a reference to "the last days," and this emphasis on eschatology continues throughout the quotation and then forms a bridge to Peter's identification of Jesus. Luke's account adds "above [ἄνω]," "signs [σημεῖα]," and "below [κάτω]" to Joel's account (Acts 2:19; Joel 3:3 LXX). These "wonders in heaven above" and "signs on the earth below" are neither extraneous items unrelated to the argument nor exhausted of their symbolic significance on the day of Pentecost. Roger Stronstad, dissatisfied with attempts to relate the symbols to the crucifixion or consummation, calls such attempts "a counsel of despair."[107] Luke's addition of σημεῖα ("signs")[108] to Joel's text and the immediate attribution of "miracles, wonders, and signs" to Jesus in Acts 2:22 indicate that the reader is to understand all the theophanic signs of Pentecost as part of the eschatological activity of God evident in Christ's ministry (2:22) and continuing through the exalted Christ. Just as God attested to Jesus with miraculous signs at his baptism (Luke 3:22) and through miracles during his earthly ministry (ἀποδεδειγμένον, "having been attested"; Acts 2:22), God also attested to Christ by raising him from the dead (v. 24). Christ's resurrection is part of the complex of eschatological signs, along with the outpouring of the Spirit and accompanying manifestations, that signals the inauguration of the kingdom. Because Pentecost launches empowered ministry characterized by signs and wonders (2:43; 4:16, 30; 5:12; 6:8; 8:13; cf. 7:36) in preparation for the consummation (Acts 1:7–8), there is no reason to believe that every manifestation cited in Joel must have complete fulfillment before or at Pentecost. Some eschatological tension remains.

What is most significant to note for this study is that all these eschatological signs point to Christ's lordship. The references to "wonders" and "signs" in Acts 2:19 and 22 connect the first segment of Peter's speech (vv. 14–21) with what follows. Peter includes the latter part of the Joel quotation because it forms a natural transition into his discussion of Jesus as Lord. Peter apparently understands the approaching "day of the Lord" (v. 20) with its cosmic signs not as only the day of Yahweh, but as the day of the Lord Jesus.[109] The prerogatives of the Κύριος ("Lord") of the

107. Stronstad, *Prophethood of All Believers*, 50n4. However, his attempt to press all of the eschatological signs into Pentecost seems rather ambitious. See pages 49–53.

108. Cf. 2:43; 4:22, 30; 5:12; 6:8; 7:36; 8:13; 14:3; 15:12.

109. So also Bock, *Theology of Luke and Acts*, 182. Cf. 1 Cor 5:5; 1 Thess 5:2.

Septuagint (Yahweh) have become those of the Lord Jesus.[110] Verse 21 introduces what becomes a recurring theme in Acts, "the name of the Lord" (e.g., 2:38; 3:6, 16; 4:10, 30; 5:28). "And it will be that whoever calls on the name of the Lord [Jesus] will be saved" (2:21). Each division of Peter's speech moves the argument toward his declaration of Jesus' royal identity.

Peter's direct address to the "Men, Israelites" (Acts 2:22) introduces the next segment, in which Peter testifies that Jesus of Nazareth has fulfilled the Psalms of David. Attention is placed on Jesus by locating him at the head of a series of phrases all referring to him in the accusative case: "Jesus the Nazarene ['Ιησοῦν τὸν Ναζωραῖον]," "a man [ἄνδρα] attested by God," "this man [τοῦτον], being determined by the will and foreknowledge of God, was handed over," and "whom [ὃν] God raised" (vv. 22–24). The phrases end with emphatic statements of direct address regarding the crowd's knowledge of Jesus' miracles ("you yourselves know"; v. 22) and their shared responsibility for his murder ("you killed"; v. 23). The contrast between "you killed" and "God raised" (v. 24) leads into the quotation of a psalm attributed to David (Ps 16:8–11) concerning God's rescue of Jesus from decay. The effect of the strategically placed references to Jesus in the accusative case is to clearly identify Jesus as the one approved of God and anticipated in the Scriptures and to heighten the contrast between his good deeds and the murderous action against him. That "God raised" him verifies the divine approval of Jesus. Peter explains that the Psalm refers to Christ, who was not left in Hades but came to know the "paths of life" (vv. 27–28). The combination of emphatic grammar and a scriptural quotation in this unit serves to identify Jesus as the one who fulfills the Davidic expectation of a risen one.

Another direct address by Peter ("Men, brothers"; Acts 2:29) introduces the third segment of his speech (vv. 29–36) and a christocentric explanation of the Psalm that leads to more biblical references and another key quotation. This explanation of Ps 16:8–11 is framed by a return to the accusative: "This [τοῦτον] Jesus God raised" (Acts 2:32). The continued employment of this literary scheme maintains the focus on Jesus' identity throughout Peter's sermon. Peter buttresses his argument for Jesus' royal identity by alluding to David's credentials as a prophet and his knowledge of God's oath to give him a royal descendant (Acts 2:30; Ps 132:11; cf. 2 Sam 7:11, 13, 16). Parallel phrases in Acts 2:30–31 (ESV) evince the

110. Hurtado also notes that Jesus is called "Lord" in places where God was the original referent (Acts 2:20–21, 25). Hurtado, *Lord Jesus Christ*, 181.

important relationship between Christ's resurrection and enthronement. Compare the two lines of Peter's reference to David:

(A) Being therefore a prophet, and knowing that God had sworn with an oath to him that he would set one of his descendants on his throne,

(B) he foresaw and spoke about the resurrection of the Christ, that he was not abandoned to Hades, nor did his flesh see corruption.

The enthronement of Christ is here pictured in terms of the resurrection. For Luke, the resurrection, ascension, and exaltation are theologically all one motion—enthronement (cf. *T. Benj.* 10:6–7). They are of necessity chronologically separate,[111] but they are theologically united. This thought is confirmed in 2:32–33: "This Jesus God raised up, to which we all are witnesses. Therefore being exalted (ὑψωθείς) to the right hand of God . . ." The "therefore" (οὖν; v. 33) ties the exaltation directly to the resurrection. Thus, when the messengers of the gospel mention resurrection (the central element of their speeches), it evokes images of Christ's enthronement as King.

The inferential particle οὖν ("therefore") occurs three times in this portion of the narrative (vv. 30, 33, 36), and a conclusion concerning Christ's resurrection follows each one.[112] In the first case, the presence of David's tomb testifies to the fact that David prophesied about someone other than himself (Ps 16:8–11), and because David knew of God's covenantal oath to seat David's offspring "on his throne" (ἐπὶ τὸν θρόνον αὐτοῦ; Acts 2:30), he looked ahead and "spoke concerning the resurrection of the Christ" (ἐλάλησεν περὶ τῆς ἀναστάσεως τοῦ Χριστοῦ; v. 31). Peter clearly refers to Ps 132:11: "The LORD swore to David a sure oath from which he will not turn back: 'One of the sons of your body I will set on your throne'" (ESV, cf. Ps 89:3–4; Heb 6:13, 16–17). This ultimately refers to the Davidic covenant in 2 Sam 7:12–13. The answer to Peter's question, "What does this mean?" (Acts 2:12), is becoming clear. It means Jesus is the resurrected Davidite.[113]

111. *Contra* Fitzmyer who sees the ascension as part of Easter. Fitzmyer, *Acts*, 259–60. Also see Fitzmyer, *Gospel According to Luke (X–XXIV)*, 1588–89.

112. Anderson, *"But God Raised Him,"* 202, 209–19. Moessner, "*Two* Lords 'at the Right Hand'?" 227.

113. Douglas Oss comments, "In Luke-Acts the Davidic reign is integrally related to the nature of the 'last days,' providing further redemptive-historical perspective on those days as a phase of the kingdom (e.g., Luke 1:32–33, 68–79; Acts 2:25–39)." Oss,

The second οὖν (Acts 2:33) assumes the theological unity between the resurrection and Christ's exaltation to God's right hand, and, based on Jesus' having received the promised Spirit, Peter concludes, "He has poured out this that you yourselves are seeing and hearing" (Acts 2:33 ESV).[114] Peter emphatically affirms ("you yourselves") that the crowd is seeing clear evidence of Peter's claims. "What does this mean?" It means that the manifestations (the sound of wind, the fiery tongues, and the speaking in tongues) are due to the resurrected, exalted, Davidic King having poured out the Spirit. Peter supports this with another mention of David and a quotation from Ps 110:1 (cf. Luke 20:42–43), from which Peter infers that David addresses Jesus as "Lord" (Acts 2:34–35): "The Lord said to my Lord, 'Sit at my right hand, until I make your enemies your footstool.'" The designation of Jesus as "Lord" provides Peter with the scriptural justification for moving to his essential point at the climax of his speech.

The third οὖν occurs in Acts 2:36, where Peter concludes, "Therefore let all the house of Israel know with certainty that God has made him both Lord and Christ, this Jesus whom you crucified." Once again Luke returns to his literary strategy of moving accusative case nouns and pronouns to the front of his phrases in order to emphasize Jesus' identity.

- καὶ κύριον αὐτὸν ("both Lord him")
- καὶ χριστὸν ἐποίησεν ὁ θεός, ("and Christ God made")
- τοῦτον τὸν Ἰησοῦν ὃν ὑμεῖς ἐσταυρώσατε. ("this Jesus whom you crucified.")

This emphatic declaration provides a fitting conclusion to Peter's speech. The insertion of the narrator's comments in verse 37 signals to the reader that the speech has reached its denouement.[115] The narrator records the crowd's interruption: "What should we do, men, brothers?" Dibelius sees similar interruptions as a literary device used in various speeches in

"A Pentecostal/Charismatic View," 267–68.

114. Some scholars see an allusion in Acts 2:33 to Ps 68:18 (67:19 LXX). Jesus' ascension is likened to Moses' ascending Mt. Sinai to receive the law. Thus, Jesus has ascended to receive and pour out the Spirit. But the clear and overwhelming Davidic context makes this identification unlikely. See the discussion in chapter 1.

115. Tannehill has a similar view: "Acts 2:22–36 is a compact, carefully constructed argument leading to the conclusion in v. 36." He also notes, "Acts 2:36 is clearly the conclusion and climax of the preceding argument and must be interpreted in light of it." Tannehill, *Narrative Unity*, 2:35, 37.

Acts: "The fact that these interruptions each occur at a significant point suggests literary technique; the speech is always allowed to reach just that point which is important to the author."[116] The crowd's enquiry sets up Peter's admonition to repent in order to receive forgiveness and his affirmation of the availability of the "gift" and "promise" (Acts 2:38; cf. Luke 11:13; 24:48; Acts 1:4; 2:33) of the Spirit,[117] but the blessings are only attainable on the basis of the royal and messianic identity of Jesus as declared in Acts 2:36.

The adverb ἀσφαλῶς ("certainty"; Acts 2:36) hints at the centrality and importance of this verse, for its cognate noun ἀσφάλειαν occurs in Luke 1:4, where Luke records that his purpose for writing was in order that Theophilus may know the "certainty" of the things of which he had received instruction.[118] This clear christological declaration serves as the pinnacle of Peter's speech, and it contains the central truth of Luke-Acts. Peter has argued on the basis of biblical texts attributed to David that Jesus is the Christ (Acts 2:31)[119] and the Lord (v. 34), and the outpouring of the Holy Spirit confirms this identity of Lord and Christ as Jesus exercises a divine prerogative in pouring out the Spirit. The divinity of Jesus is evident in his exercising of the divine prerogatives in dispensing forgiveness, salvation, judgment, and the Spirit (Luke 3:16; Acts 10:42); in his sharing of God's rule as implied by his position at God's right hand;[120] and in his title as "Lord" (κύριος). God's having made Jesus the "Lord" is

116. Dibelius, *Studies in the Acts*, 160.

117. With Christ dispensing both salvation and the gift/promise of the Spirit, it is natural to expect them to be listed closely together. However, the nature of the promise of the Spirit has been defined by Luke in the passages just alluded to and in the charismatic outpouring of Acts 2. Given this larger context, it seems gratuitous to suddenly change the definition of the promise/gift in Acts 2:38 to a non-charismatic, indwelling more akin to Paul's ontological discussions of the salvation experience. Luke does not equate salvation/forgiveness with reception of the Spirit; he does, however, emphasize that both have their origin in the exaltation of Christ.

118. This is the only location of this word in the Gospel of Luke, and ἀσφαλῶς and cognates rarely occur in Acts. In Acts it never has a theological sense except in 2:36.

119. Smalley holds that "Christ" is used as a title thirteen times in Acts and also as a name thirteen times in Acts. He views the Christology of Acts as "essentially primitive in character, yet richly embryonic in content." The term is not primarily defined by later usage, as is commonly suggested by some critical scholars, but Acts has an "undeveloped but high Christology, possibly running back to Jesus himself." Smalley, "The Christology of Acts Again," 85, 92–93.

120. Bock, *Acts*, 134. Foerster, "κύριος," 1089.

not evidence of a subordinationist[121] or an adoptionist[122] theology; it is a reflection of the limitations imposed on Jesus in his incarnation and of the historical-redemptive timing of the revelation of his identity in the full exercise of the divine prerogatives in his exaltation. The Pentecostal events, including tongues, are indicative of the Spirit's presence, which in turn, is indicative of the divine identity of Jesus. Tongues are the direct result of the exaltation of Jesus as Lord and Christ.

Programmatic texts such as Luke 4:18–19 and Acts 1:8 give both literary and theological guidance to the reader as Luke purposes to record the spread of the good news and to explain the prophetic power fueling the gospel's dissemination, but the central theological point undergirding the gospel's progress is the reign of Christ, and his reign is the spring from which the Spirit pours. Thus, if the crowd will repent and be baptized in *Jesus' name*, they too will receive "the gift of the Holy Spirit" (2:38–39). In this context, water baptism is nothing less than the demonstration of full submission to Christ's lordship. The international significance of Christ's reign is also hinted at again in the phrase "all the house of Israel" (2:36), which focuses on the Jews but addresses them as representatives of Jewish people everywhere.[123]

Luke has strategically organized samples from Peter's original Pentecostal sermon (Acts 2:40) in order to move the reader from the Pentecostal outpouring to his central christological claim ("Lord and Christ") and to a narratological invitation to join the penitent in salvation and the experience of the Spirit. Peter's sermon forms the theological bridge between the event of speaking in tongues and the explanation of its historical-redemptive significance. The crowd asks, "What does this mean?" The simple answer is that Jesus is "Lord and Christ."

Summary

In this chapter I have traced Luke's line of thought from the Pentecostal outpouring of the Spirit (Acts 2:1–4), to the reaction of the crowd (vv. 5–13), and to Peter's sermon (vv. 14–36) with its climactic declaration of Jesus' identity as Lord and Christ (v. 36). This was done in order to view

121. Contra Conzelmann, *Theology of St. Luke*, 173–84. See the discussion in Buckwalter, *Character and Purpose*, 184–91.

122. See the discussion in Bock, *Acts*, 135.

123. Tannehill emphasizes the gospel for all Jews in this passage. *Narrative Unity*, 2:27.

Pentecostal tongues within Luke's framework rather than isolating them from his larger concerns. An examination of the first segment revealed that Pentecost is a thoroughly eschatological event in line with biblical history. An emphasis on Christology surrounds the Pentecostal story, and there are various pointers to Christology in the opening verses of Acts 2. Even the theophanic language with the fiery tongues symbolizing the divine presence carries a christophanic sense to it, with the signs originating in heaven where Christ is seated at the right hand of God. The speaking in "other tongues" is attributed to the inspiration of the Spirit; Pentecost is a miracle of prophetic language in response to the exaltation of the Lord Jesus and not a "gift of ears."

The response of the crowd and the list of nations from which the people originate bring to mind the story of Babel, but Luke does not present Pentecost as a reversal of Babel. The echoes of Babel remind the reader of God's promise of blessing to all nations through Abraham. The tongues of Pentecost reflect a missiological concern and symbolize the nations who need the gospel message. This missiological interest intersects with Luke's christological focus so that tongues signify the international scope of the gospel and Christ as Lord of the nations. The latter point finds support in the vertical orientation of the tongues and their christocentric content. Peter's sermon elaborates on the central content of the tongues, as the tongues of praise relate directly to what God has done in the resurrection, ascension, enthronement, and investiture of Jesus with the promised Spirit.

In Acts 2:14–38 Peter responds to the crowd's request for an explanation of the Pentecostal signs. "What does this mean?" (v. 12). Peter commences his answer to the question by appealing to Scripture and positioning the day's events within an eschatological context. He contends that the speaking in tongues is a kind of prophetic speech as anticipated by Joel (2:28–32). This is consistent with the emphasis on inspired utterance throughout the entire episode, so that the reader understands the nature of tongues as prophetic, much as prophetic speech resulted from the Spirit's endowment in Num 11. The latter portion of the Joel quotation, with its mention of the "Lord," works well as a transition into a series of quotations from the Psalms and an emphasis on the coming of a Davidic Lord and Messiah. Peter clearly identifies the crucified and risen one as the Lord and Christ. The Pentecostal outpouring, with its speaking in tongues, evinces the enthronement of Jesus and his exercising of the divine prerogative of distributing the Spirit. The royal "Lord" (κύριος) grants forgiveness to the penitent, and the "Anointed One" (χριστός) gives the Spirit. The ultimate answer to the crowd's question is that Jesus' identity is "Lord and Christ," and this implies that he is the source of salvation and the gift of the Spirit. Consequently, speaking in tongues is a response to the enthronement of Jesus as Lord and Christ.

The speaking in "other tongues" at Pentecost entails an additional miracle not found in other passages containing glossolalia—at Pentecost the tongues are recognizable human languages. This added element helps the reader establish the symbolic significance of tongues. Tongues symbolize nations and point to Christ's universal lordship, the mission to the nations, and the empowerment of Christ's ambassadors to reach the nations (Acts 1:8). As a Spirit-inspired type of utterance, speaking in tongues is prophetic in nature. The content of tongues consists of praise oriented toward God and Christ. Speaking in tongues is an act of worship, a celebration of what God has done in Christ. Jesus rose from the dead, ascended into heaven, and sat down at the right hand of the Father. He poured out his Spirit on his waiting, obedient disciples. They received power to spread the gospel to the nations and responded to the enthroned Lord and Christ with a new form of praise that appropriately signified his universal reign and their newfound power to proclaim his name.

3

Pentecostal Literature

Acts 2 as a Type-Scene

THE CASUAL READER OF Acts does not get the impression that Luke was embarrassed by the occurrence of speaking in tongues or intent on dismissing it as merely a curious event of a bygone era. Rather, he features other tongues at the beginning of his second volume, appears to celebrate them, and supposes that Theophilus will also delight in the Pentecostal miracle. Surely Luke expects some kind of response from his readers, as biblical narratives do more than provide historical information; they capture the imagination, motivate to action, and elicit emotional and behavioral responses. In this chapter I will incorporate some insights from literary criticism in order to further demonstrate the christocentric nature of the Pentecostal event and garner additional insights about tongues.

The discussion begins with the subject of hermeneutics and a recommendation for employing a literary approach to Acts in order to lead the interpreter closer to the heart of Luke's message. The next section demonstrates how Luke employs various literary devices to draw attention to the Pentecostal event. The third section contains the bulk of the argument and introduces the concept of the literary type-scene. I propose that at least four key motifs accompany the arrival of the Spirit and form a pneumatic type-scene in the Hebrew Scriptures. In addition, Luke incorporates those motifs into his descriptions of the Spirit's coming. The outpouring of the Spirit at Pentecost constitutes a type-scene that is repeated in Acts, has at least six primary emphases, is profoundly christological, and sheds light on several issues related to speaking in tongues.

READING ACTS AS NARRATIVE THEOLOGY

Lukan scholars owe I. Howard Marshall much thanks for helping to rescue Acts from the "mere history" mentality by acknowledging its theological contribution. Marshall emphasizes the message of salvation in Acts, and he makes the contemporary application of Luke's message explicit at the close of his monograph: "Luke's task was to show what men everywhere must do in order to be saved. Thus the Book of Acts is itself a means of salvation to those who hear the gospel in it and make the same response as the Philippian jailer and many another: 'Believe in the Lord Jesus, and you will be saved.'"[1] However, in the latter years of the previous millennium some scholars continued to struggle with how much theological weight should be given to Acts because of its historical narrative genre.[2] But it was also during this time that some scholars trained in literary criticism began to see the genre of Acts as less a barrier to theology and more as a vehicle of theology.[3] In addition, more interpreters began to understand the implication of accepting Luke as a theologian, that is, that Luke does not teach theology merely as an intellectual exercise but with the intent to persuade and affect behavior. The conclusion that Luke-Acts is one literary work with two volumes reinforces the claim that Luke is promoting practical theology. His emphases on the marginalized in society, the proper use of wealth, discipleship, and prayer in both volumes surely indicates his expectation of changed thinking and behavior. Robert Tannehill captures this notion: "Readers are led to believe or to reaffirm their belief in the central character, Jesus, and are thereby influenced in complex ways—in their attitudes, controlling images, patterns of action, feelings, etc. . . . The message of Luke-Acts is not a set of theological propositions but the complex reshaping of human life, in its many dimensions, which it can cause."[4] Literary criticism

1. Marshall, *Luke: Historian*, 215.

2. Fee, *Gospel and Spirit*, 83–104. See Fee's discussion, partners in dialogue, and notes.

3. See Mittelstadt, *Reading Luke-Acts*, 82–91.

4. Tannehill, *Narrative Unity*, 1:8.

supplies additional tools that enable the interpreter to mine the practical imperatives from the narrative.

Acknowledgement of Luke as a theologian and literary artist is foundational to understanding Luke's charismatic worldview, and Pentecostals have traditionally assumed that the charismatic events in Luke's writings were there not only to impress the reader but to provide models for empowered Christian service.[5] Pentecostals had often read Acts rather uncritically but intuitively realized that charismatic phenomenon in Acts could be applied to and experienced in daily life. Literary criticism provided some "technical language" for those who had identified with the experiences narrated in Acts.[6] Donald Johns explains the benefits of narrative theology when he points out how a "theological point can be perceived directly through the story"[7] and how a story can introduce someone to a new "world" and affect change in their existing "world."[8] He suggests that Luke uses the Pentecostal story to influence his readers to have an experience where they are filled with the Holy Spirit and speak in tongues.[9] This hermeneutical approach views Acts as more than an interesting object of grammatical-historical investigation; it also perceives Luke's invitation to enter the door of salvation and partake of empowered life in the Spirit.

Tongues and the Literary Significance of Acts 2

I have argued that the goal of Luke's Pentecostal narrative is the declaration of Jesus as "Lord and Christ" (Acts 2:36). Peter's explanation of speaking in tongues ends at this goal after narrating the fulfillment of Joel's prophecies and the Davidic expectation of the Hebrew Scriptures. Therefore, Luke presents tongues as a charismatic manifestation that is christocentric in nature. Consequently, when Luke begins his narrative in earnest in Acts 2, tongues receive a substantial emphasis by nature of their relationship to Jesus' enthronement as Lord. A look at Pentecost through literary eyes reveals at least five more ways Luke emphasizes the Pentecostal event with its other tongues.

5. Menzies, *Pentecost*, 23–27.
6. Mittlestadt, *Reading Luke-Acts*, 91.
7. Johns, "Some New Directions," 154.
8. Johns, "Some New Directions," 154.
9. Johns, "Some New Directions," 156.

First, Luke creates an anticipation of Pentecost in his narratives both by recording the promises of the Spirit's coming (Luke 3:16; 11:13; 24:49; Acts 1:4–5, 8)[10] and the prophecies of the gospel's universal reach (Luke 2:31–32; 3:6; 13:28–30; 24:47; Acts 1:8). Tongues result from the outpouring of the Spirit, and tongues (languages) inherently signify the international implications of Jesus' ascent to the throne. Second, Luke's use of the word "fulfilled" (συμπληροῦσθαι) in the opening phrase of the account of Pentecost alerts the reader that the anticipated coming of the Spirit has arrived (Acts 2:1).[11] Peter's citation of Joel 2:28–32a confirms that tongues are part of the anticipated fulfillment (Acts 2:17–21). Third, Luke gives Pentecost a prominent location at the beginning of the narrative of Acts. From a literary perspective, it is what Charles Talbert refers to as the "frontispiece" of Acts.[12] Frank Macchia rightly observes that the location of tongues in Acts 2 (as well as in Acts 10 and 19) is more significant than the number of times tongues occur.[13] The frontloading of Christ's enthronement, the outpouring of the Spirit, and the accompanying tongues suggest that Luke intends his readers and auditors to interpret his second volume through this lens. Fourth, the dramatic flair in Acts 2:2–4 arrests the attention and stirs a sense of wonder and awe in the reader.[14] The sound of a forceful wind comes "suddenly" and is accompanied by vivid images of fiery tongues and miraculous speech. Luke signals to his readers that an event of great significance is unfolding.

Finally, Luke highlights the Pentecostal event and its tongues by explaining it through one of his most important literary features—a speech.[15] Luke often uses speeches to give voice to his own message; therefore, it is important to take note of the content for that reason alone,

10. Johnson notes that "the narrative suspense built by Luke is about to reach a first resolution" in Acts 2. Johnson, *Acts*, 45.

11. Tannehill points out how Luke intentionally relates Acts 2:1 to Luke 9:51 by means of his emphasis on fulfillment of prophecy in both stories (see Luke 9:22, 31, 44; 24:49; Acts 1:4–5, 8). "The prophecies have prepared us to appreciate the importance of this day." Tannehill, *Narrative Unity*, 2:26–27.

12. Talbert, *Reading Acts*, 30. Hovenden and others see Acts 2 as programmatic for Acts. Hovenden, *Speaking in Tongues*, 77; Turner, *Power from on High*, 267.

13. Macchia, "Groans Too Deep," Section 3.

14. Spencer, *Journeying through Acts*, 41.

15. Keener notices the strategic placement of tongues in Acts 2: "This speaking in tongues is more strategic for Luke's narrative because what follows hinges on it—that tongues provides the catalyst for the multi-cultural audience's recognition of God's activity (2:5–13) and the starting point for Peter's message, 'This is what Joel meant . . .' (2:16–17)." Keener, *For All Peoples*, 58.

but the speech gains added significance because one of Luke's primary characters, Peter, delivers it. The importance of the speech is also magnified by its substantial length, numerous Scripture references (including the longest Scripture quotation in the New Testament),[16] and incredible evangelistic success. When one considers that tongues provide the impetus for the speech, that they are a significant element in its content, and that Luke often places his teaching on the lips of his characters, it seems unwise to dismiss the tongues as doctrinally extraneous, immaterial, or isolated to that moment in history. Rather, the tongues of Acts 2 (as well as Acts 10 and 19) embody the central point in the climax of Peter's speech—that Jesus is both Lord of all nations and Israel's Messiah. On the basis of this integration of Christology and charismatic phenomena, one should be willing to entertain the notion that the charismatic expression of Christ's reign continues along with the expansion of his reign until he returns (1 Cor 13:8–12).

Acts 2 as a Pentecostal Type-Scene

The literary and theological prominence given to Acts 2 has significant implications for how one reads other episodes where the Spirit is poured out in the narrative. This especially holds true if one understands Pentecost as a literary type-scene. Robert Alter, inspired by research into conventional patterns identified in Homeric epics, applied the insights gained from ancient literature to the Hebrew Scriptures.[17] Alter notes that artistic communication is enabled by "an elaborate set of tacit agreements between artist and audience about the ordering of the artwork. . . . Through our awareness of convention we can recognize significant or simply pleasing patterns of repetition, symmetry, contrast: we can discriminate between the verisimilar and the fabulous, pick up directional clues in a narrative work, see what is innovative and what is deliberately traditional at each nexus of the artistic creation."[18] Based on Alter's description, one could say that a type-scene is a conventional episode in a narrative that follows a pattern and has a recurring set of motifs. The reader recognizes the literary pattern, and divergence from the pattern

16. Acts 2:17–21 quoting Joel 2:28–32.

17. Alter, *Art of Biblical Narrative*, 59.

18. Alter, *Art of Biblical Narrative*, 55.

often signals an important point in the narrative.[19] In biblical literature the type-scene does more than simply remind the reader of a familiar scene. "The type-scene is not merely a way of formally recognizing a particular kind of narrative moment; it is also a means of attaching that moment to a larger pattern of historical and theological meaning."[20] This last statement is particularly important when one views such scenes from the perspective of biblical-theological development and eschatological fulfillment in the Scriptures, for a single occurrence of a type-scene can both carry substantial theological weight and illustrate advances in the biblical story.

Alter offers various examples of type-scenes such as the scene where a patriarch makes a journey to escape famine and deceives the residents of the land about the identity of his wife.[21] He also devotes considerable attention to the pattern of a betrothal at a well,[22] and he mentions the type-scene of an announcement of the birth of a hero to a barren woman.[23] Various scholars have identified five main elements in Luke's birth narratives that are also found in the announcements in the Hebrew Scriptures: (1) the appearance of an angel, (2) fear or perplexity at the angelophany, (3) a divine message, (4) the recipient's objection, and (5) a reassuring sign.[24] In the typical cases such as with Sarai (Gen 18:1–15) and Manoah's wife (Judg 13), a barren woman receives a promise of a male child, and the child will play a significant role in redemptive history. The events with Elizabeth and Zechariah (Luke 1) have strong affinities with these two stories. This story is somewhat of a textbook type-scene that recurs in order to demonstrate the continued working of God in history through the arrival of John the Baptist. However, the type-scene has an unusual element in Mary's story (Luke 2). Mary is not barren—she does not even have a husband! The new twist in the type-scene (a virgin becomes pregnant) signifies to the reader that a major event is unfolding in history, for God is bringing an ancient pattern of his miraculous deeds to a wondrous new level. The hero to be born in this story will be like no other.

19. Alter, *Art of Biblical Narrative*, 61.

20. Alter, *Art of Biblical Narrative*, 72.

21. Alter, *Art of Biblical Narrative*, 58.

22. Alter, *Art of Biblical Narrative*, 61–75.

23. Alter, *Art of Biblical Narrative*, 58, 60.

24. For a discussion of Luke's use of this pattern from the Hebrew Scriptures, see Bock, *Luke*, 1:73; Brown, *Birth of the Messiah*, 156; Fitzmyer, *Gospel According to Luke (I–IX)*, 335; Lidbeck, *Resurrection and Spirit*, 66–70.

For the purposes of this discussion, there are two important points to note about Luke's employment of the type-scene. The first is simply that his use of the type-scene in the birth narratives demonstrates his familiarity with this literary device and his intentional incorporation of it. Tannehill has also identified the use of type-scenes in other places in Acts, such as in Paul's repeated announcement that he would turn to the gentiles in consequence of Jewish rejection of the gospel (13:46–47; 18:5–6; 28:23–28) and in what he calls an "epiphanic commissioning story" (18:9–10).[25] It is therefore entirely within the purview of Luke to portray Pentecost in the fashion of a literary type-scene. The second item to note is that Luke is fully capable of making a theological point by presenting an old pattern with a new twist. If Luke is presenting Pentecost as a type-scene, then there are important theological points to glean not only from the continuity with ancient stories, but also from the unusual elements in the new scene. In other words, the occurrence of tongues is not an embarrassing event that Luke hopes the reader will ignore, but a significant development within an ancient pattern of the bestowal of the Spirit.

The Pneumatic Type-Scene in the Hebrew Scriptures

The Hebrew Scriptures mention the divine Spirit just over 100 times,[26] and narrative passages describe an actual reception of the Spirit about twenty-three times.[27] A future reception of the Spirit is also prophesied for the Messiah (Isa 11:2; 42:1) and the people of God (Num 11:29; Isa 32:15; 44:3; Ezek 36:27; 37:14; 39:29; Joel 2:28–29). The narrative passages usually describe the Spirit's arrival rather tersely, as a coming upon (Num 24:2; Judg 3:10; 11:29; 1 Sam 19:20; 2 Chr 15:1; 20:14), a rushing upon (Judg 14:6, 19; 15:14), a clothing (Judg 6:34; 1 Chr 12:18 ET [12:19 MT]; 2 Chr 24:20), or a falling upon (Ezek 11:5).[28] This economic description

25. Tannehill, *Narrative Unity*, 2:223.

26. Hildebrandt counts 107 occurrences where רוּחַ refers to the divine Spirit. Hildebrandt, *Old Testament Theology*, 1.

27. This includes the 70 elders (Num 11:17, 24–27); Balaam (24:2); Othniel (Judg 3:10); Gideon (6:34); Jephthah (11:29); Samson (three separate occasions; 14:6, 19; 15:14); Saul (three separate occasions; 1 Sam 10:6, 10; 11:6; 19:23); David (16:13); three groups of Saul's men (19:20–21); Elisha (2 Kings 2:9–15); Amasai (1 Chr 12:18); Azariah (2 Chr 15:1); Jahaziel (20:14); Zechariah (24:20); and Ezekiel (three occasions; 2:2; 3:24; 11:5).

28. This discussion is focused on passages that directly mention the Spirit, but

of the Spirit's coming is evident in Judges, where a brief description of the Spirit's arrival is often followed by an account of military exploits and deliverance for Israel. The two dominant functions of the Spirit in the narrative accounts are the empowerment of God's chosen leaders and the inspiration of prophetic activity. The only accounts where prophetic activity is not evident are among the judges, although Gideon hears clear instructions from God in a manner reminiscent of prophets (Judg 7:1–12).[29] The concise records of the Spirit's arrival span over significant periods of Israel's history and imply a longstanding, shared knowledge of the literary pattern and theological significance of the Spirit's coming. The author of Genesis appears to have assumed such a shared knowledge among his readers when he penned the account of Joseph, where the readers are expected to recognize the prophetic inspiration of the Spirit in Joseph's dreams and interpretations (Gen 41:38).[30]

There are only a handful of detailed narrations of the bestowal of the Spirit in the Hebrew Scriptures, and they provide context for the briefer accounts. Whereas it is not always clear in the brief descriptions whether the coming of the Spirit is an initial coming or a renewed moment of prophetic inspiration (e.g., 1 Chr 12:18; 2 Chr 15:1; 20:14; 24:20), the more detailed records describe an initial filling, are more theologically nuanced, and fill several gaps in understanding such events. They include the bestowal of the Spirit on the seventy elders (Num 11), Saul (1 Sam 10), David (1 Sam 16), and Elisha (2 Kgs 2).[31] Among these, the placing of the Spirit on the seventy elders is the most significant as a type-scene that articulates the key elements of a biblical reception of the Spirit.

There are at least four key elements in the type-scene of Num 11 that are also evident in the other scenes mentioned above: the divine action of giving the Spirit, the purpose of empowering chosen leaders, the

the prophets certainly use other ways of communicating prophetic inspiration that presumably imply the activity of the Spirit. Ezekiel often reports, "The word of Yahweh came to me" (e.g., 3:16; 6:1; 7:1) or "The hand of Yahweh was upon me" (e.g., 3:22; 33:22).

29. Aside from the six accounts of Spirit reception in Judges (3:10; 6:34; 11:29; 14:6, 19; 15:14), all the other seventeen accounts exhibit strong associations with prophetic activity (Num 11:17, 24–27; 24:2; 1 Sam 10:6, 10; 11:6; 16:14; 19:20–21, 23; 2 Kgs 2:9–15; 1 Chr 12:18; 2 Chr 15:1; 2 Chr 20:14; 24:20; Ezek 2:2; 3:24; 11:5).

30. I have argued previously that Pharaoh intended a reference to the Spirit of God. Lidbeck, *Resurrection and Spirit*, 33.

31. One might also include Ezekiel's reception of the Spirit, as it includes details of his visionary experience (ch. 1) and his calling (2:1–3:9), as well as a few added details of his actual reception of the Spirit.

prophetic response to the Spirit's arrival, and an eschatological foreshadowing in the characters or the event itself.[32] The divine action is evident in Num 11:17b (cf. v. 25) when Yahweh informs Moses of his plans: "I will take of the Spirit that is on you and set [the Spirit] on them." Often God uses a human agent when he gives the Spirit—what Stronstad calls a "transfer of the Spirit."[33] This seems to be the case in all four scenes under discussion here. In Num 11 God performs the action of giving the Spirit, yet Moses' presence is significant in that the Spirit is taken from him and placed on the seventy elders. Saul receives the Spirit after Samuel anoints him with oil and after Saul is exposed to the band of prophets (1 Sam 10:1, 5–7, 9–11). Later on, three groups of Saul's men and Saul himself are overcome by the Spirit and prophetic inspiration when they come into proximity with Samuel and a group of prophets (19:18–24). David also receives the Spirit in connection with Samuel's anointing of David (16:13), but in contrast to Saul, David's endowment with the Spirit would not be forfeited as a result of rebellion (v. 14). The transfer of the Spirit from Elijah to Elisha along with Elisha's acquisition of the prophetic ministry is detailed in 2 Kings 2.[34] There are several occasions where God bestows the Spirit directly without the mention of any human agency (e.g., Judg 3:10; 6:34; 1 Chr 12:18; 2 Chr 20:14), but the common use of prophets as mediators in the giving of the Spirit leads the reader to expect such activity.

The narrative makes clear that the purpose of the placement of the Spirit on the seventy elders is to empower them to help Moses lead the people (Num 11:16–17). God's choice of them is confirmed by the prophetic sign (v. 25), but the element of choosing becomes even more prominent in the narratives of Saul and David. God's choice of Israel's king is a significant element in the anointing of Saul (1 Sam 9:15–16; 10:1) and an even more prominent feature in the narrative of David as God's choice (1 Sam 16:12; 2 Sam 7:8) in light of Saul's failures. Even Elijah cannot pass along the ministry mantle to Elisha but must leave the issue in God's hands (2 Kings 2:2). God's choice of Elisha is evidenced

32. Stronstad has described receptions of the Spirit in the Hebrew Scriptures in terms of a "transfer motif," a "sign motif," and a "vocational motif." Stronstad, *Charismatic Theology: Trajectories*, 23–27.

33. Stronstad, *Charismatic Theology: Trajectories*, 23.

34. That the Spirit of the Lord is in view and not just Elijah's spirit (2 Kings 2:9) is evident from the clear reference to the Spirit in verse 16, the inheritance of the prophetic ministry, and the miraculous dividing of the Jordan River (v. 14).

by his dividing of the Jordan River (v. 14) and the confirmation of the observing prophets (v. 15).

Prophecy clearly signals the arrival of the Spirit on the seventy elders (Num 11:25) and Saul (1 Sam 10:10). Immediately after David receives the Spirit the narrator draws attention to David's music ministry (16:13–22) and his spiritual qualification to play the harp for Saul: "And Yahweh is with him" (v. 18c). The Spirit's equipping of David as a prophetic psalmist is directly stated later in the narrative (2 Sam 23:1–2). Elisha's ministry as a prophet is apparent. In all four cases the charismatic gifting goes hand-in-hand with the concept of divine choice, as the prophetic response helps identify the one God has chosen to carry out his tasks (cf. Luke 3:22; John 1:32–34).

The story of the empowering of the seventy elders is rich in eschatological anticipation. The author highlights the significance of Eldad and Medad by telling his audience three times that they remained "in the camp" (Num 11:24–25). Their prophesying "in the camp" suggests that God's ultimate desire is to give his Spirit to the entire community and not only to a limited number of leaders.[35] This comports well with the surrounding context in which there is an emphasis on the issue of God's presence in their midst (5:3; 9:15–23; 10:33–36) and with Moses' prophetic wish "that all the LORD's people were prophets, that the LORD would put his Spirit on them!" (Num 11:29b ESV).[36]

Not only does Moses anticipate a future democratization of the prophetic Spirit in his prophetic words, but his role as a unique prophet also anticipates a greater fulfillment. Although Joshua steps into Moses' leadership role, the narrator emphatically notes that Moses is an incomparable figure among God's people. "And there has not arisen a prophet since in Israel like Moses, whom the LORD knew face to face, none like him for all the signs and the wonders that the LORD sent him to do in the land of Egypt, to Pharaoh and to all his servants and to all his land" (Deut 34:10–11 ESV). This summary reflects the unique status of Moses highlighted in Num 12:6–8, which occurs hard on the heels of the giving of the Spirit to the seventy elders. Moses prophesies that God will raise up another unique prophet: "The LORD your God will raise up for you a prophet like me from among you, from your brothers—it is to him you shall listen" (Deut 18:15), but that prophet is not Joshua. Luke reveals

35. Cotton, "Pentecostal Significance," 9.

36. For a more extensive discussion of Num 11, see Lidbeck, *Resurrection and Spirit*, 36–47.

the identity of that prophet through the mouth of Peter (Acts 3:22) and Stephen (7:37), and the prophet is Jesus. Although in his youthful zeal Joshua has a mentality of limitation when it comes to the giving of the Spirit, he apparently recognizes the unique, even royal status of Moses (Num 11:28), who foreshadows the coming of a future Messiah who will dispense the Spirit.

The author of 1 and 2 Samuel does not emphasize the eschatological significance of Saul because he obviously forfeits his favored status to David. Consequently, David becomes the anointed king who receives the promise of an enduring kingdom (2 Sam 7:11–16, 25–29) and becomes the symbol of a future Messiah (Luke 1:32–33) who is given the Spirit to pour out on others (Acts 2:33–35). Luke also depicts Christ's ascent into heaven in terms drawn from the account of Elijah's ascension (2 Kgs 2:11–12; Acts 1:9–11). The descriptions are very similar: "And Elijah was taken up by a whirlwind, as it were, into heaven" (καὶ ἀνελήμφθη Ηλιου ἐν συσσεισμῷ ὡς εἰς τὸν οὐρανόν; 2 Kgs 2:11 LXX) and "This Jesus who was taken up from you into heaven" (οὗτος ὁ Ἰησοῦς ὁ ἀναλημφθεὶς ἀφ' ὑμῶν εἰς τὸν οὐρανὸν; Acts 1:11). It appears that Luke views the ascension of Elijah and transfer of the Spirit to Elisha as a pattern fulfilled in Jesus' ascent and his pouring out the Spirit on his disciples.[37]

It is rather remarkable that the four most detailed accounts of Spirit reception in the Hebrew Scriptures serve as primary resources and patterns on which Luke depends. Jesus is the Prophet like Moses, the King in the line of David (who is presented in contrast to Saul), and the one who ascends like Elijah. Each of these are formative in Luke's understanding of the descent of the Spirit at Pentecost. Although more brief accounts of the coming of the Spirit do not always emphasize all four elements outlined in these passages, it is important to note how the four generally travel together and particularly how they often contain a christological anticipation.

The Pneumatic Type-Scene in Luke-Acts

The four travelling companions (the divine action of giving the Spirit, the purpose of empowering chosen leaders, the prophetic response, and an eschatological foreshadowing) are present when Luke describes the

37. Witherington, *Acts*, 112.

reception of the Spirit in his birth narratives.[38] The divine passive is used to describe the experience of both Elizabeth and Zechariah, as each "was filled with the Holy Spirit" (Luke 1:41, 67). Both had the proper character qualifications to serve as parents to John the Baptist and to act as prophets announcing the eschatological developments (v. 6). Both burst forth into prophesy when filled with the Spirit (vv. 42–45, 67–79), and both uttered christological content as eschatological fulfillment (vv. 42–45, 68–75). The accounts of their receiving the Spirit are brief, and Luke places most of the emphasis on the act of prophesying and the christological/eschatological significance of it. The type-scenes in the Hebrew Scriptures have paved the way, but the emphasis has become more obviously christocentric due to developments in redemptive history.

The account of Jesus' reception of the Spirit is more detailed because of the obvious significance of the event. The divine activity is evident from the direct agency of the Father's giving the Spirit, the open heavens, and the divine voice of affirmation (Luke 3:21–22). The event is an empowering experience (4:14, 18–19), and the emphasis on being a chosen leader is abundantly evident in the divine sanction: "You are my beloved Son; in you I am well pleased" (3:22b). There is no immediate prophetic statement recorded, but Jesus' identity as a prophet is not in question (7:16). The christological emphasis is clear, and the descent of the Spirit serves not only to empower Jesus but to identify him as the Messiah. Luke also adds some new emphases to the ancient type-scene. He depicts Jesus praying when the Spirit descends (3:21), and this added note prepares the way for Luke's accent on prayer in relation to the reception of the Spirit (e.g., 11:13; Acts 1:14; 4:31). The idea is not entirely new, as the Hebrew Scriptures imply that the laying on of hands and commissioning of Spirit-filled leaders was an act of prayer (Deut 34:9; 1 Sam 10:1; 16:13; cf. Acts 8:15–17; 9:12, 17; 19:6). The bold imagery of the Spirit descending in bodily form as a dove also adds a new twist to the type-scene that complements the uniqueness of the moment and the incomparableness of Christ's character.[39] The dramatic scene amounts to a theophany (Isa 64:1–2) with a christocentric focus in preparation for

38. Although Luke's comments regarding the pneumatic experiences of John the Baptist, Mary, and Simeon (Luke 1:15, 35; 2:25–27) could also be cited in support of the argument for the essential elements in the type-scene, for the moment I have chosen to focus on the texts that actually record the Spirit's coming.

39. This vivid imagery is characteristic of Luke (cf. Acts 2:2–3), as the other gospels simply have "as a dove" (Matt 3:16; Mark 1:10; John 1:32) instead of the concrete expression "bodily."

Pentecost's christophany. Luke incorporates the four motifs found in the Old Testament into his Gospel, and these four serve as the foundation for Luke's construction of a Pentecostal type-scene in Acts. He retains the old motifs and develops them into a new type-scene that serves his purposes in recording the progress of God's plan in Christ.[40]

James Edwards applied Robert Alter's literary insights regarding type-scenes in the Hebrew Scriptures to the narrative of Pentecost. He argues that the scene in Acts 2 "is the model which establishes a conventional cluster of literary motifs a reader would expect in a Pentecostal type-scene."[41] Edwards highlights "twenty-three motifs which form a conventional story-telling cluster" in Acts 2 and compares them to five other Pentecostal scenes in Acts. "Little Pentecost" (4:23–37) contains seventeen of the motifs; the "Samaritan Pentecost" (ch. 8) has seventeen; the "Damascus Pentecost" (ch. 9) has twenty; the "Caesarean Pentecost" (ch. 10) has twenty-two; and the "Ephesian Pentecost" (ch. 19) has sixteen.[42] According to Edwards, there is a cluster of eight motifs that occur in all six scenes: the unity of the participants, a concrete image of the Holy Spirit, the breaking of barriers, miracles, people are pointed to Christ, listeners are told that Jesus is the Christ, eyewitnesses of the kerygma direct the scene (except at Damascus where Christ himself appears), and the core of the kerygma is proclaimed (with particular emphasis on the resurrection).[43] Edwards identifies tongues as one of the twenty-three Pentecostal motifs and argues that, as part of the cluster, "the literary structures suggest with some force that Holy Spirit baptism necessarily involves the believer in the act of speaking in tongues."[44]

There will naturally be some variations in categorizing the themes and emphases in the passages where the Spirit is poured out, but Edwards has done scholars a service in pointing out key motifs in the type-scene. For purposes of this discussion, I have highlighted six major emphases in the Pentecostal type-scene that include several motifs numbering somewhere in the vicinity of Edwards's count of twenty-three (see the chart in the Appendix). The six main categories are: (1) the divine action of giving the Spirit, (2) Christology, (3) eschatological fulfillment, (4) the purpose

40. For a discussion on Jesus' baptism as setting a precedent for the filling of the Spirit in Acts, see Aker, "New Directions in Lucan Theology."

41. Edwards, "Initial Evidence," 4.

42. Edwards, "Initial Evidence," 4–5.

43. Edwards, "Initial Evidence," 5.

44. Edwards, "Initial Evidence," 20.

of empowering chosen leaders, (5) the prophetic/inspired response to the Spirit's arrival, and (6) missions/kerygma. The differences between the Pentecostal type-scene and the Spirit's coming in the Hebrew Scriptures is due to developments in salvation history, but the four main categories highlighted earlier remain intact.[45] Eschatological foreshadowing has become eschatological fulfillment, and the anticipation of a messiah has developed into Christology as the primary focus of the type-scene. The emphasis on preaching the gospel and missions is new in the sense that the new mission is to be Christ's witnesses and this witness is the expected result of the filling of the Spirit (Acts 1:8).[46]

Based on how type-scenes generally function in biblical literature, the reader should expect the accounts of Spirit reception in Acts to contain the core elements of the accounts in the Hebrew Scriptures and to have new developments or twists due to historical developments and theological interests. This appears to be the case with the type-scenes in Acts. If the Old Testament provides the basic pattern, one should also expect Acts to contain brief accounts of initial fillings or occasional moments of inspiration that remind the reader of other elements in the type-scene. Acts includes these kinds of moments,[47] but in the follow-

45. Hur outlines "the most discernible effects due to the Spirit-reception (which do not always occur promptly)" in the Jewish Scriptures. They include prophetic utterances, miraculous powers, esoteric wisdom, and religio-ethical sustaining power. Hur, *Dynamic Reading*, 72. His helpful list includes items that are found to characterize Spirit-endowed leaders as the stories develop. This is different from a type-scene in that the key elements of a type-scene are generally located in the immediate context of a particular scene in a narrative.

46. Of course, the concepts of mission and gospel are deeply rooted in the Hebrew Scriptures.

47. Luke briefly records both Peter (Acts 4:8) and Paul (13:9) experiencing what appears to be a renewed moment of inspiration when addressing opponents of the gospel. In both cases Luke uses the aorist passive participle of πίμπλημι ("to fill"), but the aorist participle need not refer to a previous event, as though these fillings were not new experiences. See Keener, *Acts: Exegetical*, 2:1144n973. Paul and Barnabas "were filled with joy and the Holy Spirit" (Acts 13:52), and the use of the imperfect passive form of the verb πληρόω ("to fill") also points to a fresh filling but emphasizes the duration of the experience. As part of a summary passage (vv. 49–52) that also mentions persecution, the filling with the Spirit in conjunction with joy emphasizes the uninterrupted supply of divine enablement and hope in the midst of opposition. These three passages are all refilling events and do not describe the filling experience in detail, so I have not included them as primary examples in the type-scene discussion. Luke uses the noun πλήρης ("full") to describe the spiritual condition and Spirit's enabling of the seven deacons (6:3), Stephen (6:5; 7:55), and Barnabas (11:24) in Acts. These are not descriptions of the Spirit's arrival and are not considered part of the type-scene. For additional discussion of Luke's use of terms related to the Spirit's arrival and presence,

ing discussion the focus is on examining the six scenes mentioned above where more details are given about the Spirit's filling (Acts chs. 2, 4, 8, 9, 10, 19).[48] The six scenes are analyzed in relation to the six major motifs outlined above, although it should be mentioned that the scene in chapter 4 is not an initial filling and Saul's filling is mentioned but not actually recorded. The analysis begins at Pentecost with the motif of the divine action of giving the Spirit.

Type-Scene Motifs in Six Pentecostal Scenes in Acts

At Pentecost the divine activity of giving the Spirit is implied by the passive "they were filled" (Acts 2:4). The event takes place in response to the prayerfulness (1:14) and unity (v. 1) of the believers. Both of these elements are important in other filling scenes, with prayer of some form occurring in all six.[49] The theophanic manifestation of fiery tongues and the sound of a mighty wind accompany the giving of the Spirit at Pentecost (2:2–3), the place shakes in 4:31, and scales fall off Saul's eyes (9:18). All this points to divine activity, but there does not appear to be a single, theophanic pattern that particularly characterizes the type-scene. As in the Hebrew Scriptures, the Spirit sometimes comes via a human agent, thus Peter and John lay hands on the Samaritans (8:17), Ananias lays hands on Saul (9:17), and Paul lays hands on the Ephesian disciples (19:6). However, human agency is absent on two occasions (chs. 2 and 4) and even deemphasized at Caesarea (10:44–46). The most stunning new development in the divine distribution of the Spirit is that the enthroned Lord Jesus now exercises the divine prerogative to pour out the Spirit (2:32–36). This has strong Trinitarian implications, as Peter himself later attributes the giving of the Spirit at Caesarea and at Pentecost to God (11:17).

The centrality of Christ in every reception of the Spirit in Acts merits the highlighting of Christology as a key element in the type-scene. The accounts draw attention to the exalted status of Jesus in various ways—by incorporating christological titles (Acts 4:27, 30; 9:20), alluding to the royal lineage of David (2:25, 29, 34; 4:25), including royal or

see Stronstad, *Spirit, Scripture and Theology*, 79–98.

48. The study follows Edwards in choice of passages, but the emphasis lies on the six major themes I have outlined. Edwards, "Initial Evidence," 5.

49. Acts 4:24–31; 8:15, 22, 24; 9:9, 11, 17; 10:2, 3, 4, 9, 30, 31; 19:6.

enthronement terminology (2:30, 33, 34; 8:12; 19:8), and especially by appealing to Jesus' resurrection.[50] In biblical literature, resurrection is exaltation from death to life and an act of enthronement.[51] Luke's high Christology is evident in his repeated use of the "name" of Jesus in reference to his divine authority (e.g., Acts 5:40–41). Reference to the "name" occurs in all six Spirit reception scenes.[52] What is telling about Luke's Christology in relation to his pneumatology is that every scene where the Spirit comes contains references to Jesus as "Christ" and "Lord." Thus, the pinnacle of Peter's speech in Acts 2:36 ("God has made him both Lord and Christ, this Jesus whom you crucified") articulates an essential and foundational motif present in every pneumatic type-scene in Acts.[53] The Spirit is never given without the acknowledgement of Jesus as Lord and Christ in the immediate context. The concentration on Jesus' royal, divine identity is the most prominent feature of the pneumatic type-scene, and his identity provides the context in which tongues occur; that is, they never occur outside of this christological focus (see Appendix).

It would not be an exaggeration to claim that every episode where the Spirit is given in Acts is inherently eschatological by virtue of the focus on the long-awaited Messiah, the preaching of the resurrection and kingdom, and the democratization of the Spirit. In addition to these and other eschatological pointers in the narratives (e.g., Acts 2:1; 10:42), Luke's employment of the Hebrew Scriptures to prove the identity of Jesus as the Messiah is obviously eschatological. Peter's Pentecostal speech is built on biblical quotations (Acts 2:17–21, 25–28, 34–35), and the gathered believers in Acts 4 cite a messianic passage as the basis for their prayer (vv. 25–26). Peter refers to "all the prophets" at Cornelius's home (10:43), and the lead into the Ephesian outpouring has Apollos vigorously arguing from the Scriptures that "the Christ is Jesus" (18:28). Although I have separated Christology and eschatological fulfillment

50. Acts 2:24, 27, 28, 31, 32, 36; 4:33; 9:5, 10; 10:40, 41. Even when the resurrection is not explicitly stated, it is alluded to in every one of the passages where the Spirit is given in Acts. Often the preaching of "the word" in Acts refers primarily to the resurrection of Jesus. Lidbeck, *Resurrection and Spirit*, 135–41.

51. See Brueggemann, "From Dust to Kingship," 1–18.

52. Acts 2:21, 38; 4:30; 8:12, 16; 9:14, 15, 16, 21; 10:43, 48; 19:5, 13, 17.

53. The combination of the terms in a title or close proximity is reserved for certain occasions (see chapter 1 above), but the titles often occur separately in pneumatic passages. "Christ" occurs in Acts 2:36, 38; 4:26; 8:5, 12; 9:22; 10:36, 48; 11:17; 18:28. "Lord" occurs in 2:20, 21, 36; 4:33; 8:16, 22, 24, 25; 9:1, 5, 10, 13, 15, 17; 10:33?, 36; 11:16, 17; 18:25; 19:5, 10, 13, 17, 20.

into two categories in order to highlight Luke's captivation with Christ, the two categories have their roots in the messianic predictions and prototypes in the Old Testament and are therefore of the same stock.

As with the other primary motifs in the pneumatic type-scene, the emphasis on the empowerment of God's chosen leaders contains elements of continuity with the Hebrew Scriptures and redemptive-historical progress. Luke explicitly states that the coming of the Spirit is for the purpose of empowerment, but now the empowerment is specifically for the purpose of testifying to the risen Jesus (Luke 24:46–49; Acts 1:8). The believers in Acts 4 request boldness to preach the word (v. 29) and do precisely that upon receiving the Spirit (v. 31). Luke summarizes the situation: "With great power the apostles were giving testimony of the resurrection of the Lord Jesus" (v. 33a). That witnessing power is in view in Acts 4, where Peter and John are present with the gathered believers, sheds light on the nature of the Pentecostal gift. The nearly identical expression for the giving of the Spirit is used in both locations:

a. καὶ ἐπλήσθησαν πάντες πνεύματος ἁγίου καὶ ἤρξαντο λαλεῖν ἑτέραις γλώσσαις (2:4)

b. καὶ ἐπλήσθησαν ἅπαντες τοῦ ἁγίου πνεύματος καὶ ἐλάλουν τὸν λόγον τοῦ θεοῦ μετὰ παρρησίας (4:31).

a. "And they were all filled with the Holy Spirit and began to speak in other tongues" (2:4)

b. "And they were all filled with the Holy Spirit and were speaking the word of God with boldness" (4:31).

This parallel language creates a bit of a dilemma for those who insist that Pentecost was a conversion-initiation event rather than an empowerment for proclamation, for Luke has given no indication that he has suddenly altered the definition of "filled with the Holy Spirit." Because some of the same believers were present at both events, one who holds to a conversion-initiation perspective of Pentecost would have to argue that those present at Pentecost were converted there, subsequently lost their salvation, and were reconverted in Acts 4. It is much simpler and more consistent with Lukan pneumatology to view both episodes as empowering events where the believers of Acts 2 received a fresh filling of the Spirit to meet the demands of the moment in Acts 4.[54] This is also

54. I am grateful to Douglas Oss for pointing out the implications of this parallel to me in a private conversation.

more consistent with what some characters experienced in the Old Testament when they received fresh, charismatic fillings to accomplish divine purposes (e.g., 1 Sam 11:6).

Saul's growth in power in proclaiming that "he [Jesus] is the Christ" (Acts 9:22) along with his subsequent ministry implies that the Spirit's coming was an empowering event. The language of the Spirit "falling on" (ἐπιπίπτω) the Samaritans (8:16) and the gentiles at Caesarea (10:44; 11:15) also points to empowerment, as the term seems to reflect the Spirit's "falling upon" (πίπτω) Ezekiel to give him prophetic inspiration (Ezek 11:5 LXX). The mention of "about twelve" men who received the Spirit at Ephesus (Acts 19:7) may imply that those men were filled to lead the Ephesian church (see chapter 5 below for more details).

Although the democratization of the Spirit has altered the limitations on the number of those chosen to minister under the power of the Spirit, the affirmation of divine acceptance continues in the giving of the Spirit. Joel's prophecy that God would pour his Spirit "on the male servants and female servants" (3:2 MT) becomes, "on *my* male servants and female servants" (ἐπὶ τοὺς δούλους μου καὶ ἐπὶ τὰς δούλας μου) in Acts 2:18.[55] The outpouring of the Spirit confirms God's acceptance of his people.[56] The intentionality of the alteration is evinced by the prayer of the believers in 4:29: "And now, Lord, look upon their threats and grant to *your* servants (τοῖς δούλοις σου) to continue to speak your word with all boldness." The believers had just invoked the Davidic lineage of Jesus and various christological titles in their outline of the opposition to Jesus. The Holy Spirit had spoken through "your servant, our father David" about the opposition to God "and against his Anointed One [τοῦ χριστοῦ αὐτου]" (4:25–26). Jew and gentile alike had opposed "your holy servant Jesus, whom you anointed" (τὸν ἅγιον παῖδά σου Ἰησοῦν ὃν ἔχρισας; v. 27). The answered prayer and filling with the Spirit (v. 31) effectively declare that they are God's anointed servants in the tradition of David and of God's especially chosen and anointed one, Jesus. This is not only a fresh filling and empowering, but a fresh affirmation of the community's identity.

55. Menzies points out this adjustment in the text as part of his argument that Pentecost is an empowerment event rather than a conversion-initiation event. Menzies, *Empowered for Witness*, 182–83.

56. Peter and the apostles refer to the gift of the Spirit in Acts 5:32 as reserved for those who "obey" God. The obedience appears to refer to acknowledgement of Jesus (cf. 7:39), in contrast to those who reject Jesus and disqualify themselves for the eschatological gift.

The acknowledgment of different people as accepted by God and as part of his people is intimated by the laying on of hands in other pneumatic passages (Acts 8:17; 9:17; 19:6). Saul is even called a "chosen vessel" who will carry Jesus' name to gentiles and Jews (9:15). The issue of divine acceptance permeates the entire story of Cornelius and his household. Peter comes to the realization that "God does not show partiality, but in every nation the one who fears him and practices righteousness is acceptable [δεκτὸς] to him" (10:34–35).[57] The unmediated outpouring of the Spirit confirms Peter's proclamation (vv. 44–46). It is therefore fair to say that the Old Testament motif of the Spirit's empowering God's chosen leaders continues in the New Testament as empowerment of God's chosen people and witnesses. The arrival of the Spirit empowers the believers but also signals that God has accepted them.[58]

The emphasis on inspired speech in Acts 2 is pervasive. The direct response to the Spirit's filling is speaking in other tongues, which Luke describes with a verb that often refers to an inspired utterance (ἀποφθέγγομαι; v. 4).[59] The same verb appears again in verse 14 to indicate the inspired nature of Peter's speech (vv. 14–36). Peter refers to tongues as prophetic speech in fulfillment of Joel's prophecy (Acts 2:17) and adds an extra "and they will prophesy" to emphasize the point (v. 18). The major twist in the narrative is that prophetic speech from the Hebrew Scriptures now has a specific manifestation in keeping with Christ's reign over the nations—tongues. The direct result of the Spirit's filling in Acts 4 is boldness in speaking the word of God (v. 31), and the apostles were testifying "with great power" to "the resurrection of the Lord Jesus" (v. 33). Speaking in tongues serves as clear evidence to Peter's companions that the gentiles gathered at Cornelius's home had received the Holy Spirit

57. On gentile acceptance as God's people, see Pao, *Acts*, 236–42.

58. Luke focuses primarily on the filling of communities in Acts. Groups in Jerusalem, Samaria, Caesarea, and Ephesus receive an outpouring of the Spirit en masse. The account of Paul's filling is more the exception, but Luke does not actually record Paul's filling, he only anticipates and assumes it. Luke primarily presents the Spirit as one who empowers diverse communities who are accepted by God and not as the Spirit who regenerates individuals, saving and indwelling them one by one. This is not to say that Luke in any way objects to the latter, but that this is simply not his emphasis.

59. The verb occurs in reference to an inspired utterance (whether divine or pagan) in the Septuagint of 1 Chr 25:1; Ezek 13:9; Mic 5:11; Zech 10:2. See also Philo, *Heir* 1.259; *Joseph* 1.117; *Moses* 1.176; 2.33, 253, 263. It can also mean "declare loudly" in some contexts. See Balz and Schneider, "ἀποφθέγγομαι," 147; Behm, "ἀποφθέγγομαι," 447.

(10:46), and speaking in tongues and prophesying marked the reception of the Spirit at Ephesus (19:6).[60]

At Samaria there is no clear statement as to how Simon knew the Spirit had arrived, and Luke likely omits the explanation because he expects the reader to be cognizant of the type-scene in Acts 2 and because the emphasis shifts away from the experience of the Samaritans to the compromised heart of Simon (8:18–24).[61] The introduction of Simon early in the story (v. 9), the emphasis on his magical history (vv. 9–11), and the use of the conjunctive particle "but" (δέ; vv. 9, 12)[62] to set apart Simon's exploits and contrast them with Philip's preaching of the kingdom prepare the reader for his role in the narrative. Given Luke's profound concern for the integrity of the church, especially in relation to witchcraft (19:13–20) and greed (2:44–45; 4:32—5:11), the reader should not be surprised that Luke omits some details about the filling experience in order to emphasize the utterly inappropriate nature of Simon's request to purchase the power of the Spirit (8:18–19).[63] Peter's previous experience in guarding the church from threats to its purity (Acts 5:1–11) also helps to explain why his presence was important at this event.[64]

60. See the discussion in chapter 5 regarding what Luke meant by tongues and prophecy at Ephesus.

61. Some early Pentecostals argued that speaking in tongues likely occurred at Samaria because Simon had evidently witnessed other charismatic signs previously without requesting power to perform such miracles. Presumably, his observance of the Samaritan people receiving the Spirit introduced him to tongues. Brumback, *"What Meaneth This?"* 206–7. Various scholars have suggested that tongues likely occurred at Samaria, e.g., Barrett, *Acts*, 1:412; Dunn, *Acts of the Apostles*, 111; Haenchen, *Acts*, 304; Haya-Prats, *Empowered Believers*, 116n37. MacDonald has also noticed Luke's attention to Simon's greed issue and that when Luke records the details of an initial reception of the Spirit in Acts the recipients speak in tongues. MacDonald, "Glossolalia," 130–31.

62. The particle probably has an adversative force in both verses, but it almost certainly does in verse 12.

63. Luke records: τότε ἐπετίθεσαν τὰς χεῖρας ἐπ' αὐτοὺς καὶ ἐλάμβανον πνεῦμα ἅγιον (Acts 8:17). Both verbs in this verse are imperfect verbs, suggesting that the laying of hands and the receiving of the Spirit were continuous events. Consequently, Simon's observation of this and his offer of money interrupts the impartation of the Spirit and hinders kingdom activity.

64. Various suggestions have been offered to explain the delay between the conversion of the Samaritans and the outpouring of the Spirit on them. See the discussion in Turner, *Power from on High*, 360–75. Turner does not view this as "problematic" for Luke, but he does see it as "anomalous" for him. I see it as neither "problematic" nor "anomalous," as Luke embraces the Old Testament pattern of the Spirit's falling on covenantal people to empower them. Turner is right in asserting that Philip does not lack the spiritual credentials for imparting the Spirit. Turner, *Power from on High*, 374. Philip's ministry later in the chapter is accomplished by the Spirit (Acts 8:29), and his

The Pentecostal type-scene allows Luke to proceed with addressing Simon's threat to the integrity of the fledgling church without having to give additional details about charismatic signs. There is no immediate reference to inspired utterance in response to Saul's reception of the Spirit either, but Luke does not actually record that Saul received the Spirit—he only anticipates it (9:17).[65] Where the reader expects the record of Saul's filling, Luke records that scales fell from his eyes, he recovered his sight, he was baptized, and he had something to eat (vv. 18–19). Presumably, Saul was filled with the Spirit as well, as his calling assumes empowered ministry in the face of opposition (vv. 15–16), the following narrative presents him as an empowered speaker (vv. 27–28), and the rest of Acts presents him as the equal of Peter. That Paul spoke in tongues is evident from his comments in 1 Cor 14:18, but there is a methodological problem with building a case for Lukan tongues on the basis of Paul's writings.[66] The interpreter cannot suppose that Luke's readers were all familiar with Paul's writing and that they could fill gaps in Acts from Paul's epistles. Therefore, Paul's personal testimony is important as supporting evidence but not necessarily as reflecting a Lukan agenda. Nevertheless, the reader does not need to leave Acts in order to infer that Paul spoke in tongues. Not only does the Pentecostal type-scene predispose the reader to draw such a conclusion, but Luke's presentation of Paul as equal in authority and practice to Peter also points in that direction.[67] With the latter thought in mind, the reader would naturally assume that Paul's authority to lay hands on the Ephesians with the resulting occurrence of tongues

pneumatic transportation reminds the reader of Elijah (v. 39) and elevates him to the status of a prophet. Therefore, it is possible that at least part of the explanation revolves around the practical need for Peter and John to give assistance in preserving the integrity of the church. The issue does not appear to revolve around some sort of apostolic prerogative in giving the Spirit but the role of the original eyewitnesses in guarding the message from becoming diluted by greed.

65. Menzies also observes that three of four places in Acts where reception of the Spirit is described include speaking in tongues, that tongues are implied in Acts 8:14–19, and that there is no description of Paul's reception of the Spirit. Menzies, *Speaking in Tongues*, 33, 33n10.

66. Dunn points out a similar problem in relying on the Gospel of John to establish that the Pentecostal filling with the Spirit is subsequent to salvation. Dunn, *Baptism*, 39. At the same time, it is not unreasonable to conclude that Luke's audience knew something of Paul's life and ministry, as much of the second half of Acts is concerned with defending Paul's reputation.

67. There are several parallels between Peter and Paul, including the similarities between their gospel presentations (cf. Acts 2:14–39; 13:26–41) and miraculous ministries (cf. 9:36–43; 20:7–12). See Tannehill, *Narrative Unity*, 2:236–37.

mirrors the charismatic ministry of Peter (Acts 8:14–18; 10:44–48) and entails the same charismatic qualifications held by Peter (2:4). The simple fact that tongues occur when Paul lays hands on the Ephesians implies that Paul himself had the spiritual authority and personal experience to supervise such a transfer of the Spirit (19:5–6).[68] This pattern of spiritual authority was evident in the Hebrew Scriptures as well, where proximity to a prophet resulted in prophetic experiences.

Although the emphases on inspired utterance and divine service continue from the Hebrew Scriptures, the progress of redemption results in a new expression of God's mission in the missionary efforts of the early church and the proclamation of the gospel of Jesus. There is clearly a relationship between the filling with the Spirit and the gospel for the nations. Key terms related to the kerygma often occur in the pneumatic texts, including the "word" (e.g., Acts 2:41; 4:29, 31; 8:4, 14; 10:36, 44; 19:10), the "gospel" and cognates (8:4, 12, 25; 10:36), and "faith" (2:44; 4:32; 8:12, 13; 10:43; 19:2).[69] The emphasis on the proclamation to the nations is evident from the list of nations at Pentecost (2:5–12), the location of Samaria (ch. 8), Paul's calling (9:15), the gentile audience at Caesarea (10:35), and the Asian location of Ephesus (19:1–7). The "witness" word group and concept often occur in most of these places as well (2:32, 40; 4:33; 8:25; 9:14; 10:39, 41, 42, 43). In short, the Pentecostal type-scene contains a strong missional component. The repeated emphasis on the message of Jesus Christ in the type-scenes supports the primary contention of this study of Acts that tongues are christocentric in nature and symbolic of his reign over the nations. The presence of tongues at Pentecost leads directly into the list of nations and has a strong relationship to missions, as tongues provide the symbol for the mission.

Conclusions about the Pentecostal Type-Scene

Having surveyed the six main pneumatic type-scenes in Acts, it is time to make some final observations and draw some conclusions. First, Luke situates the Pentecostal episode in a literarily advantageous position in the narrative to function as a type-scene. Second, Luke's pneumatic type-scene emerges out of a type-scene that has a substantial history in the

68. Although his arguments are not quite the same as those delineated above, MacDonald has also suggested that Paul's ministry to the Ephesians implies something about his own experience with tongues. MacDonald, "Glossolalia," 133.

69. See the chart in the Appendix for a more complete list.

Old Testament and influences both his Gospel and Acts. Third, Luke's Pentecostal type-scenes demonstrate both continuity with the ancient pattern and some new twists due to the progress of redemption—speaking in tongues is one of those new twists. Fourth, there are about two dozen recurring motifs that typify the Pentecostal type-scenes, but it is fair to summarize them in six primary themes including the divine action of giving the Spirit, Christology, eschatological fulfillment, empowering chosen leaders, prophetic or inspired utterance, and the gospel message for the nations. Fifth, of the six themes, Luke devotes about the most amount of energy to Christology and explicitly refers to Jesus as "Lord" and "Christ" in the immediate context of all six episodes. Closely related to this, he also expends a great deal of energy describing the spread of the gospel message to the nations. He intends to glorify Jesus as Lord of all nations, therefore tongues travel in the type-scene as part of this larger picture.

Sixth, the largest concentration of the recurring themes of Acts 2 is in Acts 10 (the chart in the Appendix illustrates this). The latter is clearly a pivotal text, and the recurrence of tongues there intentionally mirrors Pentecost so that the reader is assured that Jew and gentile are equal participants in the kingdom and in its benefits and mission. Seventh, as tongues do occur in the most important texts, the lack of specific mention of them in other texts does not provide the controlling factor in interpretation; rather, the Pentecostal type-scene provides the lens through which the other scenes are read. The interpreter's posture is to expect tongues, and when they are not mentioned, it is most likely because other theological concerns are dominating the narrative. The Samaritans likely spoke in tongues, but the threat to the church via Simon was Luke's primary concern. The broader narrative of Acts hints at Paul's charismatic experience with tongues, yet Luke's primary concern in Acts 9 is to show his dramatic conversion and calling. Luke never actually records Paul's filling with the Spirit. Luke assumes the reader understands what happens when people receive the Spirit in the age of the Spirit (Acts 2:4). In Acts 4:31 the believers do not receive an initial filling, so their experience is not exactly comparable to other situations. Nevertheless, inspired utterance is still in view.[70]

If one approaches Acts armed only with grammatical-historical tools, then one might dismiss the occurrences of tongues as simply

70. The same applies to Peter's refilling in Acts 4:8 and Paul's refilling in 13:9.

isolated, historical events. In that case, Luke writes only descriptively and not prescriptively, and he has no intention of encouraging the continued use of tongues in conjunction with the Spirit's coming. However, if one accepts that Luke intends to teach theology and influence praxis, and if he functions in the vein of the Old Testament in promoting his agenda through literary conventions, then one cannot so easily dismiss the possible normativity and continuation of tongues. This is especially so if tongues are specifically tied to Christology and missions.

Speaking in tongues occur in all three passages in Acts where Luke records what happens when the Spirit fills people with power to witness for the first time, and the establishment of a type-scene in Acts 2 provides the lens for interpretation in passages where the details and results of filling are not elucidated. Tongues travel via the type-scene with the gospel for the nations and the focus on Christ. Tongues cannot be separated from mission and Christ in Acts.

4

Declaring Christ is Lord in Caesarea

In the previous chapters I have reviewed the kingdom context of Luke-Acts, pointed out Luke's strategic references to Jesus as Lord and Christ, highlighted the christological context of tongues in Acts 2, and suggested that Acts 2 builds on an ancient pattern and serves as a type-scene for the outpouring of the Spirit in the rest of Acts. The Pentecostal story presents tongues as a missional symbol that points to Christ's lordship over the nations. Tongues are vertical in orientation, christocentric in content, and prophetic in nature. This chapter investigates the outpouring of the Spirit and accompanying tongues at Cornelius's household in light of Luke's Christology. The discussion compares the context and various aspects of tongues in Acts 10:1—11:18 with the Pentecostal outpouring and seeks to establish how the lordship of Christ provides the essential literary and theological context for understanding the experience of speaking in tongues. Along the way, the chapter examines the literary significance of the Cornelius story in the narrative of Acts, the question of Cornelius's spiritual state prior to reception of the Spirit, the textual issues and the emphasis on Jesus' lordship in Acts 10:36, the christological titles in the story, and Luke's depiction of a "gentile Pentecost" at Caesarea. The latter topic also covers how the Spirit "fell upon" the gentiles, the debate over the normativity of tongues, the kind of tongues spoken by the gentiles, and tongues as praise. A summary concludes the chapter.

The Significance of Caesarea

Luke incorporates a variety of literary devices to emphasize the importance of the events related to the outpouring of the Spirit on the gentiles in Caesarea. Scholars have noticed the length of this story, and Polhill comments, "Acts 10:1—11:18 is the longest single narrative in all of Acts."[1] Repetition characterizes the account both within the individual scenes (e.g., the sheet in Peter's dream descends three times [10:11–16]) and in reference to entire episodes (10:30–33) or practically the whole account (11:4–17). Peter repeats the highlights of the story again at the Jerusalem Council, where the account serves as a theological foundation for the acceptance of gentiles without ritual circumcision (15:6–11).[2] The account is also marked by the repetition of numerous gospel themes, tying it to the Pentecostal outpouring and demonstrating Luke's selectivity of material.[3]

As at Pentecost, the prominence of Peter in the story gives it a sense of gravitas. The abundance of supernatural elements in the account (including an angelic appearance, a trance, visions, guidance by the Spirit, miracles of timing, and speaking in tongues) points to the direct activity of God. It is reminiscent of the birth narrative in Luke 2, which was also characterized by a flurry of miraculous activity. Elements such as these imply that the story is important to Luke, and the inclusion of glossolalia at this significant juncture also points to its importance. Frank Macchia notes the significance of the location of tongues in Acts: "How many times tongues are mentioned in Acts is not important. . . . Where and how tongues are mentioned and what theological meaning is implied are important."[4] When one also considers the theological significance of the outpouring of the Spirit on gentiles (Acts 10:44) along with the strategic placement of the Son's identity at the head of Peter's sermon ("Jesus Christ, this one is Lord of all"; v. 36b), it becomes evident that the events of Acts 10 are of monumental importance to Luke.

1. Polhill, *Acts*, 250. See also Marshall, *Acts*, 181.

2. Dibelius, *Studies in Acts*, 109; Wilson, *Gentiles*, 177; Witherington, *Acts*, 340.

3. See the previous chapter on the Pentecostal type-scene and the chart in the Appendix. Chuen points to Luke's selectivity of material as an indicator of the importance he places on tongues. Chuen, "Acts 10," II.B.

4 Macchia, "Groans Too Deep," Section 3. Here Macchia is distancing himself from older Pentecostal arguments for a pattern in Acts based on counting the number of times speaking in tongues occurred or likely occurred.

The Spiritual State of Cornelius

Scholars have entertained the question of Cornelius's spiritual condition prior to his reception of the Spirit; that is, at what point does Cornelius experience saving faith? The question is a concern because it has implications for the debate over whether the gentile reception of the Spirit was an empowering experience, a conversion-initiation event, or both. Some scholars, particularly in the Pentecostal tradition, have argued that Cornelius was already a believer prior to the reception of the Spirit recorded in Acts 10:44; consequently, the occurrence of speaking in tongues (for some of these scholars) functions as a sign of a post-conversion Spirit baptism. Those who view the reception of the Spirit as solely a conversion event often view the speaking in tongues as an isolated occurrence given to confirm the availability of salvation for gentiles. The following discussion reviews what Luke says about Cornelius's spirituality.

The piety of Cornelius reminds the reader of the centurion in Luke 7:1–10 who had faith greater than that of the Israelites. Luke describes Cornelius and his household as εὐσεβής ("godly", "devout"), God-fearing, generous, and prayerful (Acts 10:2, 30–31).[5] The latter two are particularly mentioned by the angel in verse 4. This special mention of these two is not surprising in light of Luke's focus on prayer as an act of piety and as preparation for reception of the Spirit (Luke 2:37; Acts 1:14; 4:31) and in light of his repeated references to one's handling of wealth as an indicator of one's standing in the kingdom. On the latter point, Luke has already highlighted Judas's reward money (Acts 1:18), the sharing of the early church (2:44; 4:32–35), the generosity of Barnabas (4:36–37) in contrast to the greed of Ananias and Sapphira (5:1–11), and Simon's attempt to purchase the power of the Spirit (8:20). Cornelius's generosity testifies to the authenticity of his kingdom values and aligns him with the people of the kingdom in Luke-Acts.[6]

The narrative repeatedly refers to Cornelius's fear of God (Acts 10:2, 22, 35) and righteous character (vv. 22, 35), and his servants comment on his respectability in the Jewish nation (v. 22). Bock views the reference to the whole nation as "almost a technical phrase" in Judaism, demonstrating that "Cornelius is well known among the Jews."[7] Were it not for the

5. Tannehill notes how Cornelius is described in terms that one would expect to be applied to a devout Jew. Tannehill, *Narrative Unity*, 2:133.

6. Luke 6:24; 10:35; 11:39; 12:13–21; 16:19–31; 19:1–10; 20:47; 21:1–4.

7. Bock, *Acts*, 392.

clear references to his gentile descent, a reader would naturally assume that someone who prayed at the ninth hour (v. 3) and was so favored with an angelic visitation was a significant figure in Israelite history.[8] Stronstad argues that Cornelius was already a believer on the basis of the charismatic nature of the gift of the Spirit in Luke-Acts and Luke's "'antecedent spiritual state' narrative strategy" that depicts Cornelius and others as believers prior to their reception of the Spirit.[9] He contends that "Luke always identifies the antecedent spiritual state of the person(s) he is about to report will receive the gift of the Holy Spirit" (Luke 1:6, 41, 67; Acts 8:12, 14–17; 10:44–48; 11:17; 19:2, 6).[10] It appears that Cornelius had some level of faith prior to meeting Peter.

References to the cleanness and acceptability of Cornelius and other gentiles might also point to their spiritual state. The voice in Peter's vision urges him not to call anything impure that God has cleansed (Acts 10:15)—apparently referring to more than just unclean foods, as Peter applies the vision to persons in verse 28. Peter refers to anyone who fears God and practices righteousness as "acceptable" (δεκτός) to God (v. 35; cf. Luke 4:19, 24). However, some have argued that the acceptability in view is not the same as salvation,[11] but it is a reference to the availability of salvation to non-Jews; that is, they are "welcome to come to Christ on the same basis as Jews."[12] Peter's comment on the acceptability of the righteous from any nation follows Cornelius's announcement of eager expectation to hear Peter's message: "Now therefore we are all here in the presence of God to hear everything the Lord has commanded you" (Acts 10:33b). The "now" has a climactic tone in Cornelius's speech, and the gentile group has gathered in obedience and with a posture of worship.[13] Perhaps as a result of the angelic visitation and all that has already transpired, Cornelius possesses an awareness of the divine presence even before the outpouring of the Spirit.

8. Parsons, *Acts*, 143; Tannehill, *Narrative Unity*, 2:133.

9. Stronstad, *Charismatic Theology: Trajectories*, 64.

10. Stronstad, *Charismatic Theology: Trajectories*, 64.

11. Larkin, *Acts*, 163.

12. Peterson, *Acts*, 335.

13. Witherington notes this posture of worship and also points to a possible echo of the disciples awaiting Pentecost in Acts 1:13–14. *Acts*, 354. Kurz refers to God's presence as a "prayerful setting." He also refers to the expectant response to Peter's arrival as "evidence of the expectant faith that disposes people's hearts to receive the Holy Spirit." Kurz, *Acts of the Apostles*, 174.

Peter emphatically tells the gathered gentiles, "You know [ὑμεῖς οἴδατε] what has happened throughout all Judea, beginning from Galilee after the baptism that John preached" (Acts 10:37). Peter rehearses the key elements of the gospel of Jesus, but Martin Dibelius comments, "Nothing justifies our assuming that Cornelius 'knows' anything."[14] However, it is entirely reasonable to accept that Cornelius and his family did possess some familiarity with the message of Jesus. Luke has already referred to Cornelius's association with the Jewish nation (v. 22; cf. 26:26), and the relatively close proximity of Caesarea to Jerusalem and Galilee makes it likely that Cornelius knew what had transpired there; it is also plausible that the ministry of Philip in Caesarea had impacted Cornelius (8:40; 21:8).[15] Cornelius had knowledge of the basic story of Jesus, but it is probably going too far to say that this knowledge equates to new-covenant salvation.[16]

Peter's explanation of his sharing in fellowship with gentiles challenges the notion that Cornelius was fully converted prior to his introduction to Peter. Peter rehearses for the Jewish believers how the angel instructed Cornelius to search for Peter, "who will speak words to you by which you will be saved, you and all your house" (Acts 11:14). Likewise, at the Jerusalem Council Peter refers to the events in Caesarea and claims that God had made the choice that the gentiles would hear the gospel message through Peter's mouth and would believe (15:7). James Dunn seizes on these passages along with the climax of Peter's speech (although interrupted by the outpouring of the Spirit), in which Peter expounds on the availability of forgiveness of sins through faith in Jesus (10:43). Dunn argues that "the Spirit was not something additional to God's acceptance and forgiveness but constituted that acceptance and forgiveness."[17] Dunn is right to reject the idea that Cornelius was saved in the new-covenant sense of the word prior to hearing Peter preach, but his remarks sound more like a commentary on a Pauline passage than an analysis of Luke's charismatic pneumatology.[18] Max Turner provides a

14. Dibelius, *Studies in Acts*, 111n5. Barrett suggests that the statement does not make sense in this context, so Luke must be using traditional material. Barrett, *Acts*, 1:523. Fitzmyer thinks the "you know" must refer to the reader rather than the gentiles. Fitzmyer, *Acts*, 464.

15. Peterson, *Acts*, 337; Stanton, *Jesus of Nazareth*, 20–21.

16. Arrington cites Acts 11:18 in support of his contention that the "you know" indicates that conversion has taken place. Arrington, *Acts*, 112–13.

17. Dunn, *Baptism*, 80.

18. On various occasions in Acts a group of people receive the Spirit at the same

corrective to Dunn when he notes that "what Cornelius received was the 'Spirit of prophecy' evinced in charismatic speech: as this contains elements that are transparently 'additional' to forgiveness and acceptance, we have no reason to equate receiving the Spirit with God's forgiveness simpliciter."[19] By Dunn's logic, speaking in tongues would be part of the conversion experience. Turner ultimately concludes that "the Spirit of prophecy is simultaneously the soteriological Spirit in so far as it is the power of Zion's cleansing/restoration."[20] Turner is right to distinguish the charismatic element from conversion, but his attempt to make the Spirit's arrival also soteriological is not supported by Lukan pneumatology in general.

The structure of Peter's sermon, ending with "everyone who believes in him [Jesus]" (Acts 10:43), followed by the narrator's interruption and account of the Spirit's outpouring, implies that Cornelius's family and friends believe and enter into the new covenant during Peter's preaching.[21] Luke presents Cornelius and those with him as people of faith who hold to Jewish values and have a basic knowledge of Jesus. However, their status in regard to the new covenant in Jesus was unclear both to early Jewish believers in Jesus and to the gentiles themselves. Cornelius's household was poised for salvation and only needed clarity regarding Jewish ritual regulations and access to Christ. They needed to know the gospel applied to them and that they could enter the Christian church directly through Christ. For Peter, the gift of the Spirit serves as evidence that the gentiles are Christians and that a faith commitment has already taken place. Consequently, Peter can point to the Spirit as a gift in the same manner that the Spirit fell on the disciples who were already

---

time. If these receptions of the Spirit are understood as charismatic empowering experiences, there is no problem with groups of people simultaneously receiving the Spirit. However, if one understands Luke's pneumatology as essentially identical to Paul's teaching that the indwelling of the Spirit occurs at the moment of salvation, then it creates problems for groups of people to all receive the Spirit at precisely the same moment. It would imply that every disciple at Pentecost, every one of Cornelius's group at Caesarea, and each of the twelve Ephesian disciples received salvation at precisely the same moment. Presumably, even in groups of people the moment of salvation differs from person to person. The interpreter is left with the unenviable task of making every group reception of the Spirit some kind of exception in the narrative.

19. Turner, *Power from on High*, 381–82.

20. Turner, *Power from on High*, 387.

21. Some scholars who point to Peter's sermon or the final words of it as indicating the timing of salvation include: Harrison, *Acts*, 175; Horton, *Book of Acts*, 135; Longenecker, "Acts," 393; Polhill, *Acts*, 264.

believers in Jesus prior to Pentecost (Acts 11:17). God had purified the hearts of the gentiles by faith just as he had done for the disciples, so the gift of the Spirit did not constitute repentance or saving faith, but testified to its prior existence.[22] The outpouring of the Spirit confirmed their faith and acceptance by God and enabled them to share in the mission to the nations.

Although salvation and the gift of the Spirit occur close in time in Acts 10, Robert Menzies is right in emphasizing the distinctive nature of the gift of the Spirit in Luke-Acts and in viewing the gift of the Spirit as a testimony to the prior inward working of God's grace in the heart of the gentiles.[23] The notion of a logical distinction is grounded in Luke's reliance on an Old Testament pattern, Luke's employment of a Pentecostal type-scene, and the overall nature of Luke's pneumatology.[24] Even if conversion for the gentiles happened at precisely the same moment as reception of the empowering Spirit,[25] that would not negate the logical distinction between conversion and Spirit baptism in Luke-Acts. Consequently, speaking in tongues is not integral to conversion but evinces a prior conversion and is associated with empowered mission and declaring the lordship of Christ, but, in the final analysis, the timing of Spirit baptism and conversion does not alter the christocentric character of tongues.

The Text of Acts 10:36

After Cornelius explains why he sent for Peter, Luke starts a new unit with this introductory formula to Peter's speech: "And he opened his mouth and said" (Acts 10:34a). Peter begins by stating that God shows no favoritism "but in every nation [ἐν παντὶ ἔθνει] the one who fears him and works righteousness is acceptable to him" (v. 35). The phrase "in every nation" is emphatic, occurring at the head of the clause, and is reminiscent of Jesus' instruction to preach repentance for the forgiveness

22. See the comments by Peterson (who follows Turner somewhat). Peterson, *Acts*, 347n21. Haya-Prats and Shelton view the Spirit as testifying to faith. Haya-Prats, *Empowered Believers*, 142; Shelton, *Mighty in Word*, 133.

23. See the discussion in Menzies, *Empowered for Witness*, 215–18. Also see Cho, *Spirit and Kingdom*, 150–54.

24. See the discussion of the hermeneutical issues involved in William W. Menzies and Robert P. Menzies, *Spirit and Power*, 109–19.

25. See Keener, *Acts: Exegetical*, 2:1809; Palma, *Holy Spirit*, 121.

of sins in his name "to all nations [εἰς πάντα τὰ ἔθνη]" (Luke 24:47) and of the international emphasis in Acts 2. The following sentence (10:36) has caused a considerable stir over the Greek construction. A literal translation reads, "The word which he sent to the sons of Israel preaching good news of peace through Jesus Christ—this one is Lord of all" (τὸν λόγον [ὃν] ἀπέστειλεν τοῖς υἱοῖς Ἰσραὴλ εὐαγγελιζόμενος εἰρήνην διὰ Ἰησοῦ Χριστοῦ, οὗτός ἐστιν πάντων κύριος). C. K. Barrett remarks that the language in verses 36–38 "is so difficult as to be untranslatable," and Joseph Fitzmyer calls it "miserable Greek."[26] The problem revolves around two primary issues. First, there is textual uncertainty about the inclusion of the relative pronoun ὃν ("which"). Second, the sentence begins with "the word" in the accusative case (τὸν λόγον), but there is no immediately apparent subject and verb for "the word" as an object.

Regarding the problem with ὃν, its proximity to λόγον could explain either its accidental omission due to haplography or its addition due to dittography.[27] Omission of the relative pronoun smooths out the sentence, rendering the following reading: "He sent the word to the sons of Israel, preaching good news of peace through Jesus Christ—he is Lord of all."[28] However, the omission appears to be an attempt at amelioration, and the more difficult reading that includes the relative pronoun is more likely the original reading.[29]

Scholars have proposed a number of causes and solutions for the syntactical problem of "the word" (τὸν λόγον) occurring in the accusative. C. C. Torrey proposed that the rough Greek results from dependence on an Aramaic source.[30] Richard Longenecker mentions the possibility of Luke using a Septuagintal style, but he suggests that the difficult Greek results from Peter's attempt at using Greek to speak to a gentile audience.[31] Gerhard Schneider follows Harald Riesenfeld in proposing that

26. Barrett, *Acts*, 1:521; Fitzmyer, *Acts*, 460. See similar comments by Dodd, *Apostolic Preaching*, 27; Witherington, *Acts*, 356.

27. Metzger, *Textual Commentary*, 379. Haenchen chooses the dittography option. *Acts*, 352.

28. Johnson opts for the smoother reading. *Acts*, 191.

29. Keener, *Acts: Exegetical*, 2:1798n694; Metzger, *Textual Commentary*, 379. Also see Soards, *Speeches in Acts*, 73n180.

30. Torrey, *Composition and Date of Acts*, 35. Various scholars see some evidence of an Aramaic source. See Bruce, *Acts of the Apostles*, 225; Dodd, *Apostolic Preaching*, 27. Stanton does not see sufficient evidence for this conclusion. *Jesus of Nazareth*, 70.

31. Longenecker, "Acts," 392. Williams points to Luke's conscious employment of a Semitic style. *Acts of the Apostles*, 136.

Acts 10:36 is in apposition to verses 34b and 35.[32] In this case, "the word which he sent to the sons of Israel" (v. 36) becomes a parallel summary of what Peter realizes: "I realize that [ὅτι] God does not show favoritism, but in every nation the one who fears him and works righteousness is acceptable to him" (vv. 34b, 35).[33]

Another proposal looks in the opposite direction for a resolution and posits that the "you know" (ὑμεῖς οἴδατε) of Acts 10:37 supplies the subject and verb for "the word" in verse 36. The RSV translates the passage in this manner: "You know the word which he sent to Israel, preaching good news of peace by Jesus Christ (he is Lord of all)" (v. 36). C. K. Barrett criticizes this view, calling it "remote" and concluding that this solution only complicates the problem in verse 37.[34] Barrett also rejects reconstructions based on the notion that suspended clauses were more common in Aramaic, and he suggests that after Luke wrote that Jesus is "Lord of all," Luke simply "forgot how the sentence was intended to run."[35]

Graham Stanton notices the common language between Acts 10:36 and Ps 107:20 (106:20 LXX) and suggests that Peter's speech may originally have begun by citing this psalm.[36] Verse 19 of the Psalm mentions the Lord, and verse 20 reads, *ἀπέστειλεν τὸν λόγον αὐτοῦ καὶ ἰάσατο αὐτούς* ("he sent his word and healed them"), sharing "he sent" and "the word" with Acts 10:36 and the verb for healing with verse 38. It is possible that Ps 106:19–20 (LXX) informs Acts 10:36, but the original presence of a longer quotation is speculative and dependence on the Psalm does not fully explain Luke's Greek construction.

Another mention of "the word" occurs in Acts 10:37, where Peter begins to summarize the gospel message: "You know the word [ῥῆμα] that has happened throughout all of Judea, beginning from Galilee after the baptism that John preached." While the terms λόγος and ῥῆμα overlap somewhat in Luke-Acts, Luke uses the term λόγος much more often and commonly uses it as a shorthand term for the message of Jesus and his

32. Schneider, *Die Apostelgeschichte II*, 75–76; Riesenfeld, "The Text of Acts x.36," 191–94. Also see Bock, *Acts*, 396; Soards, *Speeches in Acts*, 73n180.

33. For an overview of the history of this interpretation, see Neirynck, "Acts 10,36a τὸν λόγον ὅν," 118–23.

34. Barrett, *Acts*, 1:522.

35. Barrett, *Acts*, 1:522.

36. Stanton, *Jesus of Nazareth*, 71, 77.

resurrection.[37] Luke uses ῥῆμα to refer to a report or an event and often as a general description of a person's words.[38] In this passage the change seems intentional; λόγος appears to refer directly to Jesus as Lord of all and ῥῆμα refers to the general events or happenings related to the gospel story.[39] The distinction in terms occurs again a few verses later, when Peter finishes speaking "these words" (τὰ ῥήματα ταῦτα) and the Spirit falls on "all those who heard the word [τὸν λόγον]" (v. 44). In both cases the term ῥῆμα has a general sense to it, and λόγος takes on a more technical use as a specific "word"—the message of Jesus' resurrection and lordship. Awareness of Luke's use of λόγος is important in this text because it helps explain why Luke would exercise himself in placing the term at the head of a sentence. The arrangement functions to emphasize that the "word" that was previously sent "to the sons of Israel" about Christ's universal lordship applies to the gentiles in Caesarea.

Perhaps the best explanation for how to render the grammar of Acts 10:36 is to understand "the word" (τὸν λόγον) as an accusative of respect.[40] A similar occurrence of this construction is found in Rev 1:20: τὸ μυστήριον τῶν ἑπτὰ ἀστέρων οὓς εἶδες ἐπὶ τῆς δεξιᾶς μου . . . · οἱ ἑπτὰ ἀστέρες ἄγγελοι τῶν ἑπτὰ ἐκκλησιῶν εἰσιν. . . . "As for the mystery of the seven stars which you saw in my right hand . . . : the seven stars are angels of the seven churches."[41] This verse begins almost like a title or heading for what follows, just as Acts 10:36 does. A Lukan passage that has very likely influenced Luke's style is found in Luke's direct quotation of Ps 117:22 (LXX) in Luke 20:17b: λίθον ὃν ἀπεδοκίμασαν οἱ οἰκοδομοῦντες, οὗτος ἐγενήθη εἰς κεφαλὴν γωνίας ("As for the stone which the builders rejected: this one has become the cornerstone").[42] This construction is

37. The term λόγος occurs thirty-two times in Luke's Gospel and sixty-five times in Acts, while ῥῆμα occurs nineteen times in Luke and fourteen times in Acts. See the discussion in Lidbeck, *Resurrection and Spirit*, 135–41.

38. Pao distinguishes between Luke's use of the two words. *Acts*, 147–48.

39. Bock also sees a distinction in the two words in this passage. *Acts*, 397.

40. Tannehill, *Narrative Unity*, 2:139; Burchard, "A Note on 'PHMA,'" 290–94.

41. I have borrowed the reference and the initial part of the translation from Wallace. He also points to other examples of the accusative of respect in Matt 27:57; John 6:10; Acts 2:37; Rom 10:5; 1 Cor 9:25; 2 Cor 12:13; Eph 4:15; Heb 2:17. Wallace, *Greek Grammar*, 204. However, note that the example in Matt 27:57 may actually be a nominative case. See also BDF §160.

42. Marshall posits that the accusative case of the "stone" results from "attraction to the relative pronoun, and is caught up by οὗτος." Marshall, *Gospel of Luke*, 732. Several scholars have suggested the same in Acts 10:36. See Bock, *Acts*, 396; Fitzmyer, *Acts*, 463; Schneider, *Die Apostelgeschichte II*, 75.

so similar to Acts 10:36 that it seems like a deliberate attempt to transfer the christological significance of the stone passage into Peter's speech (cf. 4:10–11). The emphasis on the resurrection of Jesus and his role as judge in the context of both passages increases the likelihood of this scenario.[43] Acts 10:36 could then be translated as follows: "As for the word which he sent to the sons of Israel, preaching good news of peace through Jesus Christ: he is Lord of all." Various scholars consider the latter phrase to be parenthetical but yet recognize the phrase as the central theme of the passage. This translation gives the latter phrase its proper theological place and affirms Luke's use of grammar to emphasize his theological interests. Luke intentionally places "the word" where he does in verse 36 to draw attention to the universal lordship of Jesus and the availability of the gospel for all. That this arrangement is not due to an Aramaic source or the author's clumsiness is also supported by the occurrence of related stylistic elements in Acts 10 and within other speeches in Acts.[44] In addition, "the word" serves a framing purpose in Peter's speech in Acts 10.

Regarding Luke's use of nouns and pronouns in the accusative case at the beginning of sentences or clauses for purposes of emphasis, he uses this arrangement in Acts 10:38: Ἰησοῦν τὸν ἀπὸ Ναζαρέθ, ὡς ἔχρισεν αὐτὸν ὁ θεὸς πνεύματι ἁγίῳ καὶ δυνάμει, ("Jesus from Nazareth, how God anointed him with the Holy Spirit and power"). This statement relies on the "you know" of verse 37, but translators must rearrange the initial phrase beginning with the accusative Ἰησοῦν in order to make sense of it. It also seems a little awkward at the end of verse 39 when a relative pronoun in the accusative case starts a new sentence: ὃν καὶ ἀνεῖλαν κρεμάσαντες ἐπὶ ξύλου, ("Whom also they killed by hanging him on a tree"). The sentence continues with a demonstrative pronoun in the accusative beginning a new clause: τοῦτον ὁ θεὸς ἤγειρεν ἐν τῇ τρίτῃ ἡμέρᾳ ("this one God raised on the third day"). Luke's emphatic style clearly identifies Jesus as the Christ, the one who died and rose again, and the one who is Lord of all.

To further accentuate this claim, Luke uses the demonstrative pronoun (in the nominative case this time) to identify Jesus: "Jesus Christ, this one [οὗτός] is Lord of all" (v. 36b). Luke makes a similar identification at the end of Peter's speech, forming a frame: "This [οὗτός] is the one

43. Lidbeck, *Resurrection and Spirit*, 157.

44. As I have argued above, the primary source material is not an Aramaic source but Ps 117:22 (LXX).

appointed by God as judge of the living and the dead" (v. 42b).[45] Luke's style maintains the christocentric focus throughout Peter's speech and affirms the universal lordship of Christ at the beginning and the end of the speech. Luke attributes to Jesus the divine status of universal Lord and, by use of a merism, not only affirms his lordship over all ethnicities but also over the living and the dead. Further evidence of an intentional frame may be found in the repetition of "the word" at the beginning and end of Peter's sermon. Luke uses the word λόγος and then ῥῆμα in verses 36–37, and then he summarizes by using them in reverse order in verse 44. Consequently, literary and thematic elements form a frame that identifies Jesus as the Lord, the central figure in the message (λόγος), and the one who shares the divine prerogatives in reigning, judging, and forgiving (v. 43).

Luke's emphatic style in Acts 10 recalls his similar style in Acts 2 (vv. 22–24, 32; cf. Luke 20:17; Acts 3:15; 13:37). A comparison of the key texts in each passage evinces how his style serves his christological purposes. Both passages employ the accusative style, mention Israel, use a demonstrative pronoun to clearly identify Jesus, and include the threefold designation of Jesus as Lord and Christ. Each text provides the theological centerpiece of each sermon, with the first one climaxing Peter's sermon and the second one commencing it. The focus on Jesus as Lord intensifies in the second reference as a result of the gentile context.

> ἀσφαλῶς οὖν γινωσκέτω πᾶς οἶκος Ἰσραὴλ ὅτι καὶ κύριον αὐτὸν καὶ χριστὸν ἐποίησεν ὁ θεός, τοῦτον τὸν Ἰησοῦν ὃν ὑμεῖς ἐσταυρώσατε.
>
> "Therefore let all the house of Israel know with certainty that God has made him both Lord and Christ, this Jesus whom you crucified" (Acts 2:36).

> τὸν λόγον [ὃν] ἀπέστειλεν τοῖς υἱοῖς Ἰσραὴλ εὐαγγελιζόμενος εἰρήνην διὰ Ἰησοῦ Χριστοῦ, οὗτός ἐστιν πάντων κύριος,
>
> "As for the word which he sent to the sons of Israel, preaching good news of peace through Jesus Christ: he is Lord of all" (Acts 10:36).

Consequently, Acts 2 and 10 share both a similar christological emphasis and a similar style in emphasizing that christological center.

45. Others have noticed the frame in this passage; e.g., Keener, *Acts: Exegetical*, 2:1807; *Parsons*, Acts, 155; Tannehill, *Narrative Unity*, 2:141; Witherington, *Acts*, 358.

What at first sight appears to be a Greek conundrum in Acts 10:36 is much more likely a Lukan style adapted from the Septuagint (Ps 117:22; cf. Luke 20:17b) for the purpose of emphasizing the messianic, royal, and divine identity of Jesus. The "word" (τὸν λόγον) in Acts 10:36 is the message that Jesus is Lord of all, and this christological declaration provides the context for the outburst of speaking in tongues that follows. This is entirely consistent with the emphasis on Jesus' lordship when tongues occur in Acts 2.

Lord and Christ of the Gentiles

Peter's sermon at Caesarea and the subsequent events underscore the royal and messianic identity of Jesus in a variety of ways. At the outset of Peter's sermon, he refers to the message first "sent to the sons of Israel" (Acts 10:36; cf. 2:14, 22, 36; 5:31) as good news of "peace" (Acts 10:36; cf. Luke 2:10–11, 14). The peace is not the *Pax Romana*, and the Lord is not Caesar (cf. Luke 1:79–2:1; Acts 25:26), but a Roman centurion (Cornelius) gladly hears the proclamation that Jesus is the Lord who brings peace.[46] The terminology reflects the angelic announcement in Luke 2, and the proclamation first made to the Jewish people now begins to manifest its universal character. C. H. Dodd correctly summarizes Peter's christocentric sermon to the gentiles as the proclamation of the kingdom of God.[47]

Luke specifically refers to Jesus as the "Christ" three times in the story of Cornelius (Acts 10:36, 48; 11:17), and he also draws attention to how "God anointed [ἔχρισεν] him with the Holy Spirit and power" (10:38a). The phrase is immediately preceded by "Jesus from Nazareth" (Ιησοῦν τὸν ἀπὸ Ναζαρέθ) in Luke's familiar style in order to emphasize the identity of Jesus.[48] The cognate of "Christ" reminds the reader of the identical aorist verb used in Luke's programmatic passage in Luke 4:18a: "The Spirit of the Lord is upon me because he has anointed [ἔχρισέν] me to preach good news to the poor," which is drawn directly from Isa 61:1 (LXX; cf. Ps 2:2). F. F. Bruce suggests that Jesus is identifying himself with

46. Others have also noticed the irony in this; e.g., Holladay, *Acts*, 238; Keener, *Acts: Exegetical*, 2:1800, 2:1800n715. On the commonality of the term "Lord" in the ancient world, see Barrett, *Acts*, 1:522; Keener, *Acts: Exegetical*, 2:1800; Longenecker, "Acts," 393; Thompson, *Acts: A Commentary*, 210; Witherington, *Acts*, 257.

47. Dodd, *Apostolic Preaching*, 24.

48. Bruce, *Acts of the Apostles*, 226.

the role of the Servant (Isa 42:1—53:12) and the anticipated, Spirit-filled Davidic ruler of Isa 11:1–5.[49] This is a sensible suggestion, and the terminology of anointing reminds the reader of David's anointing with the Spirit (1 Sam 16:13) and the covenantal promises made to him (2 Sam 7:11–16; cf. Luke 1:31–33; 2:26). Although the gentile context of the sermon does not require the same degree of proof that Jesus is the Davidic Messiah, Luke still alludes to Jesus' identity as a Davidite in keeping with his strong kingdom theology.[50] In so doing, he indicates that the gentile outpouring occurs within the same framework of Christ's Davidic kingship as the Pentecostal outpouring.[51]

The lordship of Christ is also expressed in Peter's summary of Jesus' healing ministry, as he "went around doing good and healing all those who were oppressed [καταδυναστευομένους] by the devil" (Acts 10:38b). The verb καταδυναστεύω ("to oppress") occurs only here and in James 2:6 in the New Testament, but the verb or its cognate noun occurs about forty times in the Septuagint. The verb describes the oppression of the Egyptians in Exod 1:13, and the noun occurs in 6:7b: "And you will know that I am the Lord [Κύριος] your God who brought you out from under the oppression [καταδυναστείας] of the Egyptians." Similarly, the healing ministry of Jesus manifests his lordship as he breaks Satan's tyrannical power.

Peter testifies to Christ's lordship again when he twice plainly asserts his resurrection from the dead. "This one [τοῦτον] God raised on the third day" (Acts 10:40a), and the disciples ate and drank with him "after he rose from the dead" (v. 41b). The resurrection of Christ was not merely a resuscitation, but a glorification and pointer to his royal and exalted status (Acts 2:23–36; 1 Sam 2:6–10).[52] He is therefore also "the one appointed by God as judge of the living and the dead" (Acts 10:42b; cf. 1 En. 38.3). As Lord of all, Jesus is also the eschatological judge of all. During Paul's sermon at Athens, he directly ties the resurrection of Jesus to his role as judge (Acts 17:31), and he uses the same Greek word (ὁρίζω)

49. Bruce, *Acts of the Apostles*, 214.

50. Peter's statement that God was with Jesus (Acts 10:38c) could apply to several Old Testament characters, but the mention of anointing could point to the distinction between Saul and David, as the Lord was with David but had departed from Saul (1 Sam 16:10–14).

51. Oss, "A Pentecostal/Charismatic View," 269.

52. See Lidbeck, *Resurrection and Spirit*, especially chapter 4.

for God's appointing of Jesus to this role as Peter uses in Acts 10:42.[53] Jesus' role as judge is also alluded to when the day of the Lord becomes the day of the Lord Jesus in Acts 2:20–21, and it is implicit in other passages in Acts (2:34–35; 3:23; 7:56)[54] and in the "Son of Man" passages in Luke (e.g., 5:24; 6:5; 9:26; 11:30–32; 12:8; 18:8; 21:27, 36; 22:69).[55] The solemnity in Peter's charge "to testify" (note the compound verb διαμαρτύρομαι; Acts 10:42) of Jesus' appointment as judge of the living and the dead is happily preceded by the mention of the acceptability of the gentiles (Acts 10:35) and followed by the provision of forgiveness through Jesus' name (v. 43). The reception of the Spirit confirms that Cornelius's household and friends are recipients of divine favor and will not experience the fiery wrath of the eschatological judge (v. 44). When Peter rehearses the story for the Jews, he asserts that Cornelius was awaiting Peter's words by which he and his family could be "saved" (i.e., from wrath; 11:14). Peter explains that the Spirit fell when he began to speak, indicating God's favor toward the gentiles and reminding Peter of Jesus' promise of a baptism in the Spirit (vv. 15–16; 1:5). The reference has its origin in John's identification of Jesus as one who would baptize in the Spirit and fire (Luke 3:16), but the fire is omitted in both Acts 1:5 and 11:16 because the disciples at Pentecost and Cornelius's household alike experienced Jesus as a divine benefactor and redeemer and would not experience him as the dispenser of raging fire.

The story of Cornelius reveals Jesus' identity as the Messiah who is Lord of all, and this identification includes his roles as the giver of peace, the judge, the forgiver of sins, the savior, and the baptizer in the Spirit. But just in case anyone missed the point in the story, Luke includes the threefold designation of Jesus one more time at the end of the entire unit (Acts 10:1—11:18). Peter concludes his defense of his actions by appealing to God's initiative in giving the same gift of the Spirit to the gentiles as he had given to the Jews who "had believed on the Lord Jesus Christ [τὸν κύριον Ἰησοῦν Χριστόν]" (11:17). The repetition of this designation is the exclamation point on the Caesarean narrative, and the repetition of Christ's identity at the beginning of Peter's speech (10:36) and at the end of the pericope exerts a controlling influence over the interpretation of the gift of the Spirit and the resulting tongues in Acts 10:44–47.

53. Bruce, *Acts of the Apostles*, 227.

54. Peterson, *Acts*, 338.

55. See also Luke 10:8–16; 12:41–48; 17:20–37; 20:18.

The Gentile Pentecost

It is little wonder that scholars have often referred to the reception of the Spirit in Acts 10:44–48 as "the Gentile Pentecost."[56] As outlined above, Luke's grammatical style intentionally mirrors that of Pentecost. The key themes that make up the Pentecostal type-scene (see chapter 3) are repeated in Acts 10, and there are numerous common emphases in both passages. They include: the arrival of the Spirit (2:4; 10:44), mention of signs/healing (2:19, 22; 10:38), prayer (1:14; 10:2, 3, 4, 9, 30, 31), unity (2:1; 10:33), "Christ" (2:36, 38; 10:36, 48; 11:17), "Lord" (2:20, 21, 36; 10:36; 11:16, 17), the "name" of Jesus (2:21, 38; 10:43, 48), the resurrection (2:24, 27, 28, 31, 32, 36; 10:40, 41), christological judgment (2:34–35; 10:42), empowerment terminology (1:8; 10:44; 11:15), acceptance of God's people (2:18; 10:34–35), the divine will (2:23, 31; 10:41), eschatology (2:1, 17–21; 10:42), fulfillment of Scripture (2:17–21, 25–28, 31, 34–35; 10:43), a Petrine speech (2:14–36; 10:34–43), nations (2:5–12, 17; 10:35), forgiveness of sins (2:38; 10:43), salvation (2:21, 40, 47; 11:14), witness (2:32, 40; 10:39, 41, 42, 43), the "word" (2:41; 10:36, 44; 11:1), faith (2:44; 10:43; 11:17), water baptism (2:38, 41; 10:48), church growth (2:41, 47; 11:14, 18), an emotional reaction (2:6, 7, 12; 10:45), the inclusion of women (1:14; 2:17–18; 11:14 [implied]), and speaking in tongues (2:4; 10:46).

In addition to the above, the pneumatological terminology in the Caesarean narrative is obviously Pentecostal. The Jews in Caesarea were "surprised" (ἐξέστησαν) that the "gift" (δωρεὰ) of the Holy Spirit "was poured out" (ἐκκέχυται) on the gentiles (Acts 10:45). This verse points to God's promise to pour out (ἐκχεῶ) the Spirit (Acts 2:17–18)—a promise Peter calls a "gift" (δωρεὰν) and makes available to the crowd in Acts 2:38 (cf. 11:17). Luke often records the emotional response to miraculous events, and he even uses the same term for "surprise" in both Acts 2:12 and 10:45.[57] The language of being baptized in the Spirit is used in

56. Longenecker notes that F. H. Chase referred to the outpouring in Caesarea as "the Pentecost of the Gentile World." Chase, *Credibility*, 79; Longenecker, "Acts," 394. Hovenden observes the general scholarly consensus that Luke intended to present the reception of the Spirit in Caesarea as a gentile Pentecost. Hovenden, *Speaking in Tongues*, 94–95.

57. Bock notes various instances where Luke employs the term for "surprise" (Acts 2:7, 12; 8:9, 10, 11, 13; 9:21; 12:16), but remarks, "The 2:12 text is important, for the description in 10:45 matches the reaction that took place at the original Pentecost." Bock, *Acts*, 400.

both contexts (1:5; 11:16), and Peter equates the gift of the Spirit that fell on the gentiles to the Pentecostal event four times (10:47; 11:15, 17; 15:8).[58] Luke records that the believers at Pentecost "began to speak in other tongues" (ἤρξαντο λαλεῖν ἑτέραις γλώσσαις) and that the Jewish audience responded, "We hear them speaking in our own tongues the great deeds of God" (ἀκούομεν λαλούντων αὐτῶν ταῖς ἡμετέραις γλώσσαις τὰ μεγαλεῖα τοῦ θεοῦ; 2:11b). Luke employs similar terminology to associate tongues with praise in Acts 10:46: "For they were hearing them speaking in tongues and magnifying God" (ἤκουον γὰρ αὐτῶν λαλούντων γλώσσαις καὶ μεγαλυνόντων τὸν θεόν). The similarities between Acts 2 and 10 are so obvious that the Western text even adds ἑτέραις ("other") to 10:46 to make the passages conform to one another even more closely.[59] Acts 2:11b and 10:46 also share the participle "speaking" and the plural noun "tongues." The mirroring of so much of Acts 2 in Acts 10 testifies to Lukan intentionality in creating theologically informative patterns in the narrative.

The centrality of Jesus as Lord and Christ in the Petrine speeches at Pentecost and Caesarea and the Lukan presentation of Acts 10 as a gentile Pentecost exerts a considerable influence over how one understands several thorny issues related to Acts 10. The discussion below addresses the nature of the Spirit's coming, the question of the evidential value and normativity of tongues, the nature of tongues (known languages or ecstasy?), and the content of tongues.

The Holy Spirit "Fell upon" Them

Luke accentuates the importance of the Spirit's descent in Caesarea by presenting it as an interruption of Peter's speech. "While Peter was still speaking these words the Holy Spirit fell on [ἐπέπεσεν] all those hearing the word" (Acts 10:44), and Peter repeats the event: "And when I began to speak the Holy Spirit fell on [ἐπέπεσεν] them just as on us in the beginning" (11:15).[60] Interruptions often occur at the declaration of Christ's lordship and/or his resurrection (Acts 2:37; 17:32; 23:7; 26:23–24), and

58. Hovenden, *Speaking in Tongues*, 95.

59. Polhill, *Acts*, 263. Witherington, *Acts*, 360. The omission of "other" tongues as well as any reference to xenolalia in Acts 10 may be significant and will be discussed below.

60. Luke also highlights the importance of the Spirit's coming by returning to the narrator's commentary here. Haya-Prats, *Empowered Believers*, 50.

in 22:21 Paul's mention of the mission to the gentiles stirs a riot among the Jews of Jerusalem. In Caesarea the interruption is clearly initiated by God and not humans, but the proclamation of Jesus' messianic and divine identity in connection with the mission to the gentiles fits well within Luke's larger interests.

The interruption also helps to convey a sense of suddenness, divine initiative, and power in the narrative that is reminiscent of Pentecost (Acts 2:4).[61] Luke's language of the Spirit "coming upon" or "falling upon" (ἐπιπίπτω) enhances this impression and places the reader in the conceptual world of Old Testament stories of the Spirit falling upon Israel's leaders. The compound Greek verb itself does not directly occur in reference to the Spirit in the Septuagint, although Ezekiel uses the aorist of the verb πίπτω ("to fall") to describe the Spirit's falling upon him and inspiring prophecy (Ezek 11:5). The compound verb is often used idiomatically to describe someone falling on someone's neck to kiss the person (Gen 45:14; 46:29; 50:1; Tob 11:9, 13; 3 Macc 5:49), and Luke also uses the term this way (Luke 15:20; Acts 20:37). The term is most commonly employed in the Septuagint to describe fear or fear and trembling falling on someone.[62] Luke also uses the term in this manor (Luke 1:12; Acts 19:17). The falling upon in the Septuagint often carries with it a sense of suddenness (e.g., Josh 11:7; Eccl 9:12; 1 Macc 1:30), as is also suggested in Acts 10:44.[63] Luke uses the term in relation to the Spirit at Samaria (8:16), and the Western text substitutes "immediately fell" (εὐθέως ἐπέπεσεν) for "came" (ἦλθεν) when Paul lays hands on the Ephesian disciples in Acts 19:6.[64] The terms are conceptually similar, as Luke also uses ἔρχομαι ("come") to describe the Spirit's coming in Luke 1:35; 2:27; and Acts 1:8.[65]

61. Menzies suggests that the timing of the interruption points to the inclusion of gentiles as prophets who testify to Jesus. He bases this on Luke's mention of the christocentric testimony of the prophets right before the outpouring of the Holy Spirit accompanied by tongues (Acts10:43–46). Menzies, *Speaking in Tongues*, 58–59.

62. Exod 15:16; Josh 2:9; Neh 6:16; Job 4:13; 13:11; 33:15; Ps 54:5; 104:38; Jdt 2:28; 14:3; 15:2; Dan 4:5: 10:7; 1 Macc 7:18; Odes 1:16. The term occurs fifty-one times in the Septuagint and eleven times in the New Testament. Luke-Acts accounts for eight of those occurrences. See Schneider, "ἐπιπίπτω," 32.

63. Kurz also notes that the verb "suggests a sudden and dramatic coming." Kurz, *Acts of the Apostles*, 180.

64. There is also a variant in Acts 8:39, where some manuscripts add that the Holy Spirit "fell upon the eunuch." Schneider, "ἐπιπίπτω," 32.

65. Keener associates Luke's "upon" language with Old Testament passages about empowerment to prophesy, lead, or exhibit superhuman strength. He avoids strictly

Although the compound "fall upon" does not occur in reference to the Spirit in the Septuagint, the verb does occur in relation to prophetic ecstasy in Gen 15:12. The author describes how "a trance fell upon Abram" (ἔκστασις ἐπέπεσεν τῷ Ἀβράμ) and then relays how a "great, terror of darkness falls on [ἐπιπίπτει] him." Luke is familiar with the terminology used for "trance," as ἔκστασις came on Peter when he was praying (Acts 10:10; 11:5; cf. 22:17), but what is noteworthy is that ἐπιπίπτω is used in conjunction with charismatic activity in the Septuagint (cf. Dan 10:7 Th.). In other words, Luke's word choice of "fell upon" to describe the Spirit's coming at Caesarea is consistent with his own depictions of the Spirit coming in charismatic empowerment, the element of a sudden coming in the Old Testament, and a coming that is associated with prophetic activity. These associations color the reader's understanding of the outbreak of tongues at Cornelius's home.

Luke does not describe the Spirit's arrival in Acts 10 as a quiet, inward transformation. The sudden coming of the Spirit is obvious to the observers, and the speaking in tongues along with the description of Jesus' ministry in the immediate context helps define the kind of reception of the Spirit Luke has in mind. God anointed Jesus with the "Holy Spirit and power," and he "went around doing good and healing all those who were oppressed by the devil" (10:38). This gift of the Spirit to the gentiles was for purposes of empowerment to share in the mission of Jesus along with the Jewish disciples. The disciples would naturally have assumed that the "Holy" Spirit (vv. 38, 44, 45, 47) would not fall upon uncircumcised, unclean gentiles (v. 45),[66] so the gift of the Spirit at once empowers them for ministry, endows them with charismatic speech, and testifies to the Jewish observers that God had already cleansed the gentiles' hearts

differentiating between the language of the Spirit coming "in" and the Spirit coming "upon," but he notes, "Still, Paul's and other early Christian 'in' passages often do evoke more the transforming activity of the Spirit characteristic of Ezek 36, whereas Luke's 'upon' passages typically evoke the more frequent OT idiom that more often refers to empowerment." Keener, *Acts: Exegetical*, 2:1810, 1810n798.

66. Nunnally suggests that "in the minds of contemporary Jews, the Shekinah (often interchangeable with the Holy Spirit) rested only on Israelites and never on Gentiles." Nunnally, *Book of Acts*, 208. See Shabbat 22b. Tannehill also notices Luke's emphasis on the Holy Spirit in a context of gentile uncleanness. Tannehill, *Narrative Unity*, 2:136. He concludes that the "issue is not whether there should be a Gentile mission—the Lord commanded his witnesses to preach to all the nations—but how that mission can be conducted in the face of a serious obstacle." He identifies gentile uncleanness as the obstacle to the mission. Tannehill, *Narrative Unity*, 2:135. Tannehill certainly has a legitimate point, but it does seem as though some of the Jewish believers still did not grasp the universality of the mission.

by faith (15:8–9). The gift of the Spirit indicates the demise of cultural and national barriers, and the speaking in tongues is a fitting expression of gentile submission to Jesus' lordship and participation in his mission.

"For They Were Hearing Them Speaking in Tongues"

Luke narrates the outpouring of the Holy Spirit in Acts 10:44–46, and his description concludes with an explanation of how the Jewish believers knew that the gentiles had received the Spirit: "For they were hearing [ἤκουον γὰρ] them speaking in tongues and magnifying God" (v. 46). The conjunction "for" (γὰρ) makes it clear that what follows provides the basis for their knowledge that the Spirit had been poured out. In other words, speaking in tongues is the observable evidence of the baptism in the Spirit at Caesarea. The imperfect verb ἤκουον ("they were hearing") suggests that the speaking was ongoing and more than a brief utterance. Donald Johns underscores the importance of the narrator's commentary here, as it provides his assessment of the event described: "The narrator in Acts 10:46 explicitly assigns evidential value to speaking in tongues and states that this was the view of Peter and his associates."[67] In general, interpreters from a classical Pentecostal perspective have viewed speaking in tongues as a "normative" sign of being baptized in the Spirit, many charismatics have seen it as "normal," cessationists have limited it to New Testament times, and some critical scholars have dismissed it as a Lukan invention. Below I will engage some of the positions that scholars have offered on the question of the "normalness" or "normativity" of tongues.[68]

John Polhill views the outpouring at Caesarea as a unique event.

> Like the Pentecost of Acts, it was a unique, unrepeatable event. It was scarcely programmatic. The sequence, for one, was most unusual, with the Spirit coming before their baptism. The pattern of a group demonstration of the Spirit invariably accompanies a new breakthrough in mission in Acts. We see it in the initial empowering of Pentecost, the establishment of the Samaritan mission (8:17–18), the reaching of former disciples of John the Baptist (19:6), and the foundation of the Gentile mission and its legitimation for the Jerusalem church.[69]

67. Johns, "Some New Directions," 152.

68. The title of Larry Hurtado's article illustrates the nature of the debate on this issue: "Normal, but Not a Norm: 'Initial Evidence' and the New Testament," 189–201.

69. Polhill, *Acts*, 264.

It is interesting that Polhill rejects a Pentecostal pattern at Caesarea because of the timing of water baptism, but he does see an overall "pattern" of the gift of the Spirit to groups in Acts.[70] However, the point of the passage is that neither salvation nor the demonstration of the Spirit's coming with charismatic signs was "unrepeatable." Polhill attempts to dismiss the notion of a normative, charismatic reception of the Spirit by explaining each event as a special group reception at key missional moments.

Richard Thomas argues along similar lines: "Luke's description appropriates Pentecost imagery to underscore that these pious Gentiles, like the Jewish believers at Pentecost, were recipients of the Holy Spirit, blessed by God's saving work. To make this specific description normative for contemporary Christians misunderstands its basic role in Acts, which links what happened here with the earlier Pentecost event."[71] Gerald Hovenden also comments on key moments of the Spirit's descent at Pentecost, Samaria, Caesarea, and Ephesus: "It would appear that Luke appeals to tongues at significant stages in the advancement of the early church—to mark the successive overcoming of religious and social barriers."[72] Although Craig Keener does not view tongues as necessarily always accompanying the gift of the Spirit, he offers a caution against viewing each occasion as an exception. "Although the recorded cases do serve literary functions, treating them all as exceptions fragments Luke's larger narrative, especially when we consider that these cases constitute a remarkably high proportion of Luke's description of people 'receiving

70. Those in the classical Pentecostal camp have often been criticized for building their theology on patterns in Acts. Some of the criticism has been valid, but many Pentecostals have intuitively discovered Luke's intended emphases, and the addition of more sophisticated hermeneutical approaches and literary criticism has aided Pentecostal scholars. E.g., Menzies, *Pentecost*, 21–39.

71. Thompson, *Acts: A Commentary*, 213.

72. Hovenden, *Speaking in Tongues*, 100. Hovenden is following Mills, *A Theological/Exegetical Approach*, 72. Mills suggests, "It is no accident that the gift of tongues is traced to the Holy Spirit in Acts 2:4, 10:46, 19:6. It was for Luke a phenomenon which legitimately validated the presence of the Spirit of God. Luke would not intend the Christians of subsequent generations should formalize the experience into a kind of religious panacea, far superior to any other manifestation of possession by God's Spirit." Mills, *A Theological/Exegetical Approach*, 73. While I agree with Hovenden and Mills that Luke carefully situates tongues speaking at key junctures in the narrative and that tongues signal the breaking of barriers, I do not agree that the occurrences are exceptional and primarily of historical and theological interest. On the other hand, I know of no modern Pentecostal scholar who sees tongues as a "kind of religious panacea" or as "far superior to any other manifestation of possession by God's Spirit."

the Spirit' for the first time in Acts."[73] An approach to Luke's record of the bestowal of the Spirit in Acts that views the events as exceptions rather than as models for contemporary experience does not do justice to Luke's constructive theology. It is precisely because Luke intentionally connects the stories that one should consider the charismatic elements as part of the package when one receives the Spirit. This is especially so if one views tongues as associated with praise,[74] symbolic of missions, and christocentric in orientation. The occurrence of tongues at missional moments does not argue for their cessation or omission from current practice. It argues for their continued use. Until the mission ceases, there is no reason for the symbol of mission to cease. As long as the Lord continues to extend his reign over the nations, it is perfectly suitable for his Spirit-endowed servants to respond to his lordship with an appropriate international symbol and form of charismatic praise.

Larry Hurtado critiques the initial evidence teaching of classical Pentecostals on various grounds. He claims that the New Testament never raises "the question of what constitutes 'the initial evidence' of a person having received the 'baptism in the Spirit.'" He suggests that the doctrine results from inferences drawn from Acts, "reflects relatively modern church struggles and group formation," and amounts to "eisegesis."[75] While the articulation of tongues in relation to the giving of the Spirit naturally reflects contemporary language, recent historical studies have also shed light on the Church's experience of tongues in history.[76] Regarding Hurtado's exegetical critique, it is, strictly speaking, true that the New Testament does not present the issue of tongues in relation to the giving of the Spirit as a specific question raised by early believers. However, although we know of no church crisis over the matter of what constitutes the sign of the Spirit's coming, the continuity of Lukan pneumatology with the Hebrew Scriptures suggests that Luke assumes an ancient understanding of Spirit reception and applies it in a New Testament context in order to instruct his readers on the matter. This understanding of Lukan continuity with redemptive history is foundational to Roger Stronstad's *The Charismatic Theology of St. Luke* and

73. Keener, *Acts: Exegetical*, 2:1813n822.

74. Thompson makes this association. *Acts: A Commentary*, 213.

75. Hurtado, "Normal," 191–92.

76. Randal Ackland provides a historical survey of tongues that includes numerous helpful resources in his notes. *Toward a Pentecostal Theology*, 410–61. See also Burgess, *Christian Peoples of the Spirit*.

also to this present work. In addition, the employment of various grammatical and literary devices employed by Luke (outlined above) points to intentionality in his description of tongues in relation to the Spirit. The Pentecostal teaching is not built merely on inference and Acts, but on pneumatological emphases in the Hebrew Scriptures, the development of those emphases throughout Luke's entire work (Luke-Acts), and the authorial intention of Luke indicated by his direct comments, record of speeches, and various literary techniques.[77]

Hurtado also argues along similar lines as those mentioned above when he opines that the tongues passages in Acts are exceptional and simply illustrate the gospel's progress; in short, the tongues passages are descriptive and not prescriptive. For support, Hurtado points to Gordon Fee's concerns with Pentecostal hermeneutics.[78] Fee questions the ability of historical narrative to demonstrate authorial intention in establishing normative teaching. A vigorous dialogue between him and Pentecostal scholars William Menzies and Roger Stronstad ensues.[79] However, the implementation of literary criticism in Lukan studies has led to what Martin Mittelstadt refers to as "the triumph of narrative theology."[80] The realization that narrative is the preferred method of teaching theology for many of the biblical writers and the utilization of theological and literary approaches to the grammatical and historical tools has resulted in some of the earlier critiques becoming obsolete. Interpreters should consider

77. In fairness to Hurtado, some of his criticism against Pentecostalism's hermeneutical methods was justified at the time he wrote the article cited. Pentecostal authors have traditionally sought to buttress their case for the normativity of tongues by counting the number of episodes in Acts where speaking in tongues occurs (Acts 2:4; 10:46; 19:6) or was likely to have occurred (Acts 8:14–19; 9:17 with 1 Cor 14:18). For a classic example of this hermeneutical approach, see Brumback, *"What Meaneth This?"* While earlier Pentecostals sometimes lacked sophisticated hermeneutical methods, their intuitive response to reading narrative was largely correct. That is, Luke surely intended his readers to have a charismatic theology and to emulate the positive characters in his narrative.

Thanks to Hurtado and others like him, Pentecostal scholars today have adopted improved hermeneutical methods.

78. Hurtado, "Normal," 193–94.

79. See Fee, *Gospel and Spirit*, 83–104. Chapter six, "Hermeneutics and Historical Precedent: A Major Problem in Pentecostal Hermeneutics," and chapter seven, "Baptism in the Holy Spirit: The Issue of Separability and Subsequence," are of particular interest. In the postscript to chapter six, Fee responds to the critiques of his article by William Menzies and Roger Stronstad. See William Menzies, "The Methodology of Pentecostal Theology," 1–14; Stronstad, *Spirit, Scripture and Theology*, especially chapters 1–2.

80. Mittelstadt, *Reading Luke-Acts*, 82.

the possibility that Luke is repeating stories containing glossolalia on purpose: "It is a common storytelling technique the world over to tell things in groups of threes: three times should be enough to tell anything. The paradigmatic effect of these stories should lead us to expect the same things in our own experience with the Spirit."[81] As Donald Johns points out, it is important to consider that Luke intends his readers to emulate certain activities and persons and to reject the negative examples of some characters. When one adds the element of the type-scene, the enormous emphasis that Luke places on the Pentecostal and Caesarean episodes, and the development of his charismatic and prophetic pneumatology throughout Luke-Acts to the discussion of tongues, there is a substantial amount of exegetical material to consider before dismissing the possibility that Luke intends his audience to experience tongues as part of a reception of the Spirit.

Some of the same responses I have offered above apply to Max Turner's position on tongues in Acts. He sees it as "very unlikely that Acts 2 presents the Pentecostal phenomena of tongues as something that should be regularly anticipated at reception of the Spirit. On the contrary, only very strong indications in the rest of the narrative could possibly incline the reader to consider initial 'tongues' as 'regular' at all."[82] The lack of tongues in relation to Jesus' reception of the Spirit at the Jordan and the lack of repetition of xenolalia after Pentecost forms part of the logic of Turner's resistance to the idea of tongues as occurring regularly. However, if one accepts that tongues are a response to Jesus as the enthroned Lord and that they symbolize his reign over the nations, then it is obvious why tongues are reserved for the new-covenant believers and why Jesus is not portrayed as one who speaks in tongues.

Regarding Turner's objection on the basis of only a single occurrence of xenolalia, the constellation of themes repeated in Caesarea can also assist the reader in discerning what is not essential to this reception of the Spirit. There are elements of Pentecost that are not repeated in Caesarea or elsewhere, that do not comprise an element of the type-scene, and that are not integral to an initial reception of the empowering Spirit. The appearance of tongues of fire, the sound of a rushing wind, and xenolalia do not recur anywhere in Acts, but that is not to say that these are insignificant, for each of them provides symbolic reinforcement to the

81. Johns, "Some New Directions," 163. Johns is referring to tongues in Acts 2, 10, and 19.

82. Turner, *Power from on High*, 357–58.

primary theological and experiential elements of the endowment of the Spirit. That is, the symbols speak to the kind of experience a baptism in the Spirit is. Speaking in tongues, however, is repeated and is integral to the experience of an initial filling because inspired, prophetic utterance is integral to the Lukan definition of what it means to be filled with the Spirit. With the enthronement of Christ, speaking in tongues provides an appropriate new variation on an old theme. Again, Luke's readers should bear in mind that he is not merely writing abstract theology but presenting a way of life to be emulated. His accounts of the reception of the Spirit are not just fascinating stories from history or concepts for systematic theology; rather, they are models for contemporary believers that create certain expectations of the kind of experience believers can have today.

Xenolalia at Caesarea?

The question of the nature of tongues after Pentecost has received considerable attention from scholars. Are the tongues in Acts 10 and 19 additional examples of xenolalia, or are the tongues ecstatic in nature and more akin to the tongues in the Corinthian church?[83] Of course, there is no universal agreement on their nature at Corinth either, but generally speaking, most scholars view the tongues at Caesarea as ecstatic.[84] The common arguments favoring the ecstatic position include the absence of "other" preceding the mention of tongues in Acts 10 and 19 (cf. 2:4), the omission of "dialect" (διάλεκτος) in reference to human languages as found in 2:6 and 8,[85] the lack of international observers who would benefit from xenolalia, the complete absence of any record of xenolalia, and the apparent occurrence of ecstatic tongues in Paul's discussion (1 Cor 12–14). Those supporting the notion that tongues throughout Acts are human languages point to the repeated use of the word "tongues" (γλώσσαις) as referring to languages,[86] Luke's intentionally establishing

83. Scholars differ in how they define "ecstatic," some even using the word as a pejorative equivalent to madness. I use the term to refer to a heightened sensitivity to the Spirit's revelation and not in reference to wild emotional displays or psychological dysfunction. In the present discussion, I use "ecstatic" to refer to Spirit-inspired language that is not a known, human language.

84. E.g., Esler, "Glossolalia," 136; Haenchen, *Acts*, 354; Larkin, *Acts*, 394; Peterson, *Acts*, 340; Williams, *Acts*, 196. Some simply say that the tongues at Caesarea were not xenolalia. E.g., Turner, *The Holy Spirit*, 219; Witherington, *Acts*, 360.

85. Williams, *Acts*, 41.

86. Keener, *Acts: Exegetical*, 2:1813.

continuity between Acts 2 and the other tongues passages,[87] the shared theological meaning of tongues as signifying "cross-cultural prophetic empowerment,"[88] and the problem of how the Jewish believers at Caesarea would recognize ecstatic tongues without previous exposure to them.[89]

The arguments in favor of viewing tongues at Caesarea as ecstatic are valid but certainly not hermetic. Several of the arguments are arguments from silence, and dependence on a disputable Pauline definition of tongues seems methodologically questionable. It is a little ironic that scholars have often critiqued Pentecostals for relying on John 20:22 to differentiate between the Spirit's coming at regeneration and in power at Pentecost but see no problem with defining Pentecost in Pauline terms or defining the Lukan phenomenon of tongues with Pauline concepts.[90] While it is certainly fair to draw from Paul for support, the primary argument for ecstatic tongues in Acts should come directly from Luke's narrative and the sources to which he refers. On the other hand, the arguments for understanding tongues at Caesarea and Ephesus as zenolalic are not entirely convincing either. It does seem odd that people would speak in known languages without anyone present to recognize the miracle, and the languages would be equally unrecognizable to the Jewish observers at Caesarea regardless of whether the gentiles spoke in earthly or heavenly languages. Occurrences of tongues in Acts after Pentecost are probably not examples of xenolalia, but perhaps it is best to emphasize what seems integral to the occurrence of tongues.[91] That is, tongues are a Spirit-inspired, prophetic form of utterance, and the international symbolism has been established at Pentecost regardless of the nature of tongues

87. Everts, "Tongues or Languages?" 73. Menzies wonders, "Why, we may ask, does Luke use the same language to describe each of the events even though they actually refer to different activities? This striking literary connection suggests that Luke has intentionally shaped his narrative in order to highlight this linkage. In other words, the pattern is important to him. Luke desired to make the connection: he desired to establish Acts 2 as a model." Menzies, *Speaking in Tongues*, 18.

88. Keener, *Acts: Exegetical*, 2:1813.

89. Keener, *Acts: Exegetical*, 2:1813.

90. Dunn, *Baptism*, 38–40.

91. Lim Yeu Chuen holds that Luke is not concerned with the kind of manifestation of tongues but that tongues evince the baptism in the Holy Spirit. Chuen, "Acts 10," Conclusion.

thereafter. Whether known or unknown languages, they at once function as a symbol of missions and a response of praise to the Lord of all.[92]

Tongues of Praise

The Jewish believers at Caesarea recognized that the Spirit had fallen because "they were hearing them speaking in other tongues and magnifying God" (ἤκουον γὰρ αὐτῶν λαλούντων γλώσσαις καὶ μεγαλυνόντων τὸν θεόν; Acts 10:46). The two participial phrases joined by καὶ ("and") appear to be parallel, suggesting that the "speaking in tongues" and "praising God" are similar, with the latter phrase providing the content of the speaking in tongues.[93] The statement is consistent with the comment of the observers in Acts 2:11, which employs the adjective μεγαλεῖος: "We hear them speaking in our own tongues the mighty deeds of God [τὰ μεγαλεῖα τοῦ θεοῦ]" (cf. 19:17; see the discussion of Luke's emphasis on praise in chapter two above). The orientation of the praise is toward God, and the specific content apparently concerns Christ at both Pentecost and Caesarea. The emphasis on the resurrection of Jesus and his identity as the divine Lord in Peter's sermon (10:34–43) gives way to the interruption of the Spirit, and the response from Cornelius and his household is inspired praise to God because they share in the gospel of Jesus. The gentiles not only receive the same Spirit as the Jewish believers (11:16–17), but they receive the Spirit in the same manner (v. 15), with the similar effect of speaking in tongues of praise, and with the same orientation and essential content of the tongues. The tongues of gentiles celebrate the greatness of God and the lordship of Jesus the Messiah.

The outpouring of the Spirit prompts Peter to urge the gentile believers to receive water baptism "in the name of Jesus Christ" (Acts 10:48). The timing of baptism after reception of the Spirit is problematic for some, but Luke's emphasis is not on the order of service but on the gentiles' new status evinced by their public identification with "the name of Jesus Christ." They are on an equal footing with the Jewish believers on the basis of their submission to the same Messiah and Lord. The speaking

92. There is no shame in allowing for an element of mystery or even diversity in the expression of the manifestation of tongues. For an approach that emphasizes the mysterious element, see Tarr, *The Foolishness of God*.

93. Keener and Peterson also identify the tongues as praise, while Turner sees the praise as additional, "related phenomena." Keener, *Acts: Exegetical*, 2:1814; Peterson, *Acts*, 340; Turner, *The Holy Spirit*, 219.

in tongues has already testified to the cross-cultural implications of the gospel, the gentiles' partnership in the mission, and the universal lordship of Christ.[94] For Jew and gentile alike, speaking in tongues is a charismatic celebration of Jesus as Lord of all.

Summary

This chapter began with an overview of the various literary devices Luke uses to give the events of Acts 10:1—11:18 a place of prominence in the narrative of Acts. This important story includes speaking in tongues, and the debate over Cornelius's spiritual state prior to his baptism in the Spirit raises questions about what tongues signify. Luke portrays him as a gentile man of faith who fears God but who has not fully entered into the new covenant because of a lack of clarity over the application of the gospel to gentiles. Cornelius and his family place their faith in Jesus during Peter's sermon, the gift of the Spirit confirms their faith and participation in the gospel, but the baptism in the Spirit does not constitute salvation. The speaking in tongues is presented as a sign of the empowerment of the Spirit and sharing in the international mission to proclaim the lordship of Jesus.

The difficult text of Acts 10:36 provides the key theological assertion of the passage and the context of the occurrence of tongues. It appears that Luke has intentionally constructed the statement to emphasize his christological interest: "As for the word which he sent to the sons of Israel, preaching good news of peace through Jesus Christ: he is Lord of all." Various elements of the grammar, and especially the emphatic use of the accusative case at the beginning of the phrase, mirrors the similar style found in Acts 2 and other speeches. The verse forms the initial part of a christological frame around Peter's speech (cf. 10:42) and finds a precedent in the stone passage of Ps 117:22 (LXX) quoted in Luke 20:17b. The emphatic nature of Jesus as Lord in Acts 10:36 combines with Luke's identification of Jesus as a Davidite and Messiah (Christ) to present Jesus in similar terms to his identification in Acts 2. Luke identifies Jesus as the Lord and Messiah at Caesarea through the language of anointing, the preaching of his resurrection, and his roles as giver of peace, judge, forgiver of sins, savior, and baptizer in the Spirit. He is the Lord Jesus

94. Macchia well expresses the significance of tongues as "the bringing together of Jew and Gentile in the diverse but unified praise and witness of the Spirit to the goodness of God." Macchia, "Groans Too Deep," Section 3.

Christ (11:17), and this identification serves as the primary context in which tongues must be interpreted.

Luke's selectivity in language, style, and themes demonstrates his intentionality in making Acts 10:44–48 a gentile Pentecost and in providing theological commentary on the event. The Spirit "fell upon" the gentiles, and the language is appropriate to an empowerment experience associated with prophetic activity. For Luke, speaking in tongues serves as a fitting symbol for those who have submitted to Christ as universal Lord, have been baptized in his Spirit, and are participants in his mission to the nations.

Acts 10:46 indicates that tongues were the observable evidence of the baptism in the Spirit at Caesarea, but there has been much debate over the continuation of tongues and the normativity of them for believers today. For some scholars, tongues are thought to be exceptions in the narrative of Acts, only serving as theological markers of gospel progress. However, the repeated connection of tongues to an initial reception of the Spirit appears intentional, and there does not seem to be appropriate justification for limiting the phenomenon to a few mile markers on an ancient road when Luke expects a series of signs along a missional highway leading into the eschaton. Advances in narratology have made some arguments against continuationism, the normalness, and even the normativity of tongues, obsolete. Tongues in Acts are part of a larger historical-redemptive picture that includes the Old Testament and the whole of Luke-Acts, and Luke employs a hermeneutic of expectation where the members of Christ's church share in this redemptive trajectory and continue to experience what others have experienced. The employment of the type-scene, the mirroring of Pentecost at Caesarea, the charismatic pneumatology of Luke-Acts, and the christological context of the outpouring of the Spirit make tongues a suitable New Testament sign of the baptism in the Spirit. As long as the mission continues, the symbol of mission continues. As long as people receive power to proclaim the lordship of Jesus to the nations, the nations will respond in tongues of praise to the Lord Jesus Christ.

5

Declaring Christ is Lord in Ephesus

THE FINAL RECORD OF speaking in tongues in Acts occurs at Ephesus, where Paul laid his hands on about twelve men and they received the Holy Spirit and spoke in tongues and prophesied (Acts 19:6–7). In order to gain a proper perspective on this event, I will examine both the stories of Apollos in Ephesus (Acts 18:24–28) and Paul's ministry to about a dozen "disciples" in Ephesus (19:1–7). These two units have received considerable discussion and numerous varying interpretations among scholars. Much of the controversy revolves around the spiritual status of Apollos and the followers of John the Baptist when they first met Paul. Some scholars place great emphasis on the conversion of the twelve after meeting Paul, so that the reception of the Spirit is viewed as chronologically and theologically closely associated with their salvation and water baptism experience. Other scholars argue that the twelve were already Christians when Paul met them; consequently, their reception of the Spirit occurred as a charismatic event and clearly subsequent to salvation.[1] In the following discussion, I argue that Luke's primary concern is to demonstrate that Jesus is Lord and Christ in Ephesus. Luke's record of speaking in tongues is directly associated with this issue, and framing the discussion in this manner sheds light on the other controversies. The discussion first addresses the christological elements in the account of Apollos (18:24–28), then the emphasis on Jesus' name in relation to

1. Not every scholar who believes that the Ephesian disciples were already Christians also adheres to the idea that they experienced a separate baptism in the Spirit for charismatic empowerment. E.g., Holladay, *Acts*, 366.

tongues at Ephesus (19:1–7), and then the significance of Jesus' lordship in relation to the cult of Artemis in Ephesus.

Apollos, the Scriptures, and the Identity of Jesus (Acts 18:24–28)

The city of Ephesus features quite prominently in the narrative of Acts. It was a port city at the crossroads of three major trade routes. It was known for its commerce and its political importance, as it was the location of the proconsul in the province of Asia.[2] Estimates of the city's population vary widely,[3] but it was a very large city with a significant Jewish population.[4] Luke's account of the riot in Ephesus testifies to its importance as a religious center (referred to as νεωκόρος ("temple keeper") of Artemis; Acts 19:35) and to the relationship between religion and commerce (vv. 23–27). For these reasons, Luke portrays Ephesus as a strategic center for the dissemination of the gospel.

The narrative of Acts emphasizes the importance of Ephesus in various ways. The events at Ephesus conclude Paul's ministry prior to his arrest and form a climax to his missionary journeys begun in Acts 13.[5] RobertTannehill suggests that there is a "ring or envelope composition" between the beginning of his ministry and Acts 19, "for themes in the last major setting of Paul's mission repeat themes at the beginning of Paul's missionary journeys." He cites the encounters with Elymas and the sons of Sceva and the demonstrations of the Spirit's power in both contexts as repeated emphases.[6] Richard Longenecker points out that Luke gives only limited details about Paul's time of ministry at Ephesus (see 19:1–12),[7] but Luke records Paul reminding the Ephesians of his three years of instruction there (20:31), which is longer than any other ministry period recorded in Acts. Ephesus remains at the center of the

2. Barrett, *Acts*, 2:893.

3. Mounce and others believe the population may have been over 250,000 in New Testament times. Mounce, *The Book of Revelation*, 67. For a list of varying views, see Keener, *Acts: Exegetical*, 3:2790n4947.

4. Bock, *Acts*, 591.

5. Parsons also views Acts 13–19 as a unit. *Acts*, 259.

6. Tannehill, *Narrative Unity*, 2:237–38.

7. Longenecker, "Acts," 491. Scholars commonly mention the lack of "we" passages in this section of Acts and suggest that Luke may not have been an eyewitness of the events in Ephesus.

narrative for an extended portion of Acts (18:19—20:38), and its prominence helps unify this portion of Acts.[8]

Luke also builds some anticipation for the ministry in Ephesus by recounting how the Spirit initially forbade Paul's entrance into the province of Asia (Acts 16:6) and then by recording Paul's brief visit and promise to return to Ephesus (18:19–21) before he finally arrives for his lengthy stay (19:1). Tannehill also notices how the brief record of Paul's trip to Antioch (18:18–23) serves as a divider highlighting the Ephesian ministry: "Ephesus is not just another stop in a series. It is Paul's last major place of new mission work; indeed, it is the sole center of mission noted in the last stage of Paul's work as a free man."[9] Tannehill also cites Luke's summary of the expansive reach of the gospel to all Asia—to both Jews and Greeks—as another indicator of the missional significance of Paul's ministry in Ephesus (19:10; cf. v. 17; 20:21).[10] Additional elements in the narrative that highlight the importance and climactic nature of the Ephesian ministry include the occurrence of "extraordinary miracles" (19:11), the public repentance from witchcraft practices (vv. 18–20), and the significant farewell speech of Paul to the Ephesian elders (20:18–38). Given Luke's attention to the Ephesian narrative, it will not suffice to merely mention Luke's account of glossolalia there in passing, for this third occurrence of tongues is placed in another highly significant location just as the previous two occurrences were (19:6; cf. 2:4; 10:46). While recording an event in a group of three is an important storytelling strategy for bringing a point across,[11] the three key locations in which tongues occur is even more telling than the number of repetitions when it comes to Luke's estimation of their importance.

Scholars usually view the stories of Apollos in Acts 18:24–28 and Paul with the twelve "disciples" (19:1–7) as connected.[12] The two passages are directly related by their location in Ephesus, the mention of Apollos in 19:1,[13] their experience of only John's baptism (18:25; 19:3), their characters gladly accepting additional spiritual assistance, and the focus on the lordship of Christ (18:25, 28; 19:5). The focus on this latter

8. Keener, *Acts: Exegetical*, 3:2797.

9. Tannehill, *Narrative Unity*, 2:231.

10. Tannehill, *Narrative Unity*, 2:235–36.

11. Johns, "Some New Directions," 163.

12. E.g., Keener, *Acts: Exegetical*, 3:2797; Menzies, *Empowered for Witness*, 220; Parsons, *Acts*, 259; Peterson, *Acts*, 523; Tannehill, *Narrative Unity*, 2:231–32

13. Haenchen, *Acts*, 552.

point in the first story naturally leads into the second and brings clarity to both narratives.

Luke informs the reader that Apollos was a "learned man" and "powerful [δυνατὸς] in the Scriptures" (Acts 18:24). "He had been taught the way of the Lord [τὴν ὁδὸν τοῦ κυρίου] and, fervent in the Spirit, was speaking and teaching [ἐδίδασκεν] accurately the things concerning Jesus [τὰ περὶ τοῦ Ἰησοῦ], knowing only the baptism of John" (v. 25). When Priscilla and Aquila heard him in the synagogue, he was speaking "boldly" (παρρησιάζεσθαι). The two took Apollos aside and "explained to him the way of God more accurately" (v. 26). Apollos then left Ephesus with the blessing of the brothers and became a great help to the believers in Achaia (v. 27) because he "vigorously refuted the Jews in public, proving through the Scriptures that the Christ is Jesus [εἶναι τὸν χριστὸν Ἰησοῦν]" (v. 28). The frame around these verses highlights Luke's primary interest in recording this episode. The frame (vv. 24 and 28) emphasizes the role of Scripture in properly recognizing Jesus as the Messiah. The phrase "way of the Lord" (τὴν ὁδὸν τοῦ κυρίου) in verse 25 sounds very much like the description of John the Baptist as one who prepares "the way of the Lord" (τὴν ὁδὸν κυρίου) in Luke 3:4 (cf. Isa 40:3).[14] Apollos, as a proper follower of John the Baptist and educated in the Scriptures, speaks and teaches accurately "concerning Jesus" (περὶ τοῦ Ἰησοῦ; v. 25). The latter phrase is significant because it is one of Luke's preferred expressions for emphasizing the christocentric nature of the Hebrew Scriptures and the preaching in Luke and Acts. Jesus explains that every category of Scripture focuses on him when he claims it is "about me" (περὶ ἐμοῦ; Luke 24:44). Luke also concludes the book of Acts in a manner that bears a striking resemblance to the description of Apollos. There Paul spends his time in Rome "preaching the kingdom of God and teaching [διδάσκων] the things concerning the Lord Jesus Christ [τὰ περὶ τοῦ κυρίου Ἰησοῦ Χριστοῦ] with all boldness [παρρησίας], unhindered" (Acts 28:31). Notice the similar terms found in verse 25 above. Luke reminds his readers that adherence to the Scriptures and the teaching of John the Baptist inevitably leads to Christ.

Luke closes the frame with the repetition of the "Scriptures" as Apollos's source and with another astounding comparison to the

14. It is likely that Luke avoids the shorter phrase "the Way" here in order to emphasize the parallel with John the Baptist rather than to draw attention to the shorter phrases used of the church in Acts (see Acts 9:2; 19:9, 23; 22:4; 24:14, 22).

teaching of Paul.[15] Apollos uses the Scriptures to prove that "the Christ is Jesus" (εἶναι τὸν χριστὸν Ἰησοῦν; v. 28), but Luke has described Paul earlier in the same chapter as "occupied with the word, testifying to the Jews that the Christ is Jesus [εἶναι τὸν χριστὸν Ἰησοῦν]" (v. 5). Attempts to pinpoint the moment of Apollos's conversion have often caused interpreters to overlook Luke's primary interest in this pericope. This episode describes Jesus as both Lord and Christ, just as Peter describes him in Acts 2:36. Luke demonstrates that the Scriptures and John the Baptist both testify to the royal and messianic identity of Jesus, thus Apollos has rightly followed these sources of revelation to their proper conclusion: Jesus. With a little help from Priscilla and Aquila, Apollos identifies Jesus as the Christ in his preaching just as Paul does.[16]

With Apollos's teaching focused on Jesus from the outset, it seems likely that Luke intends his readers to view the description of Apollos as "fervent in the Spirit" (ζέων τῷ πνεύματι; v. 25) as a reference to the Holy Spirit (cf. Rom 12:11). The christocentric nature of the Spirit's functioning in Luke-Acts supports the notion that the Spirit is already active in Apollos's teaching. C. K. Barrett rightly suggests that "it is unlikely that one as interested as Luke in phenomena due to the Spirit would use ζέων τῷ πνεύματι to mean no more than an effervescent, lively human spirit."[17] When Luke describes Apollos as "powerful [δυνατὸς] in the Scriptures" (Acts 18:24), he uses an adjective that he has elsewhere used of the ministry of Jesus ("powerful in deed and word"; Luke 24:19) and of Moses ("powerful in his words and deeds"; Acts 7:22). Stephen was "full of grace and power" and was performing "great wonders and signs" (6:8), and his opponents "were not able to stand up against the wisdom and the Spirit with which he was speaking [τῷ πνεύματι ᾧ ἐλάλει]" (6:10). This language is not far from Luke's description of Apollos speaking with fervency in the Spirit (ζέων τῷ πνεύματι ἐλάλει; 18:25).[18]

In order to recognize the significance of Luke's statement that Apollos only knew the baptism of John, it should be pointed out that Luke

15. Peterson also notes the emphasis on the Scriptures in this passage. Peterson, *Acts*, 526.

16. I agree wholeheartedly with Tannehill that "Apollos is not a problem but an asset." *Narrative Unity*, 2:232.

17. Barrett, *Acts*, 2:888. Others who understand this passage as referring to the divine Spirit include: Arrington, *Acts*, 188n1; Bruce, *Book of Acts*, 359; Dunn, *Acts of the Apostles*, 250; Keener, *Acts: Exegetical*, 3:2807; Menzies, *Empowered for Witness*, 222; Peterson, *Acts*, 525; Tannehill, *Narrative Unity*, 2:232.

18. Tannehill, *Narrative Unity*, 2:233.

does not mention any miraculous signs connected with Apollos's ministry.[19] In this regard, his experience is not parallel to Jesus, Moses, or Stephen. Also, there does appear to be some sharpening in the clarity of Apollos's identifying Jesus as the Christ after meeting with Priscilla and Aquila. Teaching "accurately about Jesus" (Acts 18:25) becomes "the Christ is Jesus" (v. 28). Scholars frequently point out that, in contrast to the "disciples" in chapter 19, Luke records no baptism of Apollos or apparent need for repentance.[20] Although this amounts to an argument from silence, the contrast does add force to the point. At the same time, acknowledging the activity of the Spirit in Apollos' life does not guarantee that he has experienced the same Pentecostal Spirit baptism as the disciples experienced, especially since Luke emphatically states that he knew "only the baptism of John" (18:25). It is possible that Apollos is thoroughly grounded in the tradition of John the Baptist in that he knew the empowering work of the Spirit, had repented of his sins, had been baptized in water under John's ministry, spoke accurately about Jesus, but still needed the full, Pentecostal blessing of the Spirit. Given the number of people who prophesied by the Spirit early in Luke (cf. 1:41–45, 46–55, 67–79; 2:25–35) and the ministry of the Twelve with "power and authority" (δύναμιν καὶ ἐξουσίαν; 9:1) prior to Pentecost, it is not unreasonable to suggest the Apollos was still a step behind in the progress of redemption. If Luke wanted to emphasize Apollos's fullness with the Spirit, he certainly could have used his more familiar fullness or baptismal language, but perhaps he wanted to recognize the activity of the Spirit but avoid the inference that Apollos had experienced the post-ascension outpouring of the Spirit.[21]

In summary, Apollos already believed in Jesus to the extent that his knowledge permitted. He did not need to repent, and the Spirit was already active in his preaching and teaching. However, he needed additional teaching in order to fully catch up to speed on the advances in

19. Keener, *Acts: Exegetical*, 3:2812.

20. In the absence of any mention of the need for repentance or faith, Bock concludes that Apollos was already a believer. *Acts*, 592. Others note that Apollos was not rebaptized. E.g., Arrington, *Acts*, 189n2; Keener, *Acts: Exegetical*, 3:2798; Nunnally, *Book of Acts*, 324; Shelton, *Mighty in Word*, 134.

21. Some scholars hold that the "disciples" of chapter 19 were influenced by Apollos. This is not at all certain, but if it were true, then this might also suggest that Apollos had not received the Pentecostal baptism in the Spirit. One would have expected him to lay hands on the men of Ephesus and pray for their filling with the Spirit if he had already had the same experience.

redemptive history, and he may also have needed a Pentecostal baptism in the Spirit. However, Luke does not primarily intend to apprise his audience of all the details of Apollos's spiritual journey. Rather, Luke informs his readers of how an important figure in the early church preaches the same gospel Paul preaches and how anyone who properly reads the Hebrew Scriptures and heeds the message of John the Baptist will ultimately acknowledge that Jesus is the Christ. The christocentric message of Acts 18:24–28 is consistent with the rest of Luke-Acts, and the final words of this segment, "the Christ is Jesus," prepare the reader for the primary issue under discussion with the men of Ephesus (19:1–7).

The Twelve Ephesians and the Name of the Lord Jesus (19:1–7)

Paul's encounter with about twelve "disciples" in Ephesus presents the researcher with a minefield of controversial issues and difficult questions. How could "disciples" not know about the Holy Spirit? Were the twelve already Christians? How does water baptism relate to the Spirit's coming? Why does Paul lay hands on the men before the Spirit comes? Why does Luke record that they spoke in tongues? This sampling by no means exhausts the list of debatable issues, but the structure of the passage points the reader in the right direction for making sense of this encounter with the Spirit. Mikeal Parsons, following Scott Shauf and Charles Talbert, outlines the chiasm in Acts 19:1–7.[22] Here is Parsons' version with slight modifications:

A Paul finds "some" disciples (19:1b)

- B Question and answer regarding Holy Spirit (19:2)
  - C Question and answer regarding baptism (19:3)
    - D Paul teaches about John's baptism and John's relationship to Jesus (19:4)
  - C′ Disciples are baptized into the name of the Lord Jesus (19:5)
- B′ Disciples receive the Holy Spirit and speak in tongues and prophesy (19:6)

A′ There are twelve disciples (19:7)

22. Parsons, *Acts*, 264; Shauf, *Theology as History*, 145; Talbert, *Reading Acts*, 167.

The center of the chiasm is revealing, as Paul explains that John told the people to believe in "the one coming after him, that is, in Jesus [τοῦτ' ἔστιν εἰς τὸν Ἰησοῦν]" (v. 4). The end of the sentence emphasizes and identifies the object of faith with Luke's characteristic use of οὗτος (see the discussion in chapters 2 and 4 above). This is reminiscent of the climactic identification of Jesus in 18:28 above—"the Christ is Jesus." Luke uses two slightly different literary schemes in the two passages under discussion, but the central point in both passages is the acknowledgment of the true identity of Jesus.

The contrast between the men's experience of John's baptism and baptism into Jesus emphasizes the identity of Jesus even more, for they are not merely baptized into Jesus, they are baptized "into the name of the Lord Jesus [εἰς τὸ ὄνομα τοῦ κυρίου Ἰησου]" (vv. 3, 5). It is the superior identity of Jesus that makes his baptism superior, and Luke intentionally piles on some of his favorite christological markers to reinforce the point. "The name" is particularly significant because it is a key element in every episode of the outpouring of the Spirit in Acts (2:21, 38; 4:30; 8:12, 16; 9:14, 15, 16, 21; 10:43, 48; 19:5, 13, 17), evincing the christocentric nature of the event. Peter's instructions to the crowd at Pentecost provide a close parallel to the passage under discussion. He tells the crowd: "Repent and be baptized, each of you, in the name of Jesus Christ for the forgiveness of your sins, and you will receive the gift of the Holy Spirit" (2:38). When Peter and John arrived in Samaria, "they prayed for them so that they might receive the Holy Spirit, for he had not yet fallen on any of them, but they had only been baptized into the name of the Lord Jesus [εἰς τὸ ὄνομα τοῦ κυρίου Ἰησοῦ]" (8:15–16). The latter phrase is identical to Acts 19:5, and in all three passages baptism in the name of Jesus indicates submission to him as the exalted Lord.[23] At Samaria baptism into the name of the Lord Jesus is clearly a distinct event from reception of the Spirit. The outpouring of the Spirit at Cornelius's house provides another comparable baptismal scene, but it also serves as a caution against making the rite of water baptism the primary focus. Peter preaches that forgiveness of sins is through Jesus' "name" (Acts 10:43), but the Spirit falls on the gentiles prior to the act of baptism "in the name of Jesus Christ"

23. Although Luke turns his attention to the reaction of Simon and the contrast between Christianity and magic, Haenchen is very likely correct to infer that the Samaritans spoke in tongues. *Acts*, 304. The parallels in Acts 2, 8, and 19 suggest this, and Luke's employment of a type-scene points in this direction. It is also likely that Simon saw something different than the miracles he had witnessed under Philip. Horton, *What the Bible Says*, 156.

(v. 48). The emphasis is on the acknowledgment of Jesus' name, that is, submission to him as Lord, and the rite expresses the faith commitment that has already occurred in the heart.[24] Therefore, in Luke's perspective, baptism in the name of the Lord Jesus does not make one a Christian but serves as a strong indicator that one is a Christian.

That "the name of the Lord Jesus" plays a significant role in Ephesus is confirmed in the episode of the seven sons of Sceva. They attempted to "pronounce" (ὀνομάζειν; literally, "name over") those who had evil spirits "the name of the Lord Jesus" (τὸ ὄνομα τοῦ κυρίου Ἰησοῦ; Acts 19:13). The exorcists received a beating and fled the scene naked because their misuse of Jesus' name along with their own lack of submission to his lordship rendered them powerless against the evil spirit (v. 16). The miserable failure of the Jewish exorcists, in contrast to Paul's performing extraordinary miracles (v. 11), resulted in the magnifying of "the name of the Lord Jesus" among both Jews and Greeks in Ephesus (v. 17). This story confirms that the baptism of the twelve men in the name of the Lord Jesus is absolutely not a mere baptismal formula or a magical incantation but an indication of right relationship with the Lord Jesus.

One must not overlook the presence of the term "Lord" (κύριος) in the description of the men's baptism (Acts 19:5). The royal term goes hand-in-hand with Paul's proclamation of "the kingdom of God" in verse 8. In addition, there is some irony in the attempt of the Jewish exorcists to use "the name of the Lord [κύριος] Jesus" (v. 13), because the man with the evil spirit literally "lorded over" (κατακυριεύσας) them (v. 16). In contrast to this demonic domination over the Jewish exorcists, the authentic Lord had actually appeared to Paul in Corinth (18:9), the name of this Lord was gaining praise in Ephesus (19:17), and the word of this Lord "was growing and becoming strong" in Ephesus (v. 20). The mention of the "Lord" occurs several times in the immediate context of the Ephesian outpouring (18:25; 19:5, 10, 13, 17, 20). In fact, the "Lord" occurs in every instance of the outpouring of the Spirit in Acts (2:20, 21, 36; 4:33; 8:16, 22, 24, 25; 9:1, 5, 10, 13, 15, 17; 10:36; 11:16, 17). This is also true of Jesus' identification as "Christ" (Anointed One), which is particularly fitting in passages where the Spirit is poured out (2:36, 38; 4:26; 8:5, 12;

24. It is at this point that the Oneness Pentecostals mistakenly reduce baptism in the name of Jesus to a mandatory formula. Luke intends to emphasize the necessity of submission to Jesus, with all the Trinitarian implications of his exalted status. Baptism in the name of the Lord Jesus also expresses Jesus' royal identity as superior to that of John and distinguishes their baptisms from each other.

9:22; 10:36, 48; 11:17; 18:28). The episode with Apollos concludes with him proving from the Scriptures that "the Christ is Jesus" (18:28). This preaching of Jesus as the anointed one naturally leads into Paul's questions to the twelve men about their experience with the Spirit, then their subsequent submission to Jesus' lordship, and then their reception of the Spirit. The central message in Ephesus is the same "Lord and Christ" preached at Pentecost (2:36).

The attention on Jesus' name and lordship in Acts 19:5 has a direct bearing on the status of the twelve men in Ephesus. Scholars have debated whether or not the twelve men were Christians prior to meeting Paul.[25] Some Pentecostals have been particularly concerned to demonstrate that they were already Christians in order to establish that reception of the Spirit is a distinct event from salvation.[26] Others have attempted to ignore the chronological markers and blend their moment of faith, water baptism, and reception of the Spirit into a single, neat, salvation package. Attempts to identify the spiritual status of the men based on Luke's reference to them as "disciples" have been inconclusive. The term refers to Christians in every other location in Acts,[27] but it refers to John's disciples on four occasions in Luke's Gospel (5:33; 7:18 [2x]; 11:1), and John is mentioned by name in Acts 19:3. Nor has James Dunn's effort to appeal to "certain disciples" (τινας μαθητὰς; v. 1) succeeded in differentiating them from Christian disciples.[28] He makes a good point

25. These scholars contend that the men already were Christians when Paul found them: Bock, *Acts*, 599; Bruce, *Book of Acts*, 363; Fitzmyer, *Acts*, 642–43; Shelton, *Mighty in Word*, 133–34. These scholars contend that the men were not Christians: Keener, *Acts: Exegetical*, 3:2815–16; Lenski, *Acts*, 783; Peterson, *Acts*, 523–24. Marshall begs the question when he comments, "These men can hardly have been Christians since they had not received the gift of the Spirit." Marshall, *Acts*, 305. Witherington argues more persuasively but in a similar fashion to Marshall. Witherington, *Acts*, 570. Kurz (and many others) faces a major dilemma in concluding that the men were not Christians "since Christian initiation entails receiving the Spirit as Jesus' disciples did at Pentecost." He later urges contemporary Christians to seek "the graces of Pentecost," but if water baptism, laying on of hands, and reception of the Spirit (which includes charismatic signs in Acts 19) are all part of one initiation, then how could modern believers receive the Spirit without charismatic signs? Kurz, *Acts of the Apostles*, 291, 292–294.

26. E.g., Arrington, *Acts*, 191; Horton, *What the Bible Says*, 159–62; Menzies, *Empowered for Witness*, 221; Nunnally, *Book of Acts*, 326; Palma, *Holy Spirit*, 125–29; Stronstad, *Charismatic Theology: Trajectories*, 79; Williams, *Renewal Theology*, 2:181–207; Wyckoff, "Baptism in the Holy Spirit," 429–30;

27. The term occurs thirty-seven times in Luke and twenty-eight times in Acts. Were it not for the presence of John in the immediate context, the argument that the term refers to Christians would be very compelling.

28. Dunn, *Baptism*, 84.

that the articular plural of μαθητής is quite consistently used of the group of believers in Acts, but the article is missing in 19:1.[29] Actually, the same pattern holds true of John's disciples and Jesus' disciples in the Gospel of Luke, except on one occasion. Luke describes "a great crowd of his [Jesus'] disciples" (ὄχλος πολὺς μαθητῶν αὐτοῦ; 6:17).[30] It appears that the lack of the article is not due to a theological concern, but it is simply omitted for stylistic reasons when the adjective immediately precedes the plural noun. This is similar to Acts 19:1 when Luke uses the indefinite pronoun τινας adjectively and places it before μαθητὰς. Given this construction, the lack of the article here proves nothing.[31] Neither does the addition of τινας definitively indicate that the disciples are not Christians, as Luke uses the indefinite pronoun of both Ananias (τις μαθητὴς; 9:10) and Timothy (μαθητής τις; 16:1).[32]

Considerable controversy has existed over Paul's question: "Did you receive the Holy Spirit after [when] you believed?" (εἰ πνεῦμα ἅγιον ἐλάβετε πιστεύσαντες; 19:2). Both sides have pointed to the aorist participle "believed" (πιστεύσαντες; v. 2) in support of their positions. Some argue that the believing action takes place prior to the action of the principal verb "receive" and should be translated as "after you believed," signifying a post-conversion reception of the Spirit.[33] Others point out that it is natural to translate it as a coincident aorist, "when you believed," supposedly inferring a reception of the Spirit simultaneous with conversion.[34] These arguments have not proven conclusive, and, in any case, they may not be as important to the debate as has been assumed. What can be stated with greater confidence is that once Luke records, "They were baptized into the name of the Lord Jesus," he has made it as clear as possible that the twelve men have come to full, new-covenant faith in

29. Dunn, *Baptism*, 84.

30. The article does not usually precede the singular μαθητής, as is evident in Luke 6:40; 14:26, 27, 33; Acts 9:10; 16:1.

31. Luke does use the indefinite pronoun τις along with the article on two occasions, and on both occasions the construction is possessive ("his disciples"), referring to John (Luke 7:18) or Jesus (Luke 11:1).

32. Arrington, *Acts*, 191; Menzies, *Empowered for Witness*, 222.

33. See the discussion in Horton, *What the Bible Says*, 159–62.

34. E.g., Barrett, *Acts*, 2:894; Bruce, *Book of Acts*, 363n8; Dunn, *Baptism*, 87; Moulton, *Prolegomena*, 131n1. Even if one accepts the coincident aorist translation, one still must demonstrate that coincident is the same as simultaneous. A person could believe and receive the Holy Spirit around the same general time period but the two events remain distinct. Ervin, *Spirit-Baptism*, 79n55. See the discussion in BDF §339.

Jesus. In short, they are full-fledged Christians by the end of verse 5 and prior to Paul's administering the laying on of hands in verse 6.

The chiastic structure outlined above pairs Paul's questioning the twelve men about their experience with the Spirit (Acts 19:2) with their actual reception of the Spirit marked by charismatic signs (v. 6). Paul inquires whether or not the men received the Holy Spirit when they believed (v. 2), and the question itself suggests at least two noteworthy items. Paul saw evidence of some level of faith in their lives, and he held out the possibility that someone could have faith without having experienced the full benefits of the new covenant, in other words, a baptism in the Spirit.[35] It is generally accepted in most quarters that their response, "But we have not heard if the Holy Spirit is" (v. 2b), is not a philosophical statement about the existence of the Spirit but an eschatological statement about the age of the Spirit.[36] Paul inquires, "Into what then were you baptized?" and the Ephesians respond, "Into the baptism of John" (v. 3). Their response affirming John's baptism helps Paul pinpoint their place in salvation history. These men gladly heeded Paul's instruction regarding the messianic goal of John's ministry and submitted to baptism "in the name of the Lord Jesus" (v. 5).[37] The combination of their ignorance, lack of baptism into Jesus, and lack of reception of the Spirit leaves the reader with the impression that they were considerably farther behind redemption's progress than Apollos was and lacked essential elements of the gospel. At the same time, they believed to the extent of their knowledge and readily caught up when Paul provided further revelation and opportunity.[38]

Upon Paul's laying on of hands, "the Holy Spirit came on them and they were speaking in tongues and prophesying" (Acts 19:6). This portion of the chiasm corresponds to Paul's question about the twelve's reception of the Spirit and defines the kind of reception of the Spirit Paul had in mind in verse 2. It does not appear to be an automatic insufflation

35. Contra Longenecker, "Acts," 493.

36. Nunnally appeals to a variety of ancient texts to establish that the men would surely have known about the Spirit's existence. He specifically points to the translations found in some ancient versions for support (e.g., Codex Bezae). Nunnally, *Book of Acts*, 327–28. See also Keener, *Acts: Exegetical*, 3:2819.

37. That ancient copyists recognized the similarities between passages such as this and Pentecost is evident in some of the additions of the Western text (D). At the end of Acts 19:5 it adds "Christ for forgiveness of sins" (Χριστοῦ εἰς ἄφεσιν τῶν ἁμαρτιῶν) in conformity with Acts 2:38. See Holladay, *Acts*, 365nf.

38. Keener, *Acts: Exegetical*, 3:2817.

that accompanies the moment of faith, but an event that more closely matches the charismatic emphases throughout Luke-Acts. There is no indication in the text how much time has elapsed between the moment of faith, baptism in the name of Jesus, and Paul's laying on of hands, but reception of the Spirit is clearly distinct from the moment of conversion just as it was for the Samaritans (8:14–17). Max Turner attempts to tie the gift of the Spirit to the conversion-initiation perspective by claiming that "no significant 'delay' is implied between 19:5 and 19:6," but in so doing he too admits there is a time distinction.[39] Gonzalo Haya-Prats observes how Luke distinguishes between the moment of water baptism and Paul's laying on of hands "by the change from the passive form ἐβαπτίσθησαν to the active form that introduces a change of subject, καὶ ἐπιθέντος αὐτοῖς τοῦ Παύλου χεῖρας. It is highly probable that the change of subject is intentional in order to emphasize that the laying on of hands was an office of Paul, while baptism would have been conferred by one of his companions."[40] Indeed, it is likely that someone other than Paul performed the baptisms, and the two events are distinct.

The laying on of hands reflects what Stronstad terms a "transfer motif" and has its origins in the Hebrew Scriptures (Num 11:16–30; Deut 34:9; 1 Sam 10:1, 10; 16:13).[41] In laying hands on the Ephesian men, Paul recognizes them as fellow believers who are eligible to participate in the Christian mission and who are in need of the Spirit's empowerment. That the laying of hands is an act of prayer is made clear by the similar event in Samaria, where Peter and John arrive to pray for the reception of the Spirit and are then depicted laying hands on the Samaritans (Acts 8:15, 17).[42] Attempts to explain away the chronological separation of the event

39. Turner, *The Holy Spirit*, 46. Peterson follows Turner in this. Peterson, *Acts*, 532. Bruce acknowledges that the Spirit is given after baptism and the laying on of hands. *Acts of the Apostles*, 355. Luke does not say who actually administered the water baptism or how long afterward Paul laid hands on the men. Given Luke's perspective on the Spirit as a benefit of entrance into the new covenant, he would likely prefer that new believers accepted their birth right as soon as possible. The idea that there is a distinction between entrance into the new covenant and an experience of the Spirit as a benefit of the new covenant does not mandate a specific time requirement between conversion and a charismatic empowering experience of the Spirit.

40. Haya-Prats, *Empowered Believers*, 151. The argument of Haya-Prats largely negates the argument of Kurz that the single sentence in the Greek text indicates that the laying of hands completes the rite of water baptism. Kurz, *Acts of the Apostles*, 292.

41. Stronstad, *Charismatic Theology: Trajectories*, 23–24, 92.

42. The scene presents Paul as functioning in the same authority and charismatic power as Peter and John did. Johnson holds that the event also had a legitimizing

of salvation and the Spirit's filling by designating such occurrences as anomalies will not suffice.[43] Along with the lordship of Christ, one of the most consistent elements in the Pentecostal type-scene is the emphasis on prayer prior to reception of the Spirit. Jesus tells his disciples to ask for the Spirit (Luke 11:13); the gathered believers pray prior to Pentecost (Acts 1:14); the Spirit refills the believers in response to their prayer (4:24–31); Peter and John pray for the new believers (8:15, 17); Paul prays and fasts for three days (9:9, 11) before Ananias lays hands on him for the filling with the Spirit (v. 17); the events surrounding the gentile Pentecost happen in response to Cornelius's prayers (10:4, 31), at the hour of prayer (vv. 3, 30), and in connection with Peter's prayers (v. 9; 11:5); and the twelve men receive the Spirit in response to Paul's prayer (19:6). These events do not align with the invisible, ontological aspect of the Spirit's bringing new life into the heart of a person at conversion.[44]

"The Holy Spirit came [ἦλθεν] upon them" (Acts 19:6; cf. Ezek 2:2; 3:24) just as he also "came upon" (ἐπέρχομαι) Mary (Luke 1:35) and the disciples at Pentecost (Acts 1:8). Prophetic speech accompanies the empowerment terminology at Ephesus just as in the other places mentioned: "and they were speaking in tongues and prophesying" (ἐλάλουν τε γλώσσαις καὶ ἐπροφήτευον).[45] The imperfect verbs are often translated as inceptive ("they began to speak in tongues and prophesy"), but this also includes the element of continuing to speak and prophesy.[46]

Craig Keener views the speaking in tongues "as clearly distinguished from prophecy here, as indicated by the emphatically double connection

purpose for Paul's ministry in Ephesus. Johnson, *Acts*, 343–44.

43. E.g., Turner, *Power from on High*, 360, 394.

44. Nor does the attempt to dismiss the charismatic events as isolated instances of corporate reception of the Spirit in the progress of redemption provide a satisfactory explanation (see the discussion in chapter 4). Presumably, Paul did not place his hands on all twelve men at once, but more likely prayed for each person individually. While new people groups receive the Spirit, the reception of the Spirit at Samaria and Ephesus does not appear to be a corporate experience per se; rather, individuals in the same geographical location receive Spirit baptism. The individual experience is not entirely overshadowed by a group outpouring that marks new stages of gospel progress.

45. Fitzmyer notices that the word "other" found in Acts 2:4 is absent here, possibly suggesting that the tongues are "ecstatic speech" or explained by the mention of prophesying. Fitzmyer, *Acts*, 644. Luke does not mention the presence of observers who require a language miracle. Stagg is uncertain, but he serves as an example of those who favor intelligibility in Acts 19:6. Stagg, "Glossolalia," 34–35. See the discussion in chapter 4 above.

46. Barrett, *Acts*, 2:898.

τε . . . καί."[47] Roger Stronstad appeals to Peter's identification of tongues as prophecy at Pentecost (Acts 2:17–18) and views the prophecy in 19:6 as essentially epexegetical.[48] Acts has far more passages with the τε . . . καί pattern than any other New Testament book, but there is no other precise occurrence of it in Acts with the use of imperfect verbs in the order of Acts 19:6.[49] Two of the closest parallels are found in 21:30 and 22:7. In the former Paul faces the crowd at Jerusalem: "And the whole city was stirred up and the people ran together" (ἐκινήθη τε ἡ πόλις ὅλη καὶ ἐγένετο συνδρομὴ τοῦ λαου). In the latter text Paul repeats his conversion story: "And I fell to the ground and I heard a voice saying to me" (ἔπεσά τε εἰς τὸ ἔδαφος καὶ ἤκουσα φωνῆς λεγούσης μοι). The connectors join two distinct events in these examples, but the events are also closely related to each other. An attempt to completely differentiate tongues and prophecy on the basis of Luke's use of connectors may place more of a burden on them than they can carry. In this case both interpretations are viable, and one's understanding will likely depend on the weight given to the account of Pentecost as the key to interpretation or to other passages in Luke-Acts where prophecy is a separate function from speaking in tongues. Pentecost as a type-scene probably gives a slight edge to understanding the tongues here as a form of prophetic speech, but one can say with confidence that Luke intends his readers to see a strong relationship between tongues and prophecy as pneumatic forms of speech. However, the more significant point is that the charismatic coming of the Spirit in 19:6 defines Paul's expectation of Spirit reception in verse 2. Luke views Paul as a charismatic who expects those who submit to Jesus as Lord to experience a charismatic filling with the Spirit as a benefit of their salvation.

The final pair in the Ephesian chiasm consists of the "certain disciples" (Acts 19:1) and the summary "And there were about twelve men in all" (v. 7). Luke often reports numbers, especially as a summary statement to cap a literary unit and for the purpose of reporting the growth

47. Keener, *Acts: Exegetical*, 3:2824. For a brief overview of the use of the particle τε, see Turner, *Syntax*, 338–39.

48. Stronstad, *Charismatic Theology: Trajectories*, 80. Menzies does not equate the tongues with prophecy. Menzies, *Empowered for Witness*, 224n4. Turner sees the difficulty but leans toward viewing the καί ("and") as "conjoining" rather than epexegetical. Turner, *The Holy Spirit*, 194.

49. Often the combination can be translated as "both x and y" (e.g., Acts 10:39), but this usually involves the simple connection of two or more nouns, such as in Acts 1:8.

of the church.[50] Luke's mention of the number twelve in the Gospel is generally consistent with usage in Matthew and Mark—with a few exceptions. For instance, Luke adds the story of Jesus in the temple at age twelve (Luke 2:42). In Acts, Luke refers to Jesus' disciples as "the twelve" (6:2), includes the twelve patriarchs in Stephen's speech (7:8), and records Paul's mention of the twelve days since arriving in Jerusalem to worship (24:11). The number most commonly refers to the twelve disciples in Luke's Gospel (6:13; 8:1; 9:1, 12; 18:31; 22:3; 22:47). Scholars debate whether or not the "about twelve" has any symbolic significance in Ephesus.[51] Some, understandably, express concern with over-interpreting what may simply be a typical element of Lukan style or just an ordinary, round number. However, Luke appears to use the number as a means of connecting the story of Jairus's daughter ("about twelve years old [ὡς ἐτῶν δώδεκα]"; Luke 8:42) to the story of the woman with the bleeding malady ("for twelve years"; v. 43). Matthew completely omits the age of the young girl (Matt 9:18–26), and Mark includes her age at the end of the story as a parenthetical comment specifying that she was of walking age (Mark 5:42). Luke's intentional use of the number twelve in these miracle stories; the chiastic structure in Acts 19:1–7; and the Ephesian location as a new, premier mission center, suggest intentional symbolism in Acts 19. The chiasm compares the "certain disciples" to the "about twelve men [ὡσεὶ δώδεκα]," and the mention of "disciples" with "twelve" simply seems too scintillating to ignore. The implication appears to be that the "disciples" have become twelve Spirit-filled followers of Jesus who represent the formation of the church in Ephesus.[52]

The twelve men may have been members of the group of leaders Paul addresses in his farewell speech to the Ephesian elders (Acts 20:17–38), although Luke does not explicitly say so. What Luke does make more explicit is his concern with missions and the establishment of Christ's lordship in Ephesus. Luke does not emphasize the ethnic background

50. E.g., 2:41; 4:4; 5:14; 6:7; 8:25; 9:35, 42; 12:24; 13:49; 16:5; 17:34; 19:20. Sometimes the numbers are specific amounts and other times the reports are more general in nature.

51. Polhill flatly rejects the idea because Luke makes no comment on it. *Acts*, 400.

52. Similarly, Menzies, *Empowered for Witness*, 225. The terminology "about [ὡσεὶ] twelve" is similar to that used in Acts 1:15 where there were "about [ὡσεὶ] 120." Concerning Acts 1:15, Kurz suggests that the number is "apparently an approximation symbolic of the restored Israel." Kurz, *Reading Luke-Acts*, 76. So also Talbert, *Reading Acts*, 13.

of the twelve men, although they appear to be Jews,[53] but he repeatedly mentions that the gospel has gone out to both Jews and Greeks in Asia. Paul's two years reasoning in the lecture hall of Tyrannus yielded these results: "All those dwelling in Asia heard the word of the Lord [κυρίου], both Jews and Greeks" (19:10). The "word of the Lord" is the message of the Lord Jesus, and its influence is touching Jew and gentile alike. When the sons of Sceva failed in their attempts to perform a deliverance by invoking Jesus' name, it "became known to all those dwelling in Ephesus, both Jews and Greeks, and fear fell on them all, and the name of the Lord [κυρίου] Jesus was magnified" (v. 17). Again, the combination of Christ's lordship and mission to the different ethnic groups converge. Luke emphasizes these points a third time when Paul summarizes his ministry to the Ephesians as "testifying to both Jews and Greeks of repentance unto God and faith in our Lord [κύριον] Jesus" (20:21). Luke summarizes in a more general manner in 19:20: "So in a powerful way the word of the Lord [κυρίου] was growing and becoming strong." The international significance of Jesus as Lord is evident at Pentecost, but the recipients of the Spirit are Jews. In Caesarea, tongues signal the lordship of Christ over the gentiles. At Ephesus, tongues represent the expansion of Christ's lordship to new regions and to both Jews and Greeks.

The chiastic structure of Acts 19:1–7 provides significant assistance in interpreting this passage. It implies that the "certain disciples" have become "about twelve" men who help form the church in its strategic location in Ephesus (vv. 1 and 7). The Spirit's arrival in response to Paul's laying on of hands and prayer explains the kind of experience Paul had in mind when he inquired about the men's reception of the Spirit. The men spoke in tongues and prophesied, that is, it was a charismatic, prophetic, and empowering reception of the Spirit (vv. 2 and 6). The men explain that they had received John's baptism, but after Paul's teaching they were baptized "into the name of the Lord Jesus" (vv. 3 and 5). The latter, christological phrase is crucial. The center of the chiasm comes when Paul explains that the goal of John's ministry is faith "in Jesus" (v. 4). The focus of the story is Jesus in Ephesus, and the Spirit comes in Pentecostal power only after the men have submitted to "the name of the Lord Jesus" (v. 5). Only upon the identification of Jesus as Lord and Christ in Ephesus does the Spirit fill the men's mouths with prophetic tongues. The close association of "Lord Jesus" and "tongues" in verses

53. See the discussion in Nunnally, *Book of Acts*, 328.

5–6 is intentional and consistent with the christological orientation of tongues at Pentecost. The location of the tongues at Ephesus is consistent with the missional symbolism of tongues at Pentecost and the concept of the expanding reign of Christ in new regions. The association of tongues with prophesy is consistent with Pentecost and reinforces the notion that tongues speech is prophetic in nature.

Artemis and Jesus—the True Lord in Ephesus

In an ironic twist, even the Greek Demetrius, instigator of the Ephesian riot, announces the progress of the gospel and proclaims that "not only in Ephesus but in almost all of Asia this Paul has persuaded and misled a large crowd, saying that things made with hands are not gods" (Acts 19:26). Demetrius also reveals his economic concerns and expresses his fears that the temple "of the great goddess Artemis" (τῆς μεγάλης θεᾶς Ἀρτέμιδος) will fall into disrepute and that "she will be robbed of her magnificence [καθαιρεῖσθαι τῆς μεγαλειότητος αὐτῆς], she whom all Asia and the world worships" (v. 27). Luke uses Demetrius's speech to contrast the reign of Jesus as Lord in Ephesus with the impotent, made-by-human-hands goddess. For two hours the Ephesian crowd shouted, "Great is Artemis of the Ephesians" (μεγάλη ἡ Ἄρτεμις Ἐφεσίων; vv. 28, 34), before the city clerk quieted the crowd and acknowledged her greatness (μεγάλης) one more time (v. 35). Luke describes the riot with Pentecostal terms, as the crowd was "in confusion" (συγκεχυμένη; 19:32; cf. 2:6)[54] and "in one accord" (ὁμοθυμαδὸν; 19:29; cf. 2:1, 46) when they rushed into the theater. Luke has masterfully contrasted the hopeless praise to a deaf goddess with the genuine majesty and greatness of the Lord Jesus. Though he seldom mentions "the kingdom" or "the kingdom of God" in Acts except for in the frame around the book (1:3, 6; 28:23, 31; cf. 8:12; 14:22), he uses both the full phrase (19:8) and the shortened phrase (20:25)[55] in the Ephesian context. When Luke summarizes the botched exorcism and how the events became known to "both Jews and Greeks," he affirms that "the name of the Lord Jesus was magnified [ἐμεγαλύνετο]" (19:17). At Pentecost the observers heard the believers speaking in their own tongues "the magnificent deeds of God" (τὰ μεγαλεῖα τοῦ θεου; 2:11),

54. The noun σύγχυσις ("confusion") is also used in Acts 19:29.

55. The Majority text, a few of the versions, and some other manuscripts have the full phrase τὴν βασιλείαν τοῦ θεοῦ at Acts 20:25.

and at Caesarea the gentiles were speaking in tongues and magnifying God" (λαλούντων γλώσσαις καὶ μεγαλυνόντων τὸν θεόν; 10:46).

Luke's characters describe Artemis with cognates of μέγας ("great") five times, and the repetition provides a clear contrast with the royal status of the first and second persons of the Trinity. Luke often uses the adjective μέγας as a simple modifier and without much theological significance attached to it;[56] however, the word group acquires more technical importance when applied to certain persons. The adjective is attributed to John the Baptist (Luke 1:15; 7:28), but more importantly, it is used positively of the deity and negatively of imposters and those engaged in self-aggrandizement. Jesus warns the disciples against pursuing self-exalting greatness (Luke 22:24, 26, 27). Simon the magician bragged about his own greatness (Acts 8:9), and his followers gladly stroked his ego with this blasphemous flattery: "This man is the power of God that is called Great" (οὗτός ἐστιν ἡ δύναμις τοῦ θεοῦ ἡ καλουμένη μεγάλη; v. 10). But Luke has pre-empted the praise of the imposters Artemis and Simon with this birth announcement: "And you will call [καλέσεις] his name Jesus. This one will be great and will be called Son of the Most High [οὗτος ἔσται μέγας καὶ υἱὸς ὑψίστου κληθήσεται], and the Lord God will give to him the throne of his father David, and he will reign over the house of Jacob forever, and of his kingdom there will be no end" (Luke 1:31b–33).[57] Mary responds appropriately: "My soul declares the greatness [Μεγαλύνει] of the Lord" (1:46). The terminology of Simon's followers is similar to that applied to Jesus, just as the attribution of greatness to Artemis represents a failed attempt to substitute an idol for the true, great, Lord Jesus.

Luke employs Pentecostal terms in his description of the riot at Ephesus, including the repetition of the "great" terms, and this description highlights the common thread that runs through all three passages where tongues are clearly in evidence. The common thread is that Jesus is declared as Lord wherever tongues occur. The expansion of his kingdom over all the earth explains the reason for the inherent missiological symbolism of tongues and the reason tongues reappear in new contexts. One should expect new tongues to appear so long as the lordship of Christ is proclaimed to those who have not heard the good news about Jesus.

56. The adjective and its cognates occur thirty-six times in Luke's Gospel and thirty-six times in Acts.

57. Jesus is referred to as a "great prophet" in Luke 7:16, and the miracles of Jesus result in an acknowledgment of the "greatness of God" in 9:43.

There may be some additional irony in the fact that Luke records the occurrence of tongues in Ephesus. Polhill notes, "The famous statue of Artemis, the centerpiece of her temple, was noted for the mysterious terms engraved on the crown, girdle, and feet of the image. Referred to as the 'Ephesian scripts,' this magical gibberish was considered to have great power."[58] If Luke's audience knew of the Ephesian scripts, the tongues speech in Ephesus adds one more way in which Luke highlights the superiority of the Lord Jesus and his miracles over Artemis and magic: the followers of Jesus speak in tongues while the followers of Artemis read engraved gibberish.

Summary

The primary emphasis in the Ephesian ministry is the recognition of Jesus as Lord and Christ in a new region. The story of Apollos does not primarily serve to record the beginning of his ministry, as important as that may be, but to emphasize his consistency with the Scriptures and with Paul in proclaiming that Jesus is the Christ. This christological affirmation emphasized through a literary framing technique leads naturally into the next story about twelve men who need to submit to Jesus to catch up with the progress of redemptive history. Luke uses a chiasm to highlight the centrality of Jesus, who is the goal of John's preaching. Luke further emphasizes his christological interests when he records how the men were baptized "into the name of the Lord Jesus" (Acts 19:5). Mention of the "name" and the "Lord" launches Luke into additional stories where Jesus' identity is acknowledged and esteemed. Even a demon acknowledges Jesus' name in a story where Jewish exorcists do not appropriately honor his name, and the message of the Lord progresses in a culture of magic.

It is in this context of Jesus' name and lordship that Paul lays hands on about twelve men who have expressed their submission to Christ's lordship through water baptism. As a result of Paul's act of prayer, the twelve speak in tongues and prophesy. The twelve men appear to represent the formation of Jesus' church in Ephesus, and their reception of the Spirit with charismatic signs prepares them to promote the gospel there. The tongues are first and foremost associated directly with the lordship of Jesus. Tongues continue to symbolize the spread of his reign to new geographical locations, and they are a prophetic form of speech.

58. Polhill, *Acts*, 405.

The use of Pentecostal terminology and the repeated insistence of the rioters in Ephesus that Artemis is "great" establish a contrast with Luke's claims about the lordship of Jesus. Luke's clear depiction of the superiority of Christ over an image made with human hands reinforces the above emphases that are embodied in tongues speech—Jesus is Lord in Ephesus and over all nations.

Part 2

A Markan Perspective on Tongues

6

A Fresh Look at the Longer Ending of Mark

THE AUTHOR OF THE longer ending (LE) of Mark (16:9–20) records Jesus saying that believers "will speak in new tongues" (v. 17). This is the only direct reference to tongues in the Gospels, and scholars have generally explained its occurrence in the disputed ending as resulting from a second-century author borrowing from Acts and other biblical sources, creating a summary ending of Mark, and placing the promise of glossolalia on the lips of Jesus. Although it is beyond the scope of this work to undertake a full-fledged examination of the textual issue, the issues of authenticity, originality, and canonicity obviously have a bearing on the subject matter. Consequently, this chapter is largely devoted to analyzing the evidence surrounding the debate over Mark's ending. However, the central argument of this book does not depend on any particular view of Mark's controversial ending. In the next two chapters, I will attempt to show that tongues in Mark are connected to the identity of Jesus as Lord much as they are in Acts, and the least one could say about the mention of tongues in Mark is that they provide an additional, second-century testimony to the christological orientation of this sign. Nonetheless, I hope to establish the christological point and contribute some fresh perspectives on the textual problem as well.

After a brief overview of the alternative conclusions of Mark and scholarly opinions on the matter, the discussion considers the external evidence for the shorter ending at 16:8 and the LE through verse 20. Following this, the discussion turns to the internal evidence; and the transition at Mark 16:8–9, linguistic elements, literary considerations, and the possibility of Lukan dependence on Mark receive attention. The resurrection language and the exaltation and lordship of Christ serve as specific touch points in Mark's Christology for examining the viability of the LE, and a discussion of these themes prepares the way for a more in-depth look at the theology of the LE in the next chapter.

The Controversy over Mark's Ending

Until the rise of critical scholarship in the nineteenth century and the awareness that Codex Vaticanus lacked Mark 16:9–20, the church had almost universally considered the twelve verses of the LE as the original and canonical ending of the book.[1] Critical scholars highlighted the textual problem, noting that the important majuscules Codex Vaticanus (B) and newly discovered Sinaiticus (א) end at verse 8 (here referred to as the shorter ending). Some manuscripts also contain a short addition to Mark 16:8 (referred to as the intermediate ending), but this ending is almost certainly spurious and occurs as the sole ending in only one Latin manuscript, Codex Bobiensis (it^{k}), dating to c. 400.[2] Some manuscripts contain both the intermediate ending and the LE, with the intermediate ending preceding the LE (L Ψ 083 099 274^{mg} 579 ℓ 1602 cop$^{sa\mathit{mss},\ bo\mathit{mss}}$ eth$^{mss,\ TH}$).[3] The LE also contains an additional insertion known as the "Freer Logion" at 16:14, as is evident in codex W and mentioned by Jerome.[4] Because the support for the Freer Logion and the intermediate ending is so limited, and the original ending obviously did not include both the intermediate ending and the LE, this study focuses on the shorter ending and the LE as potentially authentic endings.

Critical scholars of the past generally held that the original ending was lost (via mutilation or intentional suppression),[5] but the

1. Kelhoffer, *Miracle and Mission*, 6. The discovery of Codex Sinaiticus (א) by Tischendorf in 1859 further fueled the doubts about the ending of Mark, as this Codex also ends at 16:8. See the story of its discovery in Metzger and Ehrman, *Text of the New Testament*, 62–67.

2. Comfort, *Encountering the Manuscripts*, 93. The NA28 and the UBS5 include sy^{hmg} with Codex Bobiensis while others list it in support of readings that include both the intermediate ending and the LE.

3. Aland et al., *The Greek New Testament*, 5th rev. ed., 74.

4. See the translations of the various endings in Mann, *Mark*, 677–78.

5. Some have also hypothesized that Mark never completed his Gospel.

development of postmodern hermeneutics and literary criticism in the twentieth century has resulted in more scholars arguing that Mark intended to terminate his Gospel at 16:8 for dramatic effect.[6] In this case the Gospel concludes with the women at the tomb in a state of fear: "for they were afraid [ἐφοβοῦντο γάρ]." Proponents of this view have sought to demonstrate that ending a sentence or literary unit with a conjunctive γάρ ("for") was an acceptable practice in the ancient world, and although numerous examples of sentences and shorter literary units ending this way have come to light,[7] such an ending for Mark remains unlikely,[8] and there appears to be no comparable parallel to an entire work ending this way in ancient Greek literature.[9]

N. Clayton Croy, holding to the mutilation theory, has argued effectively against the notion that Mark intended to end his Gospel at verse 8: "The fundamental reason that Mark 16:8 is not likely to be the author's intended ending is the jarring lack of closure that this verse presents."[10] Croy highlights the apparent inconsistency between Mark's designation of his work as "good news" (1:1) and the continued fearful state of the women in 16:8.[11] He also argues that the mention of a resurrection (16:7) is not adequate in the Gospel's conclusion, but a resurrection appearance is central to the kerygma.[12] In addition, Peter has given somewhat of a definition of the gospel's chronological limits as including John's baptism to the ascension. This period of time was a requirement for a new witness of Jesus' resurrection (Acts 1:22). Given the traditional evidence for the relationship of Peter and Mark,[13] the opening designation of Mark's work as "the beginning of the gospel of Jesus Christ" (1:1), and the starting point at John's baptism (vv. 2–9), it seems unlikely that Mark would end without resurrection appearances and without the ascension completing the resurrection.

6. E.g., Bock, *Mark*, 382; Decker, *Mark 9–16*, 282; Hooker, *Mark*, 392–94; Lane, *Mark*, 591–92; Wallace, "Mark 16:8," 1–39.

7. Cox, *History and Critique*, 80.

8. Croy, *Mutilation*, 47–50. See also Comfort, *New Testament Text*, 162. For a response to Croy, see Iverson, "A Further Word," 79–94.

9. Lunn, *Original Ending*, 14; Witherington, *Gospel of Mark*, 45.

10. Croy, *Mutilation*, 45.

11. Croy, *Mutilation*, 51–53.

12. Croy, *Mutilation*, 54–55. See also Cranfield, *Mark*, 471; Lunn, *Original Ending*, 6–12.

13. Burgon, *Last Twelve Verses*, 260.

Croy also refers to Mark's prophecy and fulfillment scheme that raises expectations but only results in disappointment without a proper ending, to the shorter ending's departure from literary convention, and to the presence of additional endings as evidence that the shorter ending was viewed as inadequate.[14] R. T. France similarly opines that none of the attempts to argue for an open-ended conclusion of Mark are "persuasive, because they all seem to presuppose an inappropriately 'modern' understanding of literary technique both in terms of how writers wrote and of how readers might be expected to respond."[15] Leaving the reader with the women in a state of fear (v. 8) and without a resurrection appearance seems psychologically, literarily, and theologically unsatisfying.

The question remains as to whether or not the LE of Mark completes the structural and theological expectations of Mark's Gospel. While the vast majority of modern scholars reject the originality of the LE, some of these hold that the content provides an adequate ending and that the antiquity of the addition supports its canonicity. A few modern scholars, such as William Farmer, Maurice Robinson, and Nicholas Lunn,[16] have also argued for the originality of the LE. Lunn's monograph, *The Original Ending of Mark: A New Case for the Authenticity of Mark 16:9–20*, offers the most compelling case to date for the Markan authorship of the LE. Craig Evans's response to this work is noteworthy: "I will not be surprised if Lunn reverses scholarly opinion on this important question."[17] In the following discussion I will argue that the LE satisfies the expectations of Mark's readers—especially the expectation of a resurrection appearance and missionary mandate. The author of the LE was intimately familiar

14. Croy, *Mutilation*, 57. France vigorously challenges the shorter ending theory by pointing to the narrative's expectation of a resurrection and mission, arguing that "to end his gospel without an account of what everyone knew was the outcome of those predictions would have been an act not of literary artistry or of theological challenge but of frustrating anticlimax, leaving the reader waiting uncomfortably for the other shoe to fall." France, *Mark*, 672.

15. France, *Mark*, 683. For a list of arguments opposing the theory of an intended ending at 16:8, see Stein, *Mark*, 734–37. Edwards also takes exception to the notion of an intended ending at verse 8 that is grounded in reader-response theory. Edwards, *Mark*, 501. N. T. Wright, espousing the mutilation theory, suggests that there are "powerful reasons for questioning" the open-ended theory. He argues on the basis of structural considerations that Mark intended to include a resurrection appearance. Wright, *Resurrection*, 619, 620–24.

16. Farmer, *Last Twelve Verses*; Robinson, "Long Ending," 40–79.

17. Lunn, *Original Ending*, back cover.

with the structure and content of the undisputed text, and that author may very well have been Mark himself.

The External Evidence

The Greek Manuscripts

In regard to Greek manuscripts, it is well known that the fourth-century Alexandrian manuscripts (MSS) Codex Vaticanus (B) and Codex Sinaiticus (א) lack the LE;[18] however, the LE has broad geographical support from the Byzantine, Western, Caesarean, and Alexandrian manuscripts as well as much greater numerical support. The LE is included in the following uncials: A C D E F G H K M N S U V X W Γ Δ Θ Λ Π Σ Φ Ψ Ω; and it is also present in too many Greek minuscules to list.[19] Kurt and Barbara Aland suggest that the LE "is found in 99 percent of the Greek manuscripts as well as the rest of the tradition, enjoying over a period of centuries practically an official ecclesiastical sanction as a genuine part of the gospel of Mark."[20] One gets the impression from reading the comments of critical scholars that the manuscript evidence overwhelmingly favors omission of the LE, and it comes as a surprise to many that only three Greek manuscripts (B, א, and 304) lack the LE.[21] According to James Snapp, there are about 1,640 Greek manuscripts of Mark, and only the three omit the LE.[22] Of course manuscripts must be weighed and not merely counted; nevertheless, the LE does command a considerable array of supporting manuscripts.

In addition, it is possible that the space at the end of Mark in Vaticanus[23] and the decorative artwork at the end of Sinaiticus testify to the

18. See the translations of these passages in Mann, *Mark*, 677–78. Vaticanus and Sinaiticus are the oldest full Greek MSS of Mark's Gospel. Portions of Mark are contained in p45 (third century), p84 (sixth century), and the fourth century MS p88. A fragment of Mark dating to c. AD 150–250 (p137) has been published by the Egyptian Exploration Society.

19. Stein notes that "the evidence in support of this reading is too large to recite." Stein, "The Ending of Mark," 81. The list of uncials was compiled by Lunn, *Original Ending*, 25.

20. Aland and Aland, *Text of the New Testament*, 292.

21. Robinson questions whether MS 304 is a good representative of omission, as this MS contains additional commentary throughout the text. Robinson, "Long Ending," 77n129.

22. Snapp also notes that 304 is a later manuscript. *Authentic*, Loc. 183.

23. Burgon, *Last Twelve Verses*, 165.

scribes' knowledge of the LE.[24] It also seems likely that both manuscripts come from the same scriptorium,[25] which indicates that the manuscripts ending at 16:8 share in a similar time, location, and scribal tradition.

One other concern regarding the Greek manuscripts deserves mention. Bruce Metzger has commented on the presence of notes and markings at the close of Mark's Gospel: "Not a few manuscripts that contain the passage have scribal notes stating that older Greek copies lack it, and in other witnesses the passage is marked with asterisks or obeli, the conventional signs used by copyists to indicate a spurious addition to a document."[26] Upon examination of the texts in question, James Snapp concludes that the notes "tend to encourage readers to *accept*, rather than reject, the passage."[27] He continues, "Even more misleading is Metzger's claim—repeated by many commentators—that verses 9–20 are marked off with asterisks or obeli to warn readers that these verses are spurious. . . . But there is no such thing as a non-annotated Greek manuscript of Mark in which 16:9–20 is accompanied by asterisks or obeli."[28] In other words, the markings at the end of the Gospel simply point to comments in the margin or occasionally serve liturgical purposes, but they do not suggest that the LE is spurious. Lunn also takes exception to Metzger's claim: "Where then are what Metzger describes as 'scribal notes stating that older Greek copies lack it'? Plainly there are none that say such a thing. This, together with other statements like it, is nothing other than an unqualified assertion, not at all substantiated by the evidence of the notes themselves."[29] Snapp and Lunn have provided an apt reminder not to make assumptions about the evidence based on current trends in scholarship.

24. Vaticanus only leaves room for additional columns at the end of major breaks in the document, but not between two books in a unit. It appears that the scribe who concluded Sinaiticus added the artwork to prevent the addition of the LE. Lunn, *Original Ending*, 27–33. Snapp also points out that the end of Mark in Sinaiticus contains replacement pages; thus, the copyist of the Markan ending differed from the copyist of the body of Mark. Snapp, *Authentic*, loc. 428.

25. Farmer, *Last Twelve Verses*, 37–38; Elliott, "Last Twelve Verses," 86.

26. Metzger, *Textual Commentary*, 2nd ed., 103.

27. Snapp, *Authentic*, loc. 478. Emphasis original.

28. Snapp, *Authentic*, loc. 479.

29. Lunn, *Original Ending*, 37–38.

The Versions

The Old Latin manuscripts contain the LE with the exception of Codex Bobiensis, which alone contains only the intermediate ending. The Latin Vulgate also fully supports the inclusion of the LE.[30] Every Syriac authority contains the LE with the exception of the Sinaitic Syriac (Ss). Of particular interest in this group is Tatian's *Diatessaron* (c. 172), an early harmony of the Gospels evincing the LE.[31] Among the Coptic versions, the Sahidic manuscripts mostly contain the intermediate ending followed by the LE; the notable exception is Codex P. Palau-Ribes Inv. Nr. 182 (probably dating to the early fifth century), which concludes at verse 8.[32] The earliest Sahidic text probably concluded Mark at verse 8.[33] The Bohairic texts include the LE, and the largely fragmentary Fayyumic copies conclude with the LE except for one. However, the latter texts also contain the intermediate ending and/or scribal notes.[34]

The Armenian version is often cited in support of the shorter ending, as the last twelve verses are missing in "about one hundred Armenian manuscripts."[35] However, analysis of the data is complicated by the relative lateness of the extant manuscripts (the earliest dates to the late ninth century) and by the multiple historical influences on the manuscript tradition. Armenians did not have an alphabet until early in the fifth century, and the earliest translations apparently drew from Syriac texts.[36] James Snapp summarizes some of the influences on the Armenian version: "(1) the Syriac sources on which the first edition (405 to 412) was based, (2) the Greek sources taken to Armenia in 431, and (3) second thoughts of the Armenian scribes regarding their initial work

30. Elliott, "Text and Language," 255–56.

31. Aland mentions Ss as the exception. Aland et al., *The Greek New Testament*, 5th rev. ed., 74. Farmer lists Tatian, the Peshitta, the Palestinian Syriac, and the Harclean Syriac as supporting inclusion. Farmer, *Last Twelve Verses*, 49.

32. Snapp, *Authentic*, loc. 3950. See the photograph of this manuscript in Aland and Aland, *Text of the New Testament*, 202.

33. Wallace, "Mark 16:8," 20. See also Snapp, *Authentic*, loc. 3962.

34. Lunn, *Original Ending*, 47. See an overview of the Coptic versions in Aland and Aland, *Text of the New Testament*, 200–204.

35. Metzger, *Textual Commentary*, 2nd ed., 102. Cf. Comfort, *New Testament Text*, 159; Elliott, "Text and Language," 256. The classic study on this was done by Ernest C. Colwell, "Mark 16:9–20 in the Armenian Version," 369–86.

36. See the historical overviews in Aland and Aland, *Text of the New Testament*, 205; Metzger and Ehrman, *Text of the New Testament*, 117–18; and Snapp, *Authentic*, loc. 3973–4025.

after visiting Egypt."[37] Snapp's third influence listed is consistent with his proposed reconstruction in which the LE was part of the early tradition but was likely called into question and removed later on.[38] The Armenian testimony is divided between those containing the LE and those without it, but those without the LE are greater in number and generally older than those with it.[39] According to the Alands, the early Georgian translation seems to be a derivative of the Armenian version and evinces the influence of the Syriac version.[40] The history of the Georgian version is complex, the extant manuscripts are relatively late, the witness to the Markan ending is divided, but the two oldest manuscripts (897 and 913) lack the LE.[41]

Like the Armenian and Georgian versions, the Ethiopic version also has a rather tangled history, and its extant manuscripts are also rather late. However, Metzger examined numerous Ethiopic manuscripts and discovered that all the biblical manuscripts contain the LE. "In addition, what is known as the 'shorter ending' of Mark, found in several Greek and Syriac manuscripts occurs in many Ethiopic manuscripts between 16.8 and 9. Subsequently, William F. Macomber of the Hill Monastic Manuscript Microfilm Library at Collegeville, Minnesota, examined microfilms of 129 additional Ethiopic manuscripts of Mark. Of the total of 194 (65 + 129) manuscripts, all but two (which are lectionaries) have Mark 16.9–20, while 131 contain both the shorter ending and the longer ending."[42] The Ethiopic version supports inclusion of the LE.

It should be kept in mind that the versions are secondary witnesses to the ancient Greek text, that the translations often occurred at a significant chronological distance from the autographs, and that the earliest extant copies of the versions are often rather late. Thus, versional testimony has its limitations. Nonetheless, the Latin versions and the Ethiopic version strongly support the inclusion of the LE. The Syriac version also supports the LE with the exception of the Sinaitic Syriac. The Coptic versions point to instability in the textual tradition, sometimes containing

37. Snapp, *Authentic*, loc. 4027.

38. Snapp, *Authentic*, loc. 4060.

39. Colwell, "Mark 16:9–20 in the Armenian Version," 371–78.

40. Aland and Aland, *Text of the New Testament*, 205.

41. Metzger, *Textual Commentary*, 2nd ed., 102. See the discussion in Snapp, *Authentic*, 4422–69.

42. Metzger and Ehrman, *Text of the New Testament*, 120.

the intermediate ending and the LE. The Armenian and Georgian versions are related, and they both exhibit signs of textual instability.

Nicholas Lunn has observed a pattern of textual problems at the end of Mark connected to an Egyptian provenance. He views the versional textual issues in Mark 16 as consistent with the omission of the LE in Vaticanus and Sinaiticus.[43] In effect, the absence of the LE can generally be traced to a specific region, pointing to the source of the omission. On the other hand, those arguing for the originality of the short ending attribute the multiplication of manuscript evidence to later dissatisfaction with the ending and the productivity of Byzantine copyists. If Mark had intended to end his Gospel at 16:8, one wonders why early copyists were not familiar with Mark's literary techniques and insisted on adding alternative conclusions.

The Lectionaries

James K. Elliott lists lectionaries 60 69 70 185 547 883 as including the LE and lectionary 1602 as including both the LE and the intermediate ending.[44] The textual apparatus in the United Bible Society's fifth edition of *The Greek New Testament* indicates that the lectionaries support the LE.[45] One of the significant elements of the lectionary evidence is that the system had its origin in the fourth century or before; consequently, the substantial testimony to the LE among the lectionaries reflects a rather early date for the existence of the LE in the biblical manuscripts.[46] Clearly, the lectionaries support the inclusion of the LE.

Patristic Citations

The patristic testimony largely favors the inclusion of the LE, but the testimony mustered in support of an ending at Mark 16:8 primarily rests on two arguments: the silence of certain fathers and the remarks of Eusebius and of those who quoted him. The fathers most commonly cited for their

43. Lunn, *Original Ending*, 54. Farmer has also suggested that the absence of the LE relates to a problem in the Alexandrian tradition. *Last Twelve Verses*, 40. Snapp often refers to the Egyptian influence as well. *Authentic*, loc. 5583, 5628.

44. Elliott, "Text and Language," 255–56.

45. See the list of lectionaries in Farmer, *Last Twelve Verses*, 34–36. Also see the discussion in Burgon, *Last Twelve Verses*, 271–91.

46. Burgon, *Last Twelve Verses*, 275.

silence are Clement of Alexandria and Origen,[47] although some have mentioned Cyprian (d. 258), Cyril of Jerusalem,[48] and Theodoret.[49] There are two obvious problems with this line of reasoning. The first is that arguments from silence are notoriously weak, and the second is that the list of supposed witnesses is very short. Regarding Clement of Alexandria (c. 150–215), John Burgon pointed out that Clement does not cite Matthew's final chapter either.[50] According to Snapp, "Clement scarcely used the Gospel of Mark at all. It is transparently ridiculous to treat Clement's non-use of Mark 16:9–20 as evidence that his copy of Mark lacked those verses, inasmuch as he declined to use almost the entire book, other than chapter 10."[51] In addition, Lunn proposes that Clement's *Excerpta ex Theodoto* (76.3) may contain an echo of Mark 16:15–16.[52]

Concerning Origen (c. 185–254), Snapp has noted the possibility that Origen's comments recorded in *Philocalia* 1.5 may show dependence on Mark 16:15–20, but even if this is not the case, Snapp has demonstrated that Origen made only limited use of Mark's Gospel in comparison with the other Gospels.[53] Farmer has also suggested that Celsus's critical description of Mary Magdalene's emotional state after the resurrection best fits the account in the LE of Mark. As Origen responds to Celsus's critique, both men become witnesses to the LE in this scenario.[54] Allusions to the LE in Clement of Alexandria and Origen would nullify their supposed witness to the shorter ending and make them witnesses to the LE, but the possibility of the references should at least temper the tendency to make quick judgments. And given the general lack of Markan usage, one should guard against the assumption that silence indicates absence.

47. Examples of those who mention this silence in support of the shorter ending include Bock, *Mark*, 384; Elliott, *Text and Language*, 256; Metzger, *Textual Commentary*, 2nd ed., 103; Edwards, *Mark*, 497; Stein, *Mark*, 728.

48. Comfort lists Cyprian and Cyril. *New Testament Text*, 159. Snapp notes that there is insufficient use of Mark's Gospel by Cyprian to make a judgment about the LE. Snapp, *Authentic*, loc. 2260–2307. Westcott and Hort list Cyril of Jerusalem. Westcott and Hort, *The New Testament*, Appendix, 37.

49. Cox lists Theodoret. Cox, *History and Critique*, 22.

50. Burgon, *Last Twelve Verses*, 116.

51. Snapp, *Authentic*, loc. 1876.

52. Lunn, *Original Ending*, 84. See Casey, *Excerpta ex Theodoto*, 40–91.

53. Snapp, *Authentic*, loc. 2104–133, 2135–77. See Origen, *The Philocalia*, 1.5. See also Westcott and Hort, *The New Testament*, Appendix, 37.

54. Origen, *Contra Celsum*, 2.55, 60; Farmer, *Last Twelve Verses*, 31n2.

Citing Eusebius (c. 270–340) as a witness for the shorter ending has become a routine practice among scholars.[55] The comment of John Donahue and Daniel Harrington about the LE is typical: "There is no indication that Clement of Alexandria or Origen knew it, and Eusebius and Jerome claimed that it was absent from almost all the Greek manuscripts known to them."[56] The passage alluded to is found in Eusebius's *Gospel Problems and Solutions* in a section known as *ad Marinus* ("to Marinus"). In this passage, Eusebius addresses a potential discrepancy between the timing of the resurrection in Matthew and that in Mark.[57]

> Your first question was: How is it that the Saviour's resurrection evidently took place, in Matthew, "late on the Sabbath", but in Mark "early in the morning on the first day of the week"? 1. The answer to this would be twofold. The actual nub of the matter is the pericope which says this. One who athetises that pericope would say that it is not found in all copies of the gospel according to Mark: accurate copies end their text of the Marcan account with the words of the young man whom the women saw, and who said to them: "'Do not be afraid; it is Jesus the Nazarene that you are looking for, etc. . . . '", after which it adds: "And when they heard this, they ran away, and said nothing to anyone, because they were frightened." That is where the text does end, in almost all copies of the gospel according to Mark. What occasionally follows in some copies, not all, would be extraneous, most particularly if it contained something contradictory to the evidence of the other evangelists. That, then, would be one person's answer: to reject it, entirely obviating the question as superfluous.
>
> Another view, from someone diffident about athetising anything at all in the text of the gospels, however transmitted, is that there is a twofold reading, as in many other places, and that both are to be accepted; it is not for the faithful and devout to judge either as acceptable in preference to the other. Supposing the latter point of view to be granted as true, the proper thing to do with the reading is to interpret its meaning.

Eusebius continues his response by proposing that the apparent discrepancy could be resolved with appropriate punctuation in the Markan passage. He notes that the Gospel of John confirms the Markan reading

55. See the discussion in Westcott and Hort, *The New Testament*, Appendix, 30–36.

56. Donahue and Harrington, *Mark*, 462.

57. Eusebius, *Gospel Problems*, 97, 99. The text cited was translated by David J. D. Miller.

about the appearance to Mary Magdalene, and he concludes: "Thus two points of time are presented here: that of the resurrection, 'late on the Sabbath,' and that of the Saviour's appearance, 'early in the morning.' . . . Then the next words are to be pronounced after our punctuation-mark: 'early in the morning on the first day of the week he appeared to Mary of Magdala, from whom he had driven out seven devils.'"[58]

Several observations about Eusebius's response deserve mention. First, the passage only gives hypothetical responses and does not explicitly give Eusebius's opinion. Second, Eusebius seems more favorably disposed toward the latter response than to a potential textual issue. Third, the mention of a textual problem does indicate the presence of instability in the textual tradition known to him, although Marinus does not appear to be aware of the problem. Fourth, this early fourth century citation gives the first patristic evidence of the textual problem, although it is much later than the evidence from other fathers (see below). Fifth, the discussion quotes from the LE and therefore provides testimony to it from Eusebius and Marinus, who evidently had a copy of Mark containing the LE.[59] A look at the original text suggests that statements offering Eusebius as a witness are often oversimplifications in need of serious qualification.

The testimony of Eusebius is further complicated by his additional comments on Mark 16:9–20 and the lack of those verses in his Canons. In the first case, it is not at all clear exactly what position Eusebius takes on those verses because he refers to them but acknowledges that they are contained in only "some copies."[60] Regarding the Canons (a table containing parallels and independent passages of the Gospels), Eusebius evidently left Mark 16:9–20 out of them. The reason for doing so is unknown, but this omission is often viewed as reflecting Eusebius's doubts about those verses. The evidence from Eusebius is mixed, and his true opinion is difficult to ascertain, but it does appear that the LE was missing from some manuscripts known to Eusebius.[61]

58. Eusebius, *Gospel Problems*, 99.

59. Lunn, *Original Ending*, 95.

60. Eusebius, *Gospel Problems*, 113. Snapp supposes that this comment best reflects Eusebius's actual position. Snapp, *Authentic*, loc. 2857.

61. See the discussion in Lunn, *Original Ending*, 96–98. For additional treatment of Eusebius, see Farmer, *Last Twelve Verses*, 3–22; Kelhoffer, "The Witness of Eusebius' *ad Marinum*," 78–112; Snapp, *Authentic*, loc. 2763–2882.

Many have cited Jerome (c. 345–420) as a witness against the LE because of his repetition of Eusebius's comments about the absence of the last twelve verses in some Greek texts. However, it has long been recognized that Jerome simply translated Marinus's questions and Eusebius's responses from Greek into Latin and attributed the questions to a certain Hedibius, and Jerome's inclusion of the LE in his Latin Vulgate likely reflects his own opinion on the authenticity of the verses in question.[62] Snapp finds support for this position in Jerome's use of Mark 16:14 as part of the ending of Mark's Gospel.[63] Similarly, Severus and Victor of Antioch have been cited as witnesses against the LE, but they too have merely repeated Eusebius's discussion with Marinus and have actually accepted the LE.[64] The comment of Victor of Antioch is decidedly in favor of the final twelve verses:

> Notwithstanding that in very many copies of the present Gospel, the passage beginning, 'Now when [Jesus] was risen early the first day of the week, He appeared first to Mary Magdalene,' be not found,— (certain individuals having supposed it to be spurious,)—yet we, at all events, inasmuch as in very many we have discovered it to exist, have, out of accurate copies, subjoined also the account of our Lord's Ascension, (following the words 'for they were afraid,') in conformity with the Palestinian exemplar of Mark which exhibits the Gospel verity: that is to say, from the words, 'Now when [Jesus] was risen early the first day of the week,' &c., down to 'with signs following. Amen.'[65]

Consequently, closer examination of purported evidence against the LE turns out to favor inclusion of it.[66]

The list of church fathers who serve as favorable witnesses for the LE is extensive, and the work of Snapp should be consulted for a review of many of them.[67] Lunn has also compiled a list of witnesses from around the fourth and fifth centuries, including: Aphrahat the Persian, Ephrem

62. Burgon, *Last Twelve Verses*, 129–35. Jerome, *Epistle 120, To Hedibia*. See also Westcott and Hort, *The New Testament*, Appendix, 33.

63. Jerome, *Dialogue against the Pelagians*, 2.15 (*NPNF*^{2} 6:468); Snapp, *Authentic*, loc. 3792.

64. Burgon, *Last Twelve Verses*, 135–43; Lunn, *Original Ending*, 106–8.

65. Taken from Burgon, *Last Twelve Verses*, 142–43.

66. Hesychius serves as another example of a witness who purportedly supports omission of the LE but who more likely supports inclusion. Lunn, *Original Ending*, 105–6.

67. Snapp, *Authentic*, chs. 1–5.

the Syrian, Didymus the Blind, Ambrose of Milan, John Chrysostom, Augustine of Hippo, John Cassian, Nestorius, Cyril of Alexandria, Peter Chrysologus, Marius Mercator, Prosper of Aquitaine, Eznik of Kolb, Macarius Magnes, Marcus Eremita, Patrick of Ireland, Leo the Great, and Theodoret of Cyrus. References to the LE are also found in the *Apostolic Constitutions*, the *Acts of Pilate*, and the *Acts of John*.[68] Were it not for Eusebius's *ad Marinus*, there would be practically no support at all among the church fathers for the shorter ending.

Some of the most persuasive evidence in support of the disputed ending comes from the first three centuries. Hippolytus (235) probably referred to the LE,[69] and there is strong evidence that Vincentius of Thibaris (256), the *Didascalia Apostolorum* (early third century), and Porphyry (c. 270) cited or alluded to it.[70] Scholars on all sides of the dispute agree that Irenaeus of Lyons gives positive testimony to the LE. In *Against Heresies* (c. 175–85) Irenaeus directly refers to Mark as his source and then quotes 16:19: "Also, towards the conclusion of his Gospel, Mark says: 'So then, after the Lord Jesus had spoken to them, He was received up into heaven, and sitteth on the right hand of God.'"[71] There is also persuasive evidence that Justin Martyr incorporated terminology from Mark 16:20 when he wrote (c. 160) his *First Apology* (ch. 45).[72] It is also generally agreed that his disciple, Tatian, included the LE in his *Diatessaron* (c. 172). Lunn has also found evidence for familiarity with the LE in some non-canonical writings dated to the first half of the second century, including *The Gospel of Mary*, *The Gospel of Peter*, and *The Epistula Apostolorum*.[73]

Nicholas Lunn has also brought to light some possible allusions to the LE from three apostolic fathers: *The First Epistle of Clement* (late first century), *The Shepherd of Hermas* (first half of the second century), and *The Epistle of Barnabas* (c. 70–135).[74] Although the case for the latter work's support of the LE is not as compelling as for the other two, the

68. Lunn, *Original Ending*, 109–11.

69. Snapp, *Authentic*, loc. 1915–2023.

70. Farmer, *Last Twelve Verses*, 32–33; Lunn, *Original Ending*, 89–92. Lunn has also argued for Tertullian's familiarity with the LE. Lunn, *Original Ending*, 87–88. Snapp has argued in a similar manner. *Authentic*, loc. 1782–1843.

71. Irenaeus, *Against Heresies*, 3:10.5 (*ANF* 1:426).

72. Kelhoffer, *Miracle and Mission*, 64, 170–75.

73. Lunn, *Original Ending*, 71–76.

74. Lunn, *Original Ending*, 65–71.

resurrection language in *The Epistle of Barnabas* 15.9 suggests dependence on Mark 16:9–20: "This is why we spend the eighth day in celebration, the day on which Jesus both arose from the dead [ἀνέστη ἐκ νεκρῶν] and, after appearing [φανερωθεὶς] again, ascended into heaven [εἰς οὐρανούς]."[75] Although none of this language is entirely unique to Mark, the use of ἀνίστημι ("to rise") is typically Markan (16:9) and φανερόω ("to appear") is only used of Jesus' resurrection in Mark 16:12 and 14 and John 21:1 (2x) and 14. The expression "into heaven" is not unique to Mark (e.g., Acts 1:10, 11), and the occurrence without the article in *Barnabas* is not typical of the New Testament writers except for Peter (1 Pet 1:4, 12; 3:22), but Peter does not use the preposition εἰς with the plural οὐρανούς as *Barnabas* does. Although there is no perfect linguistic match for "into heaven" to any New Testament passage, it is similar to many, including Mark 16:19. The combination of terms used for Jesus' resurrection, manifestation, and ascension into heaven matches Mark 16:9–20 better than any other single, biblical passage.

The evidence for an allusion to the LE in *The Shepherd of Hermas* is stronger than that for *The Epistle of Barnabas*. Compare the language in the parable with that of the LE.[76]

> And from the eighth mountain, where there were many springs and all the Lord's creation [πᾶσα ἡ κτίσις] drank from the springs, are believers [οἱ πιστεύσαντες] such as these: apostles and teachers who preached [οἱ κηρύξαντες] to the whole world [εἰς ὅλον τὸν κόσμον] and who reverently and purely taught the word [τὸν λόγον] of the Lord [τοῦ κυρίου], and who misappropriated nothing for evil desire, but always walked [πορευθέντες] in righteousness and truth, just as they had also received the holy spirit. (*Herm.* 102.1–2)
>
> And he said to them, "Go [πορευθέντες] into all the world [εἰς τὸν κόσμον ἅπαντα] and proclaim [κηρύξατε] the gospel to the whole creation [πάσῃ τῇ κτίσει]. Whoever believes [ὁ πιστεύσας] and is baptized will be saved, but whoever does not believe will be condemned. And these signs will accompany those who believe [τοῖς πιστεύσασιν]: in my name they will cast out demons. . . ." So then the Lord Jesus, after he had spoken to them, was taken up into heaven and sat down at the right hand of God. And they

75. English and Greek texts are from Holmes, *Apostolic Fathers*.

76. The comparison here is dependent on Lunn, *Original Ending*, 68. Lunn was alerted to the passage by Charles Taylor, *The Witness of Hermas*, 60. The text of *The Shepherd of Hermas* is from Holmes, *Apostolic Fathers*.

> went out and preached [ἐκήρυξαν] everywhere, while the Lord [τοῦ κυρίου] worked with them and confirmed the message [τὸν λόγον] by accompanying signs. (Mark 16:15–17, 19–20 ESV).

Lunn gives a detailed comparison of the terms in each passage, but he especially notes how Mark 16:15 is the only place in the New Testament that combines the thought of "the whole world" and "all creation" in this manner.[77] The emphases on the lordship of Jesus, his message as "the word," the reception of the Holy Spirit (Mark 13:11; Acts 2:4), and the mission of the apostles are also evident in Acts, but the combination of these items with the language mentioned above is only found in Mark 16. There are simply too many similarities between *Hermas* and Mark 16 to dismiss the likelihood of dependence.

Among Lunn's most provocative discoveries is the similarity of context and language between Clement of Rome's summary of the disciples' preaching and that of Mark 16:9–20.[78]

> Having therefore received their orders and being fully assured by the resurrection [ἀναστάσεως] of our Lord Jesus [κυρίου . . . Ἰησοῦ] Christ and full of faith [πιστωθέντες] in the Word [ἐν τῷ λόγῳ] of God, they went forth [ἐξῆλθον] with the firm assurance that the Holy Spirit gives, preaching the good news [εὐαγγελιζόμενοι] that the kingdom of God was about to come. So, preaching [κηρύσσοντες] both in the country and in the towns . . . (*1 Clem.* 42:3–4).

> Now after he had risen [Ἀναστὰς] . . . he appeared to the eleven. . . . And he said to them, "Go into all the world and preach [κηρύξατε] the gospel [εὐαγγέλιον] to all creation. . . . And these signs will follow those who believe [πιστεύσασιν]. . . ." So then the Lord Jesus, after he spoke to them, was taken up into heaven and sat at the right hand of God. And they went out [ἐξελθόντες] and preached [ἐκήρυξαν] everywhere, the Lord working with them confirming the word [τὸν λόγον] with signs following. (Mark 16:9, 14–16, 19–20).

The contextual similarities begin with Clement's opening emphasis on "the Lord Jesus Christ" as "sent forth from God" and the origins of the

77. Lunn, *Original Ending*, 68.

78. Lunn, *Original Ending*, 65–68. He credits Charles Taylor with previously observing some of the correspondences between these texts. Taylor, "Some Early Evidence," 80.

apostles in Christ and God (42.1–2). That they "received their orders" in connection with the resurrection fits well with Mark 16:15, Matt 28:18–20, and Acts 1:3–8 (cf. Luke 24:44–49); however, Matthew mentions "doubt" (28:17) rather than faith in this context, Luke repeatedly mentions unbelief (24:11, 25, 41), and Acts 1 does not mention faith.[79] Mark has a strong emphasis on the problem of unbelief (16:11, 13, 14), but only he uses the participial form of πιστεύω ("believe") in a positive manner in this context and indicates the disciples' faith by their miraculous ministry. In addition, even though "the word" is a common expression in Luke-Acts, only the Markan ending refers to the gospel message with the singular "word" accompanied by the definite article in the resurrection narrative. The combination of terms, christological emphasis, and sending of the apostles points in the direction of the LE.[80]

Lunn has noted the similar description of the apostles' commission in Clement and Mark 16:20: "Regarding the apostles going out to preach, the particular verb chosen by Clement to describe the event (ἐξελθεῖν) is the same as that occurring in Mark 16:20 of precisely the same action. None of the other Gospel writers uses this verb in this context."[81] Lunn also notes how the apostles serve as the subjects of the verb "preach" (κηρύσσω) in both passages under discussion and how no other Gospel ending employs the term in the same manner. Additionally, the verb is followed by a location in each passage: "preaching in the country and in the towns" and "they preached everywhere" (*1 Clem* 42.4; Mark 16:20).[82] Another element that contributes to the forcefulness of the above argument is that the combination of ἐξέρχομαι and κηρύσσω is a distinctly Markan expression in the New Testament. "And they went out and preached everywhere [ἐκεῖνοι δὲ ἐξελθόντες ἐκήρυξαν πανταχοῦ]" (Mark 16:20) is very similar to the model established by Jesus: "Let us go elsewhere into other towns, so that I may preach [κηρύξω] there also, for that is why I came [ἐξῆλθον]" (1:38; cf. v. 45). Similarly, Jesus had sent the disciples on a mission to preach, cast out demons, and heal in Mark 6:12–13: "And they went out and preached [ἐξελθόντες ἐκήρυξαν] that

79. Neither the noun παραγγελία (commandment, instruction) used by Clement in 42:3 nor its cognate verb is used in any of the resurrection accounts; however, the verb does occur in Acts 1:4.

80. Lunn has also noted the similarity of setting between Clement and the LE. Lunn, *Original Ending*, 67.

81. Lunn, *Original Ending*, 67.

82. Lunn, *Original Ending*, 67.

they should repent" (v. 12). The Greek combination here is identical to that in 16:20. The combination never occurs outside of Mark in the New Testament, and the only place it occurs in a resurrection context is in the LE. Not only does this point to Clement's dependence on the LE, but it also demonstrates some consistency between the body of Mark and the LE. If Clement is drawing on the disputed ending, then it is also likely that the "firm assurance that the Holy Spirit gives" is an allusion to the signs of Mark 16:17–18.

That Clement alludes to the LE is very likely, and such an allusion places the LE in the first century, implies its earlier existence in the apostolic era, and offers a considerable challenge to the theory that a second-century author formulated and attached 16:9–20 to Mark's Gospel. The additional testimony of *The Shepherd of Hermas* and *The Epistle of Barnabas* points to an early familiarity with the disputed passage in Rome and perhaps Alexandria.[83]

In light of the external evidence surveyed here, it becomes clear that there is significant, broad support for the last twelve verses of Mark at a much earlier period than that of the short ending. Although the absence of the final verses in Sinaiticus and Vaticanus is significant, the testimony for the short ending is rather limited. The notion that the textual problem originated in Alexandria seems plausible,[84] and various reasons for the rise of textual variants have been posited,[85] but certainty on the origin of the variants is presently unobtainable.

The Internal Evidence

As challenging as it is to sift through the external evidence, in some ways analysis of the internal evidence is even more so. The difficulty of

83. The allusions mentioned here present a serious challenge to this claim: "Irenaeus and possibly Justin are the only Greek Ante-Nicene Fathers whose extant works shew traces of vv. 9–20." Westcott and Hort, *The New Testament*, Appendix, 39.

84. This line of reasoning has been argued by several scholars who support the originality or authenticity of the last twelve verses. Metzger and Ehrman have objected to William Farmer's articulation of this position in the strongest possible terms, but the basic idea that much of the manuscript uncertainty can be traced to the influence of Alexandria seems sound. Metzger and Ehrman, *Text of the New Testament*, 323n41. See Farmer, *Last Twelve Verses*, 59–75; Lunn, *Original Ending*, 113–15.

85. Various suggestions include a disruption in the completion and distribution of the Gospel, mutilation of the original text, and intentional excision of the ending. Speculation only serves to present the acceptance of the LE as a reasonable option, but it does not provide any proof for the position.

ascertaining what someone might have or would have said comes with numerous trappings. In this section, I will review some of the primary internal arguments offered for and against Markan authorship. I will refer often to the research of Nicholas Lunn, as he has presented one of the most in-depth and provocative studies of this subject to date.

The Transition at Mark 16:8–9

Even those who have supported Markan authorship of the LE have noted that the transition from verse 8 to 9 is a bit "awkward."[86] "And they went out and fled from the tomb, for trembling and astonishment had seized them, and they said nothing to anyone, for they were afraid [ἐφοβοῦντο γάρ]. Now when he rose early on the first day of the week [Ἀναστὰς δὲ πρωῒ πρώτῃ σαββάτου], he appeared first to Mary Magdalene, from whom he had cast out seven demons" (Mark 16:8–9 ESV). Philip Comfort points out the use of an active participle ἀναστὰς ("having risen") in reference to Jesus' resurrection rather than the more commonly employed passive form in the Gospels.[87] He also notes the sudden change of subject from the women in verse 8 to Jesus as the presumed subject in verse 9. He adds that "Mary Magdalene is introduced as if she was not mentioned before or was not among the women of 15:47–16:8."[88] Metzger posits that "the use of ἀναστὰς δὲ and the position of πρῶτον are appropriate at the beginning of a comprehensive narrative, but they are ill-suited in a continuation of verses 1–8."[89] Ironically, some have argued that ending verse 8 with γάρ ("for") is unusual and is evidence against Mark, while other scholars have made a substantial time investment in attempting to demonstrate that this is a perfectly acceptable way to end a book.

The first argument mentioned by Comfort is easily dismissed, as Mark never uses the verb ἀνίστημι ("to rise") in a passive form.[90] The active participle employed in 16:9 provides positive evidence for Markan

86. Terry, "Style," Section 1: Objections Based on Juncture.

87. Kelhoffer confidently asserts that Ἀναστὰς is "obviously" not Markan. Kelhoffer, *Miracle and Mission*, 179.

88. Comfort, *New Testament Text*, 159–60.

89. Metzger, *Textual Commentary*, 2nd ed., 105.

90. The verb itself never occurs in a passive form in the New Testament, and when Luke has the opportunity to use a passive form in 24:7, he uses an aorist active infinitive form. There "it is necessary for the Son of Man to be delivered [παραδοθῆναι]" and "to be crucified [σταυρωθῆναι]" and "to rise [ἀναστῆναι] on the third day."

authorship, and I will elaborate on this below. Regarding Jesus as the subject in verse 9, it is true that the author could have supplied a masculine pronoun and smoothed out the transition; nevertheless, the Gospel evinces this same practice in other places (2:13; 6:45; 7:31; 8:1; and 14:3),[91] and it is quite obvious from the context that Jesus is the one who has risen from the dead. Mary will receive attention in the next chapter, but a narrowing of the attention onto her as the first witness of the resurrection seems acceptable, and added details of her deliverance fit with Mark's emphasis on deliverance and with his literary practice.[92] Placing the spotlight on a female witness to the resurrection also fits better with the original gospel story than with a second-century milieu. Regarding Metzger's concern with using ἀναστὰς δὲ ("now having risen") and πρῶτον ("first") in verse 9, the problem vanishes when it is recognized that verses 9–20 form a new unit of material. It is one thing to acknowledge that the transition between verses 8 and 9 is not as smooth as it could be, but it is another thing to exaggerate this observation with unsustainable claims about style and to therefore conclude that the ending is spurious. I will argue in the next chapter that the LE draws heavily from the early chapters of Exodus, and dependence on sources could account for some variation in style and vocabulary without assuming a change in author.[93]

Linguistics

One of the primary arguments against the LE is the supposed excess of unique terms occurring in the last twelve verses. Metzger and Ehrman are representative of this position, referring to seventeen words unique to the LE.[94] This argument was challenged in the nineteenth century by scholars such as John Broadus, who found seventeen unique words in

91. Terry, "Style," Section 1: Objections Based on Juncture.

92. Terry cites examples of Mark adding such information about his characters after they have already been mentioned in the narrative (Mark 3:16, 17; 6:16; 7:26). Terry, "Style," Section 1: Objections Based on Juncture.

93. Burkett makes a similar argument and adds that critics of Markan style seldom define the term 'style' and make no allowances for the author as compiler. Burkett, *Rethinking*, 254–55.

94. Metzger and Ehrman, *Text of the New Testament*, 323–24. Hendrickson lists eighteen words in the LE that do not occur in the rest of Mark. Hendrickson, *Exposition of Mark*, 684. Wessel mentions 15 non-markan words. Wessel, "Mark," 792. It should also be noted that about half of the words considered to be unique to the LE "have their word root used elsewhere." Terry, "Style," Section 2: Objections Based on Vocabulary.

the preceding twelve verses also (Mark 15:44—16:8).[95] Lunn also compares the vocabulary in passages of similar length to Mark 16:9–20 and demonstrates that the number of unusual words in the LE is consistent with other passages in Mark; and the LE has even fewer unique terms than some passages.[96] He also offers cogent explanations for the degree of linguistic variation in the LE and persuasive statistical analysis showing that the absence of characteristically Markan terms is not unusual.[97] For example, the Markan term εὐθύς ("immediately") occurs forty-one times in Mark but not at all in 16:9–20. However, the distribution of this term is very uneven, with only ten occurrences in the second half of Mark and lengthy passages without it.[98] The final occurrence is in 15:1, but I believe there is a literary explanation for the decreased use of this term in the second half of Mark and for its absence after the commencement of Jesus' appearance before Pilate. Anthony Thiselton describes what I am referring to: "Mark is dominated by the shadow of the cross. The first eight chapters flash by at a rapid narrative time; the narrative slows after Peter's confession; and the passion narrative occurs as if in slow motion—all to show that the cross is the goal of Christ's life."[99] One of the major purposes of εὐθύς is to add narrative speed, but Mark slows the narrative to focus on the crucifixion and resurrection of Jesus, making the use of εὐθύς counterproductive in the ending.

Lunn also addresses the common argument that Mark consistently uses the connector καί ("and") throughout, but 16:9–20 suddenly switches to the use of δέ ("but, and"). He responds to this by noting the reality of variation within works, highlighting the similar uses of δέ throughout the body of Mark, and pinpointing passages such as Mark 13:14–23 and 14:1–9 where the ratio of καί/δέ is similar to the final twelve verses.[100] R. C. H. Lenski makes a similar observation concerning 13:9—14:1, where several sections of the Olivet discourse lack the use of καί as a

95. Broadus, "Exegetical Studies," 361. Bruce Terry has found about twenty words not used elsewhere in Mark in the twelve verses of Mark 15:40—16:4. Terry, "Style," Section 2: Objections Based on Vocabulary.

96. Lunn, *Original Ending*, 119–27.

97. Lunn, *Original Ending*, 127–57, 161.

98. Lunn, *Original Ending*, 157–58.

99. Thiselton, *The Holy Spirit*, 47.

100. Lunn, *Original Ending*, 159–60. Bruce Terry also refers to Mark 7:15–26 and 13:26–37 as passages containing very limited use of καί. Terry, "Style," Section 4: Miscellaneous Objections. Also see Burgon, *Last Twelve Verses*, 246–47.

connector.[101] As the LE records a series of resurrection appearances as well as another speech of Jesus, source considerations may account for the reduction in the use of the connector, although it is not entirely absent (e.g., 16:15). Consequently, the argument is not decisive against Markan authorship.

One of the most serious arguments against the Markan authorship of the LE is clearly articulated by Daniel Wallace. While proponents of the LE successfully point to similar examples of linguistic variety in other portions of Mark, "the most important internal argument is a *cumulative* argument."[102] He continues, "There is not a *single* passage in Mark 1:1—16:8 comparable to the stylistic, grammatical, and lexical anomalies that we find clustered in vv. 9–20."[103] Lunn produces a chart of passages that challenges this argument; he responds, "The flaw with the usual argument based upon accumulation is that it typically involves comparisons with the second Gospel *in general*, that is, with a range of linguistic features abstracted from the work as a whole. It fails to take into account the character of individual pericopes."[104] Lunn has defused the argument somewhat, although when theological, literary, and text-critical issues are added to the mix, the cumulative argument could potentially retain some force.[105] Nevertheless, the cumulative argument also works in the

---

101. Lenski, *St. Mark's Gospel*, 756.

102. Wallace, "Mark 16:8," 30. Emphasis his. See also Elliott, "Last Twelve Verses," 90.

103. Wallace, "Mark 16:8," 30. Emphasis his.

104. Lunn, *Original Ending*, 161. Emphasis his.

105. Westcott and Hort found many of the arguments based on internal considerations to be "trivial and intangible." Nevertheless, they opine, "There remain a certain number of differences which, taken cumulatively, produce an impression unfavourable to identity of authorship." In other words, the cumulative argument works against the originality of the LE. Westcott and Hort, *The New Testament*, Appendix, 48. John Burgon dismisses the cumulative argument by challenging the validity of both the external and internal evidence. He quotes Samuel Tregelles, who noted "that arguments on *style* are often very fallacious, and that *by themselves* they prove very little. But when there does exist external evidence; and when internal proofs as to style, manner, verbal expression and connection, are in accordance with such independent grounds of forming a judgment; then, these internal considerations possess very great weight." Tregelles, *An Account of the Printed Text*, 256. Cited by Burgon, *Last Twelve Verses*, 225, 249. Cox supports the position of Tregelles in this matter. Cox, *History and Critique*, 159. John Broadus also dismisses the cumulative argument (especially related to vocabulary): "It is very true that the multiplication of littles may amount to much; but not so the multiplication of nothings." Broadus, "Exegetical Studies," 360.

opposite direction when one considers the broad external evidence for the LE along with the literary and theological evidence offered below.

Lunn spends considerable time applying modern linguistic tests to the LE and analyzing the various parts of speech, participant reference, collocations, and syntactic structures. By subjecting the LE to more rigorous testing than has historically been done, he concludes that 16:9–20 "is linguistically within the Markan domain" and that the linguistic features rule out the idea of imitation by a later author.[106]

Literary Considerations

In the next chapter I discuss in some detail the important framing technique (inclusio) that Mark employs, but this section highlights a few other significant literary elements. Mark often organizes his material into triads that progress toward a climax (ABC) and sometimes end with a concluding statement (ABCX). Lunn lists several examples of this Markan structural feature and then demonstrates how the LE follows this pattern in recording three resurrection appearances (16:9–11; 12–13; 14–18) with an increasing number of witnesses (one, two, and eleven) followed by a conclusion (vv. 19–20).[107] The LE naturally lends to division into these units, as noted by others,[108] and Lunn observes how the first three paragraphs "open with a temporal adverb [Μετὰ δὲ, v. 12; Ὕστερον δὲ, v. 14] or adverbial phrase [Ἀναστὰς δὲ πρωῒ, v. 9] accompanied by the discourse particle δέ."[109] In addition, verses 1–8 also follow a similar pattern (v. 1, vv. 2–4, vv. 5–7, v. 8), with each paragraph having a corresponding parallel in verses 9–20. Thus, the pattern is A1 B1 C1 X1 // A2 B2 C2 X2. Verbal parallels confirm that the symmetry is intentional, with a form of the verb ἐγείρω ("to rise") occurring in the third paragraph of each and a participial form of ἐξέρχομαι ("to go out") in the conclusion of each. The conclusion purposely contrasts the women who went out and "said nothing to anyone" (v. 8) with the disciples who went out and "preached everywhere" (v. 20). Lunn concludes that this pattern

106. Lunn, *Original Ending*, 201. His discussion is too involved to repeat here, but see 165–208.

107. Lunn, *Original Ending*, 220–21.

108. Wessel, *Mark*, 789; Edwards, *Mark*, 504.

109. Lunn, *Original Ending*, 221.

highlights "the inadequacy of the state of affairs as left at v. 8."[110] Indeed, the pattern does seem integral to Mark.

Lunn also notes that Mark 16:1 and 9 begin with the mention of the Sabbath and Mary Magdalene,[111] and this structure indicates that the repetition of her name was not due to a blundering later editor[112] but was essential to the symmetry. Furthermore, there is a narrowing pattern centering on Mary Magdalene and then expanding to the disciples, which explains the author's clear identification of her as the one from whom Jesus expelled seven demons. In 15:40–41 Mary Magdalene, Mary the mother of James the lesser and Joses, Salome, and many other women observe Jesus' crucifixion, but only the three named make the trip together to the tomb (16:1). Then Mary Magdalene alone is named as the first witness to the resurrected Christ and the one who announces (ἀπήγγειλεν) it to the mourning disciples (vv. 9–10). This is a clear appeal to an important eyewitness.

Throughout Mark 16:7–20 there is an emphasis on declaration: "go tell his disciples and Peter" (v. 7); "just as he [Jesus] said to you" (v. 7); "and they said nothing to anyone" (v. 8); "she announced it to those with him" (v. 10); "and they went out and announced it to the rest" (v. 13); "preach the gospel" (v. 15); "they will speak in new tongues" (v. 17); "and they went out and preached everywhere" (v. 20); and "the Lord working with them and confirming the word" (v. 20). Mary Magdalene did not remain silent, but became the first proclaimer of "the word" (the message of the resurrection), thus verses 9–20 are necessary to bring to completion the proper and expected response of the universal proclamation by the believers. The emphasis on the spoken word is reminiscent of Acts 2.

The account of the raising of Jairus's daughter (Mark 5:21–24, 35–43) is of particular interest because it may foreshadow the resurrection account of Jesus. It is the only resurrection story in Mark outside of Christ's own resurrection. While some scholars may recognize a parallel between the two stories, most dismiss the LE and, consequently, do not see the extent and significance of the verbal parallels between them. Lunn notes that both resurrections are "preceded by a woman/women experiencing 'fear' (φοβηθεῖσα/ἐφοβοῦντο, 5:33; 16:8) and 'trembling'

110. Lunn, *Original Ending*, 227. See his full discussion, 221–28. See also his discussion on the macrostructure of Mark's Gospel, 228–36.

111. Lunn, *Original Ending*, 226.

112. Cranfield refers to the "clumsiness" of the juncture here. Cranfield, *Mark*, 472.

(τρέμουσα/τρόμος, 5:33; 16:8)."[113] The two accounts share similar words and phrases including ζάω ("to live"; 5:23; 16:11), σῴζω ("to save"; 5:23; 16:16), πιστεύω ("to believe"; 5:36; 16:16), κλαίω ("to weep"; 5:38; 16:10), τοὺς/τοῖς μετ' αὐτου ("those with him"; 5:40; 16:10), ἐγείρω ("to rise"; 5:41; 16:14), ἀνίστημι ("to rise"; 5:42; 16:9) and ἔκστασις ("amazement"; 5:42; 16:8).[114] This appears to be a planned parallel intended to foreshadow Christ's resurrection and present it as a climactic event.

Mark 10:33–34 (ESV) contains Jesus' prediction of his passion and resurrection, and Mark highlights the fulfillment of the predictions by using terminology similar to that in the prediction.

> See, we are going up [ἀναβαίνομεν, 10:33a; cf. 10:32] to Jerusalem, and the Son of Man will be delivered [παραδοθήσεται, 10:33b; cf. 14:41] over to the chief priests and the scribes, and they will condemn [κατακρινοῦσιν, 10:33c; 14:64] him to death and deliver [παραδώσουσιν, 10:33d; cf. 15:1] him over to the Gentiles. And they will mock [ἐμπαίξουσιν, 10:34a; cf. 15:20] him and spit on [ἐμπτύσουσιν, 10:34b; cf. 15:19] him, and flog [μαστιγώσουσιν, 10:34c; cf. Latin loan word φραγελλώσας, 15:15] him and kill [ἀποκτενοῦσιν, 10:34d; cf. ἐσταύρωσαν, "they crucified,"15:25] him. And after three days he will rise [ἀναστήσεται, 10:34; cf. 16:9].[115]

The prediction remains incomplete without the resurrection terminology in 16:9. Again, this appears to be a planned element in the story and not an afterthought. Lunn's observations concerning the resurrection not only provide forceful arguments for the originality of the LE, but they also present the resurrection in a climactic fashion. This element is particularly important to the study of tongues in 16:17, for it accentuates the resurrection context in which Jesus' prediction of tongues occurs.

Acts 10:34–48 and the Gospel of Mark

Several scholars have acknowledged a relationship of some sort between Peter's speech at Cornelius's home in Acts 10:34–43 and the outline of Mark's Gospel,[116] although some are hesitant to attribute Peter's sermon

113. Lunn, *Original Ending*, 234.

114. Lunn, *Original Ending*, 233–34.

115. Lunn, *Original Ending*, 247.

116. Keener, *Acts: Exegetical*, 2:1802. Lane, *Mark*, 10–11. Longenecker summarizes, "In scope and emphasis, the account is much like the portrayal of Jesus's ministry in

primarily to Mark rather than to Luke's own Gospel.[117] Bock notes that both Peter's sermon and Luke's Gospel follow Mark's pattern: "The outline of Peter's summary very much parallels Mark's presentation of Jesus's ministry: John the Baptist, the Galilean ministry, and then Jesus meeting his fate in Jerusalem. Luke's Gospel follows this outline as well."[118] Peterson is less enthusiastic about finding a parallel in Mark's Gospel: "If [Acts] 10:36 specifically recalls the themes of Luke's birth narratives, it may be better to view 10:36–43 as highlighting some of the main emphases of Luke's own Gospel, from the birth of Jesus to the commissioning of the apostolic witnesses in Luke 24."[119] Thus the question to address is this: Is there anything in Acts 10:34–48 to suggest that Peter's speech not only rehearses the basic content of Luke's Gospel but also includes elements particular to Mark, suggesting that Luke used Mark as an outline in his record of Peter's speech? Below I will survey the content of Acts 10:34–48 in order to determine the answer to this question. Following a discussion of how both authors use "the word" as a shorthand term for the gospel of Jesus Christ, I will follow the progress of Peter's speech in light of the pattern of Mark's Gospel.

The Word (Acts 10:36a)

The "word" is a favorite expression of Luke's, as is evident even in his Gospel prologue, where the eyewitnesses are "servants of the word" (1:2). In Acts "the word" becomes a shorthand term for the message of the gospel,[120] and the accusative singular τὸν λόγον refers to the gospel

Mark's Gospel." Longenecker, "Acts," 393. Robertson, *Word Pictures*, 3:144. Bruce enthusiastically embraces the notion of a Markan outline in Acts 10:36ff. and 13:23ff. as well as "fragments of such an outline" in 2:14ff.; 3:13ff.; 4:10ff.; 5:30ff. Bruce, *Acts of the Apostles*, 224–25. Bruce cites the work of C. H. Dodd, who proposed that the various pericopae of Mark's Gospel were organized according to a skeletal frame which approximated the *kerygma* of the early church. Dodd, "The Framework of the Gospel Narrative," 1–11. D. E. Nineham, arguing on the basis of form critical presuppositions, attempts to refute Dodd. Nineham, "The Order of Events," 223–39. Guthrie provides a good analysis of the debate. Guthrie, *New Testament Introduction*, 63–66.

117. Fitzmyer, *Acts*, 464. Tannehill sees Acts 10:36–43 as a summary of Luke's Gospel. Tannehill, *Narrative Unity*, 2:140.

118. Bock, *Acts*, 397.

119. Peterson, *Acts*, 337.

120. Important examples include: Luke 2:41; 4:4, 29, 31; 6:2, 4, 7; 8:4, 14, 21, 25; 10:36, 44; 11:1, 19; 12:24; 13:5, 7, 26, 44, 46, 48, 49; 14:3, 12, 25; 15:7, 35, 36; 16:6, 32; 17:11, 13; 18:5, 11; 19:10, 20; 20:7, 32.

message (often of the resurrection in particular) in every instance of its twenty-seven occurrences. This is certainly the case when Peter introduces the gospel as "the word" in 10:36 and when the Spirit falls "on all those hearing the word" during his sermon (v. 44). The "word" is used less frequently in Luke's Gospel (8x), occurring three times in the parable of the sower and parallel to Mark (8:12, 13, 15 par. Mark 4:15, 16, 20),[121] once in reference to giving "an account" (Luke 16:2), twice in passages unique to Luke (10:39; 11:28), and twice in passages where Luke expands on existing stories (5:1; 8:21). Both 8:21 and 11:28 emphasize hearing and obeying God's word.[122]

Mark uses the expression more often than any of the other Gospels (16x),[123] and this is particularly noteworthy given the relative brevity of Mark. He uses it more often (7x) and more consistently in the parable of the sower than Luke or Matthew,[124] but the associations Mark establishes with "the word" are even more telling. The cleansed leper "began to preach much and spread the word" (1:45). Jesus "was speaking the word to them" (2:2; 4:33). In Mark 8:31 Jesus describes the essential elements of his mission: "And he began to teach them that the Son of Man must suffer many things and be rejected by the elders and the chief priests and the scribes and be killed, and after three days rise again" (ESV). In the following verse Mark summarizes, "And he was speaking the word plainly" (*καὶ παρρησίᾳ τὸν λόγον ἐλάλει*), and this editorial note is conspicuous by its absence in Matthew (16:21–22) and Luke (9:21–23). Not only is the death and resurrection central to what constitutes "the word" here,[125] but this "bold" or "plain" speech sounds very much like the

121. Lunn argues forcefully for Lukan dependence on Mark by comparing the two versions of the parable of the sower. "In certain of the details Luke is seen to be following Mark's version of the parable and its interpretation, not his own parable as he had just recorded it." Lunn, *Original Ending*, 285. See Lunn's detailed linguistic argument for this claim on pages 284–87.

122. Matthew contains ten occurrences of τὸν λόγον, but only three are independent of Mark (Matt 15:12; 19:11, 22), and there is no indication that Matthew uses the term in any technical sense. John's thirteen uses of τὸν λόγον differ from Luke's use of it in Acts in that John often uses possessive pronouns with "the word" (4:41; 5:24, 38; 8:43, 52, 55; 14:23; 15:20; 17:6, 14), emphasizes keeping the word (8:52, 55; 14:23; 15:20; 17:6), and does not focus on spreading the word.

123. Only two of Mark's mentions of "the word" do not refer directly to the message of God or Christ (5:36; 7:29).

124. Luke changes ὁ σπείρων τὸν λόγον σπείρει ("The sower sows the word"; Mark 4:14) to ὁ σπόρος ἐστὶν ὁ λόγος τοῦ θεοῦ ("The seed is the word of God"; Luke 8:11).

125. Also note that "the word" is connected with the resurrection in Mark 9:10.

request of the persecuted believers for the Lord to grant them the ability "to speak your word with all boldness" (μετὰ παρρησίας πάσης λαλεῖν τὸν λόγον σου; Acts 4:29) and much like the answer to their prayer: "And they were speaking the word of God with boldness" (καὶ ἐλάλουν τὸν λόγον τοῦ θεοῦ μετὰ παρρησίας; v. 31). The believers appeal to the Lord for "signs and wonders" in Acts 4:30, and one cannot help but recall how the disciples went out and preached everywhere, the Lord confirming τὸν λόγον ("the word") with "signs" following (Mark 16:20). Considering Luke's own statement that he relied on sources for the composition of his Gospel (Luke 1:1–4), it is reasonable to expect Acts sometimes to reflect Markan language.

In light of the above, some observations are in order. First, Acts and Mark share a common use of τὸν λόγον, which reinforces the notion that a strong affinity exists between these two works. They both use the expression as a means of summarizing the gospel of Christ, including his death and resurrection. Second, although one may see the seeds of this terminology in the Gospel of Luke, Mark's use of τὸν λόγον is much more defined and evident, suggesting that Luke may have been inspired by Markan usage when he wrote Acts. Passages such as Acts 4:29–31 point in this direction. Third, the use of τὸν λόγον in Mark 16:20 is entirely consistent with the rest of Mark. Fourth, given the consistent and common use of τὸν λόγον in Mark, it seems more likely that Luke has taken his ques in framing Peter's speech in Acts 10 from all of Mark than that a later editor borrowed from Acts and appended "the word" at Mark 16:20. One could argue that an editor imitated Mark, but this is neither necessary nor the most natural reading of the text. Finally, the tongues in Acts 10 and Mark 16 share a remarkable contextual similarity in relation to both the gospel as τὸν λόγον and the spread of τὸν λόγον.

The Gospel of Peace (Acts 10:36b)

Peter commences his sermon with a description of "the word" as a "preaching good news of peace [εὐαγγελιζόμενος εἰρήνην] through Jesus Christ: he is Lord of all" (Acts 10:36). This good news message finds its origin in Isa 52.[126] In contrast to the other Gospels, Luke shows

126. "I am present as an hour upon the mountains, as the feet of one who brings the good news of peace (εὐαγγελιζομένου ἀκοὴν εἰρήνης), as the one who brings the good news of good things; for I will make your salvation heard, saying, 'O Zion, your God will reign!'" (Isa 52:6c–7 LXX; cf. Nah 2:1). Translation from Rick Brannan et al., eds.,

a significant interest in this "peace," with the term εἰρήνη occurring twenty-one times in Luke and seven times in Acts but only six times in John, four times in Matthew, and one time in Mark.[127] Thus, the beginning of Peter's summary of the gospel message appears to be thoroughly Lukan. Even the following phrases are reminiscent of Lukan concepts: "through Jesus Christ [Ἰησοῦ Χριστοῦ], this one is Lord of all [πάντων κύριος]" (Acts 10:36b), yet the combination of words and concepts, taken as a whole, reflects the content of Mark 1:1–3 as well as any individual passage in the Gospel of Luke.[128] "The beginning of the gospel of Jesus Christ [τοῦ εὐαγγελίου Ἰησοῦ Χριστοῦ], the Son of God. As it is written in Isaiah the prophet, . . . 'Prepare the way of the Lord [κυρίου].'"[129] Although the phrase "Jesus Christ" occurs fairly commonly in Acts (11x), it never occurs in Luke's Gospel but is very pronounced in Mark 1:1.[130] However, the close combination of "gospel," "Jesus Christ," and "Lord" as found only in Mark's Gospel does not provide the only parallel to Acts 10 (see the discussion of Luke's structure in chapter 1), for the angel of Luke 2:10 preaches good news (εὐαγγελίζομαι) of joy for "all people" (cf. "every nation" in Acts 10:35) because of the birth of "Christ the Lord" (χριστὸς κύριος; Luke 2:11). The heavenly armies join in praise and declare "peace" (εἰρήνη) upon men with whom God is pleased (v. 14).

Determining sources is complex, and caution is in order when making claims about who borrowed from whom, but it appears that Luke both borrowed from Mark and developed his own emphases when structuring Luke-Acts. The sharing of core ideas by Luke, Peter, and Mark suggests that the early church was familiar with and transmitted at least a basic outline of the gospel message from its inception.

The Baptism of John (Acts 10:37–38)

In Acts 10:37 (ESV) Peter continues, "You yourselves know what happened [ῥῆμα] throughout all Judea [ὅλης τῆς Ἰουδαίας], beginning from Galilee after the baptism that John proclaimed [τὸ βάπτισμα ὃ ἐκήρυξεν

The Lexham English Septuagint.

127. For a study of peace, see Mittelstadt, "Spirit and Peace," 7.

128. The titular style of Acts 10:36 also reminds one of Mark 1:1.

129. See Lane's comparison. *Mark*, 11.

130. Lunn also points out the significance of the phrase "Jesus Christ" in the two passages under analysis. Lunn, *Original Ending*, 292–93. Matthew also contains "Jesus Christ" in his introduction (1:1, 18), but he uses it in relation to the genealogy of Christ.

Ἰωάννης].” This sentence is thoroughly Lukan, reflecting his typical language and content in his Gospel, but Mark also records John “preaching a baptism [κηρύσσων βάπτισμα] of repentance for the forgiveness of sins” (1:4; par. Luke 3:3) and mentions that “all the country of Judea [πᾶσα ἡ Ἰουδαία χώρα] was going out to him” (1:5).[131] While the terminology is not an exact fit between Acts 10 and Mark 1, there is enough verbal similarity and developing structural and conceptual similarity with Peter's speech to give one pause. Mark also highlights the beginning of Jesus' proclamation of the gospel in Galilee (1:14) as Peter does. Mark contains several of the essential elements of Acts 10:37.

The likelihood of dependence of Peter's speech on Mark increases in Acts 10:38: “how God anointed Jesus of Nazareth with the Holy Spirit and power, who went around doing good and healing all those who were oppressed by the devil, because God was with him.”[132] There are certainly several typical Lukan characteristics here,[133] but the phrase “Jesus of Nazareth” (Ἰησοῦν τὸν ἀπὸ Ναζαρέθ) has some important similarities to Mark's “Jesus of Nazareth” (Ἰησοῦς ἀπὸ Ναζαρὲτ) in 1:9. First, although Luke identifies Jesus as from Nazareth seven times in Acts, only here does he use the proper noun Ναζαρά instead of his usual Ναζωραῖος.[134] Mark employs the phrase “Jesus of Nazareth” more frequently (5x) than the other Gospels but usually uses the adjective Ναζαρηνός (1:24; 10:47;

131. See the comparison in Lunn, *Original Ending*, 292.

132. Some scholars see in this passage “the primitive Christology of Mk.” Bruce, *Acts of the Apostles*, 226. While I share Bruce's view that this passage reflects the influence of Mark and Peter, the high Christology of Christ's lordship mitigates the argument that statements regarding God's anointing of Jesus or presence with Jesus indicates a lower Christology. See Peterson, *Acts*, 397. What is more likely represented here is a consistent Lukan pneumatology with Jesus as the “Christ” (Acts 10:36) who is “anointed” (v. 38; cf. Luke 4:18) with the Spirit.

133. Luke emphasizes the anointing (cf. Luke 4:18) and “the Holy Spirit and power” (cf. Luke 1:17: 4:14; Acts 1:8). The term “healing” (ἰάομαι) occurs fairly often in Luke's Gospel (11x) but is used only once in Mark (5:29), and Luke refers to the devil as διάβολος five times in his Gospel and twice in Acts and uses the identical phrase “by the devil” in Luke 4:2. Mark, however, never employs this designation. Luke also makes certain that his readers know of the importance of Nazareth (Luke 1:26; 2:4, 39, 51) and that Jesus grew up there (4:16).

134. Ναζωραῖος occurs with “Jesus” in Acts 2:22; 3:6; 4:10; 6:14; 22:8; 26:9. Luke uses it only once in his Gospel (18:37) in a text parallel to Mark 10:47. Although it may be a bit of an overstatement, Bauer recognizes a Lukan pattern when he says, “Where the author of Lk-Ac writes without influence fr. another source he uses Ναζωραῖος.” BDAG, 664. Luke uses the proper noun Ναζαρά five times in his Gospel, but there it is always preceded by the preposition εἰς (1:26; 2:39, 51; 4:16) or ἐκ (2:4). On two occasions Luke uses the adjective Ναζαρηνός (4:34 par. Mark 1:24; Luke 24:19).

14:67; 16:6). Significantly, only in Mark 1:9 does he use the proper noun Ναζαρά. In addition, Luke never uses the preposition ἀπό ("from") in "Jesus of Nazareth" except in Acts 10:38, and neither does Mark except in 1:9.[135] The uniqueness of this combination of Jesus, ἀπό, and the proper noun Ναζαρά in Mark and Acts makes it an attractive possibility that Luke had a copy of Mark 1:9 before him when he recorded Peter's speech.[136]

Both the Second and Third Gospels record the origins of Jesus and his ministry in Nazareth and Galilee, and both contain an account of his reception of the Spirit (Mark 1:10; Luke 3:22), but the close proximity of Γαλιλαίας ("Galilee"; Acts 10:37), βάπτισμα ("baptism"; v. 37), Ναζαρέθ ("Nazareth"; v. 38) and anointing with the πνεύματι ἁγίῳ ("Holy Spirit"; v. 38) in summary form is not found in Luke but in Mark. Luke uses the dative phrase πνεύματι ἁγίῳ as a recollection of the baptismal scene, as he uses it elsewhere only in this context (Luke 3:16; Acts 11:16). Among the Gospels the dative phrase is rare and only occurs in relation to Jesus as the Baptizer (Mark 1:8; Luke 3:16; Matt 3:11; John 1:33). But notice the agreement of terms and concepts at Jesus' baptism with Mark 1:8–9 (ESV). "'I have baptized you with water, but he will baptize you with the Holy Spirit [ἐν πνεύματι ἁγίῳ].' In those days Jesus came from Nazareth [Ἰησοῦς ἀπὸ Ναζαρὲτ] of Galilee [Γαλιλαίας] and was baptized [ἐβαπτίσθη] by John in the Jordan." Mark 1:10 then records the descent of the Spirit as a dove. It is not that these elements are absent from Luke's Gospel (which may have also borrowed from Mark), but that the tight arrangement of them in Acts 10:37–38 more closely approximates Mark 1:8–10 than any single passage in Luke.

The summary of Jesus' empowered ministry of healing the oppressed in Acts 10:38 resembles Luke 5:17, with its emphasis on the power (δύναμις) of the Lord to heal (ἰᾶσθαι). But conceptually speaking, no less could be said of Mark's emphasis on deliverance. Lane well describes Mark 1:16—10:52 as "dominated by narratives describing healing and exorcism, demonstrating the power of God at work in Jesus's

135. Matthew uses it only one (21:11) of the two times he uses "Jesus of Nazareth" (cf. 26:71), and John uses it only one (1:45) of the four times he uses the phrase (18:5, 7; 19:19). See the chart and additional comments on the Petrine-Mark use of "Jesus of Nazareth" in Lunn, *Original Ending*, 292–93, especially 293n47.

136. The question of Luke's possible use of prosopopoeia arises here. However, it is not necessary to conclude that Peter's speech is a Lukan fabrication because Luke used Petrine-related sources to provide terminology for his Petrine speeches.

ministry."[137] Mark describes how Jesus "healed many who were sick with various diseases and cast out many demons" (1:34) and, similarly, how the Twelve went out preaching repentance and "cast out many demons, and anointed many sick people with oil and healed them" (6:12–13).

Jesus' miraculous deeds include "healing all those who were oppressed [καταδυναστευομένους] by the devil" (Acts 10:38).[138] The same verb occurs in Exod 1:13, and its cognate noun occurs in 6:7, where the Septuagint records that God bought the Israelites out "from under the oppression [καταδυναστείας] of the Egyptians." Although this term has no equivalent in either the Gospel of Luke or in Mark, it is significant because it so forcefully connects a Lukan passage containing tongues with the exodus theme so prevalent throughout Mark. As David Pao has shown, Luke shares with Mark the heavy emphasis on the new exodus theme.[139] Furthermore, the association of deliverance, healing, the early chapters of Exodus, and tongues in Mark 16 finds a conceptual parallel in Acts 10.[140]

Witnesses of Jesus' Life and Resurrection (Acts 10:39–43)

Consistent with Luke's emphasis on testimony to the resurrection, the word "witness" and its cognates occur four times in Acts 10:39–43 (vv. 39, 41, 42, 43) along with three mentions of the resurrection (vv. 40, 41) and the claim that the disciples "ate and drank with him after he rose from the dead" (v. 41). This section has all the earmarks of Lukan concepts and phraseology, just as the previous verses do.

None of the above terms are particularly revealing, but the other resurrection term used in Acts 10:40 is noteworthy. Peter says that God "caused him to appear" (ἔδωκεν αὐτὸν ἐμφανῆ γενέσθαι), and the adjective ἐμφανής is rarely used in the Scriptures, never used in a resurrection scene, and used only in Rom 10:20 in the New Testament. One is hard-pressed to find a parallel use of this term even among its cognates. The cognate verb ἐμφανίζω occurs ten times in the New Testament, and five of them are in Acts (23:15, 22; 24:1; 25:2, 15), but only Matthew

137. Lane, *Mark*, 11.

138. The summary of Jesus' work here is also reminiscent of the programmatic passage in Luke 4:18–19 (cf. Isa 61:1–2; 42:7). For a discussion of Luke's employment of Old Testament themes in this passage see Bock, *Luke*, 1:404–11.

139. Pao, *Acts*.

140. Themes from the exodus in Mark 16 are detailed in the next chapter.

27:53 provides a potential candidate for comparison. There Matthew records that after Jesus' resurrection many resurrected saints came out of their tombs and "appeared [ἐνεφανίσθησαν] to many," but the term is not applied directly to Jesus. In Luke, Herod's confusion over the identity of Jesus is due to rumors that John had "risen [ἠγέρθη] from the dead" (9:7), or that "Elijah had appeared [ἐφάνη]," or that an ancient prophet had "risen [ἀνέστη]" (9:8). This passage combines cognates of two of the three resurrection terms used in Acts 10:40–41 with φαίνω, which is a cognate of ἐμφανής. But this passage does not fit Peter's description of Jesus' resurrection. It seems that the only viable candidate for close comparison with Peter's summary is found in Mark 16:9, where Jesus "appeared [ἐφάνη]" to Mary and where both ἐγείρω (v. 6) and ἀνίστημι (v. 19) occur in close proximity to ἐφάνη as they do to ἐμφανῆ in Acts 10:40–41.[141]

Lane concludes his comparison of Peter's sermon and Mark's Gospel at Acts 10:41 and Mark 16:8 based on the assumption that the LE is inauthentic,[142] but the above observations concerning resurrection language point in another direction. First, the line has already been crossed into Mark 16:9 based on the constellation of resurrection terms. Second, Peter's speech continues through Acts 10:43, and there is no reason not to investigate farther and see if the agreement between the texts continues through the rest of the speech and into the response to Peter's sermon.

It must be affirmed that Luke continues to develop his own previously established themes, but the question of reliance upon Mark is not an either/or but a both/and, for the Markan pattern provides the skeletal structure that Luke fleshes out. Mark's emphasis on preaching has been discussed earlier, but Peter's assertion that "he commanded us to preach [κηρύξαι]" (Acts 10:42) is reminiscent of Jesus' command to preach (κηρύξατε) in Mark 16:15. The imperative of κηρύσσω only occurs four times in the New Testament (Matt 10:7, 27; Mark 16:15; 2 Tim 4:2), and only in Mark 16:15 does the plural imperative occur in a resurrection account.[143]

141. Lunn opines, "The formal resemblance (both showing the root φαν-) as well as the semantic relationship between the two is striking." Lunn, *Original Ending*, 294.

142. Lane, *Mark*, 10–11. The trend among scholars has been to limit all comparisons to Peter's speech only (omitting the record of the Spirit's outpouring), and often expunging the final two verses of the speech (10:42–43). This approach also disallows any potential input from the resurrection narrative of the LE.

143. Lunn makes a similar observation. *Original Ending*, 294, 294n50.

There are other conceptual and verbal similarities to Mark's ending, such as the exalted position of Jesus as judge (Acts 10:42) and enthroned Lord (Mark 16:19), the specifying of the name of Jesus (Acts 10:43, 48; Mark 16:17), and the designation of the gospel message as "the word" (Acts 10:44; Mark 16:20). But the phrase that stands out is "everyone who believes [τὸν πιστεύοντα] in him" (Acts 10:43), which, in this passage, turns out to be "all those who heard the word" (v. 44). No such promise of forgiveness or salvation is present in the Lukan or Matthean resurrection accounts, but in Mark "he who believes [ὁ πιστεύσας] and is baptized will be saved" (16:16; cf. 1:4). And Peter's command that the gentiles be baptized (βαπτισθῆναι; Acts 10:48; cf. v. 47) establishes another point of contact between the two passages, with the passive voice emphasizing the role of the baptisands over the baptizers in both places.[144]

A Glossolalic Ending (Acts 10:44–48)

One of the most outstanding features toward the close of each text under discussion is speaking in tongues. Luke's narration of the Spirit's interruption of Peter's speech offers speaking in tongues as clear evidence that gentiles had received the gift of the Spirit, "for they heard them speaking in tongues [λαλούντων γλώσσαις] and magnifying God" (Acts 10:46). Peter's command that they be baptized "in the name of Jesus Christ" (v. 48) closes the christological frame (cf. v. 36), but the baptism only acknowledges the obvious truth that these gentiles have already submitted to the Lord Jesus Christ and are already praising God for his salvific work through Christ.

Mark's glossolalic terminology occurs as a promise of a future sign: "they will speak in new tongues [γλώσσαις λαλήσουσιν καιναῖς]" (16:17), but it is similar to Luke's and shares with Luke a signifying purpose. The outpouring of the Spirit with the sign of tongues in Acts 10 is not part of Peter's speech but interrupts it, yet it still appears that Luke's record of the event gives a real-life illustration of Mark's outline—an outline that includes the LE. Luke's account appears to reflect Mark's resurrection terminology (16:9), the command to preach (v. 15), the promise of salvation to those who believe (v. 16), the mention of baptism (v. 16), and the sign of speaking in tongues (v. 17).[145] If it could definitively be proven that

144. Lunn, *Original Ending*, 294.

145. Throughout the above discussion I have independently examined the potential

Acts 10 depends on the LE, then the issue could be finally resolved in favor of it; however, it is probably best to consider the evidence offered here as a strong pointer in the direction of the originality of the LE.

Resurrection Language in Mark 16

A study of the resurrection language in Mark 16 provides a suitable sampling for testing the credibility of the LE, but more importantly, it highlights the resurrection context in which tongues occur. In this segment I will analyze the various resurrection terms in Mark 16:9–20 and compare them to the terms used in the resurrection narratives of the other Gospels.

Ἀνίστημι ("To Rise")

The first word in the contested ending is ἀναστὰς ("after he had risen"), the aorist participle of the verb ἀνίστημι (v. 9). This word is entirely consistent with Mark's usage, as it occurs sixteen other times in the Gospel, of which nine are in reference to a resurrection.[146] That this term provides a suitable climax to the narrative is evident from its occurrence in Jesus' clear predictions of his own resurrection (8:31; 9:9, with v. 10; 9:31; 10:34).[147] In addition, there is nothing objectionable about how verse 9 begins: Ἀναστὰς δὲ πρωῒ πρώτῃ σαββάτου ἐφάνη πρῶτον Μαρίᾳ τῇ Μαγδαληνῇ ("Now after he had risen early on the first day of the week he appeared first to Mary Magdalene"). Similar constructions with verbs using aorist participles and δέ occur in several other places in Mark, and the above construction is not unlike Ἐκεῖθεν δὲ ἀναστὰς ἀπῆλθεν ("And

parallels between Acts and Mark but have benefited from the parallels highlighted by Lane and Lunn. See Lane, *Mark*, 10–11; Lunn, *Original Ending*, 292–94.

146. Mark 5:42; 8:31; 9:9, 10, 27, 31; 10:34; 12:23, 25. The word is missing in some important MSS of 12:23 but is probably original. See Metzger, *Textual Commentary*, 2nd ed., 110–11.

147. Lunn rightly criticizes Kelhoffer for insisting that the use of ἀναστὰς actually supports the argument against Markan authorship because this occurrence would be the only time the NT uses this verb as an aorist participle in reference to the resurrection. If the exact duplication of every verb form is required to establish authorship, there would be no end to the number of New Testament passages under suspicion. That the identical aorist participle is used five other times in Mark of "rising" in a general sense should be sufficient to establish that the participle is within Mark's range of terms. Lunn, *Original Ending*, 137; Kelhoffer, *Miracle and Mission*, 67–68.

he arose from there and went"; 7:24).[148] Luke uses ἀναστὰς δὲ on several occasions (Luke 4:38; Acts 5:17, 34; 9:39; 11:28; 13:16), while neither Matthew nor John ever use it. Luke 24:12 is of interest because it records a resurrection day event: Ὁ δὲ Πέτρος ἀναστὰς ἔδραμεν ἐπὶ τὸ μνημεῖον ("But Peter arose and ran to the tomb"). The shared use of this construction between Mark and Luke along with the similar constructions occurring in resurrection contexts (Mark 16:9; Luke 24:12) adds impetus to the notion that there is a particularly strong relationship between the two Gospels.

The similarity between Mark 1:35, Καὶ πρωῒ ἔννυχα λίαν ἀναστὰς ("And rising very early in the morning, while it was still dark"; ESV) and 16:9, Ἀναστὰς δὲ πρωῒ πρώτῃ σαββάτου ("Now when he rose early on the first day of the week"; ESV), also supports the argument for the originality of the LE; for not only is there a reoccurrence of the same word, but there is a collocation (what Lunn defines as a "co-occurrence of words")[149] consisting of the adverb πρωῒ and the aorist participle ἀναστὰς. Jesus' rising up early to pray in 1:35 seems to anticipate his later rising from the dead, for, apart from the collocation, there are some significant thematic and verbal echoes in 16:15–20 of 1:35–39. Jesus wants to go "elsewhere" (ἀλλαχοῦ) "to the neighboring towns" in order to "preach" (κηρύξω; 1:38; κηρύσσων; v. 39), for that is why he "came out" (ἐξῆλθον; v. 38). Mark records in 1:34 that Jesus had healed many people and cast out many demons, and in verse 39 he once again summarizes Jesus' ministry as characterized by deliverance. The commission in Mark 16 includes the command to preach (κηρύξατε; v. 15) and the promise that believers will cast out demons (v. 17) and heal the sick (v. 18). The disciples then "went out and preached everywhere" (ἐξελθόντες ἐκήρυξαν πανταχου; v. 20). All three of these words match either linguistically or conceptually with 1:38. This observation not only points to a purposeful structure in Mark that incorporates the LE, but it also connects a nexus of themes to the term ἀναστὰς and to Jesus' resurrection.

148. Lunn, *Original Ending*, 137.

149. Lunn, *Original Ending*, 183.

Φαίνω ("To Appear")

The next term used to designate a resurrection appearance in the LE is ἐφάνη ("he appeared," an aorist passive of φαίνω; 16:9).[150] This word is not unique to the LE, occurring in 14:64, but there it connotes "appear" in the sense of "to seem" rather than to make a physical appearance such as in a resurrection. Kelhoffer suggests, "There is no evidence that this use of ἐφάνη points to the imitation of Markan or other NT material," but in his note he points to "the distinctiveness of the LE's vocabulary."[151] This is a typical example of the quandary faced by some who reject the LE, for consistency with the rest of Mark indicates imitation, and divergence signifies spuriousness; however, the occurrence of ἐφάνη in 16:9 poses no problem for Markan authorship.

The three appearances of Jesus (to Mary, 16:9; the two walking in the country, v. 12; and the eleven, v. 14) are essentially parallel to each other, so that all three terms designating his appearance are third person aorist passive verbs. Thus, ἐφάνη in verse 9 is conceptually related to its cognate ἐφανερώθη ("appeared") in verses 12 and 14, and this is consistent with John's use of ἐφανερώθη in 21:14 (cf. 21:1; Mark 4:22).[152] Luke 9:7–8 offers an interesting parallel to Mark 16 because three terms related to resurrection occur together (ἐγείρω, φαίνω, ἀνίστημι). "Now Herod the tetrarch heard about all the things happening and was perplexed because it was said by some that John had risen from the dead [ἠγέρθη ἐκ νεκρῶν; cf. Mark 16:6], and by some that Elijah appeared [ἐφάνη; cf. Mark 16:9], and by others that a certain prophet of old had risen [ἀνέστη; cf. Mark 16:9]." That ἐφάνη is sandwiched between two resurrection terms in Luke 9 gives it a strong sense of association with resurrection, therefore its occurrence in Mark 16:9 is quite consistent with Luke's use of the term, and the variety of resurrection terms in Mark 16:6–9 is also consistent with Luke and encompasses both sides of the supposed break at verse 8.[153]

150. The term occurs a total of 31 times in the New Testament. Among its cognates only φῶς ("light," 73x) and φανερόω ("to manifest," 49x) occur more often in the New Testament. See Trenchard, *Complete Vocabulary Guide*, 116.

151. Kelhoffer, *Miracle and Mission*, 68, 68n88.

152. Louw and Nida list φαίνομαι and φανερόω within the same semantic domain and adjacent to each other (24.18; 24.19), although they distinguish between φαίνω ("shine") and the deponent verb φαίνομαι ("to appear, to become visible") and see the latter term as the proper root in Mark 16:9. L&N, 1:279. For examples where φαίνω is used to indicate the miraculous appearance of some personage, see Matt 1:20; 2:13, 19; 24:30.

153. Mark 6:14–16 parallels Luke 9:7–8, but Mark does not use the variety of

The above arguments show that there is nothing objectionable about the idea that Mark used φαίνω in the LE. In fact, some diversity in resurrection language is to be expected when one compares Mark's resurrection accounts with those of the other Gospels.

Ἐγείρω ("To Raise")

All four Gospels use ἐγείρω, with the Synoptics each using it in a parallel text along with the phrase οὐκ ἔστιν ὧδε ("he is not here"; Matt 28:6; Mark 16:6; Luke 24:6). Matthew repeats the aorist passive form of ἐγείρω to emphasize the reality of the resurrection (28:7), and John uses a participial form of the verb in a later appearance to the seven disciples at the Sea of Tiberias (21:14). Mark also uses the perfect passive participle of the verb in 16:14. The term ἐγείρω is commonly used of resurrection in the New Testament, so its occurrence in both the LE and in 16:6 is entirely consistent with the New Testament, the Gospel resurrection narratives, and the rest of Mark (5:41; 6:14, 16; 12:26; 14:28).

Ὁράω ("To See"), Θεάομαι ("To Behold, To Look At")

The term ὁράω ("to see") in its various forms is the word most frequently used to describe a resurrection appearance in the resurrection narratives (10x). Matthew (28:7) and Mark (16:7) use the second person plural future ὄψεσθε in a parallel prediction of a Galilean appearance. Matthew repeats the term in the third person (ὄψονται; 28:10) when Jesus himself tells the women that the disciples will see him in Galilee. Matthew frequently gives attention to a meeting in Galilee (26:32; 28:7, 10, 16), Mark has less interest in it, and Luke creates no such anticipation. This comparatively reduced interest in Galilee by Mark may explain why it is not mentioned in the LE, although a Galilean location may be implied at the commissioning of the disciples.[154]

The third occurrence of ὁράω in Matthew (28:17) occurs when the gathered followers of Jesus meet him on the mountain in Galilee, but the

resurrection language Luke does, and Mark makes it clear that Herod opted for the opinion that John the Baptist had been raised. The Matthean parallel is brief (14:1–2).

154. See Lunn's detailed analysis of this issue and his suggestion that Mark telescoped some of the final appearances into a briefer account. Lunn, *Original Ending*, 319–25.

LE does not specify the location of its commission.[155] Typical of Markan style, 16:15 begins with the conjunction "and" (καὶ εἶπεν αὐτοῖς; "and he said to them"), which does not necessarily imply that what precedes occurs simultaneously with what follows.[156] It appears that the LE compresses various appearances of Jesus into brief accounts without clear chronological and geographical markers. As Lunn notes, this is reminiscent of Luke's telescoping in his final chapter (24:36–53).[157] Without a close parallel between Matthew and Mark, there is no reason to expect there to be a particular shared term in the LE's brief account.[158]

Despite the absence of ὁράω ("to see") in the disputed ending, it is not devoid of visual terminology, for Jesus chides the eleven because "they did not believe those who had seen [θεασαμένοις] him after he had risen" (v. 14). And where Mary testifies, "I have seen the Lord [ἑώρακα τὸν κύριον]" in John 20:18, Mark narrates that Jesus "was seen by her [ἐθεάθη ὑπ' αὐτῆς]" (v. 11). But if an insufficient number of particular terms in a passage be deemed a suitable test for authenticity, then Matthew's resurrection account must be suspect, for the word ἀνίστημι occurs in resurrection contexts in the body of all four Gospels (e.g., Matt 12:41; Mark 8:31; Luke 16:31; John 6:39) and in the resurrection accounts in Mark 16:9, Luke 24:7, 46, and John 20:9, yet this term is completely absent from Matt 28.

About eight different expressions are used to describe the resurrection in Mark 16. Of the six occurring in the LE, only φαίνω ("to appear") and θεάομαι ("to look at"; v. 11) are unique to Mark among the resurrection accounts. Wilhelm Michaelis confidently asserts that the use of θεάομαι in verses 11 and 14 "helps to show that this is not the true ending

155. Wenham suggests that the commission recorded in Mark 16:15–18 is probably not a parallel version of Matthew 28:16–20, as the two scenes have very few verbal similarities and Mark's account seems more suited to a Jerusalem setting nearer to the time of Pentecost. Wenham, *Easter Enigma*, 120.

156. Wenham, *Easter Enigma*, 120.

157. Lunn, *Original Ending*, 322–25.

158. Luke twice uses the imperative ἴδετε ("look"; v. 39) when Jesus encourages the disciples to see him and touch him at his first resurrection appearance to the gathered disciples. John uses ὁράω ("to see") of various resurrection appearances (20:18, 20, 25, 29). Wenham suggests that because Luke (24:39) and John (20:20) are concerned with demonstrating the materiality of Jesus in his resurrection, they use vivid terminology for Jesus' appearances. Wenham, *Easter Enigma*, 106. In John, Jesus responds to Thomas's "unless I see" with visual and physical proof, thus John employs an aorist participle of ὁράω (ἰδόντες; v. 29). The LE only briefly summarizes the appearance to the eleven on Easter (16:14) and does not record the episode with Thomas at all.

to Mk."[159] This word frequently occurs on the lists of terms found in the LE but absent in the rest of Mark that supposedly provide evidence that the LE is spurious. Comparisons with the other resurrection accounts also demonstrate that the LE has a perfectly acceptable number of unique terms describing a resurrection appearance. While the LE contains φαίνω and θεάομαι, only Matthew says that "Jesus came [προσελθὼν] and spoke to them" (28:18) and that "Jesus met [ὑπήντησεν] them" (v. 9). The latter term occurs only one other time in Matthew (8:28) and only a total of ten times in the New Testament. Only Luke says that "Jesus himself came near and walked along with them" (αὐτὸς Ἰησοῦς ἐγγίσας συνεπορεύετο αὐτοῖς; 24:15).[160] Only Luke summarizes the complex of Jesus' resurrection and ascension as an entering into his glory (εἰσελθεῖν εἰς τὴν δόξαν αὐτοῦ; v. 26). Only Luke says of the two travelers that "they recognized [ἐπέγνωσαν] him" (v. 31) and that he "vanished" (ἄφαντος ἐγένετο; v. 31). Not only is ἄφαντος unique among the resurrection accounts, but it is also a *hapax legomenon* in the New Testament and the Septuagint. John prefers to present Jesus as standing among his observers (20:14, 19, 26; 21:4; cf. Luke 24:36), and only he says, "Jesus came [ἔρχεται] . . . and stood in the midst" (20:26).

It is debatable whether θεάομαι (Mark 16:11, 14; 22x in the NT) has a distinct definition from the more common term θεωρέω (58x). Louw and Nida list them together with a single definition: "to observe something with continuity and attention, often with the implication that what is observed is something unusual."[161] But Michaelis holds that θεάομαι "has its own nuance" and "is colourless only when there is alternation between θεάομαι (cf. Ac. 22:9) and θεωρέω (Ac. 9:7)."[162] Mark uses θεωρέω seven times prior to the LE (3:11; 5:15, 38; 12:41; 15:40, 47; 16:4), so one might expect its use in the LE rather than θεάομαι. But Michaelis notes that Luke's use of θεάομαι in 23:55 "as compared with θεωρέω in Mt. 28:1 par. Mk. 15:47 lays stress on the element of love and intimacy"[163] of the women who "saw the tomb and how his body was laid" (Luke 23:55). Of

159. Michaelis, "ὁράω, εἶδον, κτλ.," 345.

160. Although ἐγγίζω is a common term in Luke's Gospel (18x), συμπορεύομαι is a rare term in the NT (4x). Luke uses it three times (7:11; 14:25), so his use of it in 24:15 is entirely consistent with the rest of his Gospel. Nonetheless, it shows that other Gospel writers also use rare terms that do not have a parallel in the other resurrection accounts.

161. L&N, 1:279.

162. Michaelis, "ὁράω, εἶδον, κτλ.," 344.

163. Michaelis, "ὁράω, εἶδον, κτλ.," 345.

Mark's seven uses of θεωρέω, only two of them have Jesus as the object. In 3:11 the demons see Jesus (but "love and intimacy" does not seem to properly describe their response), and in 15:40 the women watch the events of the crucifixion from afar. While it is not necessary to explain any author's use of a few different words, it seems reasonable to suggest that Mark reserved the word θεάομαι to describe Jesus' personal and climactic resurrection appearances to Mary (16:11) and to the eleven (v. 14).[164] As Luke uses θεάομαι to describe the disciples' observance of the ascension (Acts 1:11), and John uses this term to emphasize the eyewitness testimony to the resurrection (1 John 1:1), the use of θεάομαι in the LE is fitting.

Φανερόω ("To Manifest"), Ζάω ("To Live")

Two other resurrection words create no problem for the LE because they both occur earlier in Mark as well as in the resurrection accounts of other Gospels. The first, φανερόω ("to manifest"), occurs in Mark 4:22 as well as in 16:12, 14 and in John 21:1 (2x), 14. The second, ζάω ("to live"), occurs in Mark 5:23 and 12:27 as well as in Mark 16:11 and Luke 24:5, 23.

All of this leads to the conclusion that each of the Gospels presents us with a variety of terms describing the resurrection and each one contributes some vocabulary that is peculiar among the resurrection accounts and sometimes peculiar within its own narrative. That the LE has two resurrection terms that are distinctive to it but shares several with other Gospels is what one would expect of a credible resurrection narrative. In terms of theology, Mark 16:17 shares with Acts the mention of tongues in close proximity to multiple references to Christ's resurrection.

Ascension and Exaltation Language in Mark 16

The disputed ending of Mark clearly records the resurrection of Jesus but does not stop there; it also emphasizes the ascension, the session, and the lordship of Jesus. Below I examine Mark 16:19–20 to see if it is consistent with the rest of Mark and with teaching on Christ's ascension and session in other New Testament texts. This section examines the Christology of

164. Lunn argues in a similar fashion. See his additional points on this matter. *Original Ending*, 145.

the LE to see if it provides a similar context for tongues to what is found in Luke-Acts.

Μὲν Οὖν ("So Then")

Mark clearly signifies a transition from Jesus' commissioning words to the disciples (16:15–18) to his concluding remarks with the phrase Ὁ μὲν οὖν κύριος Ἰησοῦς ("So then the Lord Jesus"; v. 19).[165] The expression μὲν οὖν seldom occurs in the New Testament except for in Acts, where it appears twenty-seven times and seems to be a favorite Lukan expression.[166] Bruce comments on οἱ μὲν οὖν in Acts 1:6 and notes that the phrase is "a favourite formula in Ac. for opening a new section of the narrative, connecting it with the preceding section." [167]

The most striking feature of this phrase is its use as a division marker or summary specifically in passages that highlight the spread of the gospel, as in Mark 16:19–20 and in Luke-Acts. Although the ascension and session are squeezed in between Mark's opening phrase and his record of the disciples going out and preaching the word (τὸν λόγον) everywhere with the accompanying signs, the thematic similarity to Luke-Acts is noteworthy. "So with many [Πολλὰ μὲν οὖν] other exhortations he preached good news to the people" (Luke 3:18 ESV). "Now those [Οἱ μὲν οὖν] who were scattered went about preaching the word [εὐαγγελιζόμενοι τὸν λόγον]" (Acts 8:4 ESV). "Now when [Οἱ μὲν οὖν] they had testified and spoken the word of the Lord [τὸν λόγον τοῦ κυρίου], they returned to Jerusalem, preaching the gospel to many villages of the Samaritans" (Acts 8:25 ESV; cf. 2:41; 11:19; 13:4; 14:3; 17:12, 17).[168] The use of this transition phrase says little in and of itself regarding authorship of Mark, but the associations it shares with Luke-Acts places it squarely in a typical

165. The phrase μὲν οὖν rarely occurs in the canonical Septuagint (Gen 43:4; Exod 4:23; 9:2; Esth 8:14; Dan 3:23) and, apart from one occurrence in Wisd. of Sol. 13:16, is only used in the remainder of the Septuagint in 2, 3, and 4 Maccabees. See 2 Macc 3:22; 4:20; 7:42; 9:28; 10:22; 11:18, 19; 3 Macc 2:1, 31; 3:6, 11; 4:15; 5:9; 6:29; 4 Macc 1:7, 10, 22; 3:9.

166. Some passages provide a close linguistic and stylistic parallel where μὲν οὖν is preceded by the nominative singular ὁ and is followed by the subject and where the phrase serves as a transition marker (2 Macc 9:28; 3 Macc 2:1; Acts 12:5; 23:22; cf. 25:4; 28:5).

167. Bruce, *Acts of the Apostles*, 70. John's use of μὲν οὖν in 20:30 provides another clear NT example of a major division marker in a narrative.

168. Note particularly the association with signs and wonders in Acts 14:3.

New Testament sphere of functioning. It also suggests the possibility of a relationship between Mark and Luke.

This phrase is important in this study because it serves as the hinge highlighting the Lordship of Jesus and connecting his identity with the previous commission to preach and the subsequent obedience of the disciples in preaching. The promised charismatic signs and the experienced signs are joined by Ὁ μὲν οὖν κύριος Ἰησοῦς ("So then the Lord Jesus"; Mark 16:19), as will be demonstrated in the next chapter. Also, such a major transition recalls the transition in 16:9 and creates a tie between "Now after he had risen" (Ἀναστὰς δὲ) and the parallel phrases "he was taken up into heaven" (ἀνελήμφθη εἰς τὸν οὐρανὸν; v. 19) and "he sat at the right hand of God" (ἐκάθισεν ἐκ δεξιῶν τοῦ θεοῦ; v.19). Thus, the resurrection is directly connected to the ascension and session, and the absence of clear chronological markers at the commencement and completion of Jesus' speech (vv. 15, 19 in contrast to vv. 1, 9, 14) forms a theological bridge between them. The use of "after" (μετὰ) in verse 19 provides sequence but is ambiguous regarding time lapse, as it is not precision in chronology that is important in v. 19, but the linking of the resurrection appearances and commission with the ascension and exaltation of Christ. This is theologically consistent with Acts 2 and 10.

Κύριος Ἰησοῦς ("Lord Jesus")

It is precisely at this important hinge that the author first designates the Christ as "the Lord Jesus" (Ὁ μὲν οὖν κύριος Ἰησοῦς).[169] Although a textual issue makes inclusion of Ἰησοῦς uncertain, it is likely that the Nestle-Aland reading (followed here) has it right. It appears that Luke and Mark have followed a similar line of thought in including the "Lord Jesus" in their resurrection narratives (cf. Luke 24:3). Luke-Acts accounts for 211 of the 717 occurrences of κύριος in the New Testament, but early in Luke's Gospel the Lord in view is usually the Lord God (1:6, 11, 16, 28, 38, 45, 68, et al.). However, on a couple of occasions Luke uses κύριος to hint

169. There is a textual problem with Ἰησοῦς in this phrase. Metzger's committee rated the variant used in the NA and UBS text as "C" for very doubtful. The MS evidence is quite evenly divided between the variants κύριος Ἰησοῦς and κύριος. Both show a broad range of geographical diversity. The latter has the Byzantine MS Alexandrinus in its favor while the former reading has the original hand of Codex Ephraemi Rescriptus in its favor. Perhaps the support of some of the early versions tips the scales slightly in favor of the NA/UBS reading. The following discussion also lends evidence in favor of inclusion. See Metzger, *Textual Commentary*, (1971), 127.

to the reader that Jesus is also the Lord (1:43, 76) before he completely expels every shadow of doubt with the angelic announcement, "For a Savior has been born to you today in the city of David; he is Christ the Lord (χριστὸς κύριος)" (2:11). Although this truth remains hidden to the participants in Luke's story, this announcement provides the reader with the necessary lens through which to read the developing narrative and prepares him or her for Peter's climactic announcement in the Pentecostal text: "God has made this Jesus whom you crucified both Lord and Christ" (2:36).

After the birth narratives, when the characters in Luke's story call Jesus "Lord" it is generally in a lesser sense than the divine Lord. However, Jesus himself often hints at his own identity as Lord,[170] and the Lukan narrator prefers to call him Lord.[171] A turning point comes in the narrative when the women find the tomb empty and Luke narrates, "They did not find the body of the Lord Jesus [τοῦ κυρίου Ἰησοῦ]" (24:3). Luke has reserved the phrase "Lord Jesus" in order to highlight the close connection between Jesus' resurrection and the recognition of him as Lord. In Acts 1:21 Peter refers to him as "the Lord Jesus," and from there forward this phrase becomes a common designation for Jesus in Acts.[172]

Mark uses κύριος ("Lord") eighteen times, and, as in Luke, it is used as a general term of respect (7:28), as a designation for the Lord God (11:9; 12:9, 11, 29, 30; 13:20), and by Jesus himself to point to his own identity (2:28; 11:3; 12:36–37; 13:35). In regard to the latter, two passages are particularly instructive. First, in 2:28 Jesus affirms, "So the Son of Man is Lord even of the Sabbath" (ὥστε κύριός ἐστιν ὁ υἱὸς τοῦ ἀνθρώπου καὶ τοῦ σαββάτου). This text associates Jesus with David (2:25) and also directly connects Jesus' lordship with "the Son of Man." As James Edwards notes, κύριός takes the emphatic position at the beginning of the sentence and accentuates the identity of the Son of Man as the Lord of the Sabbath.[173] Thus, although "Son of Man" often connotes the human side of Jesus and provides a non-controversial self-designation for Jesus, it is never entirely devoid of divine connotations in the Gospels.[174] Second,

170. See Jesus' use of "Lord" in 6:5; 12:36–37, 42–43, 45–47; 13:8, 25; 19:16, 18, 20, 25, 31; 20:42, 44.

171. See 7:13, 19; 10:1, 39, 41; 11:39; 12:42; 13:15; 17:5–6; 18:6; 19:8; 22:61.

172. The phrase is used only the one time in Luke (24:3), but it is used 15x in Acts: 1:21; 4:33; 7:59; 8:16; 11:17, 20; 15:11; 16:31; 19:5, 13, 17; 20:24, 35; 21:13; 28:31.

173. Edwards, *Mark*, 97.

174. *Contra* Hurtado, *Lord Jesus Christ*, 305. "The Son of Man" with the article

Mark links Jesus with David, the Christ, and the Lord via Jesus' quotation of Ps 110:1 in 12:35–37 (cf. Matt 12:42–44; Luke 20:41–44; Acts 2:34).

As in the Gospel of Luke, Mark depicts the struggle of the characters in coming to grips with who Jesus is, but, unlike Luke, the narrator (as opposed to the characters' "Sir") never calls Jesus "Lord" in the body of his Gospel. The only time the narrator calls Jesus "Lord" is in his introductory quotation of Isa 40:3, "Prepare the way of the Lord," (Mark 1:3) and in 16:19–20. So, Mark announces at the outset that the Lord for whom John prepares the way is none other than "Jesus Christ, the Son of God" (1:1; cf. Luke 2:11).[175] Both Mark and Luke announce Christ's divine lordship early in their Gospels, reserve the phrase "Lord Jesus" for their concluding and climactic resurrection narratives, and frame their Gospels with reference to the divine Lord. Because Mark does not use the word "Lord" nearly as often as Luke does (18x vs. 104x) and only allows it to fall from the lips of the narrator in 1:3 and 16:19–20, the effect of "Lord Jesus"[176] in verse 19 and "Lord" in verse 20 is far from an argument against Markan authorship, but rather, is strong evidence of a planned structure somewhat similar to Luke's.[177] If anything, the Markan

never occurs outside the Gospels (except for Acts 7:56) and is never used after the resurrection of Christ except for when the angel quotes Jesus' own prediction of his resurrection in Luke 24:7. "Lord" is the preferred designation for Jesus after the resurrection and only Jesus had used "The Son of Man" for himself in the first place. The exception in Acts 7:56 is significant because Stephen purposely draws attention to the fulfillment of Jesus' prediction in Mark 14:62 and Luke 22:69 that the Son of Man will sit at God's right hand (i.e., as Judge) and come on the clouds of heaven. Therefore Acts 7:56 identifies Jesus as the Judge who has been vindicated and does indeed reign at God's right hand. Stephen's allusion ties together the human suffering of Christ before his judges and his vindication as the enthroned Judge, showing again that the Son of Man terminology is never far removed from royal implications. See Bock, *Acts*, 311–13.

175. "Son of God" is absent from a couple important MSS, but its inclusion in the NA28 is justified because the phrase is consistent with Mark's theology and because textual support for it is reasonably strong and diverse. See Edwards, *Mark*, 25n8; Metzger, *Textual Commentary* (1971), 73. Rikki Watts argues that Mark's citation of Isa. 40:3 is part of Mark's heading and is programmatic for the Gospel. He further asserts that "as it is written" is "epexegetical of v. 1: the 'gospel' of Jesus Christ is the gospel about which Isaiah wrote." Watts, *Isaiah's New Exodus*, 56. His observations show the close tie between the Christ of verse 1 and the Lord of verse 3.

176. The inclusion of the phrase "Lord Jesus" in Mark 16:19 has the weighty support of the following MSS: p75 ℵ A B C L W Δ Θ Ψ 070 f1 f13 28 33 157 180 205 565 597 700 892 1006 1010 1243 1292 1342 1424 1505 *Byz* [E F G H]. UBS5 apparatus. Also see Metzger, *Textual Commentary* (1971), 183.

177. Mark and Luke are not alone in using "Lord" in a climactic fashion, for during Jesus' resurrection appearance to Thomas the former doubter makes this majestic declaration, "My Lord and my God!" (20:28). John Broadus also comments on the

frame is even more pronounced in Mark than in Luke.[178] It is "the Lord Jesus" who commissions the disciples and prophesies their charismatic ministries, particularly, that they will speak in new tongues (v. 17).

Ἀνελήμφθη ("He Was Taken Up")

The summary of the Lord Jesus' ascension and session is brief in Mark 16:19, but it is quite consistent with the general teaching of the New Testament. "So then the Lord Jesus, after he had spoken to them, was taken up [ἀνελήμφθη] into heaven and sat at the right hand of God." The uncompounded λαμβάνω ("to take") occurs twenty times in Mark; other compounds appear in various passages (e.g., 4:36; 7:33; 8:23; 14:8, 33, 48) but the compound verb ἀναλαμβάνω occurs only in 16:19.[179] However, Luke uses the same aorist passive form of the verb in reference to ascension in Acts 1:2, 22 (as does Paul in 1 Tim 3:16). It is also used of Enoch's ascension in Sir 49:14 and in reference to Elijah in 1 Macc 2:58.

The latter reference along with the repetition of ἀνελήμφθη in the Septuagint of 2 Kings 2:9, 10, 11 may provide the primary backdrop for the term in Mark 16:19. Lunn highlights the Elijah motif in Mark (6:15; 8:28; 9:4, 5, 11, 12, 13; 15:35, 36) and then compares the terminology in 16:19 with 2 Kings 2:11.

> When Elijah was taken up, witnessed by Elisha his successor, the LXX text says "As they were walking along talking [ἐλάλουν] . . . Elijah was taken up [ἀνελήμφθη] in a whirlwind as into heaven [εἰς τὸν οὐρανόν]" (2 Kgs 2:11). This exhibits the same words as used in Mark's ending with reference to Jesus's ascension (16:19), "the Lord Jesus, after he had spoken [λαλῆσαι] to them, was taken up [ἀνελήμφθη] into heaven [εἰς τὸν οὐρανόν]." The sequence ἐλάλουν . . . ἀνελήμφθη . . . εἰς τὸν οὐρανόν in 2 Kings is matched by λαλῆσαι . . . ἀνελήμφθη εἰς τὸν οὐρανὸν in Mark. Since each contains three related elements occurring in the same order, with the verb in identical form, the similarity is not likely to be purely coincidental.[180]

---

appropriateness of the designation "Lord" after the resurrection in Mark 16. Broadus, "Exegetical Studies," 359.

178. If there is a borrowing of this structure, it is more likely that Luke, who already claimed to use sources, would borrow from the strong christological frame in Mark.

179. Lunn, *Original Ending*, 156.

180. Lunn, *Original Ending*, 264.

This suggests that 16:19 is thematically consistent with the rest of Mark and draws its vocabulary primarily from the Septuagint. The author's careful choice of ἀνελήμφθη does not create a problem for the LE but adds to the likelihood of its authenticity. In addition, there is no one dominant term for "ascension" in the New Testament, and even Luke uses a variety of terms for it (ἀνεφέρετο, 24:51; ἀνελήμφθη, Acts 1:2, 22; ἀνέβη, Acts 2:34). And as Mark uses a term particular to the LE in his Gospel, so Luke's use of ἀνεφέρετο in 24:51 is particular to his resurrection narrative in Luke-Acts.[181]

Ἐκάθισεν ἐκ Δεξιῶν τοῦ Θεοῦ ("He Sat at the Right Hand of God")

The statement that Jesus "sat at the right hand of God" (ἐκάθισεν ἐκ δεξιῶν τοῦ θεοῦ; Mark 16:19) is not at all surprising in light of Jesus' prophecy that "you will see the Son of Man sitting at the right hand of power [ἐκ δεξιῶν καθήμενον τῆς δυνάμεως] and coming with the clouds of heaven" (14:62; cf. Matt 26:64; Luke 22:69). The narrator draws on Ps 110:1: "The Lord says to my Lord, 'Sit at my right hand until I make your enemies a footstool for your feet.'" Jesus has already quoted this passage in Mark 12:36 (par. Matt 22:44; Luke 20:42), and several other New Testament authors either directly associate this text with Christ's session (Acts 2:33–35; Heb 1:13; 10:12–13) or at least allude to his reign at God's "right hand" (Acts 5:31; 7:55–56; Rom 8:34; Eph 1:20; Col 3:1; Heb 1:3; 8:1; 12:2; 1 Pet 3:21–22). The closest verbal parallel to ἐκάθισεν ἐκ δεξιῶν τοῦ θεοῦ is found in Heb 10:12 (ἐκάθισεν ἐν δεξιᾷ τοῦ θεοῦ), but other texts picture the complex of resurrection, ascension, and session together in a manner similar to that found in Mark 16:19 (Acts 2:32–35; 5:30–31; Rom 8:34; Eph 1:20; 1 Pet 3:21–22).[182]

One other passage in Mark deserves attention at this point. Jesus' Palm Sunday entrance into Jerusalem provides a proleptic glimpse of Jesus sitting on the throne (11:1–12). Jesus instructs his disciples to obtain a tied colt (cf. Gen 49:11) upon which no one has ever "sat" (ἐκάθισεν; Mark 11:2).[183] In the event that the disciples are questioned, they are to say specifically that "the Lord [ὁ κύριος] needs him" (v. 3)—a barely veiled

181. Lunn, *Original Ending*, 156.

182. Rom 8:34, Eph 1:20, and Acts 5:30–31 mention resurrection and session but not ascension. Ascension is often assumed when the resurrection is mentioned.

183. For a discussion on the messianic significance of this event, see Lane, *Mark*, 395–96.

allusion to Jesus' lordship from his own lips. Jesus then "sat" (ἐκάθισεν; v. 7) on the colt and received the adulation of the crowds in the words of the psalmist: "Hosanna! Blessed is the one who comes in the name of the Lord!" (v. 9; Ps 118:25–26). The crowds continued, "Blessed is the coming kingdom of our father David! Hosanna in the highest!" (Mark 11:10). Although the crowds may not have understood the full significance of this picture in light of Zech 9:9, Mark certainly expects his readers to see the messianic implications. The mention of "kingdom" and "David" along with "Lord" and the picture of Jesus sitting on the colt prepares the reader for Christ's exaltation and even causes the reader to expect it. Mark 16:19 satisfies this expectation.

In relation to other New Testament books, Acts 2 presents the closest conceptual parallel with Christ's session in the LE, but verbal parallels are necessarily limited by the fact that Luke records an extended Petrine inaugural sermon while the narrator in Mark 16 concludes his Gospel in a summary fashion. More parallels will be discussed below, but, for now, notice that both authors focus on Christ's lordship (16:19, 20; Acts 2:34, 36); both incorporate Ps 110:1 and the right hand of God (16:19; Acts 2:33–35); both speak of the ascension "into heaven" (16:19; Acts 2:34; cf. 1:2, 9–11, 22); both specify that the Lord is Jesus (16:19; Acts 2:36); both include glossolalia in relation to Christ's exaltation (16:17; Acts 2:4–13); and both view charismatic evangelism as the result of Christ's exaltation (16:20; Acts 2:32–33, 40–43). These two authors were certainly cut from the same theological cloth. The obvious implication for this study is that speaking in tongues seems to occur in response to Christ's lordship in Mark 16 as well as in Acts.

Summary

Given the opposition to the originality of the LE, it is surprising to find that the external evidence for the LE is well represented among the versions, numerically overwhelming among the Greek manuscripts, strongly supported among the lectionaries, and much more ancient than the variants among the patristic witnesses—to the point of encroaching on the first century. There are also surprises in regard to the internal evidence. Upon closer examination, many of the standard arguments against the LE lack potency. Arguments based on disjuncture at Mark 16:8–9 seem exaggerated, supposed excessive linguistic anomalies have been overstated, consistent literary features have gone almost unnoticed, and the possible dependence of Peter's sermon in Acts 10 on the LE has not received due consideration. In addition, the language and concepts related to the resurrection, ascension, session, and royal identity of Christ in the LE are consistent with Mark's Christology and provide a suitable, structurally consistent closing to his Gospel. This ending includes some of the same christological emphases that occur in Luke's theology and in charismatic passages containing Petrine speeches (Acts 2, 10). The Christology of the Markan ending will receive more treatment in relation to speaking in tongues in the next chapter.

Some major questions regarding theological and literary elements in the LE remain. For example, how does one account for the strange reference to taking up serpents in Mark 16:18? The next chapter will treat such issues in depth, and the exegesis of the LE will shed light on both the sources of the LE and Mark's charismatic theology.

7

The Charismatic Theology of St. Mark

TODAY IT IS WIDELY acknowledged that the introduction of an ancient literary work was of utmost importance for informing the reader of the content of the work.[1] Opinions as to the extent of Mark's prologue vary, but one must certainly consider 1:1–15 as having great significance for what follows.[2] It is reasonable to expect an authentic conclusion of Mark to reflect the themes presented in the introduction. John Burgon argued for such a literary frame around Mark long before the more recent studies on literary criticism. Burgon highlighted the repetition of baptism (1:4, 5, 8, 9; 16:16), preaching (1:7; 16:20), preaching the gospel (1:14; 16:15), and belief in the gospel (1:15; 16:11, 13, 14, 17) at the end of Mark.[3] He also observed a strong connection between 1:9–20 and 16:9–20, listing the parallel elements of Jesus' manifestation or appearance (1:9–11; 16:9–11, 12–14), Satan's defeat (1:12, 13; 16:17, 18), "the Pentecostal gift" (1:8; 16:17), the preaching of the gospel with the admonition to believe (1:14, 15; 16:15, 16), emphasis on the kingdom (1:15; 16:19), and a calling to ministry (1:16–20; 16:20).[4] While one may differ with Burgon on

1. Watts, *Isaiah's New Exodus*, 54.

2. The change in location from verse 13 to verse 14 suggests a division, but the content of verses 14–15 seems theologically tied both to what precedes and what follows. Along with Watts, I see verses 14–15 as transitional. Watts, *Isaiah's New Exodus*, 91–95. My discussion assumes that the traditional beginning of Mark has not been lost. For an opposing perspective, see Croy, *Mutilation*, 113–36.

3. Burgon, *Last Twelve Verses*, 262.

4. Burgon, *Last Twelve Verses*, 263–64. The "Pentecostal gift" Burgon mentions is in verse 8 and not quite in the range of verses 9–20. He opines that that the parallels are too profound to have been done by an imitator. Burgon, *Last Twelve Verses*, 263, 265.

some of his perceived parallels, his overall argument is sound and his point well taken. Nicholas Lunn also argues along similar lines, citing some of the same elements as Burgon as well as providing additional evidence for an inclusio.[5]

In the following discussion, I will highlight several themes found in the introduction (especially baptism in the Spirit), determine whether they are consistent with the Longer Ending (LE), and demonstrate how they might shed light on the reference to tongues in Mark 16:17. The following topics are of particular interest: the proclamation of the gospel, faith, and the Holy Spirit. After examining key Markan themes in relation to the LE, the specific signs of Mark 16 and the christological comments in verses 19–20 receive an in-depth look. The discussion pays particular attention to possible parallels between the LE and the story of Moses' calling in Exodus. This discussion provides the biblical and theological context for Mark's doctrine of signs and the claim that believers will speak in "new tongues" (Mark 16:17). The discussion closes with a summary of Mark's teaching on tongues and an overview of the implications of this study for the status of the LE and the relationship of tongues in Mark to those in Luke.[6]

The Gospel Proclamation

One can hardly miss the prominence Mark gives to the gospel (τοῦ εὐαγγελίου) in his opening line: "The beginning of the gospel of Jesus Christ, the Son of God" (Ἀρχὴ τοῦ εὐαγγελίου Ἰησοῦ Χριστοῦ υἱοῦ θεοῦ). The noun εὐαγγέλιον ("gospel") only occurs in Acts 15:7 and 20:24 in Luke's writings, but the cognate verb εὐαγγελίζω occurs quite frequently (10x in Luke's Gospel and 15x in Acts). John does not use any form of "gospel" at all; Matthew uses it five times and Mark seven times (1:1, 14, 15; 8:35; 10:29; 13:10; 14:9) plus one time in the controverted ending (16:15). But the statistics are not nearly as significant as the location of these references. In Mark the first three appear toward the beginning, and the one in 8:35 follows shortly after Peter's confession (8:29). In 10:29 the disciples are assured of rewards for sacrificing for Jesus and the gospel. Jesus' anticipation of the coming mission (13:10) holds a prominent

5. Lunn, *Original Ending*, 210–14.

6. For ease in the discussion, I will at times simply refer to the content of the LE as part of Mark's Gospel.

position at the center of verses 5–23 in the Olivet discourse: "And it is necessary for this gospel to be preached [κηρυχθῆναι τὸ εὐαγγέλιον] first to all the nations." According to Lunn, this segment "has a definite inverted parallel structure" in which verses 5–6 correspond to verses 21–23 in warning about deceivers, verses 7–8 correspond to verses 14–20 in cataloging various troubles, and verse 9 corresponds with verses 11–13 in highlighting persecution and testimony.[7]

Regarding the woman who anointed him at Bethany, Jesus promises that "wherever the gospel is preached [κηρυχθῇ τὸ εὐαγγέλιον] in the whole world, also what she has done will be spoken of in memory of her" (14:9). The placement of this statement at the end of this story suggests that Mark not only includes this event to foreshadow Jesus' betrayal and death, but to highlight the universal proclamation of the gospel. In combination with 13:10, this passage causes the reader to expect some kind of fulfillment or later statement to satisfy the anticipation Mark creates.

Finally, in 16:15 Jesus commands the disciples: "Go into all the world and preach the gospel [κηρύξατε τὸ εὐαγγέλιον] to the whole creation." This commission is consistent with the emphasis on the universal proclamation found in 13:10 and 14:9. In addition, the combination of κηρύσσω and εὐαγγέλιον in these three passages reflects the beginning of Jesus' ministry in Galilee, where he came "preaching the gospel of God" (κηρύσσων τὸ εὐαγγέλιον τοῦ θεοῦ; 1:14). Also, the summary in 16:20 matches the rest of Mark well: "And they went out and preached everywhere" (ἐκεῖνοι δὲ ἐξελθόντες ἐκήρυξαν πανταχοῦ), just as the report about Jesus "went out . . . everywhere" (ἐξῆλθεν . . . πανταχοῦ; 1:28) and as Jesus explained that the reason he "went out" (ἐξῆλθον) was to "preach" (κηρύξω; 1:38; cf. 6:12).

The word κηρύσσω ("to preach") is particularly prominent in Mark, the verb occurring fourteen times.[8] As with "gospel," κηρύσσω is prominent in the beginning of the Gospel (1:38, 39, 45), especially in the introduction (1:4, 7, 14). The object of Jesus' preaching is sometimes simply referred to as "the word." After Jesus prophesied his suffering, rejection, death, and resurrection, Mark summarizes, "And he was plainly speaking the word [τὸν λόγον]" (8:32). Luke often speaks of the resurrection message/gospel in a similar manner in Acts (e.g., 2:41; 4:4, 29, 31; 10:44). When Jesus announces in Mark 8:35 that whoever

7. Lunn, *Original Ending*, 269–70.

8. It does not occur in John but occurs nine times in Matthew, nine times in Luke, and eight times in Acts.

loses his life for him and the gospel will save it, he also parallels this with the shame rewarded to those who are ashamed of him and his words. Thus, the gospel is parallel with Jesus' "words" (λόγους; 8:38). Ironically, the cleansed leper became an unsolicited evangelist when he "went out and began to preach [κηρύσσειν] much and to spread the word [τὸν λόγον]," (1:45).[9] This is significant for the LE because in 16:15 the disciples are told to "preach the gospel," but when the author summarizes what the disciples did, he says they "preached everywhere" and "the Lord . . . confirmed the word [τὸν λόγον]" (v. 20). The terminology here is consistent with the rest of Mark.

Some observations are in order. First, the preaching of the gospel spoken of in 16:15–20 is very much what one would expect of Mark's ending in light of the strong emphasis on gospel preaching at key points in his narrative and, particularly, in his introduction. Second, the preaching of the gospel frames the entire Gospel and, therefore, appears to be a designed element rather than an afterthought. Third, when one joins the gospel preaching frame to the lordship of Jesus frame (1:3; 16:19, 20), even greater impetus is added to the notion that the LE has been purposely and integrally designed to provide proper closure to Mark. Fourth, the author locates the sign of tongues squarely within a context of the universal proclamation of the good news about Jesus' resurrection in light of the enthronement of Jesus as Lord; this suggests both missiological and christological associations with speaking in tongues.

Those Who Believe

Several scholars have observed the emphasis on belief and unbelief in the LE.[10] Hooker, although rejecting the LE, comments on the unbelief of the disciples found in 16:14: "To this extent at least these verses are in agreement with the rest of Mark: by their failure to believe the reports of those who have announced the resurrection, the disciples have once again demonstrated their lack of faith and hardness of heart."[11] Similarly, Cole comments on 16:10–11: "The unbelief of the disciples has been a constant theme of Mark's Gospel: they are still the same, even after the

9. Similarly, the man healed of deafness and a speech impediment and those who witnessed his healing disregarded Jesus' instructions and "preached [ἐκήρυσσον] it all the more" (Mark 7:36).

10. E.g., Cranfield, *Mark*, 472; Edwards, *Mark*, 504–5.

11. Hooker, *Mark*, 389.

resurrection of Jesus, showing that the picture given is true."[12] However, the emphasis on the unbelief of the disciples in the LE is commonly attributed to a later editor's dependence on Luke 24:11 and 41 rather than to Mark himself.[13]

Mark first highlights the necessity of faith in the introduction of Jesus' preaching ministry, where "the gospel of God" is parallel with "the kingdom of God" and where Jesus proclaims that people must "repent and believe [πιστεύετε] in the gospel" (1:14–15). Throughout his Gospel Mark focuses on the heart condition of those who hear the message. The religious leaders often receive Christ's censorship due to their hard and errant hearts (3:5; 7:6–7; 8:11–13; 12:1–12). Some in Mark's narrative have substantial faith (2:5; 10:52), while others struggle with unbelief (9:24) and fear (5:15, 36). The disciples do not fare well in the narrative, as they are rebuked for their fearfulness (4:40–41), hard heartedness (αὐτῶν ἡ καρδία πεπωρωμένη; 6:52; πεπωρωμένην ἔχετε τὴν καρδίαν ὑμῶν; 8:17), and unbelief (ἄπιστος; 9:19).[14] Thus it comes as little surprise that this pattern continues into the LE, though it is surprising that unbelief still characterizes the disciples after the resurrection.

The author of the LE twice registers unbelief with the verb ἀπιστέω ("to not believe"; vv. 11, 16; cf. Luke 24:11), once with the noun ἀπιστία ("unbelief"; v. 14; cf. 6:6; 9:24), and twice by negating the verb πιστεύω ("to believe"; vv. 13, 14; cf. 11:31; 13:21). The author also speaks of those who believe (with a positive connotation) with πιστεύω (vv. 16, 17), so that the various cognates of belief occur seven times. As Edwards notes, "The longer ending presents three testimonies to the disbelieving disciples in an order of increasing authority: one female witness (vv. 9–11), two male witnesses (vv. 12–13; the Greek pronouns are masculine), and the resurrected Jesus himself (v. 14)."[15] The appearance of Jesus to the disciples "reclining at the table" (v. 14) could be the Easter Sunday evening encounter, but the author records a more severe rebuke of the

12. Cole, *Mark*, 336.

13. Evans, *Mark 8:27—16:20*, 548. Wessel, however, says the disciples' disbelief in 16:13 is not dependent on Luke. Wessel, "Mark," 789.

14. C. S. Mann suggests the word "unbelief" (ἀπιστία), as found in 16:14, is "confined in Mark to critics and enemies," but surely the disciples are considered among those with unbelief in 9:19, as they were unable to expel the demon. Also, in 9:24, which Mann specifically references, the father of the demonized boy is neither a critic nor an enemy and yet has unbelief. This unfounded comment seems to be intended only to cast doubt on the LE. Mann, *Mark*, 675.

15. Edwards, *Mark*, 505.

disciples than what Luke mentions (although both record the unbelief, Luke 24:41). In 16:14 Jesus rebukes them for "their unbelief [ἀπιστίαν] and hardness of heart [σκληροκαρδίαν]" because "they did not believe [ἐπίστευσαν] those who had seen him after he had risen." Although Mark does not use the noun σκληροκαρδία of the disciples in 6:52 and 8:17 (but see his use of it in 10:5), there is a close conceptual link between these passages and 16:14.

The brevity of the resurrection appearances in the LE is reminiscent of what Maurice Robinson refers to as the "staccato" style of Mark's introductory events,[16] but this brevity makes it challenging to identify the setting of the commission in 16:15–18 and to determine the degree to which events have been compressed.[17] The tone changes considerably as Jesus commands the disciples to preach the gospel and as the author summarizes the obedient response (v. 20). Just as the reader can justifiably anticipate that the fearful women will not remain silent forever (vv. 8–9), so the reader assumes from the context (and perhaps life experience in the first century) that the disciples finally do believe. Jesus now speaks to them not about their own faith, but about the belief or unbelief of those who hear their message: "The one who believes and is baptized will be saved, and the one who does not believe will be condemned" (v. 16).[18] Likewise various signs will characterize the disciples and all believers: "And these signs will follow those who believe" (v. 17), as the gospel goes to "all the world" and "all creation" (v. 15). William Hendrickson cites B. B. Warfield to support his position that these charismatic signs were limited to the apostles during the formative years of the Church, but such a conclusion can only be applied to verse 17, not drawn from it.[19]

Mark has already primed the pump in expectation that believers will lead lives characterized by charismatic signs. Mark's famous intercalation or "sandwich" in 11:12–26 warns of coming judgment on the temple and its Messiah-rejecting religious system. But when Peter remarks on the withered fig tree, Jesus offers no further direct comment about Israel but turns the episode into a lesson on faith. "Have faith [πίστιν] in God"

16. Robinson, "Long Ending," 64. See also Lenski, *St. Mark's Gospel*, 756.

17. See the previous chapter on the possibility that the author compressed more than one resurrection appearance into Mark 16:14–18.

18. The close connection between faith and baptism is not unique in the New Testament (e.g., 1 Pet 3:21), but the second portion of the verse emphasizes faith as the determining factor at the judgment. Baptismal regeneration is not in view.

19. Hendrickson, *Exposition of Mark*, 690. See Warfield, *Counterfeit Miracles*. For a strong rebuttal to Warfield see Ruthven, *On the Cessation*.

(v. 22). The mountain will move if the speaker does not doubt in the heart but believes (πιστεύῃ; v. 23). The person who prays must believe (πιστεύετε; v. 24).

The word "faith" (πίστις) and its cognates occur sixteen times outside the LE, but the highest concentration of the term comes in contexts involving miraculous signs: the woman with the bleeding disorder and the synagogue ruler's daughter (5:34, 36), the demonized boy (9:19, 23, 24 [2x]), and the encouragement to faith mentioned above (11:22, 23, 24). In the latter passage the miracles are for "whosoever" (v. 23), and this is entirely consistent with Jesus' description of those who believe in 16:17, especially in light of his exalted status and his continued working (vv. 19–20). Speaking in tongues, then, is one of the signs that characterizes those who have departed from unbelief, have embraced the resurrection of Christ, and now preach his gospel to all creation. Speaking in tongues is directly associated with missions and missionaries.

The Holy Spirit

The Holy Spirit is only directly mentioned six times in Mark, but this is not due to the humility of the Spirit or because of any inconsistency between glory and a suffering Messiah.[20] Actually, the Spirit takes a prominent position in the prologue. Mark declares "the beginning of the gospel of Jesus Christ [Χριστοῦ]" in 1:1 and follows this reference to one anointed with the Spirit with three clear references to his pneumatic identity and ministry (vv. 8, 10, 12).[21] These early references govern what follows.[22] The anointed Messiah himself (v. 10) will baptize his followers with the Holy Spirit (v. 8), and, like their Lord (vv. 12–13), believers will also engage in spiritual warfare. It is well recognized that Luke offers more extensive treatment of the Holy Spirit in his Gospel ("Spirit" occurs about 17x) and especially in Acts (about 57x), but he also emphasizes the importance of the Spirit by frontloading his Gospel with explicit and programmatic references to the Spirit (1:15, 35, 41, 67; 2:25–27; 3:16, 22;

20. See the discussion in Thiselton, *The Holy Spirit*, 37–40.

21. Studies on pneumatology sometimes overlook the pneumatic implications of the term "Christ" and omit important references to the Spirit's activity. Jesus is called Christ on seven occasions in Mark (1:1; 8:29; 9:41; 12:35; 13:21; 14:61; 15:32). Jesus' identity as the Christ is strongly emphasized by Mark.

22. So also Keener, *Spirit in the Gospels*, 50.

4:1, 2, 14, 18). Only a handful of direct references to the Spirit remain in the body of Luke's Gospel.

The word πνεῦμα ("spirit") occurs frequently in Mark's Gospel (23x), but usually unclean spirits are in view (14x). The body of the Gospel contains three references to the Holy Spirit (3:29; 12:36; 13:11) and the LE contains none. All of the references to the Spirit in Mark have parallels in Matthew and Luke, except in Mark 12:36, where Luke has the location "Book of Psalms" (20:42) instead of the inspiration of the "Holy Spirit" for David's royal prediction. Below I will examine Mark's teaching on the Spirit to see how it aligns with speaking in tongues in the LE and how it might contribute to our understanding of this sign.

An Overview of "Spirit" in the Prologue

The first reference to the Spirit falls from the lips of John the Baptist: "I baptized you with water, but he will baptize you in the Holy Spirit" (ἐγὼ ἐβάπτισα ὑμᾶς ὕδατι, αὐτὸς δὲ βαπτίσει ὑμᾶς ἐν πνεύματι ἁγίῳ; 1:8). The brief account in Mark lacks the "and fire" found in Matt 3:11 and Luke 3:16 as well as the context of divine judgment that accompanies it.[23] The effect of this brief account is to keep the emphasis on the identity of the one greater than John and to maintain a simple focus on future empowerment for believers, in keeping with Mark 12:36 and 13:11.

Mark gives significant attention to John the Baptist's place in salvation history (1:2–3), his garb (v. 6), and his preaching (vv. 4, 7). John's attire is important because he is presented as the eschatological prophet in the tradition of Elijah. In regard to his attire and diet of locusts, Keener comments, "By presenting John as a special holy man, Mark's tradition presents John's witness that Jesus is the harbinger of the Spirit as all the more credible."[24] Hooker notes that John's "prophecy that Jesus will baptize men and women in the Holy Spirit is not fulfilled in the course of Mark's gospel; presumably he is thinking of an experience such as that described by Luke in Acts 2."[25] Of course Matthew has the same omission, unless one sees in Jesus' ministry a purifying baptism "in the Holy Spirit and fire" (3:11). The addition of Acts to Luke suggests

23. Some view the "fire" as a reference to sanctification or cleansing, e.g., Turner, *The Holy Spirit*, 25–27. Warrington views it as both cleansing and judgment. "The Synoptic Gospels," 94–96.

24. Keener, *Spirit in the Gospels*, 53.

25. Hooker, *Mark*, 38.

that Pentecost was necessary to fulfill the prophecy, but in the interest of maintaining a focus on the resurrection story and providing a timely and concise closure to a gospel, an author would have to omit the fulfillment, settle for an allusion to a coming empowerment, or provide a brief account of Pentecost. Matthew gives his readers a reference to Christ's authority and continued presence as a basis for fulfilling his commission (28:18–20). The reader must supply the rest from personal experience and an awareness of events that have transpired since Christ's ascension. One would also expect Mark's ending to contain some sort of closure to the expectation raised by John in Mark 1:8, even if it is only a general allusion to a Spirit baptism.

Watts holds that Mark begins his Gospel with reference to Exod 23:20, Mal 3:1, and Isa 40:3 in order for his readers to understand this work in terms of an Isaianic new exodus based primarily on Isa 40–66.[26] Watts believes Mark's prologue evinces this by its use of εὐαγγέλιον ("gospel"; 1:1, 14), which appears in its verbal form in Isaiah's comfort passages (40:9; 52:7; 60:6; 61:1). And the rending of the heavens along with the Spirit's descent upon Christ in Mark 1:10 (Mark's second reference to the Spirit) seems to fulfill the longing of Isa 63:7—64:12.[27] Various scholars have also pointed out the significance of "the way" in Isaiah 40:3 and how Mark depicts Jesus' progress on "the way" to Jerusalem (1:2, 3; 10:32). Other pointers include Jesus' forty days in the wilderness, apparently a recapitulation of Israel's period of testing in the wilderness, and Jesus' conflict with Satan, which reflects the Yahweh-Warrior motif in Isaiah (40:10–11; cf. Exod 15:3).[28] The latter emphasis is particularly important in relation to the Spirit because the third reference to the Spirit describes him compelling Jesus to go into the wilderness and confront Satan (Mark 1:12). That the blasphemy against the Spirit is directly related to the source of Jesus' power to deliver makes it explicit that the Spirit empowers Jesus' exorcisms (3:22–30).

26. Watts, *Isaiah's New Exodus*, 90.

27. Watts, *Isaiah's New Exodus*, 119.

28. Watts, *Isaiah's New Exodus*, 140. Watts treats the demonic theme in Mark quite extensively in light of Isaiah.

A Markan Baptism in the Spirit

What expectations would a reader of Mark likely have for a baptism in the Spirit? In Mark there is no suggestion that baptism in the Holy Spirit has a cleansing purpose, despite some associations with cleansing both in the Old Testament (Ezek 36:27) and in later Judaism (*Jub.* 1:21, 23; 1QH VIII, 12). Keener rightly sees two primary streams of the Spirit in Judaism in the centuries prior to and after the New Testament: purity and prophecy.[29] The Old Testament also contains these two streams, and in Mark the prophetic or empowerment stream dominates. Upon reception of the Spirit, the Spirit "immediately" thrusts the Messiah into the wilderness to combat Satan (1:10–13). Preaching (v. 14), casting out demons (vv. 21–28), and healing (vv. 29–34) soon follow. Attributing Jesus' Spirit-empowered exorcisms to Satan constitutes blasphemy against the Holy Spirit (3:29),[30] and Mark asserts that David's prophecy about the coming reign of the Messiah was spoken "by the Holy Spirit" (12:36). When Jesus prepares the disciples to preach the gospel to all nations (13:10), he encourages them not to premeditate what they will say in the face of opposition: "But speak whatever is given to you at that time; for it is not you speaking, but the Holy Spirit" (v. 11). Thus, it is fair to expect the baptism in the Spirit to involve inspired utterance and empowerment to proclaim the gospel in the face of opposition.

It is also appropriate to view Jesus as the primary role model of how a Spirit-baptized person functions, in which case Spirit baptism involves miraculous signs. Jesus' experience with the Spirit is unique in some ways because of his unique identity as God's "beloved Son" (Mark 1:11; cf. Gen 22:2; Ps. 2:7; Isa 42:1).[31] He is the Bearer of the Spirit prophesied about in the Hebrew Scriptures (Isa 11:2; 42:1; 61:1, 2),[32] the baptizer in the Spirit (Mark 1:8; cf. Joel 2:28–29), and the one who inaugurates the eschatological age of salvation. Perhaps the dove points to the

29. Keener, *Spirit in the Gospels*, 1.

30. The additional material in Matt 12:22–32 and Luke 11:14–23 and 12:10 gives each of them a slightly different nuance. In Matthew the accusation arises in response to the crowd's wondering whether Jesus might be "the Son of David" (12:23). Luke arranges his material differently and contrasts the blasphemy against the Spirit with speaking by the Spirit in the face of opposition (12:10–11).

31. There is much dispute over whether or not the voice from heaven is the *bat kol*, the "daughter of a voice" from Judaism. Witherington opposes the notion. *Gospel of Mark*, 75. So does Hooker, *Mark*, 47. Keener favors the idea. *Spirit in the Gospels*, 55.

32. Notice the title Χριστός (Mark 1:1). France, *Mark*, 77.

eschatological new creation, as it was associated with the new creation after the flood (Mark 1:10; Gen 8:12).[33] But although Jesus' anointing with the Spirit plays an important role in identifying him as "Jesus Christ the Son of God" (Mark 1:1), the fact that he will baptize others in the Spirit indicates that he also serves as the model of Spirit-filled life for others to follow. His own empowered ministry stresses the functional role the Spirit plays in Mark, and this is the pattern the believers must follow.

Spirit Baptism and Unclean Spirits

The functional aspect of the Spirit in Mark is highlighted by the continual clash with demons. As noted above, πνεῦμα ("spirit") only occurs six times in reference to the Spirit, but fourteen times in reference to unclean spirits. In addition, "demon" (δαιμόνιον) or "demonize" (δαιμονίζομαι) occur another fifteen times outside the LE in Mark. The Beelzebul pericope (3:20–30) highlights the functional aspect of the Spirit by contrasting τὸ πνεῦμα τὸ ἅγιον ("the Holy Spirit"; v. 29) as the source of Jesus' power with πνεῦμα ἀκάθαρτον ("an unclean spirit"; v. 30). In this pericope the enemy is directly mentioned seven times in terms of Beelzebul, the ruler of the demons, demons, Satan, or an unclean spirit. The statement that "the Spirit drives [ἐκβάλλει] him [Jesus] into the wilderness" (1:12) where he engages in a conflict with Satan invites comparison with Jesus' ministry of casting out demons. The verb ἐκβάλλω ("to cast out") is used in this connection on ten occasions outside of the LE (1:34, 39; 3:15, 22, 23; 6:13; 7:26; 9:18, 28, 38).[34]

The disciples have a similar calling to that of Jesus, as Mark clearly delineates when Jesus summons them: "And he appointed twelve, whom he also named apostles, that they might be with him and that he might send them out to preach [κηρύσσειν] and to have authority to cast out [ἐκβάλλειν] demons" (3:14–15). In 6:7 Jesus gives them the authority to cast out unclean spirits, and Mark records (6:12–13) how "they went out and preached [ἐξελθόντες ἐκήρυξαν]" and "cast out many demons"

33. Keener, *Spirit in the Gospels*, 60. Warrington sees an association with creation and new life. See his summary of various interpretations. "Synoptic Gospels," 88–89. It is probably wise not to be too dogmatic about the symbolism of the dove, given the lack of a clear historical pointer. France comments, "Thus we are not aware of any ready-made dove symbolism at the time of Mark, and it seems futile to try to provide one." France, *Mark*, 79. Stein holds a similar view to that of France. Stein, *Mark*, 57.

34. The verb occurs a total of 18 times in Mark, including two in the LE (16:9, 17).

(δαιμόνια πολλὰ ἐξέβαλλον) and "were anointing many sick people [ἀρρώστους] with oil and healing them [ἐθεράπευον]."[35] The constant references to unclean spirits provides such a stark contrast to the Holy Spirit in Mark that one gains an understanding of the mission and the function of the Spirit in both Jesus and his disciples; that is, the Spirit empowers Jesus and his followers to overthrow demonic forces and the kingdom they represent. In Mark, baptism in the Spirit signifies miraculous ministry, and especially power over demons.[36]

Given this emphasis on exorcism, perhaps scholars should not be quite so dismissive of the opening verse of the LE (16:9): "Mary Magdalene, from whom he had cast out seven demons" (Μαρίᾳ τῇ Μαγδαληνῇ, παρ' ἧς ἐκβεβλήκει ἑπτὰ δαιμόνια). Kelhoffer follows many others in assuming that the author borrows the detailed identification of Mary (cf. 16:1) from Luke 8:2b, "Mary the one called Magdalene, from whom seven demons had come out" (Μαρία ἡ καλουμένη Μαγδαληνή, ἀφ' ἧς δαιμόνια ἑπτὰ ἐξεληλύθει).[37] However, the use of the preposition παρά ("from"; Mark 16:9) with the genitive is consistent with Markan usage (despite Kelhoffer's attempts to dismiss it),[38] and the use of the verb ἐκβάλλω ("to cast out") fits better than ἐξέρχομαι ("to come out") in Mark's demonology. The phrase is distinctly Markan and not merely a patchwork of Lukan passages.

This identification of Mary Magdalene may not be an unnecessary and clumsy addition from Luke, but rather part of Mark's careful habit of certifying the timing of (14:12; 15:25, 33, 42; 16:1), witnesses of, and participants in the events surrounding Christ's death and resurrection.

35. Keener sees the ministry of the disciples here as "a paradigm for later Christian evangelism." Keener, *Spirit in the Gospels*, 69.

36. This element is also present in Luke. Much is made of Luke's "finger of God" terminology in 11:20, but the stark contrast between God's children asking the Father to give them his Holy Spirit (v. 13) and the statement "Now he was casting out a demon" (v. 14) informs the reader's understanding of the Beelzebul conflict that follows (vv. 15–26). The mention of the Holy Spirit in v. 13 provides the hermeneutical key both for interpreting the "finger of God" and for discerning which character in the story is truly the child of God, that is, the one who has the Spirit, who has not received a "serpent" or a "scorpion" (vv. 11–12), and who casts out demons. See the discussion in Turner, *Power from on High*, 256–59.

37. Kelhoffer, *Miracle and Mission*, 70. E.g., Edwards, *Mark*, 504; Cranfield, *Mark*, 472; Mann, *Mark*, 674.

38. Kelhoffer, *Miracle and Mission*, 70. There are six places in Mark where this preposition occurs with the genitive: 3:21; 5:26; 8:11; 12:2, 11; 14:43. See Farmer's comments on Mark's use of this preposition. Farmer, *Last Twelve Verses*, 85.

Judas is "one of the twelve" (14:10, 43); Simon the Cyrene is the "father of Alexander and Rufus" (15:21); and Mary is "the mother of James the lesser and Joses" (15:40).[39] Mary is certainly an important eyewitness, and it is also wonderfully ironic that one who had experienced deliverance from Jesus has become one of the believers who may participate in casting out demons in Jesus' name (16:17). Lunn offers an explanation for the fresh identification of Mary based on various texts related to the conquest of Canaan (Exod 3:8, 17; 23:20, 23; 33:2 LXX). "Jewish readers could not fail to detect the allusion to the casting out of the *seven* Canaanite nations, foretold in the Pentateuch and enacted for the most part at the time of Joshua. For this expulsion the Greek translation frequently uses the same verb ἐκβάλλειν (e.g., Exod 34:11, 24; Deut 11:23; Josh 24:18), and the number of nations is explicitly given as 'seven' (Deut 7:1; cf. Josh 24:11). The phrase 'seven nations' was to become Judaism's standard description of the original occupants of Canaan (cf. Acts 13:19)."[40] Lunn gives a detailed explanation of his theory, but whether one follows him on this or not, suffice it to say that there are plausible reasons for the author of the LE to identify Mary the way that he does.

If Mark's narrative teaches that a baptism in the Spirit empowers believers to preach and to cast out demons, then 16:17 fits the description well, and verse 20 assumes that Christ's followers have received such a baptism. "And these signs will follow those who believe: in my name they will cast out demons [δαιμόνια ἐκβαλοῦσιν], they will speak in new tongues, . . . they will lay hands on sick people [ἀρρώστους], and they will get well" (vv. 17–18). "And they went out and preached [ἐξελθόντες ἐκήρυξαν] everywhere" (v. 20a). Kelhoffer has also noticed the close correspondence between the Greek words here and those in 6:12–13 (see above), but he assumes that the correspondence is due to a second-century author's "conscious imitation" of Mark.[41] This "imitation" extends to the words "in my name," which he sees as stemming from the same phrase occurring in 9:38. He comments, "If the evangelist Mark were to write the first sign in 16:17b, this is exactly how one would expect him to do so."[42] Because Kelhoffer has completely ruled out the possibility of Mark's own hand in this, he can scarcely see any alternative to intentional

39. For a good discussion of the naming of people in the Gospels, see Bauckham, *Jesus and the Eyewitnesses*, 39–66.

40. Lunn, *Original Ending*, 261–62.

41. Kelhoffer, *Miracle and Mission*, 104.

42. Kelhoffer, *Miracle and Mission*, 105.

imitation. But it is easier to simply view the "name" as another indicator of a consistent train of thought throughout, seeing as the author emphasizes operating in the name of Jesus earlier in the narrative (9:37, 38, 39, 41; 13:6, 13). However, the name of Jesus is particularly tied to the mission (13:13) and miracles (9:38–39) both in Mark and in Acts (2:21; 3:6, 16; 4:10, 12; et al.). In Acts 2:21 "the name of the Lord" from Joel 2:32 is now the name of the Lord Jesus, and this becomes evident as Peter's Pentecostal sermon progresses. So, the connection between "the name" in Mark 16:17, speaking in tongues, miraculous signs, and the exaltation of Jesus as Lord is theologically consistent with Acts 2–3.[43] The author of the LE was not a good imitator; he was a good theologian.[44]

Although the LE does not use a phrase such as "baptism in the Spirit" or even "Holy Spirit" (and neither does Luke 24), the author has placed exorcism at the top of his list of missionary signs and shown that power over the kingdom of darkness is part and parcel to what it means to be baptized in the Spirit. Furthermore, the association with the Lord's exaltation and his confirming the word with signs demonstrates that the believers did eventually receive a baptism in the Spirit. Speaking in tongues is one of the signs resulting from this baptism.

The Spirit and Christocentric Utterances

A closer look at Mark 12:36 and 13:11 helps further clarify what a Markan baptism in the Holy Spirit entails. The reference to David speaking by the Spirit in 12:36 is surrounded by christological and Davidic references. Jesus has just finished telling one of the scribes that he is "not far from the kingdom of God" (12:34). Jesus then asks why the scribes claim that "the Christ is the Son of David" (ὁ χριστὸς υἱὸς Δαυίδ ἐστιν; v. 35). Jesus quotes Ps 110:1, which focuses on Christ as "Lord" (Mark 12:36,

43. One is justified in associating "in my name" in 16:17 with all the signs listed because Jesus himself broadens the application of casting out demons in his name (9:38) to performing any miracle in his name (v. 39). But the phrase most naturally accompanies δαιμόνια ἐκβαλοῦσιν ("they will cast out demons"; 16:17), and connecting "in my name" to the taking up of serpents and drinking anything deadly makes for very awkward grammar (the subjunctive conjunction κἂν ("and if") does not follow "in my name" well; v. 18).

44. As will be discussed later in this chapter, it seems more likely that Luke used the entirety of Mark as a source than it does that an unknown author crafted the LE in imitation of Acts. The similar theological emphases could be due to Luke's dependence on the LE.

37) and his session at God's "right hand" (v. 36). Clearly David's utterance by the Spirit is christocentric, and Mark is emphatic that "David *himself* spoke by the Holy Spirit" (v. 36) and "David *himself* calls him Lord" (v. 37). This passage is a key part of Mark's increasing emphasis on Christology, especially since Peter's confession in 8:29, and Mark highlights Jesus' identity as a Davidite.

The terminology used in the latter half of the Gospel demonstrates the increasing focus on Christology. The word "Christ" (Χριστός) has a prominent place in the opening of Mark (1:1) but disappears until Peter's confession (8:29), after which the title appears five more times in the narrative (9:41; 12:35; 13:21; 14:61; 15:32). The phrase "the kingdom of God" appears only four times prior to Peter's confession, but ten times afterward. Jesus calls himself "The Son of Man" only three times early in Mark, but he uses this designation twelve times from 8:31 forward. Jesus is referred to as "the Son of God" or the "Son" four times in the first half of Mark but six times in the second half. Along with the title in 1:1, the centurion's announcement in 15:39 is crucial: "Truly this man was the Son of God." Jesus is referred to as David's Son only later in Mark (10:47, 48; 12:35, 37), and David is only mentioned once in the early part of Mark (2:25) but six times in the latter half. When one adds to these elements the prophecies of Christ's resurrection (8:31; 9:9–10, 31; 10:34; 14:28) and, especially, the references to the Psalms and Daniel,[45] the reader begins to expect Christ's exaltation. Thus, the role of the Spirit as one who inspires proclamation of Christ's lordship fits well into Mark's developing story as the death and resurrection of Christ draw near.

In the Olivet discourse Jesus speaks of the divine necessity (δεῖ) of the universal proclamation of the gospel (13:10), followed by instruction in facing opposition. "And when they bring you to trial and hand you over, do not worry beforehand what you will say [λαλήσητε], but speak [λαλεῖτε] whatever is given to you in that hour, for it is not you speaking [λαλοῦντες], but the Holy Spirit" (v. 11). In Mark the Spirit is prophetic, both revealing what to say and inspiring the bold (without "worry") proclamation of the gospel. The description of the disciples preaching everywhere with the Lord's signs of confirmation certainly fits this picture (16:20). And since the Spirit inspires christocentric utterances in both the Old Testament (Ps 110:1 in Mark 12:36) and among Christ's

45. Mark 11:9–10 with Ps 118:25–26; Mark 12:10–11 with Ps 118:22–23; Mark 12:36 with Ps 110:1; Mark 13:26 with Dan 7:13–14; Mark 14:62 with Dan 7:13; Mark 15:34 with Ps 22:1.

missionaries, it is reasonable to conclude that the Spirit also inspires the speaking predicted by Jesus in 16:17: "They will speak [λαλήσουσιν] in new tongues." The emphasis on Christ's exaltation and lordship in the immediate context (vv. 19–20) further supports the notion that the speaking in tongues is in some sense christocentric. In short, the speaking in tongues is another example of a christocentric, Spirit-inspired form of utterance.

The Signs of Mark 16

Having surveyed some of the Markan themes related to the LE, the discussion now focuses on the signs listed in Mark 16:17–18. The central argument is that Mark 16 draws several parallels from Moses' encounters with God and Pharaoh—in keeping with his new exodus theme—and crafts his account of the disciples' commissioning in terms borrowed largely from the Septuagint of Exod 3–7. This observation may provide an interpretive key for explaining much of the content of Mark 16, including the signs of speaking in new tongues, taking up serpents, and drinking deadly drinks without harm. The following discussion highlights the centrality of God as Lord in the exodus narrative and Christ as Lord in Mark 16.

James Kelhoffer observes some parallels between the LE and the early chapters of Exodus. He mentions that Exod 4:1–5 shares with the LE an emphasis on establishing the credibility of the messengers and on a miraculous sign involving picking up snakes.[46] Kelhoffer also notices the common emphasis on the function of signs to encourage faith, but despite these strong parallels, he dismisses them, highlights some of the differences, and concludes that "the author of Exodus 4 and 7 was significantly less interested in the importance of picking up the snake as he was in demonstrating Moses' divine calling and power."[47] However, the latter point seems very similar to what the author of the LE intended to convey.

Nicholas Lunn does not fail to see the significance of the parallels, and he argues for the dependence of the LE on the account of Moses, especially on Exod 4. He sees parallels between Jesus' appearance to the disciples (Mark 16:14) and the Lord's appearance to Moses (Exod 3:16;

46. Kelhoffer, *Miracle and Mission*, 390. Although the signs follow the messengers in the LE, the primary emphasis is not on the confirmation of the messengers but on the confirmation of the message (Mark 16:20).

47. Kelhoffer, *Miracle and Mission*, 390–91.

4:5) and between the commissioning of the disciples to go preach (Mark 16:15) and Moses' commissioning to go to Egypt (Exod 3:10). There are parallel emphases on belief or lack thereof, signs, taking up serpents by hand, obedience in preaching with accompanying signs (Exod 4:20, 30–31; Mark 16:19–20), hardness of heart, and casting out corrupt nations (Exod 3:8; 34:24) or demons (Mark 16:9).[48] Some of these parallels receive treatment in the following discussion, and more potential points of contact are added to the list. I will also argue that Exod 7 provides an important aspect of the structure of Mark 16.

Hardness of Heart and Faith

The seven uses of πιστεύω ("to believe") or its cognates in the LE are entirely consistent with the other eighteen occurrences in Mark as well as with the concern over belief in Exod 4. The verb occurs five times in Moses' commissioning account (Exod 4:1, 5, 8, 9, 31 LXX), where Moses expresses concern that the people will not believe that God appeared to him and will not listen to him.[49] Thus, God grants signs so that the people will believe that the Lord God appeared to him (ἵνα πιστεύσωσίν σοι ὅτι ὦπταί σοι κύριος ὁ θεὸς; 4:5 LXX). The word "sign" also occurs six times in Exod 4 (vv. 8 [2x], 9, 17, 28, 30 LXX; cf. Mark 16:17, 20).[50] The problem of unbelief is often addressed in Mark (e.g., 4:40; 6:6; 9:19, 24), but the dullness of the disciples is clearly expressed when they do not believe that Jesus appeared to Mary (16:10–11) and when they reject the testimony of Jesus' manifestation to two others (vv. 12–13). Jesus scolds them for "their unbelief and hardheartedness" (τὴν ἀπιστίαν αὐτῶν καὶ σκληροκαρδίαν; v. 14) in failing to believe the testimonies of resurrection appearances. The choice of σκληροκαρδίαν ("hardheartedness") also points to dependence on Exodus. The term is rarely used in the Bible (Deut 10:16; Jer 4:4; Matt 19:8) but is used one other time in Mark (10:5), where Jesus gives a stinging rebuke to the Pharisees for their hardheartedness regarding marriage and divorce. In light of the previous reference, its application to the disciples in 16:14 is particularly poignant. As if this were not enough, the concept is similarly expressed throughout

48. Lunn, *Original Ending*, 263.

49. Moses' unbelief is also evident in his resistance to the call, even though the term is not directly applied to him in this account.

50. There is a textual variant for "sign" at verse 28.

the exodus story, where Pharaoh's condition is described with the combination of the verb σκληρύνω ("to harden") and the noun καρδία ("heart") thirteen times.[51] For example, in Exod 7:3 God promises, "And I will harden the heart [σκληρυνῶ τὴν καρδίαν] of Pharaoh and multiply my signs [τὰ σημεῖά μου] and wonders in the land of Egypt." The author of the LE apparently draws on this tradition, highlights the contrast between belief and unbelief, and makes an appeal with a real sense of gravitas when he writes, "He who believes and is baptized will be saved, but he who does not believe will be condemned" (16:15).

The exodus narrative does not limit the unbelief to Pharaoh, as Moses also has more than his fair share of doubts (Exod 3:11; 4:1, 10), but his doubts give way to full obedience when he and Aaron confront Pharaoh and do "just as the Lord commanded" (7:6). Similarly, after Jesus rebuked the disciples, commanded them to go and "preach the gospel to all creation" (Mark 16:15), and ascended into heaven, the disciples "went out and preached everywhere" (v. 20).

"Signs" in Exodus and Mark

The word "sign" (σημεῖον) only occurs five times in Mark outside the two occurrences in the LE, but the generally negative connotation with the word has led some scholars to conclude that Mark opposes signs. Three of the five are found in 8:11–12, where the Pharisees seek a sign and Jesus refuses to accommodate them. Mark says the Pharisees were "testing him" (πειράζοντες αὐτόν), indicating that the problem was not with signs as such, but with the heart of the tempters. The remaining two references are found in the Olivet discourse, where the disciples ask for a sign indicating the time of the temple's destruction (13:4) and Jesus warns of signs from false prophets (13:22). This small sampling makes it difficult to develop a full-fledged doctrine of signs,[52] especially when other Gospels contain both the negative elements found in 8:11–12 (Matt 12:38–39;

51. Exod 4:21; 7:3, 22; 8:15; 9:12, 35; 10:1, 27; 11:10; 14:4, 8, 17.

52. The assertion that Mark has a negative view of signs in general could be substantiated with a limited use of the term if it were clearly employed in such a way as to make it emphatic in the narrative structure (e.g., the term could be presented in a negative light in the introduction). But this does not seem to be the case, and Mark's real concern seems to be with disbelief of the signs.

16:1–4; Luke 11:16, 29–30; John 4:48; cf. 2:18) and favorable uses of sign as well (Matt 24:30; Luke 2:12; John 2:11; 4:54).[53]

While signs are somewhat of a mixed bag in the Gospels, but often mentioned due to an obsession on the part of unbelieving people, Luke certainly presents the term in a positive light in Acts (2:22, 43; 4:16, 22, 30; et al.). In light of the numerous miraculous signs in all the Gospels and Jesus' clear admonishment to faith that moves mountains (Mark 11:20–25), Mark does not view signs negatively per se,[54] so the attention to signs presents no particular difficulty in the LE. The author emphasizes the importance of them by placing the word σημεῖα at the head of his description of the five signs (16:17) and as the final word of the book (σημείων; v. 20). By closely associating these terms with compounded forms of ἀκολουθέω ("to follow"; vv. 17, 20), the author signals the structural unity of vv. 17–20 and concludes the Gospel with a sense of irony—the followers are followed by signs.[55]

The mention of signs in Mark 16:17 is immediately connected with faith: "And these signs will follow those who believe [πιστεύσασιν]." Cognates of the verb πιστεύω occur repeatedly in the immediate resurrection context (vv. 11, 13, 14 [2x]), including in the promise of salvation to the believing and condemnation to the unbelieving in verse 16. This is consistent with the emphasis on signs and faith in Exod 4. The word sign (σημεῖον) occurs more often in Exodus (19x) than any other book in the Greek Bible, and eight of these occurrences are in Exod 3, 4, and 7 (3:12; 4:8 [2x], 9, 17, 28, 30; 7:3, 9). Likewise, the verb πιστεύω occurs eight times in Exodus, and six of them are in Exod 4 (vv. 1, 5, 8 [2x], 9, 31). In Exod 4 Moses expresses his concern that the Egyptians will neither believe him nor listen to him (v. 1). The Lord reassures him by providing the signs of turning his staff into a snake and making his hand leprous. At this point the words "believe" and "sign" converge: "And if they do not

53. The definition offered for a sign sometimes excludes miracles such as Jesus performed, but this can only potentially be substantiated by omitting the LE, the book of Acts, and the Gospel of John from the discussion. According to Stein, the miracles in the Synoptic Gospels are referred to "not as 'signs' but as 'mighty works.'" Stein, *Mark*, 375.

54. Keener, *Spirit in the Gospels*, 69. Cole notes that Mark does not use sign in reference to Jesus' miracles, but he overstates the case when he says, "This may also show a later date, and certainly suggests non-Marcan authorship for the longer ending." Cole, *Mark*, 338.

55. The author uses ἀκολουθέω 18 times plus two compounds in the uncontested portion of Mark.

believe [πιστεύσωσίν] you or listen to the voice of the first sign [σημείου], they will believe [πιστεύσουσίν] you at the voice of the last sign [σημείου]. And it will be that if they do not believe [πιστεύσωσίν] you because of these two signs [σημείοις] or listen to your voice, take from the water of the river and pour it on the dry ground . . . and it will be blood on the dry ground" (Exod 4:8–9a LXX). Mark's language reflects that of the exodus, and this becomes even more evident in the signs he lists.

The Sign of Casting out Demons

The first sign that Jesus says will follow believers is that "they will cast out demons" (δαιμόνια ἐκβαλοῦσιν) in his name (Mark 16:17). The use of ἐκβάλλω ("to cast out") is entirely consistent with the rest of Mark, where it occurs sixteen other times in the undisputed text and one other time in the LE. On several occasions it is used of driving out a person or persons (1:12, 43; 5:40; 11:15; 12:8), but it is more commonly used of driving out demons or Satan (1:34, 39; 3:15, 22, 23; 6:13; 7:26; 9:18, 28, 38; 16:9, 17). The internal consistency is adequate to explain its occurrence at this point, but the reference to Mary Magdalene as the one from whom Jesus "had cast out seven demons" (ἐκβεβλήκει ἑπτὰ δαιμόνια) points to the exodus story as establishing the pattern for divine deliverance ministered by Jesus and his followers.[56] The "cast out" terminology is used repeatedly of the Canaanite nations in Exodus (23:28, 29, 30, 31; 33:2; 34:11, 24). The Septuagint of 23:18 reads, "For when I have cast out the nations before your face" (ἐκβάλω ἔθνη ἀπὸ προσώπου σου), and this line is not found in the Masoretic text. However, the additional line in the Septuagint is consistent with the Lord's angel going before their face (33:2; cf. 23:20) or God himself going before their face (34:11, 24) to cast out the nations. Mark refers directly to this context when he quotes Exod 23:20 in Mark 1:2 (cf. Exod 23:23).[57] Thus, the first sign of the disciples is

56. See the discussion earlier in this chapter. Lunn points to the use of ἐκβάλλω to describe the casting out of the seven nations of Canaan. The number seven is specifically used of the seven nations listed in Deut 7:1, and, in Exod 3:8 and 17, the Septuagint lists seven nations that will be driven out, whereas the Masoretic text lists only six. Lunn also points to the mention of seven nations in Acts 13:19 and the common reference to the seven in Rabbinic literature. Lunn, *Original Ending*, 261–62.

57. Lunn, *Original Ending*, 262. Mark attributes the quotation in 1:2–3 to Isaiah but cites Exod 23:20, Mal 3:1, and Isa 40:3 (LXX). Stein suggests Mark is satisfied to mention only his most important source. *Mark*, 42.

already illustrated in Mary Magdalene's life and grounded in the exodus story.

Not only does Mark's use of "cast out" reflect the language of the exodus story, but it is also conceptually consistent with the abundance of oppression and deliverance language surrounding Moses' calling (e.g., Exod 3:7–12). Luke also employs the language of the exodus when he speaks of Jesus as "healing all those oppressed [καταδυναστευομένους] by the devil" (Acts 10:38). The term is not common in the Old Testament, but the verb describes the oppression of Egypt in Exod 1:13 and the noun does the same in 6:7. Both Luke and Mark view the exodus as an appropriate backdrop for deliverance in the New Testament.

The Sign of Speaking in New Tongues

Until one observes the dependence of Mark 16 on the exodus story, the combination of exorcism, tongues, taking up serpents, and deadly drink appears rather improbable. However, the calling of Moses even sheds light on Mark's second promised sign: "they will speak in new tongues" (γλώσσαις λαλήσουσιν καιναῖς; 16:17). The glossolalic terminology is consistent with other passages in the New Testament, but the occurrence is also unique in that Jesus personally predicts the tongues speech (cf. Acts 2:4; 10:46; 19:6) and calls the tongues "new" (καιναῖς).[58] Jesus' direct teaching on this subject is not inconceivable considering the lengthy period of instruction between the resurrection and the ascension (Acts 1:1–5) and the possibility of dependence on the exodus narrative. The author, writing post-Pentecost, certainly had the Pentecostal phenomenon in view, but the author also saw a historic precedent for transformation from slowness of speech to inspired utterance in the exodus account. The Markan ending welcomes a comparison between the fearful women who said nothing (Mark 16:8), the disciples who were slow to believe and preach, and Moses who was slow of speech.

Upon hearing the call of God, Moses voices his concern that the people will "not believe" (μὴ πιστεύσωσίν) him and will say that "God has not appeared to you" (οὐκ ὦπταί σοι ὁ θεός; Exod 4:1 LXX). In response

58. If one argues that this record is not an historic account of what Jesus actually said or close to what he said, within the parameters of acceptable literary practices for Scripture, then one would justifiably have serious questions about the integrity of the author of the LE. One could argue that it was extremely presumptuous for a later author to place these words in Christ's mouth.

the Lord gives him the signs of turning his staff into a snake, the leprous hand, and the turning of the water into blood (vv. 2–9). These "signs" (σημείοις; v. 9) do not allay Moses' fears, so he complains about his lack of speaking ability: "Please, Lord, I am not able; I was not able yesterday, in the past, or since you came to speak [λαλεῖν] to your servant; I am weak in voice and slow in tongue" (ἰσχνόφωνος καὶ βραδύγλωσσος ἐγώ εἰμι; v. 10b LXX). Moses' "I am" is emphatic and in direct contrast with the Lord's affirmation that he is the creator of man's faculties and the source of his capacities. The Lord assures Moses that he will assist him and teach him what "to speak" (λαλῆσαι; v. 12). Moses continues to resist, and God appoints Aaron, reassuring Moses that when Aaron "speaks, he will speak for you" (λαλῶν λαλήσει αὐτός σοι; v. 14 LXX).

The narrative in Exod 4 emphasizes the divine enabling to speak in contrast to Moses' insecurities and unwillingness to obey. This scene provides a parallel for Mark's disciples who, after passing from unbelief to faith in the risen Christ, will go out and preach and will perform the miraculous signs and fulfill Jesus' prophetic command. The combination of the noun γλῶσσα ("tongue") and the verb λαλέω ("to speak") in Mark 16:17 may be drawn from the Exod 4 passages highlighted above (vv. 10, 12, 14). While λαλέω occurs often in the Septuagint, there are only a handful of occurrences of γλῶσσα and its cognates that could reasonably provide a point of direct comparison for New Testament tongues. Considering only Old Testament passages where both terms occur reduces the options even more. Given the exodus context of Mark 16, the emphasis on speaking for God in Exod 4, and the unusual occurrence of the term βραδύγλωσσος ("slow in tongue") in Exod 4:10 (found only here in biblical literature), it is likely that the author of the LE intended to reference this passage. The promise of this sign amounted to somewhat of a play on words; that is, the fearful disciples who were slow of tongue like Moses would be characterized by divinely inspired, miraculous speech.[59] The miraculous nature of the speech is indicated by its designation as one of the "signs" and its association with the miraculous signs of the exodus.

The reticence of Moses to speak in response to his initial call (Exod 4:10–17) also becomes a significant feature of the exodus story after

59. Powers holds that the "new tongues" are new in the sense of an eschatological new creation and that the "new" element refers to the heavenly nature of the tongues. However, the "new" element in Mark primarily seems to indicate bold, miraculous, Spirit-inspired speech in place of human failure to speak. Powers, "Missionary Tongues?" 51.

Pharaoh refuses to meet Moses' demands during the first confrontation (5:1–5). Moses' complaint that he is ἄλογός ("lacking in eloquence"; 6:12 LXX)[60] forms part of the frame surrounding the family records of Moses and Aaron (6:13–27).[61] Upon giving an emphatic identification of Moses and Aaron, the story resumes with the repetition of Moses' self-assessment as speech-challenged, and the term ἰσχνόφωνός ("weak in voice"; 6:30 LXX) helps signal the closing of the frame and recalls the same term used in his original calling (4:10 LXX). The similar terminology is evident:[62]

> *καὶ πῶς εἰσακούσεταί μου Φαραω; ἐγὼ δὲ ἄλογός εἰμι.* (6:12b LXX)
>
> and how will Pharaoh listen to me? And I am not eloquent.

> *ἰδοὺ ἐγὼ ἰσχνόφωνός εἰμι, καὶ πῶς εἰσακούσεταί μου Φαραω;* (6:30b LXX)
>
> Behold I am weak in voice, and how will Pharaoh listen to me?

From a literary perspective, the genealogical record is ideally situated immediately before the signs and wonders begin and clearly identifies the main characters (6:13–27).[63] From a theological perspective, the human weakness of Moses is contrasted with God's resounding "I am the Lord" (ἐγὼ κύριος) and his charge to Moses to speak to Pharaoh (6:29 LXX). The mighty deliverance takes place by God's initiative and power, and the proper role of Moses is that of obedient servant. The author of Mark incorporates these emphases into the closing of his Gospel.

The constellation of terms and the order of events in Exod 6:28—7:24 provide somewhat of a roadmap for the Markan ending. Aaron will serve as Moses' "prophet" (7:1); God commands Moses to obey (v. 2); God will harden Pharaoh's heart (v. 3); God will multiply signs and wonders (v. 3); God will be recognized as Lord (v. 5); Moses and Aaron obeyed (v. 6); Moses' staff becomes a snake (vv. 8–13); and the water of the Nile becomes undrinkable (vv. 14–24). Some of the parallels with Mark 16 have already been pointed out, but it should be noted here that

60. LSJ, 72.

61. For a summary of seven practical purposes of the genealogical material, see Stuart, *Exodus*, 175–76.

62. The Hebrew text uses the expression "uncircumcised lips" in both texts.

63. Stuart, *Exodus*, 175.

the divine enabling to speak and the title of Aaron as "prophet" is consistent with Mark's emphasis on inspired utterance (12:36; 13:11) and with speaking in new tongues (16:17). The discussion to follow also highlights the parallels with Mark's taking up serpents, deadly drink, and the centrality of lordship.

The Sign of Taking up Serpents

This sign has presented considerable difficulty to many readers of the LE: "And they will take up serpents in their hands" (καὶ ἐν ταῖς χερσὶν ὄφεις ἀροῦσιν; Mark 16:18b).[64] Commentators often locate the source of this statement in Acts 28:3–6,[65] but Lunn points out that, linguistically speaking, the Markan text has little in common with Paul's encounter with a viper that had latched onto him. There are practically no verbal parallels, and Paul does not "pick up" the viper (ἔχιδνα for "serpent," not ὄφις as in Mark 16:18).[66]

When Moses threw down his staff it became an ὄφις (Exod 4:3). "So Moses stretched forth his hand and took hold of its tail, and it became a staff in his hand [ἐν τῇ χειρι]" (v. 4b LXX). In the Septuagint of 4:17 three key words found in Mark 16 are combined in one verse: "And this staff which was turned into a serpent [ὄφιν] you will take in your hand [ἐν τῇ χειρί] and do the signs [τὰ σημεῖα] by it." Lunn points out that the purpose of the signs is "that they may believe that the Lord God . . . has appeared to you" (ἵνα πιστεύσωσίν σοι ὅτι ὤπταί σοι κύριος ὁ θεὸς; v. 5; cf. Mark 16:9, 12, 14).[67] Of course, in Mark the one who appears is the Lord Jesus. This constellation of terms and concepts seems far too close to Mark's ending to be accidental, and, along with the order of events in Exodus 6:26—7:24 (as outlined above), it challenges the common notion that the content of the LE is merely a hodgepodge of ideas gathered from the other Gospels[68] and unknown sources during the second century.

64. The phrase καὶ ἐν ταῖς χερσὶν is missing from some manuscripts but is probably original. See Metzger, *Textual Commentary* (1971), 127.

65. Evans, *Mark 8:27—16:20*, 549. Mann, *Mark*, 675. Moloney, *Mark*, 361.

66. Lunn, *Original Ending*, 260. Kelhoffer also questions the likelihood of the reference. *Miracle and Mission*, 402. It is possible, however, that Luke later included his viper story as somewhat of an illustration of the statement in the LE.

67. Lunn, Original Ending, 259–60.

68. For example, the "signs" are often thought to be borrowed from John. Evans, *Mark 8:27–16:20*, 549.

The primary purpose of including the taking up of serpents in the list of signs is to present Jesus' followers as charismatic preachers performing signs in the tradition of Moses. Thus, the author is not advocating that believers in Jesus handle snakes, but he is indicating that they will perform various miracles as Moses did.

The Sign of Protection from Deadly Drink

The fourth sign follows hard on the heels of the sign of taking up serpents: "And if they drink anything deadly, it will certainly not harm them" (κἂν θανάσιμόν τι πίωσιν οὐ μὴ αὐτοὺς βλάψῃ; Mark 16:18b). Scholars have also strained to find a parallel to this in ancient texts. For example, there is the report of Eusebius, which dates a miracle of protection from poison to the time of the apostolic period.[69] "That Philip the Apostle resided in Hierapolis with his daughters has already been stated, but now it must be pointed out that Papias, their contemporary, recalls that he heard an amazing story from Philip's daughters. For he reports that in his day a man rose from the dead, and again another amazing story involving Justus, who was surnamed Barsabbas: he drank a deadly poison and yet by the grace of the Lord suffered nothing unpleasant."[70] More recently, Robert Menzies has suggested that Job 20:16 serves as the "interpretive key" to understanding Mark's reference to snakes and poison:[71] "And may he suck the wrath of dragons, and may a snake's tongue kill him" (θυμὸν δὲ δρακόντων θηλάσειεν ἀνέλοι δὲ αὐτὸν γλῶσσα ὄφεως; NETS, LXX). The ESV translates the Hebrew text: "He will suck the poison of cobras; the tongue of a viper will kill him." Menzies compares Mark's drinking of deadly poison to the first half of the verse and the taking up serpents to the second half. Menzies acknowledges that, in Mark, this passage has a new meaning, as Jesus reverses Job's message of judgment on an ungodly person.[72] Menzies points to the mention of γλῶσσα ("tongue") in Job 20:16 in support of his view that this passage provides the biblical backdrop of this passage. "The order of the signs in Mk 16.17–18 reflects the *Stichwort* connection (common in Jewish interpretation) between

69. Evans, *Mark 8:27—16:20*, 265.

70. Eusebius, *Church History*, 3.39.9. English translation from Holmes, *Apostolic Fathers*, 567.

71. Menzies, *Speaking in Tongues*, 74.

72. Menzies, *Speaking in Tongues*, 74–75.

the believers' 'new *tongues*' and the following sign of 'handling snakes', which draws upon the '*tongue* of a snake' in Job 20.16. In other words, the *Stichwort* connection that hinges on the term 'tongue' explains why the signs from Job 20.16, handling snakes and drinking poison, follow the reference to 'new tongues' in the list of signs in Mk 16.17–18."[73] Menzies fills out his argument by drawing support from Lukan texts that connect serpents to satanic power.

There are several weaknesses in adopting Job 20:16 as the passage on which Mark depends. First, there are only two significant words ("snake" and "tongue") that the two texts share in common, so the evidence is by no means overwhelming. Second, the required transformation of the essential meaning of the text lessens the likelihood that Jesus intended to cite Job. Third, the transformation of a serpent tongue to speaking in new tongues seems to require too much revision. Fourth, the context of Job 20:16 offers no supporting evidence suggesting that Mark draws from this passage. In addition, this view requires substantial illumination from another Gospel (Luke) in order to receive clarity.

Another possible interpretation points to a conceptual parallel found in a miracle performed by Elisha. After Elijah's ascension, Elisha threw salt into a polluted spring and pronounced the waters healed by the Lord (2 Kings 2:19–22). It is thought that Mark may be relating to this story in some general way, but this suggestion lacks clear, supporting evidence.

Once again, Mark's dependence on the exodus narrative provides the most plausible interpretation of the deadly drink. One should remember that Mark's text does not refer to poison as such, but to drinking "anything deadly," and protection from such drink is called a "sign." This language is consistent with Moses' turning the Nile's water into blood, which was one of the first three signs (along with turning his staff into a serpent and his hand becoming leprous) that God specifically instructed Moses to perform when God first called Moses (Exod 4:9; 7:19–24). In Exod 7, the sign of turning the Nile's water into blood immediately follows the sign of the staff becoming a serpent (vv. 8–24). Moses repeats the Lord's words and forecasts that the Egyptians "will not be able to drink [πιεῖν]" from the river (v. 18). It happened just as predicted, and the Egyptians were "unable to drink [πιεῖν]" the water (v. 21). The Egyptians tried to dig around the Nile in order "to drink [πιεῖν]," but they were

73. Menzies, *Speaking in Tongues*, 77. Emphasis his.

"unable to drink [πιεῖν]" from the river (v. 24). God's treatment of the Egyptians is opposite of how he treats his followers, who will suffer no harm "if they drink [πίωσιν] anything deadly" (Mark 16:18b).

One may point out that the LE parallel is not precise, as the Israelites apparently did not drink anything deadly. This is true, but the exodus story itself provides the essential element of a distinction between the ungodly and the people of God. Presumably, the Hebrew people still had drinking water, and later plagues specify that God did distinguish between his people and the objects of his plagues (Exod 8:22–23; 9:4–7, 26; 10:23; 11:7). This distinction is made clear when safe drinking water becomes an issue at Marah, where Moses uses a piece of wood to make the water sweet (Exod 15:22–25). There God promises, "If you will diligently listen to the voice of the LORD your God, and do that which is right in his eyes, and give ear to his commandments and keep all his statutes, I will put none of the diseases on you that I put on the Egyptians, for I am the LORD, your healer" (v. 26 ESV). The episodes revolving around drinking water provide a ready illustration of how God's basic posture toward his people is not that of judgment but of healing. Mark continues to draw on the exodus account to provide an historical basis for God's favor on the messengers of Christ and to emphasize the charismatic and miraculous nature of the Christian community. Perhaps the association between wholesome drinking water and the revelation of Yahweh as healer also forms a natural bridge between Mark's sign of protection from deadly drink and the sign of miraculous healing.

The Sign of Miraculous Healing

The fifth sign that falls from Jesus' lips in Mark 16 is miraculous healing: "They will lay hands on the sick, and they will become well" (ἐπὶ ἀρρώστους χεῖρας ἐπιθήσουσιν καὶ καλῶς ἕξουσιν; 16:18b). Such a sign is not too surprising, given the abundance of healings recorded in the Gospels and Acts. Mark himself emphasizes the healing ministry of Jesus,[74] and on several occasions he records the instrumentality of hands as part of the healing event (1:31, 41; 5:23, 41; 6:5; 7:32–33; 8:23, 25; 9:27). Jairus implores Jesus to come and lay hands (ἐπιθῇς τὰς χεῖρας) on his daughter

74. Mark 1:29–34, 40–45; 2:1–12; 3:1–6, 10; 5:21–43; 6:1–6, 13, 53–56; 7:31–37; 8:22–26; 10:46–52. Some passages combine deliverance and healing (e.g., 8:14–29), making Mark's inclusion of deliverance and healing as the first and last of the five signs quite appropriate.

(5:23); people appeal to Jesus to lay his hand on (ἐπιθῇ αὐτῷ τὴν χεῖρα) a deaf and speech-impaired man (7:32); and twice Jesus lays his hands on a blind man (ἐπιθεὶς τὰς χεῖρας αὐτω; 8:23; cf. v. 25). The terminology of Jesus' ministry in Nazareth is instructive. Jesus was unable to do many miracles "except that he laid hands on a few sick people and healed them" (εἰ μὴ ὀλίγοις ἀρρώστοις ἐπιθεὶς τὰς χεῖρας ἐθεράπευσεν; 6:5). This text shares three terms in common with Mark 16:18: ἐπιτίθημι ("lay on"), the plural form of χείρ ("hand"), and ἄρρωστος ("sick"). Thus, the final sign of laying hands on sick people in the Markan ending is entirely consistent with Jesus' ministry in the body of the Gospel.

It is also possible that the close proximity of taking up serpents in their "hands" and laying "hands" on the sick in Mark 16:18 finds some inspiration in Exod 4. The Septuagint uses χείρ ("hand") 103 times in Exodus, and the thirteen occurrences in chapter 4 are all associated with Moses' performing signs. In 3:8, 19, 20 there is a clear contrast between the hand of God and the hand of the Egyptians/Pharaoh, implying that the signs given to Moses are an extension of the hand of God. Many of the references to "hand" in the remainder of Exodus are in reference to the miraculous signs performed during the exodus. In 4:4 Moses stretches out his hand to take up the serpent and it becomes a rod again in his hand. In 4:6–7 Moses' hand becomes leprous, and then his hand is restored when he places it in his cloak a second time. The repetition of "hand" in reference to taking up serpents and then laying hands on sick people in Mark may reflect the repeated reference to Moses' hands in Exod 4. It appears that the author of Mark 16:18 views the signs of the believers in continuity with the miracles of Jesus and Moses.

Signs and the Centrality of Jesus as Lord

Central to the exodus narrative is the repeated emphasis on the identity of Yahweh as Lord (κύριος; LXX).[75] God reveals himself as the κύριος at the calling of Moses (Exod 3:15, 16; cf. 6:2, 3); God gives the sign of taking up the serpent in order that the Israelites may believe that "the Lord, the God of their fathers, the God of Abraham, and the God of Jacob" appeared to Moses (4:5); the Lord claims sovereignty over human health and ability when Moses claims to be slow of tongue (vv. 10–11);[76]

75. The Greek term is used 389 times in the Septuagint of Exodus.

76. The manuscripts of the Septuagint have the κύριος speaking in Exod 4:11;

it is the Lord who speaks (e.g., 5:1; 8:1, 16 LXX); and there are repeated statements where phrases similar to this occur: "And all the Egyptians will know that I am the Lord [ἐγώ εἰμι Κύριος]" (7:5; cf. 6:7; 7:17; 8:6, 18; 9:29; 10:2 LXX).[77] The signs clearly serve the purpose of pointing to the identification of God as the Lord. In addition, the Greek word for "name" (ὄνομα) occurs in reference to the name of the Lord in the exodus narrative as well (3:13, 15; 5:23; 6:3; 9:16; 15:3). This is significant not only because the title κύριος is attributed to Jesus in Mark 16:19–20, but also because Jesus affirms, "In my name [ἐν τῷ ὀνόματί μου] they will cast out demons" (v. 17).

A glance at the structure of Mark 16:15–20 confirms that the signs of the LE testify to the lordship of Christ in a manner similar to how they function in the exodus narrative. The opening "And he said to them" in verse 15 introduces the main thought: "Go into all the world and preach the gospel to all creation" (πορευθέντες εἰς τὸν κόσμον ἅπαντα κηρύξατε τὸ εὐαγγέλιον πάσῃ τῇ κτίσει). The three main components here are the aorist participle πορευθέντες ("going"), the imperative aorist verb κηρύξατε ("preach"), and the universal extent of the gospel. Although the participle πορευθέντες takes on imperatival force, the accent is clearly on the imperative "preach." These components are mirrored in verse 20a: "And they went out and preached everywhere" (ἐκεῖνοι δὲ ἐξελθόντες ἐκήρυξαν πανταχου). The aorist participle ἐξελθόντες is followed by the aorist verb ἐκήρυξαν and the far-reaching extent of the preaching. A reference to "signs" follows each of these verses and takes a prominent position. After Jesus tells the disciples to go and preach the gospel, his next word of encouragement to them is that "these signs will follow" (v. 17). In like manner, the summary of the preaching in verse 20 concludes with the Lord confirming the word through "signs [σημείων] following." "Signs" heads the sentence in verse 17 and concludes the ending in verse 20. The order consists of a participle "going," a verb "preach," and "signs" that "follow" in verses 15–18 and again in verse 20. A universal element accompanies the going in verse 15 and the preaching in verse 20.

Sandwiched between these parallel elements is this verse: "So then, the Lord Jesus [κύριος Ἰησοῦς], after he spoke to them, was taken up into heaven and sat at the right hand of God" (16:19). The main verbs "preach"

---

however, only the Alexandrinus text substitutes κύριος for θεός in οὐκ ἐγὼ ὁ θεός ("Is it not I, God?). Alexandrinus more closely reflects the Hebrew text.

77. Several other passages emphasize that God is the Lord in the early chapters of Exodus. E.g., 6:6, 29; 7:16; 8:22–23; 9:1, 13; 10:3 LXX.

and "preached" frame the statement that the Lord Jesus "sat" (ἐκάθισεν). The structure of verses 15–20 looks like this:

a. going / preach / universal gospel / signs will follow

b. The Lord Jesus

a. went / preached / universal gospel / signs following.[78]

When the author adds to this structure the statement that it was "the Lord" (τοῦ κυρίου) who was working with them and confirming the word with signs (v. 20), it becomes readily apparent that all of the signs listed in verses 17–18 are christocentric. They are accomplished because Christ is Lord, as indicators that he is the resurrected Lord, and by the Lord through his followers. It appears that Mark draws from the exodus narrative in order to provide a sense of continuity with and fulfillment of the Hebrew Scriptures in Jesus' resurrection appearances and commission to his disciples. The signs have a clear precedent in the exodus, and their ultimate purpose to identify Yahweh as Lord is now transferred to Jesus in order to identify him as Lord.

The Significance of the Signs of Mark 16

In keeping with the new exodus emphasis throughout Mark's Gospel, the ending incorporates several elements of the exodus narrative. Hardness of heart to believe Yahweh is a major concern in the exodus account, and even as Moses must guard against unbelief, so the disciples must believe in the resurrected Christ and obey his commission. The five signs Jesus lists in Mark 16 all find some degree of precedent in the exodus narrative. As the Lord delivered Israel from oppression and cast out seven nations before them, so the Lord has delivered Mary Magdalene from seven demons. The disciples will do likewise in Jesus' name. Moses was resistant to the call and complained of being "slow of tongue" at first; so also, the disciples will be empowered to speak in new tongues. Moses performed the sign of turning his staff into a serpent and converting it back into a staff when he picked the serpent up with his hand. Likewise, the disciples will take up serpents with their hands. That is, they will perform mighty miracles. As God distinguished between Israel and Egypt, plaguing Egypt

78. The universal extent of the preaching is emphasized by repetition in verse 15; consequently, the disciples go "into all the world" and they "preach the gospel to every creature." The fulfillment of the command in verse 20 lacks the first universal element.

with unfit drinking water but providing sweet water for Israel, so the Lord's miraculous and protective favor will rest on the disciples. Finally, as God made himself known as Israel's healer and manifested his hand of power in performing miracles with Moses' hand, so the disciples will follow the example of Jesus and lay hands on sick people to make them well. The above linguistic and conceptual parallels between Mark 16 and the exodus narrative point to Mark's dependence on that narrative.

Not only does Mark draw heavily from the content of Exodus, but he arranges his material to also climax at the enthronement of Christ (16:19). Mark has anticipated the clear identification of Jesus as Lord (1:3; 2:28), but only after his resurrection and in the closing words of his Gospel does he give him the designation "Lord Jesus" (16:19) and then repeat the title "Lord" (v. 20). As the signs point to the identification of Yahweh as the Sovereign Lord in the exodus story, so the signs point to the Lord Jesus in Mark 16.

Viewing the Markan ending in light of the exodus story suggests the following conclusions about Mark's understanding of tongues. First, Mark finds a precedent for miraculous speech in Moses' call. No other New Testament passage on tongues makes this specific connection, suggesting that Mark is not borrowing from other writers on this point. It is very likely that Mark knew all about Pentecost and alludes to the event, but his unique perspective separates him from other authors. Second, there is also evidence that Markan tongues are prophetic in nature. The divine enablement granted to Moses and his title as prophet provide the backdrop for the new tongues of the disciples. In this respect, Markan tongues exist in the same conceptual sphere of prophecy as Lukan (Acts 2:17–18) and Pauline tongues (1 Cor 12:10). Finally, the most significant point is that Markan tongues are listed among signs that point to the lordship of Christ. In this way, Mark's brief mention of tongues accomplishes the same central purpose of tongues in Acts 2: they signify the exalted status of the risen, ascended, and enthroned Lord Jesus.

Tongues in Luke and Mark Compared

Although the primary purpose of this study is not to argue for the originality of the LE, I have attempted to show that the LE provides a reasonable and proper conclusion to Mark, fulfills reader expectations, completes integral structures, and contributes theologically consistent closure. If Mark did indeed author the LE, then his ending was likely a source for Luke. But even if Mark was not the original author, or if there was some sort of disruption in the publication process, it still seems that the antiquity of the text, traditional use by the church, and orthodox account of the resurrection is sufficient to merit its acceptance as part of the canon.[79] Disruption theories (e.g., that Mark authored the ending at a later date than the body of the book) are so speculative in nature that, given the evidence offered above, I find it easier to assume that Mark wrote the LE as part of his original design.[80] In this scenario, Luke drew from the entirety of Mark but expanded on both the introduction and the conclusion to provide a fuller account for Theophilus. Luke probably sought out eyewitnesses such as Mary the mother of Jesus and Cleopas to flesh out Mark's account and address questions current in his day.

Parallels between Luke's two volumes and Mark suggest a significant relationship between the two authors, and this relationship extends into the LE. Historical realities may account for some of the similar charismatic and christological emphases in Acts 2 and 10 and Mark 16; that is, Peter likely served as a source for Mark, and Peter certainly features prominently in Acts 2 and 10. However, the similar gospel pattern between the events at Cornelius's household and the Gospel of Mark suggest dependence of Luke upon Mark (see chapter six).

The acknowledgment that Acts 10 and the Markan ending are associated with one another historically and theologically implies several conclusions for this study. First, that Luke follows the general outline of Mark all the way through the LE points to the antiquity and authenticity of the LE. Second, Luke's dependence upon Mark leads the reader to expect some significant parallels between the two works, and Luke shares several charismatic threads with Mark. It is not unlikely that Luke has built on Mark's promise of new tongues and recorded full-fledged accounts of their occurrence for clarity and instruction.

Third, interpreting the two texts in tandem clarifies the nature of baptism in the Spirit. John the Baptist prophesies that Jesus will baptize with the Spirit (Mark 1:8), and Mark implies that baptism in the Spirit accounts for the signs following the believers (16:17–20). But these signs clearly function through believers who are engaged in missions. Mark's

79. For a discussion of the position that the LE is non-Markan but canonical, see Thomas and Alexander, "'And the Signs are Following': Mark 16.9–20," 147–70.

80. See Snapp's reconstruction for an example of a disruption theory. *Authentic*, chapter 10.

narrative distinguishes between the role of signs in missions and the salvation/water baptism experience of the new believer (16:14–16, 20). The Lukan narrative (Luke 24; Acts 1) confirms what the reader assumes in Mark 16:14—that when Jesus himself appears to the disciples and chides them for their unbelief, they finally believe. For Mark, baptism in the Spirit serves a functional purpose in the ministry of believers, enabling them to perform signs. With Mark's account and Lukan themes informing the interpretation of Acts 10:44–48, the outpouring of the Spirit is best understood as an empowering experience of gentiles who have already exercised saving faith during Peter's preaching (Acts 11:14, 17; 15:7–9). The Spirit arrives with his accompanying sign of tongues not for purposes of conversion/initiation or individual regeneration, but as an empowering agent who inspires tongues as a charismatic sign typical of missionaries.

Fourth, in both of the texts under consideration speaking in tongues is associated with healing and deliverance—signs that strongly echo God's activity through Moses in the exodus. In the wake of Christ's fulfillment of the Old Testament types, his missionaries now perform wonders and speak in new tongues as they go out and proclaim his deliverance to the nations.

Fifth, a fusion of Christology, missions, and charismatic utterance is shared by Mark 16 and Acts 10:34–48. Despite the chronological and situational differences between the two passages, the theological similarities are remarkable, and the basic pattern evident in both places suggests that speaking in tongues was not an exceptional activity but a typical activity characteristic of those in submission to Christ's lordship and carrying out Christ's mission. Furthermore, the expectation of an expanding group of missionaries in both places ("those who believe" and "gentiles") suggests that speaking in tongues should not be relegated to ancient times.

Sixth, Luke's portrayal of tongues as a symbol of international missions in Acts 2, 10, and 19 is consistent with the emphasis on missions in Mark 16. Although Luke has the advantage of additional papyri to develop this theme, it is fair to say that the more obvious missiological symbolism of tongues occurring among the gentiles in Acts 10 is inherent in the fabric of Mark 16.

On the whole, the similarities between the tongues passages in Acts and Mark are rather impressive, especially in regard to christological orientation, missions, and even inspired proclamation. Yet there are some differences in degree of theological development and emphasis. The addition of Acts obviously affords Luke more room for expansion and the recounting of actual events that Mark can only anticipate. Both authors draw from Exodus, Isaiah, and various Davidic passages, although Mark contains more contextual markers associating tongues with the events of the exodus than Luke does. Luke more clearly associates tongues with prophetic praise and expends more energy associating tongues to prophecy in his two volumes than Mark does. Tongues serve a signifying purpose to both authors, especially regarding Christology and the believing state of Christ's missionaries, but Luke more directly notes how tongues evince the outpouring of the Spirit (Acts 10:46).

Interpreters of Mark and Luke benefit from various literary conventions including the authors' clever use of inclusio, repetition, Old Testament references, arrangement of material, direct speeches, and the narrator's commentary in the tongues passages. Both authors place their charismatic texts in prominent places where a preacher or narrator offers theological commentary. Such commentary verifies what the reader discovers by implication in the narrative and informs the reader of important details; consequently, the teaching about glossolalia in Mark and Luke has a surer footing than what some have realized when relegating narrative literature to a secondary theological or doctrinal status. In Mark, the mention of speaking in new tongues even falls from the lips of Jesus himself. The prominence these authors grant to tongues is largely due to the christological and missiological implications of speaking in tongues, but their treatment of this subject also presupposes the continuation of tongues as a typical activity among believers. According to Mark and Luke, as long as Jesus is Lord and the gospel is preached, believers will speak in tongues and signify that Jesus Christ is the promised and reigning Davidic King.

Summary

The themes and theology of the LE match quite well with the introduction of Mark and appear to form a frame around the book. In this regard, the LE forms a surprisingly suitable ending for Mark—regardless of who wrote it—although the traditional attribution of authorship to Mark still seems like the simplest explanation.

In this chapter I have highlighted the similar emphases on the gospel, its proclamation, and the necessity of faith in the introduction and the ending of Mark. These themes both frame the Gospel and typify the content throughout the narrative. The combination of these emphases and the framing element of Jesus' lordship establishes strong missiological and christological associations for charismatic signs and, particularly, for speaking in tongues.

The three direct references to the Spirit and the designation of Jesus as the Christ in the opening chapter establish a pneumatological lens for interpreting the charismatic actions of Jesus and his followers in the rest of the narrative. In Mark's story the Spirit identifies Jesus as the Messiah, empowers miraculous signs, enables victory in spiritual conflict, and inspires prophetic and christocentric utterances. Mark presents Jesus as a model of anointed ministry, and the charismatic signs at the end of Mark are consistent with what the reader expects of one who is baptized with the Holy Spirit. Speaking in "new tongues" implies the inspiration of the Holy Spirit.

The ending of Mark not only forms a thematic frame around the book, but it also continues to employ references to the exodus. Parallels with the early chapters of Exodus and the call of Moses seem too numerous and vivid to ignore. The Markan ending shares with Exodus an emphasis on hardness of heart, faith, signs, the expulsion of enemies, and inspired speech. Moses' slow tongue (βραδύγλωσσος; Exod 4:10) may very well provide the biblical precedent for the disciples' transition to speaking in new tongues (γλώσσαις λαλήσουσιν καιναῖς; Mark 16:17). Other parallels include a miracle involving serpents, a sign involving contaminated drink, miracles performed with the hands, the divine name, and the purpose of the signs in identifying the Lord. The ending of Mark makes this identification emphatic by repeating the word "Lord," reserving the designation "Lord Jesus" for the ending, and locating the "Lord Jesus" between two summaries of the disciples' mission. Their mission involves going out, preaching, the universal gospel, and signs that follow.

Five important elements about tongues in the Markan ending should be borne in mind. First, as in Acts, tongues in Mark occur in a context where the resurrection and lordship of Christ is central. Both the literary structures throughout Mark's Gospel and the resurrection vocabulary in the ending accentuate this resurrection context. The focal point of this link is the "Lord Jesus" (16:19), whose royal title is anticipated in the prologue and creates a christological center for the mission and its accompanying signs. Theologically connected to the resurrection, the ascension and session of the Lord Jesus at the right hand of God fulfills the Markan expectation of a coming Davidite. Jesus' "in my name" at the beginning of the list of signs applies primarily to casting out demons, but broadly speaking, also ties the signs to Christ's authority. For the "name" is the name of "the Lord Jesus," who is in a position of authority as the risen, ascended, and seated Lord.

Second, the author places glossolalia in a context of the universal proclamation of the good news about the one who is Lord of all. Speaking in tongues is closely associated with the missionaries and the mission, as it is a sign following "those who believe" as they spread the gospel. The promise of glossolalia in a context promoting the universal proclamation of the gospel is consistent with the international symbolism of tongues in Acts 2, 10, and 19.

Third, when Mark associates speaking in tongues with other signs typical of his functional portrayal of the Spirit (such as empowering exorcism and healing), he implicitly attributes speaking in tongues to the Spirit as well. The record of the disciples' charismatic ministry in 16:20 assumes the fulfillment of John's prophecy that Jesus "will baptize you with the Holy Spirit" (1:8).

Fourth, and closely related to the above, Mark's emphasis on a universal mission is accompanied by an accent on the spoken word, and his narrative attributes both prophetic utterances and empowered proclamation to the Holy Spirit. In 12:36 the prophetic utterance is directly connected with David's christological affirmation that God's Son is Lord, and in 13:11 Jesus foretells how the Spirit will speak through his disciples in the face of opposition. Thus, the missiological and christological emphases in Mark 16 imply that the Spirit is also responsible for the speaking in "new tongues." Throughout the Gospel it is clear that the mission does not progress without the Spirit's empowerment, and the missionaries experience this functional role of the Spirit in enabling various signs such as exorcism and speaking in tongues.

Fifth, the signs of Mark 16 have a biblical precedent (cf. Acts 2:16–21), as they reflect the miraculous calling and work of Moses. As the hand of God performed wonders through the hand of Moses, so the hand of Jesus confirms the message of his evangelists by doing miracles through their hands. At first the disciples were unbelieving and hesitant to preach. Like Moses, they were "slow of speech," but with their newfound faith they would no longer be characterized by slowness of speech but by powerful preaching and speaking in new tongues.

Mark never expounds on the content of tongues, but in a context where such signs are accomplished because Christ is Lord, in response to his enthronement as Lord, as indicators that he is the resurrected Lord, and by the Lord through his followers, there can be no doubt that tongues are christological.

Part 3

A Pauline Perspective on Tongues

8

Confessing "Jesus is Lord" in Corinth

It is difficult to imagine that the tongues of Corinth are phenomenologically distinct from those of Acts and Mark. The differences in emphasis and practice are most naturally accounted for by the occasional nature of Paul's letter to the Corinthians and the more missiological contexts of Acts and Mark.[1] While it is relatively easy to observe the varying contexts in which tongues occur, the common theological thread that unites the diverse passages on tongues has often escaped the reader. Just as Luke and Mark have given prominence to the lordship of Jesus in their tongues passages, so Paul records a christological confession in 1 Cor 12:3 that towers over his entire discussion of the gifts and, particularly, over his teaching on tongues: "No one is able to say, 'Jesus is Lord,' except by the Holy Spirit."

This chapter highlights Paul's emphasis on Christology in 1 Corinthians, and especially in the epistle's opening (1:1–9) and in the introduction to chapters 12–14 (12:1–3). It is argued that Paul's teaching on tongues is best understood when viewed in relationship to his Christology. The first segment of this chapter surveys some of Paul's references to Jesus as Lord and Christ as a repeated theme in 1 Corinthians and as a means of resolving the various problems at Corinth. The second segment covers the thorny issues related to pneumatology, knowledge, idolatry, the curse formula, and the christological confession in 12:1–3. A Summary concludes the chapter and emphasizes how crucial the

1. Keener's comparisons of Luke and Paul on tongues are of considerable help. Keener, *Acts: Exegetical*, 1:814–15.

christological confession that "Jesus is Lord" is to the entire discussion on tongues.

Paul, Christology, and the Corinthian Problem

Topical studies on tongues in 1 Corinthians run the risk of missing the foundational elements in the discussion by omitting Paul's emphases in chapter 1, especially his focus on Christology. While it is difficult to identify a single thread that explains the diverse Corinthian problems, Paul's continual references to the Lord Jesus go a long way in explaining his approach to resolving different issues.

Paul's Employment of "Lord" and "Christ" in 1 Corinthians

The introduction in many ancient works sets forth issues or themes to be addressed later in the work, and 1 Corinthians is no exception to that common practice.[2] Such themes in Paul's opening in 1 Cor 1:1–9 include: Paul's apostleship (1:1; cf. 9:1–2), the importance of calling (1:1, 2, 9; cf. 7:15–24), the greater church context (1:2; cf. 4:17; 7:17; 11:16; 14:33; 16:1, 19), the issues of speech (λόγος) and knowledge (γνῶσις; 1:5; cf. 4:19–20; 12:8), the spiritual gifts (1:7; cf. 12:4),[3] the eschatological hope (1:7–8; cf. 13:10–12; ch. 15), and the Lord Jesus Christ.[4] Paul refers to "Christ Jesus" three times (1:1, 2, 4), "our Lord Jesus Christ" three times (vv. 2, 7, 8), "the Lord Jesus Christ" (v. 3), "Christ" (v. 6), and "his Son Jesus Christ our Lord" (v. 9). Paul calls Jesus "Lord" (κύριος) a total of five times and "Christ" a total of nine times in only nine verses. None of Paul's other letters has such a dense concentration of christological terms in the introduction.

2. Talbert, *Reading Corinthians*, 15.

3. Soeng Yu Li cautions against viewing the introduction as a "table of contents" and anachronistically reading Paul's later discussion of the gifts back into chapter 1. While the caution is well taken, the combination of terms related to speech and knowledge (1:5; 12:8) and Paul's recognition that they do not lack in any gift (χαρίσματι; 1:7; 12:4) surely anticipates the lengthy segment in chapters 12–14. Paul knew from the outset what he needed to address. Li, *Paul's Teaching*, 56–63.

4. This multiplication of christological terms has long been observed by commentators. E.g., see Robertson and Plummer, *First Corinthians*, 7; Severian of Gabala, "Severian of Gabala," 14.

First Corinthians contains a total of sixty-four occurrences of Christ and sixty-six of Lord, of which about sixty refer to the Lord Jesus.[5] The numerous christological references and the issues raised in Paul's letter lead Gordon Fee to suspect that a christological problem involving "a diminished view of who Christ is" lies at the root of the Corinthians' behavioral issues.[6] If this is so (and it probably is), then one should expect the identity of Jesus as Lord to play a significant role in Paul's discussion of tongues. However, the biblical authors employ Christology in varying ways to address individual concerns. Although Luke and Mark work to persuade their audiences of Jesus' lordship in order to inspire faith, Paul focuses on this identity as a presupposition in order to alter behavior, yet the issue of Jesus' lordship looms large in tongues passages among all three authors.

Paul's solution for virtually every problem at Corinth centers on a proper view of Christ or application of his work to the Christian life.[7] In the opening section on division (1 Cor 1–4), Paul appeals to the Corinthians in "the name of our Lord Jesus Christ" to end divisions (1:10). His message is "Christ crucified" (1:23), for he is "the power of God and the wisdom of God" (v. 24). Christian leaders, however, should be regarded as "servants of Christ" (4:1). When Paul urges the Corinthians to bring discipline to a sexually perverse man, he instructs them to carry it out when they are gathered "in the name of our Lord Jesus" (5:4). Likewise, they should be able to judge minor cases among themselves rather than injuring one another, as they were "justified in the name of the Lord Jesus Christ" (6:11). The Corinthians should also avoid sexual vice because the body is "for the Lord" (6:13), and even one's marital status is a matter of the Lord's calling (7:15–23).

The Lord Jesus Christ remains at the center when Paul shifts to discussing issues related to worship in 1 Cor 8–14. Regarding food offered to idols, an idol is nothing because there is only one God and "one Lord Jesus Christ" (8:6). When Paul defends his apostleship, his defense

5. Only Paul's reference to "many lords" in 1 Cor 8:5 clearly could not refer to Jesus. On five occasions Paul refers to the "Lord" in connection with Old Testament quotations that primarily refer to the Lord God, but even some of these refer to the Lord Jesus (1:31; 2:16; 3:20; 10:26; 14:21). There are about nineteen occasions where Paul does not specify that the Lord Jesus is in view but where the context and his frequent use of the term for Jesus makes it very likely that he has the Lord Jesus in mind.

6. Fee, *Pauline Christology*, 86.

7. As Richard Hays observes, "From beginning to end Paul interprets every issue in light of 'the testimony of Christ.'" Hays, *First Corinthians*, 9.

begins with his claim to have seen the Lord (9:1). Idolatry amounts to tempting Christ (10:9), and propriety in worship requires that the church remember that the head of every man is Christ (11:3). Paul cautions the Corinthians not to sin against "the body and blood of the Lord" when they partake of the Lord's Supper (v. 27). Paul repeatedly uses "Christ" as practically the equivalent of a name when he argues for the future resurrection in chapter 15. There the entire basis for the resurrection of believers is the resurrection of Christ. Finally, the letter ends as it begins—with a repeated emphasis on the Lord. "If anyone does not love the Lord, let him be accursed. Our Lord, come! The grace of the Lord Jesus be with you. My love be with all of you in Christ Jesus" (16:22–24).[8]

It then comes as no surprise when an examination of 1 Cor 12–14 reveals that Paul's entire discussion of tongues and the gifts is firmly rooted in Christology. That Paul begins his argument with a strong christological confession in 12:3 ("Jesus is Lord") and ends this unit with another strong statement in 14:37 ("what I write to you is a command of the Lord") is not accidental. Paul has a habit of multiplying christological titles for emphasis and placing them at advantageous locations for literary and theological purposes. They often define the limits of a unit (Rom 5:1 with v. 11; Gal 1:3 with 6:18; Eph 1:1–2 with 6:23–24),[9] serve as a climax to a discussion (Rom 2:16; 6:23; 2 Cor 3:16–18; Phil 2:11), or reinforce an important teaching (Rom 5:21; Gal 6:14; 1 Thess 1:10; 2:19; 3:13; 4:17; 5:23).[10] These and similar features are found in 1 Corinthians. The multiplication of christological titles in the introduction places each topic mentioned within the context of the lordship of Christ. For example, Paul immediately reminds the Corinthians that they are part of a larger community of believers who call "on the name of our Lord Jesus Christ in every place." Jesus is "their [Lord] and ours" (1:2). The lordship

8. Ciampa and Rosner have compiled a similar list, noticing that "in almost every case Paul pits Christ against the prevailing culture." Ciampa and Rosner, *First Corinthians*, 33.

9. The phrase "through our Lord Jesus Christ" (Rom 5:1, 11) frames Paul's discussion of the benefits of justification. The only place in Galatians where the triple designation "Lord Jesus Christ" is used is in the introduction (1:3) and at the closing of the letter (6:14, 18).

10. Paul uses christological terms (and especially "Lord") in conjunction with eschatological terms to close out several paragraphs in 1 Thessalonians. The christological terms perform double duty in reinforcing eschatological hope and climaxing his discussion. Paul often seems to favor the term Lord in discussions of eschatology.

of Jesus over the entire Christian community reinforces Paul's exhortations to conform to generally accepted practices among believers.

When Paul instructs the Corinthians to discipline a sexually immoral man in the church, he adds a sense of solemnity to the occasion by bringing to bear "the name of our Lord Jesus" and "the power of our Lord Jesus" to the situation (1 Cor 5:4). Similarly, Paul employs the phrase "in the name of the Lord Jesus Christ and by the Spirit of our God" to serve as a climax to his argument against lawsuits among believers and to mark the end of the topic (6:11). Paul closes his lengthy instruction on the resurrection by reminding the Corinthians that believers have the victory "through our Lord Jesus Christ" (15:57) and must always abound "in the work of the Lord" because they know their "labor is not in vain in the Lord" (15:58). The "Lord" is literally the final word in the argument, just as the "grace of the Lord Jesus" and "Christ Jesus" conclude the entire book (16:23–24).

The Problem at Corinth

Opinions vary over the primary problem at Corinth and over the primary purpose of the letter, but any explanation devoid of Christology will certainly be deficient. Paul employs Christology to correct worldly thinking (chs. 1–3), unholy praxis (ch. 6), and flawed doctrine (ch. 15), and he does so by taking full advantage of the literary methods at his disposal. Whatever issue arises, Paul's constant emphasis on Christ's lordship suggests that, at a minimum, the Corinthians failed to apply the implications of Christ's identity and work to their daily lives and corporate worship. And given the resurrection discussion in chapter 15, it is also likely that at least some of the Corinthians suffered from a weakened or distorted doctrine of Christ.[11]

Older views of the problem at Corinth such as the influence of incipient gnosticism or of a "Cephas Party"[12] have largely fallen out of favor. Several scholars have posited the influence of an overrealized eschatology,[13] but even Anthony Thiselton has qualified his original

11. Martin sees a misunderstanding of eschatology contributing to a "defective understanding of Christ the Lord." Martin, *Spirit and the Congregation*, 52.

12. Sweet, "A Sign," 246.

13. Carson, *Showing the Spirit*, 16; Fee, *First Corinthians*, rev. ed, 12; Thiselton, "Realized Eschatology at Corinth," 510–26. Martin suggests that an overrealized eschatology is evident in the Corinthian view of tongues. Martin, *Spirit and Congregation*, 43.

argument for this view by also acknowledging the cultural influences of the city of Corinth.[14] So many scholars have adopted some version of the problem of corrupt social influence at Corinth that Roy Ciampa and Brian Rosner have observed the emergence of a "rough consensus" on the issue.[15] Paul Gardner sees this influence particularly in the area of "the seeking after knowledge and sophistry, and the desire for community status, belonging, and acceptance."[16] David Garland also perceives a problem with "secular wisdom" as well as with "a *lack* of a clear eschatological vision of the defeat of the powers of this age and the final judgment of God looming on the horizon."[17] Bruce Winter also blames the Roman culture, which the Corinthians "had grown up in, and imbibed" prior to their conversion to Christ.[18]

In light of the breadth of issues raised in 1 Corinthians, some scholars have opted not to settle on a single, over-arching ideology, teaching, or cultural influence, but to allow for a "combination of influences" at Corinth.[19] This is a sensible approach, but although there may be a plethora of cultural and religious influences impelling the problems at Corinth, Paul's solution is less complex. The Pauline response is the Lord Jesus Christ.

Even if one acknowledges a variety of contributing factors to the array of Corinthian issues, there still remains the difficulty of measuring both the extent of each influence and the severity of each problem. Virtually all scholars recognize that there was division at Corinth (1:10), but to what extent did this affect other matters in the epistle? Scholars have generally backed away from the idea of an overrealized eschatology, but Paul's sarcasm for the sake of argument in 4:8 (they had already begun to reign!) surely points to that type of mindset, whether that perspective exerts a controlling influence throughout the entire epistle or not. Paul directly confronts worldly thinking regarding status at the Lord's Supper (11:17–22), but it is another question whether or not a similar mentality drives the abuse of tongues at their gatherings. And if there is an air of elitism in the operation of the gifts, is it primarily expressed in a condescending attitude toward Paul, each other, or both?

14. Thiselton, *First Corinthians*, 40.

15. Ciampa and Rosner, *First Corinthians*, 4.

16. Gardner, *1 Corinthians*, 36.

17. Garland, *1 Corinthians*, 7, 14. Emphasis his.

18. Winter, *After Paul Left Corinth*, 27.

19. Moo, *Theology of Paul*, 113. Similarly, Talbert, *Reading Corinthians*, 10.

Fee sees "the basic theological problem" between Paul and the Corinthians as "what it means to be *pneumatikos* ('spiritual' = people of the Spirit). The problem here is not so much a matter of elitism among themselves—there is not a hint of such in the long passage where this matter is taken up (chaps. 12–14; i.e., that some feel superior to others because of their gifts, or that others feel inferior for the lack thereof). This habitually given answer is not based on anything explicit in the text but is read in from the outside."[20] Hovenden suggests that the problem was disunity between the Corinthian church and other churches, not elitism within the Corinthian church.[21] On the other hand, Forbes and others argue that the elitism was between the Corinthian church members themselves.[22] The differences of opinion are not merely academic but have practical significance in relation to the contemporary believer's expectations regarding the commonality of speaking in tongues today. Turner supposes that a problem of elitism between members of the Corinthian church implies a limitation of the practice of tongues, as there could be no elitist problem if all or most of the Corinthians practiced this charism.[23] Menzies accepts the premise that some degree of elitism exists, but counters Turner by suggesting that Paul advocates the potential universality of tongues to correct the elites (1 Cor 14:5).[24]

As the discussion turns to a more detailed look at chapter 12, it will touch on the matters mentioned so far, but a handful of items are considered to be fundamental to the conversation. First, the realization and application of Jesus' lordship is the essential element for bringing correction and restoring balance in the Corinthian church. Second, the opening line of chapter 12 identifies the nature of the problem Paul addresses: "Now concerning spirituals [Περὶ δὲ τῶν πνευματικῶν (*pneumatikōn*)]." It appears that the Corinthians had a basic problem with the definition of "spiritual," and Paul intends to redefine it for them.[25] Third, the worldly influences on the church were substantial, but it is neither possible nor necessary to know every cultural wind blowing through the church. Still, Paul has given sufficient instruction from his overall narrative and in the

20. Fee, *First Corinthians*, rev. ed., 11.

21. Hovenden, *Speaking in Tongues*, 157.

22. Forbes, *Prophecy*, 171–75; Turner, "Tongues: An Experience for All?" 235–37.

23. Turner, "Tongues: An Experience for All?" 237.

24. Menzies, *Speaking in Tongues*, 90–93.

25. Fee was right to point out that this was a major problem at Corinth. *First Corinthians*, rev. ed., 11.

passage at hand to know how to properly exercise the gift of tongues and other gifts in the local assembly.

Confessing Christ: The Foundation of Spirituality (1 Cor 12:1–3)

First Corinthians 12:1–3 serves as an introduction to chapters 12–14.[26] This introduction is extremely important as a foundation for the discussion on the use of gifts in the church, so it receives detailed treatment below. This section highlights Paul's literary strategy, definition of "spirituals," employment of knowledge terms, reference to "mute idols," and the acclamations of anathema and "Jesus is Lord."

A Spiritual Inclusio (1 Cor 12:1–3; 14:37–40)

Paul continues addressing matters generally related to worship in 1 Cor 12–14,[27] but he notifies the reader that he is moving to a new topic at 12:1 by employing at least five different means. First, he concludes the previous subject matter by saying he will give further instructions later (11:34). Second, he uses his familiar "now concerning" phrase (Περὶ δὲ; 12:1) to indicate a new division (7:1, 25; 8:1; 16:1, 12). Third, he uses direct address ("brothers"; 12:1), as he often does at transitions (e.g., Rom 12:1; 1 Cor 2:1; 3:1; 16:15; 2 Cor 13:11). Fourth, he does not want them "to be ignorant" (ἀγνοεῖν; 12:1). Paul often mentions knowledge or lack thereof in combination with "brothers" when he introduces a new subject or advances an argument.[28] Paul's use of two additional verbs for "to know" and "to make known" (οἶδα; 12:2; γνωρίζω; v. 3) indicates an intentional

26. So also Woyke, *Götter, 'Götzen', Götterbilder*, 258.

27. First Corinthians 12:1 begins at least the third section on worship. He has already spoken to the issue of head coverings in 11:2–16 and the Lord's Supper in 17–34. Talbert, *Reading Corinthians*, 103. If one includes the teaching on idolatry as part of the emphasis on worship, then chapters 12–14 are the final segment in a unit beginning at 8:1. Fee, *First Corinthians*, rev. ed., 631.

28. Paul uses ἀδελφοί with the verb γινώσκω in Phil 1:12. He often uses the phrase "I do not want you to be ignorant, brothers" or something similar (Rom 1:13; 7:1; 11:25; 1 Cor 10:1; 12:1; 2 Cor 1:8; 1 Thess 4:18). The statement contains a collocation with the verb ἀγνοέω and the plural noun ἀδελφοί. He also combines γνωρίζω with ἀδελφοί to say, "I want to make known to you, brothers" (or similar) on three occasions (1 Cor 15:1; 2 Cor 8:1; Gal 1:11). Sometimes he uses οἶδα ("to know") with ἀδελφοί (1 Cor 15:58; 1 Thess 1:4; 2:1; 5:1–2; cf. 1 Cor 16:5; 1 Thess 5:12).

word choice for a particular interest. Finally, Paul introduces his next topic with the use of πνευματικῶν (12:1): "Now concerning spirituals, brothers, I do not want you to be ignorant [Περὶ δὲ τῶν πνευματικῶν, ἀδελφοί, οὐ θέλω ὑμᾶς ἀγνοεῖν]."[29] In this manner Paul alerts the reader to the issue under discussion. In verse 3 he twice mentions the Spirit and "makes known" to them that "no one speaking [λαλῶν] by the Spirit [πνεύματι] of God says: 'Jesus be cursed,' and no one is able to say, 'Jesus is Lord,' except by the Holy Spirit [πνεύματι]," pointing to the true definition of spirituality.

That Paul intentionally addresses spirituality, knowledge, speech, and the Lord in his opening verses and will integrate them into his discussion directly or by way of presupposition is confirmed at the end of this unit. These emphases are repeated when Paul concludes, "If anyone thinks he is a prophet or spiritual [πνευματικός], let him acknowlege [ἐπιγινωσκέτω] that what I write to you is a command of the Lord [κυρίου]. And if anyone ignores [ἀγνοεῖ] this, then he will be ignored [ἀγνοεῖται]. So, my brothers [ἀδελφοί], be zealous to prophecy and do not forbid to speak [λαλεῖν] in tongues; but let everything be done properly and in an orderly manner" (1 Cor 14:37–40). And to confirm that Paul has reached a conclusion, he begins the next segment this way: "Now I make known to you, brothers, the gospel that I preached to you" (15:1). By repetition of key words and topics, Paul has framed his entire argument.[30] Not only does this inclusio establish the limits of his argument, but it also confirms what subjects are essential to it. Paul is concerned to define true spirituality, and his version of it involves the right kind of knowledge—a knowledge that causes one to submit to the lordship of Jesus. Proper speaking (including prophesying and speaking in tongues), then, will reflect these realities.

"Now Concerning Spirituals" (1 Cor 12:1)

First Corinthians 12:1–3 acts as the introduction to chapters 12–14 and is the first of four units in chapter 12 (12:1–3; 4–11; 12–26; 27–31). The initial verses are fraught with difficulties and competing opinions among

29. I have not capitalized "spiritual" and related pneumatic terms, but the strong relationship between these words and the Holy Spirit is understood throughout the discussion.

30. For additional examples of Pauline frames, see Talbert, *Reading Corinthians*, 2–3.

scholars. One of the first issues involves what Paul means when he says, "Now concerning spirituals" (πνευματικῶν/*pneumatikōn*; 12:1). The adjective (used as a noun) could be either genitive masculine (people of the Spirit) or neuter (spiritual things). In the latter case, Paul may have spiritual gifts in mind. Another question arises over the relationship between πνευματικός and the χαρισμάτων ("grace gifts") mentioned in verse 4. Are these two terms used interchangeably? Does Paul prefer one term over the other?

In regard to the first issue, most Bible versions read the substantival adjective as neuter, translating it as "spiritual gifts" (ASV, ESV, NASB, RSV, NRSV) or "gifts of the Spirit" (NIV 2011, NJB). Many scholars also side with this reading,[31] often pointing to the neuter τὰ πνευματικά in 14:1 and a perceived parallel between πνευματικῶν and χαρίσματα.[32] Others argue that Paul has in mind people rather than gifts. Paul Gardner directs attention to 1 Cor 2:15, 3:1, and 14:37 as examples where spiritual people are in view. In addition, 12:2–3 emphasizes the character and confession of truly spiritual people.[33] Yet others simply cannot decide,[34] and some, such as Barrett, feel no compulsion to choose: "It seems impossible to find objective grounds for a decision between the two possibilities, and little difference in sense is involved—spiritual persons are those who have spiritual gifts."[35] Ciampa and Rosner understand the term more broadly and suggest that a translation of "spiritual gifts" at 12:1 is premature, as the discussion is only beginning.[36]

The term πνευματικὸς ("spiritual") occurs nowhere in the Septuagint, and twenty-four of the twenty-six occurrences in the New Testament are in Pauline books. The term has varied uses and is employed to describe a "gift" (χάρισμα; Rom 1:11), the law (7:14), blessings or benefits (15:27; Eph 1:3), a contrast with material things (1 Cor 9:11), the nature of the resurrection body (15:44, 46), and songs (Eph 5:19; Col 3:16). Paul also uses the word to describe the state of persons as spiritual (1 Cor

31. E.g., Carson, *Showing the Spirit*, 22; Conzelmann, *1 Corinthians*, 204; Fitzmyer, *First Corinthians*, 457; Hodge, *First Corinthians*, 239; Schatzmann, *Pauline Theology*, 31–32. Fee also leans in this direction but does not believe the term should be understood too rigidly. Fee, *First Corinthians*, rev. ed., 638. Similarly, Li favors a neuter reading but does not think the term means "spiritual gifts." Li, *Paul's Teaching*, 116.

32. Carson, *Showing the Spirit*, 22; Conzelmann, *1 Corinthians*, 204.

33. Gardner, *1 Corinthians*, 526–27.

34. Garland, *1 Corinthians*, 558.

35. Barrett, *First Corinthians*, 278.

36. Ciampa and Rosner, *First Corinthians*, 562.

2:13, 15; 3:1; 14:37; Gal 6:1).[37] At times there is a strong christological emphasis in the immediate context. The spiritual person is not subject to the judgment of others, as this person has the "mind of Christ" (1 Cor 2:15–16). Paul cannot speak to the Corinthians as spiritual people, as they are worldly and "babes in Christ" (3:1). The source of spiritual food and drink to the Israelites was a spiritual rock: "and the rock was Christ" (10:3–4). Every spiritual blessing of the Ephesians is "in Christ" (1:3), Paul prays that the Colossians will have spiritual wisdom and understanding "to walk worthy of the Lord" (1:9–10), and he admonishes them to "let the word of Christ dwell in" them by singing "spiritual songs" (3:16). Paul conceives of a spirituality that is directly related to Christ.

It is also revealing that several passages where the term occurs have a direct connection with the Spirit (πνεῦμα). After Paul mentions the Spirit seven times in Gal 5:16–26, he charges those who are οἱ πνευματικοὶ ("Spirit people") to restore any fallen brother "with a spirit of gentleness [πνεύματι πραΰτητος]" (6:1). That Paul has attributed gentleness to the Spirit in 5:23 suggests that the Spirit is still in view. Douglas Moo opts for the human spirit in 6:1, drawing support from 1 Cor 4:21 and translating, "in a gentle manner."[38] Fee prefers "the inelegant 'S/spirit' as a way of catching Paul's nuance."[39] The issue raises a real dilemma for translators who desire to show the connection between the cognates, but, with Fee, I find it hard "to imagine that this connection would have been lost on the Galatians themselves."[40]

When Paul commands the Ephesians to "be filled with the Spirit [πνεύματι]" (Eph 5:18), one of the five participles following the imperative includes "speaking" in "spiritual songs [ᾠδαῖς πνευματικαῖς]" (5:19). The grammar and the cognate adjective point to songs that have their origin in the Spirit. When Paul prays for the Colossians to "be filled with the knowledge of his will in all wisdom and spiritual [πνευματικῇ] understanding" (1:9), it follows hard on the heels of his complementing them for their "love in the Spirit [πνεύματι]" (v. 8). In the space of only seven verses (1 Cor 2:10—3:1), Paul mentions the Spirit (πνεῦμα) six times, the term "spiritual" (πνευματικός) four times, and the adverb "spiritually" (πνευματικῶς) once. Again, it would be difficult to believe

37. The gender of πνευματικοῖς is uncertain in 2:13, but it likely refers to "spiritual people."

38. Moo, *Galatians*, 375.

39. Fee, *God's Empowering Presence*, 462.

40. Fee, *God's Empowering Presence*, 462.

that the Corinthian auditors and readers would not realize the relationship among terms and conclude that Paul is attempting to help them find the correct definition of spirituality in the Spirit. After reminding them that "we have the mind of Christ," he continues, "And I, brothers, was not able to speak to you as to people of the Spirit [πνευματικοῖς] but as fleshly [σαρκίνοις], as babes in Christ" (3:1). For Paul, maturity in Christ is directly related to spirituality, and the Corinthians exhibited a lack of both by their jealousy, strife, and divisive pride over certain leaders (vv. 1–9).

This Pauline way of thinking is no less evident when we return to 1 Cor 12. Following the initial occurrence of "spirituals" (πνευματικῶν; v. 1), Paul names the Spirit eleven times in the following twelve verses (vv. 2–13). The context essentially makes the determination of the adjective's gender a moot point.[41] The Corinthians will necessarily hear the term "spirituals" explained in terms of the Spirit, and this explanation will also immediately center on the identity of Jesus as Lord (vv. 3 and 5). In addition, Paul explains that the christological confession that makes each individual a person of the Spirit also gives the believers a new corporate identity as the body of Christ (vv. 12, 27). What Paul has done in other places and contexts, he does again. That is, he draws from a Christ-exalting pneumatology as a basis for proper behavior in the church.[42] Without this foundation in place, the reader misses important elements in Paul's correction of aberrant practices related to speaking in tongues.

Regarding the relationship between πνευματικός ("spiritual") and the χαρισμάτων (*charismatōn*; "grace gifts"), some scholars argue that the terms are used interchangeably. Paul's use of *charismatōn* in 1 Cor 12:4, where the term introduces the list of gifts in verses 8–10, would imply that the *pneumatikōn* of verse 1 are spiritual gifts. Support for the position that the terms are synonymous is found in the parallel framing around chapter 13: ζηλοῦτε δὲ τὰ χαρίσματα ("but earnestly desire the *charismata*"; 12:31) and ζηλοῦτε δὲ τὰ πνευματικά ("and earnestly desire the *pneumatika*"; 14:1).[43] With the notion that the two words are used

41. If pressed, I would lean in the direction of a neuter adjective, but Paul apparently felt no compulsion to make this clear, as this was not where his interests lay.

42. Karl Maly is right to point out that Paul is not merely introducing a discussion on gifts of the Spirit, but 12:1–3 is a heading introducing the various effects of the Spirit. Maly, "1 Kor 12,1–3," 93.

43. Brookins and Longenecker, *1 Corinthians 10–16*, 62; Schatzmann, *Pauline Theology*, 32. The framing of chapter 13 does not require that the terms have an identical meaning, even if they are closely related. In addition, *pneumatika* has some degree of diversity of use even within 1 Corinthians.

synonymously in 1 Cor 12 is the added notion that Paul prefers the term *charismata* over *pneumatika*,[44] as the latter was likely a Corinthian term and possibly associated with ecstasy.[45] Earle Ellis distinguishes between the terms and suggests that *charisma* is more broad and can be used of any gift while *pneumatika* "appears to be restricted to gifts of inspired perception, verbal proclamation and/or its interpretation."[46] Li holds that "the semantic relationship between χαρίσματα and πνευματικά can best be understood as meronymy. . . . The implication of meronymy is that all parts contribute to a better understanding of the whole."[47] In this view, the grace gifts, ministries, and workings of 12:4–6 are parts of the larger concept of the *pneumatika*, and chapters 12–14 are primarily about this larger concept.[48] Although I would not care to make the sharp distinctions Li makes between the grace gifts, ministries, and workings, her essential argument that *pneumatika* is the more general term and that it is directly related to the *pneuma* is on point.[49]

Paul employs χάρισμα (*charisma*) sixteen times in his writings, and seven of these occurrences are in 1 Corinthians. In 1:7 the term anticipates the discussion in 12:4; and the gift in mind in 7:7 relates to singleness and marriage. The term is used in the plural in 12:9, 28, and 30 to describe gifts of healings, and Paul encourages the Corinthians to eagerly desire the greater gifts in verse 31. Although the term has a broad use and is applied to the gift of eternal life (Rom 6:23) and Israel's "gifts" and calling (11:29), it is also used in other passages in association with what are commonly termed the "spiritual gifts" (Rom 1:11; 12:6; cf. 1 Tim 4:14; 2 Tim 1:6). As Fee notes, the term comes from χάρις ("grace") "as a way of concretely expressing the abstract noun."[50] To emphasize the divine source of the gift, Garland applies the expression "grace-gift."[51] The term is not inherently related to the Spirit, but the association with

44. Dunn, *Jesus and the Spirit*, 208. Witherington, *Conflict and Community*, 255.

45. Schatzmann, *Pauline Theology*, 32.

46. Ellis, *Prophecy and Hermeneutic*, 24. Also Martin, *Spirit and Congregation*, 8.

47. Li, *Paul's Teaching*, 191.

48. Li attempts to obtain more precision in defining the relationships between the terms, but her attempt to outline 1 Cor 12:7–30 based on Paul's mention of grace gifts, ministries, and workings is difficult to demonstrate. Li, *Paul's Teaching*, 224.

49. Li, *Paul's Teaching*, 201, 261.

50. Fee, *God's Empowering Presence*, 33.

51. Garland, *1 Corinthians*, 575.

the Spirit occurs in the context of several passages mentioned above.[52] This is particularly the case in Rom 1:11, where Paul desires to impart some "χάρισμα . . . πνευματικὸν" ("spiritual gift").

Fee argues that *pneumatikos* "functions primarily as an adjective for the Spirit, referring to *that which belongs to, or pertains to, the Spirit*."[53] He points to the -ικός ending in support of this definition and to Pauline usage in both the masculine and neuter forms of the word.[54] Viewed this way, the *pneumatikōn* of 1 Cor 12:1 introduces the core issue under discussion: What does it mean to be "spiritual"?,[55] and the specific problem at hand involves the use of *charismata* (grace-gifts). The major concern, then, is with what it means to be people of the Spirit, and the operation of one of the Spirit's grace-gifts, speaking in tongues, must conform to Paul's christological definition of spirituality.

In Terms of Knowledge

Paul's use of three terms related to knowledge in 1 Cor 12:1–3 provides additional assistance to the reader in focusing on the topic at hand. Paul does not want the Corinthians to be ignorant (ἀγνοεῖν) of *pneumatikōn* (1:1), and he asserts their knowledge ("You know"; Οἴδατε) of their pagan past when they were led astray by mute idols (v. 2). Finally, Paul concludes, "Therefore I make known [γνωρίζω] to you that no one speaking by the Spirit of God says, 'Jesus is Anathema,' and no one is able to say, 'Jesus is Lord,' except by the Holy Spirit" (v. 3). Paul does not generally incorporate large numbers of knowledge terms in his epistles (unlike the Gospel of John), but the Corinthian letters do contain an unusual number of such terms within the Pauline corpus. He uses a variety of terms in the γνῶσις ("knowledge") family, including this term, which occurs ten times in 1 Corinthians—more than any other New Testament book. Second Corinthians adds another six uses. First Corinthians has sixteen occurrences of γινώσκω ("to know"), four of ἀγνοέω ("to be ignorant"), two of γνωρίζω ("to make known"), three of only nine New Testament occurrences of γνώμη ("opinion"), four of the compound ἐπιγινώσκω ("to know, recognize"), and one of συγγνώμη ("concession").

52. Fee, *God's Empowering Presence*, 33.

53. Fee, *God's Empowering Presence*, 29. Emphasis original.

54. Fee, *God's Empowering Presence*, 31.

55. So also Fee, *God's Empowering Presence*, 30.

Paul commonly uses the verb οἶδα ("to know") for rhetorical purposes in his epistles, but 1 Corinthians includes this verb twenty-five times—an inordinately high number for Paul. He especially likes to use the second person plural οἴδατε ("you know"), which occurs twenty-seven times in the Pauline corpus with twelve in 1 Corinthians alone.[56] Often the term is part of Paul's penetrating rhetorical question, "Do you not know?" (Rom 6:16, 11:2; 1 Cor 3:16; 5:6; 6:2, 3, 9, 15, 16, 19; 9:13, 24). The term loses some of the polemical edge when Paul simply asserts the knowledge of others, but he is also capable of adding emphasis to it with "you yourselves know" (1 Thess 2:1; 3:3; 5:2; 2 Thess 3:7). The "you know" in 1 Cor 12:2 lacks the impassioned flavor the verb has in other contexts; Paul is not chiding the Corinthians so much as reminding them of their past in verse 2. It is the combination of three knowledge terms, building on the problem of corrupt knowledge already addressed in the epistle, that gives this text a bit of pungency. While the overall tone lacks the same level of energy as Paul's correction of sexual vice in chapter 6, the additional comment regarding cursing Jesus maintains some intensity in this section. Paul is not quite angry, but he is very serious.

The two basic knowledge verbs (γινώσκω and οἶδα) may not be synonymous, as Axel Horstmann maintains that the first "was originally an inceptive" verb "representing the acquisition of knowledge ('come to know')," and the second "denotes the theoretical possession of knowledge (*know*; *be acquainted with*)."[57] But more importantly, Paul is clearly piling up the knowledge terms for rhetorical effect and building on his earlier corrections to a Corinthian obsession with knowledge. In the introduction Paul affirms that they were "enriched" in Christ, "in all speech [λόγῳ] and all knowledge [γνώσει]" (1:5). Paul consistently rejects worldly wisdom and knowledge in favor of the knowledge of Christ and his cross (vv. 21–23; 2:2, 8–16). He continues developing this theme of proper knowledge in his discussion of food offered to idols, where various terms for knowledge occur eleven times in eleven verses (8:1–11). The opening of this chapter provides a helpful parallel to 12:1–3. "Now concerning food offered to idols, we know [οἴδαμεν] that 'we all have knowledge [γνῶσιν].' Knowledge [γνῶσις] puffs up, but love builds up; if anyone thinks he has come to know anything [ἐγνωκέναι], he has not yet known [ἔγνω] as he ought to know [γνῶναι]. But if anyone loves God, he

56. See also the compound σύνοιδα ("to know, be aware of") in 1 Cor 4:4.

57. In his review of the terms, he suggests that the "classical distinction" between the terms holds in most passages in the New Testament. Horstmann, "οἶδα," 494.

is known [ἔγνωσται] by him" (8:1–3).[58] In this passage, Paul advocates love as the basis for proper behavior and warns against the pride associated with the acquisition of knowledge; he is not here confronting an incipient Gnosticism.[59]

There are several similarities between 1 Cor 8:1–3 and 12:1–3 and their surrounding contexts in addition to the "now concerning" transitional phrase and repetition of various knowledge terms. Both passages affirm in principle the existing knowledge of the Corinthians. Idols are nothing, and there is only one God (8:4); thus, "we all have knowledge" (8:1) is true as far as it goes. In 12:2 Paul affirms their knowledge that mute idols led them astray in the past.[60] However, in both cases their knowledge is deficient in some way, and this deficiency is not merely a matter of intellectual, factual, of theoretical knowledge, but is a matter of relational knowledge and behavior. Not all the Corinthians do, in fact, share the same knowledge (8:7), so the proper response is love (v. 1), sensitivity to the weak believer, and a relinquishing of personal rights (vv. 7–13). In 12:3 the new knowledge is actually a realization of how speech under the influence of the Spirit operates—it exalts Jesus. Based on this realization, Paul's lengthy discussion promotes love (ch. 13) and the edification of Christ's body in the use of gifts.

Although the topic differs between the two texts, both make the lordship of Jesus a central point. In 8:6 Paul uses the Corinthian knowledge of one God to his advantage and adds that there is "one Lord, Jesus Christ, through whom are all things and through whom we live." The triple designation of Jesus is intentional; it makes Jesus' lordship emphatic and presents the true authority and model of loving behavior (cf. vv. 11–12).[61] Even though the surface problems of eating food offered to idols and misuse of the gift of tongues seem very different, the underlying

58. Various translations (e.g., ESV, CSB, NIV 2011, NRSV) use quotations around the phrase "we all have knowledge," viewing it as a Corinthian slogan. Also, I have used masculine pronouns in my translation in order to maintain a more literal reading and to avoid the awkwardness of applying the plural pronoun "they" to a singular "anyone." Paul's intention is certainly gender inclusive. Regarding the text-critical issues in verse 3, see Fee, *First Corinthians*, rev. ed., 405–7.

59. In agreement with Fitzmyer, *First Corinthians*, 338, and contra Bultmann, "γινώσκω, γνῶσις, κτλ.," 709.

60. Brookins and Longenecker also detect a connection between the Corinthians' knowledge in 8:1 and 12:2. *1 Corinthians 10–16*, 62.

61. There are other similarities in the passages. For example, both contexts mention the problem of limited knowledge and the concept of being known by God (8:2–3; 13:12).

issues turn out to be quite similar. Paul must redefine what knowledge is and what it means to be people of the Spirit. He accomplishes this by offering a christocentric definition of knowledge that entails not only an acknowledgment of Jesus' lordship, but the practical implementation of Christ's love among the members of Christ's church. The topic has changed in chapter 12, but the redefining of terms and adjusting of behavior in light of Christ continues.

Led Astray to Mute Idols (1 Cor 12:2)

As Paul moves from the term "ignorant" (1 Cor 12:1) to what the Corinthians already know (v. 2), the exegete is confronted with a number of difficulties. "You know that when you were pagans, you were led astray to mute idols, whenever you were led" (Οἴδατε ὅτι ὅτε ἔθνη ἦτε πρὸς τὰ εἴδωλα τὰ ἄφωνα ὡς ἂν ἤγεσθε ἀπαγόμενοι; v. 2). The first difficulty arises with the ellipsis in the text; if "you were" is part of the "when" clause, no finite verb remains to complete the sentence. Most scholars supply a second "you were" verb as a simple and acceptable solution.[62]

A major difference among interpreters concerns Paul's intention in referring to the influence of "mute idols." Is he alluding to the activity of demonic spirits behind the idols? There is no clear statement of this in 12:2, but some scholars suggest that Paul's previous references to sacrificing to demons (1 Cor 10:19–22) suggests they are in view here.[63] Some take this influence a step farther and suggest that Paul is beginning to refute the influence of pagan ecstasy in the operation of tongues in the assembly. The latter perspective has had wide support among critical commentators of the past. Martin embraces this view and gives a typical articulation of it: "Now Paul touches on another trouble-spot, the uncontrolled abandon to spiritual ecstasy, implied in the verb 'you were led {astray}' (v. 2). The feature of a trancelike state that characterized the Corinthians' former pagan life (see Gal. 4:3, 8, 9) was carried over into their worship services."[64] Although a definition of "ecstasy" is seldom given, scholars in this camp usually intend the word to imply a frenzied

62. Fee, *First Corinthians*, rev. ed., 639; Gardner, *1 Corinthians*, 527; Robertson, *Word Pictures*, 4:167; Thiselton, *First Corinthians*, 911. For a survey of grammatical options, see Brookins and Longenecker, *1 Corinthians 10–16*, 63; Li, *Paul's Teaching*, 202–8.

63. E.g., Robertson, *Word Pictures*, 4:167.

64. Martin, *Spirit and the Congregation*, 9.

state where the participant is not in control of his or her faculties.[65] This implies more than a heightened sensitivity to spiritual things.

Dunn's re-creation of the circumstances at Corinth relies heavily on the language of 1 Cor 12:2 and incorporates the notion of ecstasy: "We may assume from the implied rebuke of 12.2 that this frequently involved the assembly (or certain members) working themselves up into a state of spiritual excitement, leaving themselves open to passions and powers (spirits?) which swept them away (ἤγεσθε ἀπαγόμενοι—12.2) in an outpouring of glossolalic ecstasy, and which brought no benefit to other believers let alone unbelieving outsiders."[66] This perspective usually looks to the term μαίνεσθε ("to be mad" or "insane") in 14:23 for support.

This articulation of the problem with tongues at Corinth enjoyed wide acceptance among scholars until it came under closer scrutiny by Christopher Forbes and others. Forbes examined the potential parallels to tongues in the Hellenistic world, including the practices of the Delphic oracle and Delian Apollo, the cults of Dionysus and Cybele, and various popular religious movements.[67] Forbes concludes that "nowhere in the world of pre-Christian Hellenism has a substantial parallel for early Christian glossolalia been found. Those phenomena claimed to be parallels in the modern scholarly debate have suffered from either or both of two major defects: they have been drawn from periods and sources which do not predate Christianity, and the phenomena themselves can be shown to be substantially different from glossolalia as it was understood and/or practised within early Christianity."[68] Forbes dismisses the supposed scenario in which tongues at Corinth are identified in some way with pagan ecstasy in favor of a view where tongues have been introduced by Paul and are fundamentally distinct from pagan practices. Forbes identifies the problem at Corinth as related to elitism, not ecstasy.[69]

It is possible that Paul alludes to the demonic inspiration of the past in 1 Cor 12:2, but the notion that tongues are analogous to pagan ecstasy or that such ecstasy has crept into the Corinthian church seems gratuitous

65. Soards attempts to differentiate between pagan ecstasy (emotionalism) and christocentric "enthusiasm." Soards, *1 Corinthians*, 254. The two may not always be easily differentiated, but the christological confession distinguishes them. Grudem also offers four tests for ecstasy. Grudem, *Gift of Prophecy*, 150–51.

66. Dunn, *Jesus and the Spirit*, 234.

67. Forbes, *Prophecy*, 103–81.

68. Forbes, *Prophecy*, 169–70. For similar conclusions, see Hovenden, *Speaking in Tongues*, 6–30.

69. Forbes, *Prophecy*, 170–75.

and more than the text itself can support. The scenario offered by Terrance Paige is more plausible. He points out that the Corinthians were not led "by" the idols but "towards" the idols.[70] Paige suggests, "The language of v. 2 evokes the image of a cultic festival procession (the πομπή) in which the participants normally proceeded along a sacred route, led by priests and other celebrants, those carrying cult objects or a cult image."[71] Such a procession (*pompē*) often "ended at a sanctuary where sacrifices were offered to the god."[72] Paige notes that *pompai* were part of the festivals connected with Apollo, Dionysus, and Isis at Corinth, that the word ἄγω ("to lead") was used with reference to the priests leading the processions, and that animals led to sacrifice in the procession may provide Paul with an image for describing the captivity of the devotees to dark powers.[73] Paige's proposal is sensible, yet the supporting evidence in 12:2 is too meager to conclude so much.

Although pinpointing a particular pagan practice may prove difficult, there are clues in the text to Paul's main interests. The phrase ἤγεσθε ἀπαγόμενοι ("you were led" and "led astray") is emphatic in its use of ἄγω ("to lead") with the compound verb ἀπάγω ("to lead away"). In addition, the phrase ὡς ἂν ἤγεσθε ("whenever you were led") has an iterative force to it, emphasizing that the Corinthians had repeatedly been misled in the past.[74] Ciampa and Rosner have well summarized the point when they remark that the pagan past of the Corinthians was "thoroughly marked by deception"; and "whether Paul has cultic processions, demons, or self-deception in mind, the Corinthians' experience of idolatry was not one that prepared them to discern the true nature of spiritual experiences."[75] Paul also gives prominence to the "mute idols" by locating the prepositional phrase before the final verb and participle (πρὸς τὰ εἴδωλα τὰ ἄφωνα ὡς ἂν ἤγεσθε ἀπαγόμενοι). In this way Paul can underscore the futile direction of their former lives ("to mute idols") while emphasizing the deceptive influence at work.

70. Paige, "1 Corinthians 12:2," 58.

71. Paige, "1 Corinthians 12:2," 59.

72. Paige, "1 Corinthians 12:2," 59.

73. Paige, "1 Corinthians 12:2," 60–63.

74. On the iterative force of this, see BDF §367; Brookins and Longenecker, *1 Corinthians 10–16*, 63; Fitzmyer, *First Corinthians*, 457–58. Cf. BDAG, 95. For an in-depth discussion of the syntax of 1 Cor 12:2, see Li, *Paul's Teaching*, 202–8.

75. Ciampa and Rosner, *First Corinthians*, 564.

The "mute idols [τὰ εἴδωλα τὰ ἄφωνα]" is a typical attributive adjective, and the location of the phrase early in the sentence is more significant than the order of the words "idols" and "mute."[76] The syntagma reflects the Old Testament and Jewish disdain for idols (I Kings 18:26; Pss 115:5; 135:16; Isa 46:7; Jer 10:5; Gen. Rab. 84:10; *m. Sanhedrin* 7b; 3 Macc 4:16; Jos. Asen. 8:5; 11:8; 12:5; 13:11).[77] Habakkuk 2:18–20 is particularly illuminating, as this fifth in a series of five woes to Babylon highlights Babylon's "speechless idols" (אֱלִילִים אִלְּמִים; v. 18). Ironically, the metal image teaches lies (v. 18) but is unable to teach (v. 19); that is, there is something deceptive about idols, even though they are only material objects that can provide no revelation.[78] Regarding the image, "there is no breath in it at all" (וְכָל־רוּחַ אֵין בְּקִרְבּוֹ; v. 19); the image is completely devoid of life.[79] As is typical in such passages, the silent idols are contrasted with the living Lord: "But the LORD is in his holy temple; let all the earth keep silence before him" (v. 20 ESV).[80]

The above elements shed light on 1 Cor 12:2–3, as the "mute idols" of verse 2 are understood against the backdrop of a living and speaking God who imparts speaking gifts that operate by his Spirit. God gives revelation, and the presence of revelation is evident in the acclamation that "Jesus is Lord." The deception evident in verse 2 may very well be due to demonic influence, but this is not where Paul's emphasis lies. He is not suggesting that demonic influence has crept into the church via pagan ecstasy; he is asserting the vanity and folly of pagan life devoid of God, the Spirit, revelation, and submission to the Lord Jesus. The pagan life is a Spirit-less life, but life in Christ begins with a revelation and inspired confession that "Jesus is Lord." Paul's discussion of the gifts of utterance springs from this understanding of the Spirit's activity in exalting Jesus as Lord.

76. In other words, "speechless" is not de-emphasized by its location after the noun; it reflects the traditional phraseology as found in Hab 2:18 (εἴδωλα κωφά; LXX).

77. Woyke is right to bring out the broader implications of τὰ εἴδωλα τὰ ἄφωνα and to find its significance in the Hebrew Scriptures and Judaism. Woyke, *Götter*, 264. Woyke is followed by Li, *Paul's Teaching*, 210–11.

78. Robertson, *Nahum, Habakkuk, and Zephaniah*, 210.

79. Barker and Baily, *Micah, Nahum, Habakkuk, Zephaniah*, 349. I agree with Woyke (followed by Li) that this is a significant element in understanding Paul's point. Woyke, *Götter*, 267; Li, *Paul's Teaching*, 211.

80. The Septuagint brings out the idea of contrast with the adversative δὲ. The word for "Lord" in the Septuagint of this verse is κύριος. The final reference to "silence" adds another note of irony to the passage.

"Anathema Jesus" Vs. "Lord Jesus"

The progression of thought moves from Paul's comment on ignorance in 1 Cor 12:1, to what the Corinthians know (v. 2), to what Paul makes known to them (v. 3): "Therefore I make known to you that no one speaking by the Spirit of God says, 'Jesus is anathema,' and no one is able to say, 'Jesus is Lord,' except by the Holy Spirit" (διὸ γνωρίζω ὑμῖν ὅτι οὐδεὶς ἐν πνεύματι θεοῦ λαλῶν λέγει· Ἀνάθεμα Ἰησοῦς, καὶ οὐδεὶς δύναται εἰπεῖν· Κύριος Ἰησοῦς, εἰ μὴ ἐν πνεύματι ἁγίῳ).[81] The sudden appearance of the anathema in this text has baffled scholars and spawned numerous interpretive theories. Thiselton lists twelve distinct explanations of the enigmatic phrase.[82] W. C. Van Unnik argues that the anathema is actually a positive phrase; that is, it points to Jesus' sacrificial death and his becoming a curse in order to pay for sin.[83] However, Van Unnik's attempt to explain why such an anathema cannot be uttered by someone speaking by the Spirit seems unconvincing. Walter Schmithals suggests that some gnostic Christians cursed Jesus and attributed this to the inspiration of the Spirit.[84] The gnostic dualism between flesh and spirit required the cursing of the physical Jesus while exalting the spiritual Christ, but this imposition of a second-century problem into Paul's context is anachronistic. Barret proposes that Paul is "referring to the cries of Christian ecstatics who were resisting the trance or ecstasy they felt coming upon them" in a manner similar to the Greco-Roman ecstatics.[85] But it is difficult to imagine believers cursing Jesus, and the previously mentioned critiques of the ecstatic view preclude such a reading. Winter looks to the Corinthian culture and the discovery of "twenty-seven ancient curse tablets" found in that area for an explanation.[86] Winter then translates, "Jesus [grants or gives] a curse" and concludes that "some Christians were invoking Jesus to punish, restrain or disadvantage others."[87] However, this reading seems grammatically strained and not entirely in keeping

81. I take the preposition ἐν as an instrumental dative "by" because the verb δύναται ("is able") implies an enabling that fits better with instrumentality than it does with location.

82. Thiselton, *First Corinthians*, 918–24.

83. Van Unnik, "Jesus: Anathema or Kyrios (1 Cor 12:3)," 119–20.

84. Schmithals, *Gnosticism in Corinth*, 124–30. See Origen, *Contra Celsum*, 6.28.

85. Barrett, *First Corinthians*, 280. Dunn holds a variation of this view, as mentioned earlier in this chapter. Dunn, *Jesus and the Spirit*, 234.

86. Winter, *After Paul Left Corinth*, 164.

87. Winter, *After Paul Left Corinth*, 176, 179.

with the overall context of 1 Cor 12–14. The above views suffer from too much speculation coming from outside the immediate context.

Jouette Bassler suggests that Paul may be alluding to his own former lifestyle as an opponent of Christ, while others believe Paul refers to Jews in general.[88] Hays sees the anathema as a "hypothetical counterexample" to the confession to follow but also leaves room for a possible reference to Paul's prior life.[89] David Aune well articulates the perspective of those who see the curse as a literary device, viewing it as a "hypothetical Pauline construct created as an antithesis to the distinctively Christian exclamation 'Jesus is Lord!'"[90]

While it is hard to imagine that any Christian could utter the anathema, it is also difficult to explain why Paul would introduce such a startling curse formula if there were not some basis in reality for it.[91] In addition, some scholars have struggled with the Jewish nature of the term anathema when verse 2 emphasizes the idolatry of the gentiles. As the term simply meant a votive offering in the Hellenistic world (cf. Jdt 16:19; 2 Macc 2:13),[92] the use of the term as something that is cursed by God is more consistent with its typical use in the Septuagint (e.g., Deut 7:26; Josh 6:17–18; 7:1, 11–13).[93] Consequently, some scholars struggle with a perceived disconnect between pagans in verse 2 and Jews in verse 3, but this presumption is unnecessary. Paul expects the Corinthians to understand his very Jewish reference to "mute idols" in verse 2, so one need not assume their unfamiliarity with Jewish curse terminology in verse 3 (cf. 5:7; 10:1–11). Thus, the professing of a curse need not be limited to Jews but could potentially apply to anyone opposed to Christ, and it most likely and directly applies to the pagans mentioned in verse 2.[94]

The parallelism between the two confessions suggests a translation of anathema as "Jesus is cursed" rather than "Let Jesus be cursed." Paul

88. He also appears to be advocating the idea that the curse is a literary device. Bassler, "1 Cor 12:3—Curse and Confession," 415–21. Robertson and Plummer include Jews in general as those speaking the anathema. *First Corinthians*, 261. Garland points to a Jewish use of anathema as important to interpretation here. *1 Corinthians*, 570.

89. Hays, *First Corinthians*, 208.

90. Aune, *Prophecy in Early Christianity*, 257. So also Keener, *1–2 Corinthians*, 100.

91. Fee, *God's Empowering Presence*, 156.

92. BDAG, 63. See the discussion in Thiselton, *First Corinthians*, 918.

93. Behm, "ἀνατίθημι, προσανατίθημι, ἀνάθεμα, κτλ." 354.

94. Ciampa and Rosner see the curse as likely limited to Jews. *First Corinthians*, 566. So also Talbert, *Reading Corinthians*, 103–4.

clearly uses the latter, imperatival construction with anathema on three occasions (1 Cor 16:22; Gal 1:8, 9), but he indicates this with an accompanying imperatival verb.[95] Outside 1 Cor 12:3, the only remaining Pauline use of the anathema term is in his wish that he could be accursed and cut off from Christ for Israel's sake (Rom 9:3). Paul's employment of the term in 1 Cor 16:22 holds the most promise for purposes of comparison with 12:3. Paul concludes his letter: "If anyone does not love [φιλεῖ] the Lord [τὸν κύριον], let him be anathema [ἤτω ἀνάθεμα]. Lord come [μαράνα θά]! The grace of the Lord Jesus [κυρίου Ἰησοῦ] be with you. My love be with all of you in Christ Jesus [Χριστῷ Ἰησοῦ]" (16:22–24). The emphasis on Christology is obvious, but there are some surprises in this conclusion, including the unique mention of loving the Lord,[96] the rare use of the verb φιλέω to express the love,[97] and the presence of the anathema and maranatha terms (employing paronomasia).

The unusual occurrence of a curse in a Pauline conclusion arrests one's attention and strongly implies that this anathema is somehow connected with 1 Cor 12:3. It also reinforces the notion that the curse in 12:3 is not merely hypothetical.[98] It may also be related to the closing frame around chapters 12–14, where Paul requires those who think they are prophets or spiritual to recognize the Lord's authority in Paul's writing (14:37). He continues, "But if anyone is ignorant, let him be ignorant" (v. 38). It is likely that this is a warning of judgment for anyone who lacks true, christocentric spirituality and rebels against the Lord's command. The phrase "if anyone does not love the Lord" (16:22), accompanied by the curse, serves as a general warning to pagans who curse Jesus (12:2), but it may also be a shot across the bow for those in the congregation who oppose the Lord (and Paul) under the pretense of spirituality. Paul not only disallows the curse in 12:3, but he ultimately reverses it: the cursers will be cursed. The maranatha expression is a call for Jesus to return and bring judgment to those who do not love him (16:22) and to bring eschatological rescue to those who are already experiencing his grace (v. 23).

95. The noun ἀνάθεμα only occurs six times in the New Testament (cf. Acts 23:14), and five of these are in Paul's letters.

96. This is the only place in Pauline literature where love for Jesus is mentioned. Fee, *Pauline Christology*, 85.

97. See Thiselton, *First Corinthians*, 1351.

98. With Fee, *Pauline Christology*, 120.

The closing verses of 1 Cor 16 echo elements found in the epistle's introduction (1:1–9); for example, one finds the repetition of Paul's identification, mention of the broader church, grace, the Lord's return, eschatological judgment ("the day of our Lord Jesus Christ"; 1:8), and an emphasis on the Lord Jesus.[99] Paul concludes with a tender word of his love for the Corinthians "in Christ Jesus" (16:24), but clearly, all is not well at Corinth, and the repeated references to the lordship of Jesus and warnings of eschatological judgment featuring him suggest that evil influences are not only applying pressure in the areas of ethics and community practices, but also in the area of Christology (e.g., ch. 15 on the resurrection). Consequently, every topic in the epistle is addressed with Christ in view, and Paul emphatically insists that the lordship of Jesus is foundational to his discussion of spirituals in chapters 12–14. Christology, of course, is where Paul excels anyway.

The anathema, therefore, although certainly constructed in a literarily advantageous manner alongside the confession of Jesus' lordship, is not merely stylistic but reflects opposition to Jesus in the larger Corinthian setting. Of the various explanations offered for the inclusion of the anathema in 1 Cor 12:3, those scholars emphasizing the role of the Holy Spirit are moving in the right direction,[100] as the topic remains the *pneumatikōn* (v. 1), the "mute idols" (v. 2) are breathless (Hab 2:19), the *pneuma* is mentioned nine times in 1 Cor 12:4–13, and the *pneuma* occurs twice in verse 3. The Spirit is clearly the source and agency of inspiration. The "therefore" (διὸ) in verse 3 directly connects the deceptive life of breathless, mute idols with what Paul desires to "make known" to the Corinthians—the inspiration of the Spirit in confessing the Lord Jesus. Paul frames the opposing acclamations with reference to the Spirit: "No one speaking by the Spirit of God says, 'Jesus is anathema,' and no one is able to say, 'Jesus is Lord,' except by the Holy Spirit" (οὐδεὶς ἐν πνεύματι θεοῦ λαλῶν λέγει· Ἀνάθεμα Ἰησοῦς, καὶ οὐδεὶς δύναται εἰπεῖν· Κύριος Ἰησοῦς, εἰ μὴ ἐν πνεύματι ἁγίῳ; v. 3). By specifying the Spirit "of God" Paul includes all three members of the Trinity in verse 3, preparing the way for the Trinitarian source of the graces, ministries, and workings in verses 4–6. The "Holy Spirit" is a fitting expression to describe the sanctity of the christological confession in contrast to the curse uttered in

99. There is even a final charge to "know" or "recognize" the godly members of the church (16:18).

100. E.g., Fitzmyer, *First Corinthians*, 458–59; Kistemaker, *First Corinthians*, 415–16; Li, *Paul's Teaching*, 208–18; Maly, "1 Kor 12, 1–3," 84, 93–95.

the absence of divine inspiration. This framing technique in verse 3 creates a strong tie between the Spirit and the realization and acclamation of Jesus' identity as Lord (cf. 2:12–16).

A subtle change in the language between the two confessions is significant. The curse is introduced with "no one . . . says," but the christological confession is introduced with "no one is able [δύναται] to say."[101] This implies that more than mere words are involved in the confession; it is a divine enabling that includes the illumination of the human heart to the reality of Jesus' identity (cf. 8:1–6; Rom 10:9; Phil 2:9–11). The Spirit's enabling the initial confession of faith becomes paradigmatic for Paul; every aspect of the believer's life has its origin in and enabling by the Spirit (1 Cor 6:11), and the Spirit's work is always Christ-centered. The Corinthians must remember their pneumatic initiation into Christ in order to properly function in the various graces.

Although the confession of Jesus' lordship is much more than words, verbal inspiration is also important in a context where a local church's use of the verbal gifts has gone amuck. Consequently, 1 Cor 12:1–3 incorporates several references to appropriate speech. This relates well to Paul's earlier emphasis on the Spirit's power in proclaiming the gospel rather than on human wisdom and eloquence (2:4–5). In 12:2 the idols are "mute." In 12:3 no one "speaking" by the Spirit "says," and no one is able "to say" the confession without the Spirit. In addition, both the curse and the christological confession are spoken acclamations. While mere words are not in view, inspired speech certainly is in view. This emphasis anticipates the discussion on tongues and prophecy.

An understanding of 1 Cor 12:1–3 requires a view that integrates Paul's emphasis on the Spirit, knowledge, speech, and the lordship of Jesus and explains the reference to idolatry in verse 2, the curse in verse 3, and the connection to the entire unit (chs. 12–14). Paul introduces his topic as concerning matters related to the Spirit. However the Corinthians define this, Paul defines the work of the Spirit as fundamentally connected with the recognition of Jesus' lordship. Paul moves the discussion forward from explaining his desire that the Corinthians not be ignorant, to what they already know, to what they must come to know. They already know about their idolatrous past where they were led astray

101. Maly has also noticed the importance of this word: "Δύναται weist auf die Befähigung, die der Geist geben muß. Menschliche Einsicht und Urteilskraft reichen allein nicht aus, um zum Bekenntnis Jesu als des «Herrn» zu führen." Maly, "1 Kor 12, 1–3," 90.

to mute idols—idols that had no breath in them. Paul helps the Corinthians realize that the Spirit played no part in the pagan cursing of Jesus; rather, the Spirit inspires and enables people to declare the lordship of Jesus. This declaration by the Spirit becomes paradigmatic for the life of every Christian. When it comes to the gifts of the Spirit, and especially to tongues and prophecy, the pneumatic exaltation of Christ must be the foundation for every utterance and every practice in the church. The christological confession is more than a test to discern the origin of utterances in the church (though it also applies to that): the recognition of Jesus' lordship serves as the context for all behavior.

Summary

The acclamation "Jesus is Lord" in 1 Cor 12:3 is part of a larger emphasis that runs throughout the entire epistle. The introduction (1:1–9) anticipates several themes that occur later in the work, but no theme receives more emphasis than the Lord Jesus Christ. At Corinth, the solution to virtually every problem is the Lord Jesus, and when Paul wants to drive home an important teaching or bring a unit to completion, he often does so by multiplying christological titles (e.g., 16:22–24). Scholars have suggested numerous reconstructions of the problem at Corinth, but it seems best to recognize an assortment of cultural influences infecting the church, resulting in a lack of submission to the lordship of Jesus in doctrine, ethics, and corporate worship practices. The one solution to the various problems is the re-establishment of Christ's lordship. The Corinthians need a new definition of spirituality: a truly spiritual person (a person of the Spirit) submits to Jesus as Lord.

This redefining of spirituality is an essential component of 1 Cor 12–14, and an inclusio at 12:1–3 with 14:37–40 highlights Paul's concern with the adoption of Christ-centered functioning as pneumatic people. Such people will also have Christ-centered knowledge and Christ-centered speech. Paul's profound interest in this spirituality is evident in his repeated references to the Spirit (12:3–13; cf. 2:9—3:1) and in his transitional phrase: "Now concerning *pneumatikōn*, brothers" (12:1). Whether *pneumatikōn* is masculine or neuter has little bearing on Paul's main interest, which is to redefine what it means to be spiritual in terms of Jesus' lordship. Consequently, spiritual people (i.e., people of the Spirit), will use the grace-gifts (*charismatōn*) in a Christ-honoring manner. The larger category and concern is that of spirituality, and Paul urges the Corinthians to properly implement the use of the grace-gifts under the umbrella of a christocentric spirituality.

Paul also incorporates knowledge terms in 1 Cor 12:1–3 in order to show the progression of his argument and make explicit the Christ-cursing nature of paganism and Christ-exalting nature of the Spirit. Paul's reference to mute idols (v. 2) has its roots in the Old Testament (especially Hab 2:18–19) and highlights the irony of how mute, breathless idols lead pagans astray. Idols are deceptive, yet they are devoid of spirit. This is in direct contrast to the Spirit of God, who inspires believers to confess the resurrected Lord Jesus.

Multiple explanations of the presence of the anathema in 1 Cor 12:3 have been offered, but a natural interpretation views the pagans in verse 2 as cursing Jesus. Paul uses Jewish terms throughout 1 Corinthians and in reference to mute idols in 12:2, so this explanation faces no substantial obstacle. Paul's use of anathema in his closing of the epistle, along with the maranatha expression and other references to the Lord Jesus (16:22–24), sheds light on the curse in 12:3. The parousia reverses the curses; the pagans who curse Jesus will ultimately receive the curse. In 12:2–3 those led astray to breathless, mute idols curse Jesus, but those who have the Holy Spirit confess his lordship. This confession, in keeping with Rom 10:9–10, points to the moment of salvation when someone submits to Jesus' lordship and becomes paradigmatic for the Christian life. The repeated references to how one speaks and the acclamations of cursing and confession anticipates Paul's discussion of the utterance gifts of prophecy and speaking in tongues. The double mention of the Spirit in 1 Cor 12:3 contrasts with the uninspired nature of mute idols, defines true spirituality in submission to the lordship of Jesus, and prepares the audience for a discussion of verbal grace-gifts that is grounded in the lordship of Jesus.

First Corinthians 12:1–3 serves as the introduction to chapters 12–14, and it provides the theological foundation for the proper expression of the grace-gifts, and particularly speaking in tongues. Without this pneumatic Christology in place, the interpreter and practitioner loses his or her mooring, misses the fundamental point of this unit, and interprets tongues outside of Christ.

9

Tongues and the Body of Christ in Corinth

FROM THE OUTSET OF 1 Corinthians Paul has insisted that there is only one Lord Jesus Christ, and from the knowledge of this Lord proceeds proper behavior, sound doctrine, and a communal perspective. The confession "Jesus is Lord" (1 Cor 12:3) was already in view when Paul addressed his letter to those who "have been sanctified in Christ Jesus, called to be saints, with all those calling on the name of our Lord Jesus Christ in every place, their [Lord] and ours" (1:2).[1] For Paul, pneumatic activity is Christ-centered activity (12:3), and this principle guides his discussion in 1 Cor 12–14. Although the titles of Jesus occur relatively infrequently in these chapters (12:3, 5, 12, 27; 14:37), they are strategically positioned for maximum impact, and allusions to Jesus and the implications of the introductory confession are felt throughout the charismatic conversation.

The following discussion picks up at 1 Cor 12:4 and begins with Paul's introduction to tongues within the broader context of Christ as one body. Topics in this section include tongues as one of a variety of gifts, baptism into the body of Christ, and the greater gifts in the body of Christ (ch. 12). The next two major sections cover "the tongues of men and of angels" (13:1) and tongues and the eschaton (vv. 8–13). The phenomenology of tongues and the issue of cessationism receive attention in these sections. The centrality of Christology is highlighted throughout the discussion, and a summary concludes the chapter.

1. Cf. Rom 1:5; 10:13; 15:9, 20; 1 Cor 1:10, 13, 15; 5:4; 6:11; 2 Cor 9:13.

Christ as One Body with Many Members (1 Cor 12:4–31)

Charles Talbert has noted the ABA′ pattern in 1 Cor 12:4—14:40: spiritual gifts (12:4–30), the love motivation for their use (12:31–14:1a), and spiritual gifts again (14:1b–40).[2] He rightly observes a similar ABA′ pattern within chapter 12 (vv. 4–11; 12–27; 28–30),[3] where lists of gifts surround an emphasis on the multiple members of Christ's body. In this structure, 12:1–3 is understood as the introduction to the entire unit (chs. 12–14). The discussion to follow approaches the text with these divisions in mind.

Tongues as One of Many Gifts (1 Cor 12:4–11)

Paul has set forth the general topic and christological principle for addressing the Corinthian problem, but he has not yet specified that speaking in tongues is the particular issue that requires attention. He introduces this topic within the broader context of a diversity of gifts bestowed by the one divine source (1 Cor 12:4–11). From the mention of the three members of the Trinity in verse 3 comes an anaphora of "varieties" (διαιρέσεις; v. 4) in which Paul attributes varieties of "gifts" (χαρισμάτων), "services" (διακονιῶν), and "workings" (ἐνεργημάτων) to the "same" Spirit, Lord, and God, respectively. Some scholars have opted to translate διαιρέσεις as "distributions"[4] or "allotments" rather than "varieties," drawing support from the use of the verb διαιρέω ("to distribute") in verse 11,[5] but most translations have employed "varieties" (ESV, NRSV, NASB) or "different" (NIV 2011, CSB, NJB, NET) in keeping with the variety of gifts listed in verses 8–10.[6] This translation is consistent with the idea that Paul wants to emphasize that there is a diversity of gifts but one divine source.

2. Talbert, *Reading Corinthians*, 103. Also Ciampa and Rosner, *First Corinthians*, 560; Fee, *First Corinthians*, rev. ed., 632–33. Garland sees a similar pattern, but adds the parallel introduction (12:1–3) and conclusion (14:37–40). Garland, *1 Corinthians*, 559–60.

3. Talbert, *Reading Corinthians*, 104.

4. Barrett, *First Corinthians*, 283.

5. Collins, *First Corinthians*, 452.

6. The term διαιρέσεις is used only in 1 Cor 12:4, 5, and 6 in the New Testament. It occurs more often in the Septuagint, where it is commonly used in references to divisions of land (Josh 19:51) or peoples (1 Chr 24:1).

The Lord and the List of Good Gifts

Paul's correlation of Jesus as "Lord" (κύριος) with "services" (διακονιῶν) is appropriate to Christ's own model of ministry (Matt 20:26; 23:11) and Paul's own view of service (1 Cor 3:5). The risen Lord graciously invites people to participate in serving in different capacities. Paul grounds his argument in the generosity of the Triune God (12:4–6), who himself embodies diversity within his own identity.[7] Implicit in this reference is the arrival of a new eschatological age. The Corinthians have left their former lives (v. 2) to enter into the age where Jesus is Lord and God is pouring out his Spirit (cf. Joel 2:28–32). The repeated references to the Spirit (1 Cor 12:3–13), in keeping with the topic of "spirituals" (12:1), serve as continual reminders of this new state of affairs. Verse 7 encapsulates the point of the gift list to follow: "Now to each one is given the manifestation [φανέρωσις] of the Spirit for the benefit of all."[8] For Paul, every reference to the Spirit is inherently eschatological (1:7), and his concern for "the benefit of all" underscores the communal interests of the Spirit in the age of Christ. The emphasis on diversity and corporate edification prepares the way for Paul's correction of the misuse of tongues. It is common for scholars to see in Paul's reference "to each one" the idea that Paul is emphasizing that every believer has a gift. Often paired with this emphasis is the notion that Paul is refuting tongue-speaking elitists who think that only they are the gifted in Corinth.[9] Whether or not everyone has a gift is not Paul's primary concern; rather, he is concerned to demonstrate the Spirit's generosity in giving a variety of manifestations to the church.[10]

7. Fee, *Pauline Christology*, 125.

8. The only other use of the noun φανέρωσις in the New Testament is found in 2 Cor 4:2, but the cognate adjective φανερός is found eighteen times. Perhaps Paul's use of φανέρωσις may also be a reminder of his eschatological comment regarding factions at the Lord's Supper (1 Cor 11:17–19; cf. vv. 26, 32). Paul refers to their differences as necessary "to make manifest [φανεροὶ γένωνται] those who are approved among you" (v. 19). On an eschatological interpretation of 1 Cor 11:19 over Pauline irony, see Gardner, *1 Corinthians*, 505–6.

9. As John Poirier notes, "There really is no reason to assume that the problem with the gift of tongues at Corinth was related to glossolalists flaunting their gifts before non-glossolalists." Poirier, *Tongues of Angels*, 57.

10. I agree with Fee that "this pronoun is the distributive (stressing the individualized instances) of the immediately preceding collective ('in all people'), which emphasizes the many who make up the community as a whole." *First Corinthians*, rev. ed., 653. Contra Brookins and Longenecker, *1 Corinthians 10–16*, 68; Fitzmyer, *First Corinthians*, 465–66; and Gardner, *1 Corinthians*, 531.

Various schemes have been offered to categorize the list of gifts, and Paul's alternating use of two demonstrative pronouns for "another" (ἕτερος and ἄλλος) may point to intended divisions at 1 Cor 12:9a and 10d (ἕτερος with "faith" and "kinds of tongues") or may simply be stylistic, but the change to ἕτερος in verse 10 probably highlights the introduction to "different kinds of tongues."[11] It appears that Paul intentionally lists the "word of wisdom [λόγος σοφίας]" and "word of knowledge [λόγος γνώσεως]" first, as wisdom and knowledge feature so prominently in the Corinthian context and knowledge terms frame the entire discussion (12:1–3; 14:37–38). Paul anticipates the gifts discussion in 1:7 (χαρίσματι) and specifically mentions "all speech and all knowledge [παντὶ λόγῳ καὶ πάσῃ γνώσει]" (v. 5). His brand of speech is Christ-centered, and Christ did not send him to preach with rhetorical eloquence and human wisdom (σοφίᾳ λόγου), "lest the cross of Christ be emptied of its power" (1:17). "For the message of the cross [Ὁ λόγος γὰρ ὁ τοῦ σταυροῦ] . . . is the power of God" (v. 18). This combination of "word" or "message" and "wisdom" continues in 2:1, 4, and 13, and Paul rejects the message of those who are "puffed up" (4:19), "for the kingdom of God is not in word [λόγῳ] but in power" (v. 20). While many scholars struggle to find any clear difference between a word of wisdom and a word of knowledge,[12] the importance of the two gifts lies in Paul's turning around two sources of Corinthian pride, baptizing them into Christ, and listing them as forms of Spirit-given, verbal revelation for the church. These gifts reinforce the notion that all the gifts are subsumed under the lordship of Jesus and that the Spirit functions christologically. Applying these principles to the utterance gifts suggests that tongues operate with boundaries—they function christocentrically and for purposes of edification.

The list of gifts in 1 Cor 12:8–10 is *ad hoc*, with the verbal gifts occupying the beginning and end of the list. Some of the gifts occur in the plural: gifts of healings, workings of miracles, discernings of spirits,

11. Brookins and Longenecker point out that the UBS5/NA28 texts have the conjunction δὲ with each occurrence of ἄλλος but with neither occurrence of ἕτερος, although there is textual uncertainty over the conjunction in verse 10. This may point to intentional divisions, although Brookins and Longenecker view this as merely stylistic. *1 Corinthians 10–16*, 69.

12. E.g., Conzelmann, *1 Corinthians*, 209; Dunn, *Jesus and the Spirit*, 221; and Hodge, *First Corinthians*, 245. If there is any significant difference between the gifts, the difference may be found in the definitions of "wisdom" and "knowledge." Hodge simply defines them as "the gift of speaking or communicating wisdom" and "the gift of communicating knowledge." Hodge, *First Corinthians*, 245. The christocentric element should be added to any definition proffered.

and different kinds of tongues (vv. 9–10). The plurals give the sense that there is diversity within diversity; that is, there seems to be a variety of ways these gifts function or manifest in practical use. That tongues occur last in the list (along with the interpretation of tongues) is not because this gift is an unwanted step-child, but because it is, as Fee so appropriately expresses it, the "problem child."[13] The list of scholars who have attempted to besmirch, diminish, or advocate the cessation of this gift is considerable,[14] but correcting a misuse of a gift is far from relegating it to the ash heap or supposing that God offers inferior, embarrassing gifts. Along with interpretation of tongues, it occurs at the end of the list again in 12:30 because it is the topic under discussion. Similarly, it is first in the list in 13:1–2, not because it is the greatest gift, but because it is the main gift requiring attention. It appropriately follows prophecy and its companion gift, discerning of spirits (12:10), in preparation for the lengthy discussion of prophecy and tongues in chapter 14. Moreover, if lesser gifts are listed last, then prophecy must also be inferior to other gifts listed prior to it, but this flatly contradicts Paul's strong encouragement to prophesy in chapter 14 (cf. 12:28).

"Kinds of Tongues" and "Interpretation of Tongues" (1 Cor 12:10)

Paul never explicitly mentions tongues (*γλωσσῶν*) outside of 1 Cor 12–14, but in this unit, he employs the term twenty-one times and draws the term "other tongues" (ἑτερογλώσσοις) from the Septuagint on one occasion (14:21; Isa 28:11). He uses the phrase "kinds of tongues" (*γένη γλωσσῶν*) twice (1 Cor 12:10, 28), "interpretation of tongues" (*ἑρμηνεία γλωσσῶν*) once (v. 10), variations of "speak in tongues" (*λαλεῖν γλώσσαις*) eight times (12:30; 13:1; 14:5 [2x], 6, 18, 23, 39; cf. Acts 10:46; 19:6), variations of "speaking in a tongue" (*λαλῶν γλώσσῃ*) five times (1 Cor 14:2, 4, 13, 19, 27), "tongues" (*γλῶσσαι*) alone twice (13:8; 14:22), and "tongue" (*γλῶσσα*) three times (14:9, 14, 26).[15] Acts 2:4 also has the phrase "to speak in other tongues" (*λαλεῖν ἑτέραις γλώσσαις*) and Mark 16:17 has "they will speak in new tongues" (*γλώσσαις λαλήσουσιν καιναῖς*). Given

13. Fee, *First Corinthians*, rev. ed., 655, and similarly, 634.

14. E.g., Beare, who refers to tongues as of "inferior value" and "childish" and claims that "the main purpose of Paul is to discourage the practice of speaking with tongues among Christians." Beare, "Speaking with Tongues," 124.

15. At times there are other words intervening between the mention of tongues and the verb "speak."

the similar expressions, and especially the nearly identical use of "to speak in tongues" multiple times in 1 Corinthians and in Acts 2:4, 10:46, and 19:6, Anthony Palma rightly concludes "that the expression *lalein glōssais* is a *terminus technicus* of the New Testament."[16] One might also include Mark 16:17 in this assessment.

The initial references to tongues in each book (there is only one in Mark) have an additional descriptor (Acts 2:4: "other"; Mark 16:17: "new"; 1 Cor 12:10, 28: "kinds") suitable to each context. Thiselton emphasizes Paul's plural γένη ("kinds"), translating it as "species." This definition allows him to underscore the idea of "family resemblances" among species of tongues, and these resemblances both differentiate the tongues family from prophecy and explain the difficulty in defining "a phenomenology of tongues."[17] In other words, it is difficult to define precisely what tongues are because Paul himself has stated that there are different species of tongues. Forbes also ponders whether Paul's "kinds of tongues" might refer to the various phenomena described by Paul and Luke.[18] Brookins and Longenecker suggest the phrase may refer "to various dialects of 'angelic speech' (cf. 13:1), or to a multiplicity of foreign languages, such as we find in Acts 2:5–12; possibly, it is a mixture of the two, although ch. 14 points to the first possibility."[19] More attention will be given to the controversy over phenomenological considerations later, but Paul simply does not elaborate on what he means by "kinds of tongues" in 1 Cor 12:10. Consequently, it may be best to note the plurals as part of his overall emphasis on diversity and be satisfied in knowing there are various expressions of tongues.[20]

The companion to the gift of tongues is regularly translated as "interpretation of tongues" (ἑρμηνεία γλωσσῶν; 1 Cor 12:10). The noun "interpretation" and its cognates occur seven times in the unit under

16. Palma, "Tongues and Prophecy," 24.

17. Thiselton, *First Corinthians*, 970–71.

18. Forbes, *Prophecy*, 71.

19. Brookins and Longenecker, *1 Corinthians 10–16*, 71. Similarly, Bruce views the "kinds" in reference to the known languages of Pentecost and the gift requiring interpretation in 1 Corinthians. Bruce, *1 and 2 Corinthians*, 119. Palma draws from 1 Cor 14 and suggests that "kinds" may refer to "different modes of expression for glossolalia—speaking, praying, singing." I am not sure that "kinds" is the appropriate term to describe "modes." Palma, "Tongues and Prophecy," 62.

20. The parallel between "kinds of tongues" and "interpretation of tongues" in 12:10 may also point to an understanding of "kinds" as related to languages needing interpretation. However one defines "languages" here, this parallel may point to a diversity of them.

discussion (12:10, 30; 14:5, 13, 26, 27, 28), and the definition of the term is particularly important to scholars such as Robert Gundry, who argues that tongues are human languages in need of translation.[21] In this view, Paul has in mind "translation of tongues," and this allegedly implies that tongues are not some sort of ecstatic, or heavenly language, but a human language. Not only is there a logical leap from language in general to specifically human language, but the normal definitions of terms may acquire some nuance in a discussion of miraculous tongues that are not normal. In addition, Thiselton has demonstrated that ἑρμηνεία could also mean something to the effect of "to put into words."[22] Dunn sees ἑρμηνεία and its cognates as referring mainly to the idea of translation in biblical Greek, but the broader semantic range of διερμηνεύω ("interpret, explain"; 1 Cor 12:30; 14:5, 13, 27) suggests that a broader definition than just "translation" is in order (cf. Luke 24:27).[23] Fee looks to the immediate context in 1 Corinthians and concludes, "In this context it probably means to articulate for the benefit of the community what the tongues-speaker has said."[24] This seems like a reasonable definition, given the possible range of meaning of the terms and the unusual nature of the gift of tongues.

It is important to note that the combination of kinds of tongues and interpretation of tongues in 1 Cor 12:10 assumes a corporate setting. There would be no need for interpretation were the corporate body not in view. This is significant because scholars such as Carson have argued that Paul is emphatically denying that all could potentially speak in tongues privately and that Paul's rhetorical questions in verse 30 constitute a rejection of the emphasis on tongues in the modern Pentecostal and charismatic movements.[25] Turner admits that there is a general context of corporate worship in chapters 8–14, that 12:28 concerns the church (ἐκκλησίᾳ), and that the gathered assembly is repeatedly mentioned (14:19, 23, 28, 33b, 35), but he points to the church universal as the context in the list of the gifts in 12:28–30 in order to avoid the implication that Paul is referring to the corporate use of tongues when

21. Gundry, "'Ecstatic Utterance,'" 300.

22. However, I do not agree with the conclusion Thiselton draws from this suggested definition, as he claims, "Ideally, speaking in tongues should not occur at all in public." Thiselton, "'Interpretation' of Tongues," 15, 16.

23. Dunn, *Jesus and the Spirit*, 247.

24. Fee, *First Corinthians*, rev. ed., 663.

25. Carson, *Showing the Spirit*, 41–50.

he asks, "Do all speak in tongues?" (v. 30b).[26] Of course Paul expects a negative answer to the question, and he expects the same of the next enquiry: "Do all interpret?", but Turner fails to note this close listing of tongues and interpretation as preparation for correcting a public problem. Turner posits, "So it is not clear that anything prepares the reader to think Paul's question, 'Not all speak in tongues do they?' refers exclusively or primarily to the use of tongues in public worship."[27] However, at this stage in the argument, readers would expect nothing but a corporate application to Paul's words. Paul is not denying the potential that all may speak in tongues privately (cf. 14:5, 28), but he is encouraging the incorporation of a variety of gifts in the Corinthians' assemblies and affirming that not everyone will exercise the use of tongues in this setting.[28] Although Turner is correct to see Paul's list of gifts as having application well beyond the Corinthian setting, Paul's primary interest lies with the Corinthian congregation and with the gifts at the end of his list—tongues and interpretation of tongues. The combination negates Turner's attempt to dismiss the implications for the corporate body at Corinth and place limitations on the private use of tongues.

Fee points to Paul's desire that all might speak in tongues (1 Cor 14:5), his admonition to desire the gifts (especially prophecy; 14:1), and his comment that "all may prophesy in turn" (14:31) as a basis for recognizing that "such gifts are potentially available for all."[29] Menzies builds on the idea that prophecy serves as a template for a broader use of tongues. He argues that, if scholars can reconcile Paul's question, "Are all prophets?" (12:29), with his suggestion that all may prophesy, then they should also be able to differentiate between tongues functioning in a corporate setting and use in a private setting.[30] Fee adds that Paul's "rhetoric does not mean, '*May* all do this?' to which the answer would probably be, 'Of course.' Rather, it means, '*Are* all? *Do* all?' to which the answer is, 'Of course not.'"[31] Consequently, Paul does not intend to shut off the Spirit's gift spigot, but he seeks to diversify the corporate use of the gifts for the benefit of the entire body.

26. Turner, "Tongues: An Experience for All?" 238–39.

27. Turner, "Tongues: An Experience for All?" 240.

28. Turner also attempts to mitigate the force of Paul's wish that all might speak in tongues in 14:5. "Tongues: An Experience for All?" 243–47.

29. Fee, *First Corinthians*, rev. ed., 689.

30. Menzies, *Speaking in Tongues*, 94.

31. Fee, *1 Corinthians*, rev. ed., 689. Emphasis his.

Despite the differences in emphasis between Luke and Paul, the close association of prophecy, discerning of spirits, tongues, and interpretation of tongues (1 Cor 12:10) points to a basic category of revelatory gifts that Luke would feel comfortable designating as prophetic.[32] One might include the word of wisdom and the word of knowledge under this big umbrella (v. 8), as all of these involve a revelation followed by an inspired declaration of some sort. Unfortunately, the Corinthian problems do not afford Paul the luxury of expounding more on prophecy broadly conceived; rather, Paul must emphasize the diversity of gifts and their distinctive functions in order to correct practices gone awry. Nevertheless, the association of tongues, prophecy, and their companion gifts in 1 Cor 12–14 does point to what might be referred to in Lukan terms as prophetic in nature.

Paul concludes his introduction to the problem by reinforcing the one Spirit's role in distributing a variety of gifts: "And one and the same Spirit works all these, distributing to each one just as he determines" (1 Cor 12:11). Paul has placed the entire discussion under the activity of the Triune God, and the Spirit's activity is rooted in the confession that "Jesus is Lord." Paul has not departed from this perspective, as the next segment of the discussion begins with the communal implications of having Christ as Lord.

Baptism by (ἐν) one Spirit into the Body of Christ (1 Cor 12:12–13)

Paul begins the next stage of his argument with an image of Christ as the body: "For [γὰρ] just as the body is one and has many members, and all the members of the body, though many, are one body, so also is Christ" (1 Cor 12:12). Paul's development of this metaphor keeps the focus centered on Christ, and he frames this unit with a second, emphatic reference to Christ in verse 27: "Now you are the body of Christ, and each of you is a part of it."[33] The conjunction γὰρ in verse 12 indicates that Paul is not done with the preceding emphasis on the Spirit and the diversity of gifts

32. For a similar appraisal, see Forbes, *Prophecy*, 219.

33. The way Paul articulates the argument in 12:12 further emphasizes the centrality of Christ, as one expects him to say "so also is the church" rather than "so also is Christ." Godet, *First Corinthians*, 207. Alternatively, Garland may be right that the abruptness of the expression is simply due to Paul's using shorthand ("Christ") for the body of Christ. *1 Corinthians*, 590. Either way, "Christ" is accentuated. Fee also sees this as metonymy. Fee, *First Corinthians*, rev. ed., 668.

but will now add further explanation. The metaphor of Christ as body is similar to that in Rom 12:4–8 and is not uncommon in Paul's writings (cf. 1 Cor 10:17; Eph 1:23; 4:4, 16; Col 1:24), although it is slightly different from the image of Christ as head as found in 1 Cor 11:3; Eph 5:23; and Col 1:18.[34] Some scholars see the image as having ontological implications for the church,[35] but others see it as only a metaphor and as "organic rather than ontological."[36] The metaphorical understanding seems more in line with Paul's point. The important element to note is that the acknowledgment of Jesus' lordship (1 Cor 12:3) also has horizontal implications, and verses 12–26 focus on the necessity of proper regard for the recipients of grace in the exercise of the gifts. The various gifts in verses 8–10 are distributed to persons who are part of a single body, and verses 12–14 lay the theological foundation for diversity and unity, while verses 15–20 focus on diversity and verses 21–26 emphasize unity.[37]

First Corinthians 12:13 emphasizes the common experience of the Spirit shared by the members of Christ's body, regardless of society's status markers: "For also by [ἐν] one Spirit we all were baptized into [εἰς] one body—whether Jews or Greeks, slaves or free—and were all given one Spirit to drink." Translations vary over whether to take the preposition ἐν as an instrumental dative, expressing the means ("by" or "with" the Spirit) of the baptism (CSB, KJV, NASB 1995, NIV 2011), or as locative, expressing the location or element ("in" the Spirit) of the baptism (ESV, NJB, NRSV). Some have also taken the preposition as expressing not only instrumentality, but agency, also employing "by" in translation and making the Spirit the agent who baptizes. Thus, the translation "by" in the various versions mentioned above could be understood as either instrumental or expressing agency.

34. The "body" (σῶμα) is mentioned eighteen times in 1 Cor 12:12–25 out of a total of ninety-one occurrences of the term in the traditional thirteen books of Paul. The body metaphor was widely used in the Greco-Roman world to encourage political unity. See especially Keener, *1–2 Corinthians*, 102–4. Also see Barrett, *First Corinthians*, 287; Bittlinger, *Gift and Graces*, 55; Conzelmann, *1 Corinthians*, 211n7–8; Collins, *First Corinthians*, 458–62; Thiselton, *First Corinthians*, 992–93.

35. E.g., Hays points to the expectation that Paul would say, "so also is the church," in verse 12 as grounds for believing that "Paul seems to press beyond mere analogy to make an ontological equation of the church with Christ." Hays, *First Corinthians*, 213.

36. Keener, *1–2 Corinthians*, 103. Barrett also sees it as a metaphor only. *First Corinthians*, 291–92. Also Fee, *First Corinthians*, rev. ed., 667n175.

37. Fee, *First Corinthians*, rev. ed., 666.

This text has received considerable attention from scholars with varying interests. Some have taken a sacramental approach, finding an emphasis on water baptism in the verb "baptized" and a reference to the eucharist in the verb "given to drink."[38] The idea that Paul refers to the eucharist has little exegetical foundation. A reference to water baptism is more plausible, but even if Paul were referring to it by association, he is not expounding on water baptism or suggesting that Spirit baptism "coincides with water baptism"[39] but using the verb metaphorically to emphasize the role of the Spirit in forming a single body. It is the Spirit that has been in view throughout 1 Cor 12:1–11 and that occupies Paul's attention in relation to both aorist passive verbs in verse 13.

Dunn has forcefully argued against any notion that 1 Cor 12:13 contains a baptism "by" the Spirit (conversion) that is distinct from a post-conversion baptism "in" the Spirit. He sees this passage as "crucial for the Pentecostal"[40] and supposes that Pentecostalism is undermined by his view of ἐν as locative: "Thus, unless recourse is had to semantic sleight-of-hand with ἐν or εἰς, there is no alternative to the conclusion that the baptism in the Spirit is what made the Corinthians members of the Body of Christ, that is Christians."[41] Dunn argues that "in the NT ἐν with βαπτίζειν never designates the one who performs the baptism; on the contrary, it always indicates the element in which the baptisand is immersed (or with which he is deluged)."[42] He also notes that "the Spirit is the element used in the Messiah's baptism in contrast to the water used in John's baptism" in the other passages mentioning Spirit baptism (Matt 3:11; Mark 1:8; Luke 3:16; John 1:33; Acts 1:5; 11:16).[43] Some modern Pentecostal scholars are in general agreement with Dunn's handling of

38. Calvin, *Corinthians*, 406–7; Collins, *First Corinthians*, 458; Käsemann, *Perspectives*, 103–4.

39. Schweizer, "πνεῦμα, πνευματικός, κτλ.," 427n626. Barrett argues that water baptism is in view in both the reference to baptism and in the drink metaphor. *First Corinthians*, 289.

40. Dunn, *Baptism*, 127. Many Pentecostals would not agree with Dunn that this passage is "crucial" to Pentecostal theology.

41. Dunn, *Baptism*, 129. Pentecostals have generally agreed with Dunn that conversion is in view in the first part of this verse, and many would agree with him that the latter half of the verse is a parallel expression of the same thought.

42. Dunn, *Baptism*, 128.

43. Dunn, *Baptism*, 128.

this passage,[44] but the syntax and theology of the passage is complex and needs reviewing.

Dunn's claim that the combination of ἐν with βαπτίζειν "always indicates the element" is generally true,[45] although Acts 10:48 does not fit with this claim: "And he commanded them to be baptized in the name of Jesus Christ" (προσέταξεν δὲ αὐτοὺς ἐν τῷ ὀνόματι Ἰησοῦ Χριστοῦ βαπτισθῆναι).[46] Nigel Turner lists six categories of use of the preposition ἐν, one of which he refers to as "peculiarly Christian usages."[47] Turner expounds on the difficulty of defining phrases such as "in Christ" or "in the Lord," and he comments, "The inventiveness of Christian usage is seen also in their frequent resort to similar expressions, such as *in the truth, in the Spirit, in the Name.*"[48] Consequently, "in the name of Jesus Christ" is difficult to categorize, and the expression "in one Spirit" in 1 Cor 12:13 could also create difficulties for the translator. Turner cautions, "In the Koine all the prepositions become increasingly elastic and their sense has to be determined more often by the context than was earlier the case. This is notably so with εἰς, ἐν and ἐκ. Such elasticity makes it dangerous to press doctrinal distinctions as though our authors were writing classical Greek."[49] Turner's comments are particularly relevant in 1 Cor 12, as there are several prepositions used in connection with the Spirit.

As Howard Ervin mentions, all of the other passages concerned with baptism in the Spirit are part of the tradition of John the Baptist,[50] and there are no such similar Spirit baptism passages in Pauline literature to compare with 1 Cor 12:13. This makes it necessary to look closer at other potential parallels lacking Spirit baptism language, and 10:1–4 has several noteworthy elements in common with 12:13. Paul reminds the Corinthians of the necessity of discipline in the Christian life and

44. E.g., Fee, *First Corinthians*, rev. ed., 668–72; Macchia, *Baptized in the Spirit*, 29.

45. In reference to baptism in water, see Matt 3:6, 11; Mark 1:4; John 1:25, 31. In reference to baptism in the Spirit, see Matt 3:11; Mark 1:8; Luke 3:16; John 1:33; Acts 1:5; 11:16. "In the name of Jesus Christ" occurs in Acts 10:48. "In the cloud and in the sea" is in 1 Cor 10:2.

46. Dunn allows for such exceptions. *Baptism*, 128.

47. Turner, *Syntax*, 260–65.

48. Turner, *Syntax*, 262. Emphasis original. BDF also notes that Paul's "in Christ" phrase "utterly defies definite interpretation." BDF §219.

49. Turner, *Syntax*, 261.

50. Ervin, *Conversion-Initiation*, 99. He infers from this isolation to a single tradition that the evidence supporting the locative baptism "in one Spirit" in 1 Cor 12:13 is not as substantial as one might suppose.

uses the exodus story as an example. Paul repeatedly uses the term "all" in describing how the Israelites were "under the cloud" and "passed through the sea" (10:1). "And all were baptized into [εἰς] Moses in [ἐν] the cloud and in [ἐν] the sea, and all ate the same spiritual food, and all drank the same spiritual drink; for they were drinking from the rock that was following them, and the rock was Christ" (vv. 2–4). Some of the parallels include the emphasis on many sharing a common experience, a metaphorical baptism, a baptism "into" (Moses or a body/Christ), the use of ἐν (figuratively of the cloud, sea, and Spirit), a participation in a drink, allusions to the Spirit (πνευματικός three times in 10:3–4),[51] and a focus on Christ (12:12). The similarities seem too numerous to dismiss, and the dominant idea common to the two passages is the shared experience of many in becoming a united people, and associated with this is a participation in Christ. Perhaps Paul likens incorporation into Christ to a new exodus and therefore finds the figurative language of baptism in both passages as perfectly suitable and connected in some fundamental way. The preposition ἐν used with the cloud and the sea could be locative and provide support for a locative baptism ἐν at 12:13, but the parallel is not perfect, as the Israelites were not baptized in the Spirit nor actually in a cloud or the sea, and Paul likely employs the baptismal imagery as a result of the mention of the "sea" in 10:2.[52] Nonetheless, the passages share an emphasis on the unity of many people sharing a common, Christ-centered experience of salvation.

William Atkinson points out the common problem of confusing the agency with the instrumentality of the preposition ἐν—a confusion that is compounded by the English use of "by" with a passive verb to translate both the activity of an agent and the means of an instrument.[53] Wallace finds the dative of agency to be "an *extremely rare* category in the NT" and gives a definition of it requiring that the noun in the dative be personal and "must also be the agent who performs the action."[54] The dative is commonly used to express means, but the instrument used to express means can be a person, in which case the person functions as the

51. The cloud in 10:1–2 may also be an allusion to the Spirit (Num 11:25). See Hildebrandt, *Old Testament Theology*, 72–76.

52. Gardner, *1 Corinthians*, 426.

53. Atkinson, *Baptism in the Spirit*, 98. Atkinson specifically mentions some Pentecostal authors who have confused agency with instrumentality.

54. Wallace, *Greek Grammar*, 163. Emphasis original. Wallace also gives guidelines for identifying a dative of agency, including the presence of a perfect passive verb, as is found in every clear example. *Greek Grammar*, 164.

instrument of another. This is not the same as a dative of agency.[55] Not surprisingly, several of the passages debated by scholars involve the use of the dative case with the Spirit (e.g., Gal 5:16), but Wallace maintains that translating such texts with the Spirit as agent is a result of imposing later, fully developed articulations of the Spirit's personhood onto earlier texts. "It should be noted that, in all probability, none of the examples involving πνεύματι in the NT should be classified as agency."[56] When it comes to employing ἐν plus the dative, Wallace finds no "unambiguous" examples of this dative of agency in the New Testament. He translates 1 Cor 12:13 as baptism "by one Spirit," where Christ acts as the implied agent who uses the Spirit as the instrument or means (even though he is a personal being) of baptizing people into one body.[57]

It is easy to see why there is confusion between agency and instrumentality when the instrument is often a personal agent, but the situation becomes even more difficult when the supposed agent is also a divine being. The issue goes beyond basic grammar and quickly touches on theology, as is evident in Wallace's cautions about Trinitarian theology. It leads one to ask: How much difference is there between agency and instrumentality when the Spirit is the instrument? Is it not implied that, as a divine being, he is in some sense also an active agent? To shed more light on this, it is necessary to examine the prepositions in the immediate context of 1 Cor 12:13 to see if Paul has established a preference for agency, instrumentality, or location.

Some scholars have pointed to the prepositions in 1 Cor 12:1–11 in support of the Spirit as agent in verse 13.[58] From the outset, Paul has been discussing what it means to be a person of the Spirit (12:1). The first two uses of ἐν come in verse 3: "Therefore I make known to you that no one speaking by the Spirit of God [ἐν πνεύματι θεοῦ] says, 'Jesus is anathema,'

55. Wallace, *Greek Grammar*, 164. He also lists some examples of datives of agency on page 165.

56. Wallace, *Greek Grammar*, 166. He lists the following verses in note 77 as likely dative of means: Rom 8:13, 14; 1 Cor 14:2; Gal 3:3; 5:5, 18, 25; Eph 1:13; 1 Pet 3:18. Wallace is not denying the personhood of the Spirit.

57. Wallace, *Greek Grammar*, 374. However, there are some places where the dative πνεύματι with the preposition seems to indicate agency (Luke 4:1 supported by Mark 1:12; Eph 3:5), and others where it is likely or at least possible (Luke 2:27; Rom 15:16; Eph 3:5). See Horton, *What the Bible Says*, 216.

58. Baker, "'Two-Stage' Spirit Reception," 46; Ervin, *Conversion-Initiation*, 99; Horton, *What the Bible Says*, 216; Palma, *Holy Spirit*, 100–105. Ervin seems to confuse instrumentality and agency. Horton equates "through" (means) with agency, but otherwise gives noteworthy arguments for agency.

and no one is able [δύναται] to say, 'Jesus is Lord,' except by the Holy Spirit [ἐν πνεύματι ἁγίῳ]." A locative use of ἐν ("in the Spirit") seems very unlikely, given the emphasis on the enabling of the Spirit. From a contextual perspective, either a dative of means ("by means of the Spirit" or "through the Spirit") or agency ("by the Spirit himself") is possible. One could argue that the mention of God in "Spirit of God" might imply that God is the active agent and the Spirit is the means by which one cannot curse Jesus but confesses him as Lord. However, even the passive voice of δύναται ("is able") seems to relate more directly to the Holy Spirit, and the repetition of the Spirit more naturally lends to envisioning the Spirit as the active agent.

The parallel presence of the Spirit, Lord, and God in 1 Cor 12:4–6 only confirms the difficulty of differentiating between agents within the Godhead. The Spirit is specifically connected to the gifts (v. 4), but God becomes the subject who "works all things in everyone" (v. 6), and the divine passive δίδοται ("is given") in verses 7–8 most naturally refers to God. The preposition διὰ with the genitive in verse 8 ("through [διὰ] the Spirit is given") points to the instrumentality of the Spirit. Paul changes the preposition again in relation to the word of knowledge (κατὰ, "according to"; v. 8) but continues to emphasize "the same Spirit." He returns to the use of ἐν two times in verse 9: "To another faith by [ἐν] the same Spirit, and to another gifts of healings by [ἐν] the one Spirit." Either instrumentality or agency could be in view in verse 9, and Paul dispenses with the prepositions for the remainder of the gifts, but the conclusion of the segment strongly leans in the direction of agency. It is "the one and the same Spirit" who serves as the subject who "works" all the gifts, "distributing to each one just as he determines" (v. 11). It is no wonder that scholars struggle to distinguish agency from instrumentality when the Spirit is in view, as Paul himself seems to allow for some literary and theological latitude in his writing.

What has not been in view in the immediate context is the locative use of ἐν or its equivalent with another preposition. In addition, the emphasis on agency in 1 Cor 12:11 leads into what follows with the phrase "for just as," suggesting that Paul is not done with emphasizing the activity of the Spirit. One expects that the continued emphasis on the Spirit will be akin to what precedes, so verse 13 employs ἐν ("by") as agency or instrumentality: "For also by one Spirit [ἐν ἑνὶ πνεύματι] we all were baptized into one body."[59] If the preposition expresses means, then the implied agent is God and not Christ, as Christ is the one body into which people are baptized.[60] Douglas Oss also points out that the syntax of the verse lends to a reading of the phrase as expressing agency: "The syntax of the Greek construction demands that the prepositional phrase 'into one body' function as the immediate referent of 'we were all baptized,' not 'in one Spirit.'"[61] This is an important point, as the sentence flows quite well and keeps the syntactical arrangement in order with the translation "For also by one Spirit we were all baptized into one body" (καὶ γὰρ ἐν ἑνὶ πνεύματι ἡμεῖς πάντες εἰς ἓν σῶμα ἐβαπτίσθημεν).

The latter portion of 1 Cor 12:13 has also received considerable discussion. Dunn has argued that the phrase "and all were given one Spirit to drink" (καὶ πάντες ἓν πνεῦμα ἐποτίσθημεν) is a reference to Isa 29:10 and is an agricultural metaphor for watering or irrigating, referring to an outpouring of the Spirit,[62] that is, a saturation by the Spirit or a drenching in the Spirit. However, Fee rejects this view and comments, "The most crippling blow to this position is the accusative ἓν πνεῦμα; the LXX of Isa. 29:10 has the dative, which one would certainly expect here had Paul intended πνεῦμα to be instrumental."[63] The drinking metaphor may also draw from the similar metaphor in 1 Cor 10:4. Paul contends that believers benefit from the one Spirit's involvement in making them one body in two ways: the Spirit baptizes them into the body, and believers enjoy the blessing of participation in the Spirit; the latter emphasizes the experiential aspect of the relationship and refers to the blessings and gifts enumerated in the context.[64] To say that Paul has in mind a post-conversion filling with the Spirit would go beyond what the context explicates, but the drinking metaphor at least suggests the ongoing vitality of the Spirit in the believer's life and in no way excludes other experiences. The parallel aorist passive verbs (ἐβαπτίσθημεν, "were baptized"; ἐποτίσθημεν, "were given to drink") certainly point to conversion and build on the

59. Palma is correct that "the immediate context in 1 Corinthians 12, which contains four such phrases, is determinative." *Holy Spirit*, 102.

60. Contra Wallace, *Greek Grammar*, 374. Atkinson argues for an instrumental use of ἐν with a divine passive, implying that God is the agent. Atkinson, *Baptism in the Spirit*, 98.

61. Oss, "A Pentecostal/Charismatic View," 258n34.

62. Dunn, *Baptism*, 130–31. Also Carson, *Showing the Spirit*, 46.

63. Fee, *First Corinthians*, rev. ed., 670n191.

64. Gardner is right to point out that the gifts are still in view, but he carefully excludes any reference to a post-conversion event. *1 Corinthians*, 541.

christological confession of 12:3: "Jesus is Lord,"[65] in which Jew, gentile, slave, and free all find their common identity. But on the basis of the common experience of drinking of one Spirit, Paul explains the value of the many members of the body (vv. 13–20), thereby affirming the value of every gift and implicitly confirming the ongoing drinking of the Spirit in the practice of the gifts.

The preposition ἐν should probably be taken as expressing agency, but even an instrumental use of the preposition still expresses some degree of the agency of the Spirit. The sense of agency expressed in 1 Cor 12:3 and possibly verse 9, the active role of the Spirit throughout the immediate context, the easy flow of the text with this reading, and the syntax make this the likely intention of Paul. At the same time, the cautions of placing too much emphasis on a preposition and the difficulty of describing divine activity are appreciated. But, as others have noted, the Pentecostal position does not depend on a particular reading of the preposition, as the Corinthian context differs substantially from that of Luke-Acts and the authors have very different agendas.[66] They share an emphasis on Christ, yet they assign him different functions in their contexts. Christ baptizes with the Spirit in Acts 2, but Christ is the body into which believers are baptized in 1 Cor 12.

First Corinthians 12:12–13 lays the theological foundation and provides the christological imagery for Paul's detailed discussion of a united people functioning in a variety of gifts in a loving manner. The one Spirit who distributes gifts has also baptized each member into the one body of Christ. The gifts have their origin in the deity, and the mention of Christ reminds the Corinthians of their initial confession (v. 3) and implies certain practical considerations in the functioning of the gifts. The drinking of the Spirit reinforces the baptism by the Spirit and also implies an experiential component of the Christian life and ongoing participation in the gifts. All this establishes the christocentric boundaries within which the gifts must operate in order to specifically address the misuse of tongues in the corporate body.

65. Gardner, *1 Corinthians*, 591. See his review of various positions on "given to drink." At times scholars have placed too much emphasis on the aorist verbs, suggesting that the aorist tense necessarily indicates a specific point in time in the past. Recent scholarship has highlighted the undefined nature of the aorist; consequently, the reference to conversion is based more on the context than on the aorist verb tense. In addition, caution is in order when placing emphasis on the aorist ἐποτίσθημεν, as the aorist does not necessarily limit the Spirit's drink to conversion.

66. E.g., Oss, "A Pentecostal/Charismatic View," 259.

The Body of Christ and the Greater Gifts (1 Cor 12:27–31)

The mention of division (σχίσμα) in 1 Cor 12:25 indicates that Paul has never completely left behind the discussion of class divisions in chapter 11 or the problems of division mentioned earlier in the book (1:10). The "body" remains the primary metaphor in Paul's insistence on mutual care in the congregation (12:25–26) and in his frame with the body of Christ in 12:27: "Now you are the body of Christ, and each of you is a part of it." In this way, Paul keeps Christ at the center of his discussion of all the gifts, and the emphatic "you are" (Ὑμεῖς δέ ἐστε) reinforces the notion that Christ remains the standard for church ethics and relationships. The final verses of the chapter (vv. 27–31) reflect the emphases from earlier in the discussion and include the christological frame (12:12, 27), a list of gifts (vv. 8–10, 28), a reference to gifts as *charismata* (vv. 4, 31), and "kinds of tongues" toward the end of the list (vv. 10, 28).

Paul's advocating the importance of all the gifts has left scholars wondering why he seems to rank the gifts in 1 Cor 12:28: "And on the one hand [Καὶ οὓς μὲν] God placed [ἔθετο] in the church first apostles, second prophets, third teachers, then [ἔπειτα] miracles, then gifts of healings, helps, leadership, kinds of tongues." It appears that Paul does not complete his intended μέν-δέ ("on the one hand," "but") construction, unless he returns to it after his list of rhetorical questions: "But [δὲ] eagerly desire the greater gifts" (v. 31).[67] However, Brookins and Longenecker have noted that ἔπειτα ("then") "frequently serves as a correlative to μέν when items are listed."[68] They also point out that the ordinal adverbs (first, second, third) modify ἔθετο ("placed") and not the apostles, prophets, and teachers.[69] The emphasis is on God's sovereign placing or appointing, as in 12:4–11, 18. The shift to ἔπειτα in verse 28b separates the apostles, prophets, and teachers from the rest of the list, and the enumeration ceases shortly thereafter. The implication of this is that the apostles, prophets, and teachers play a significant role in establishing

67. Brookins and Longenecker suggest this as a possibility but reject it because of the extensive intervening material between 12:28 and 12:31. Brookins and Longenecker, *1 Corinthians 10–16*, 82. Robertson and Plummer suggest that Paul abandoned the enumeration, but they emphasize the position of tongues in last place. Robertson and Plummer, *First Corinthians*, 278–79.

68. Brookins and Longenecker, *1 Corinthians 10–16*, 82. They cite Heb 7:2 and Jas 3:17; cf. John 11:6–7.

69. Brookins and Longenecker, *1 Corinthians 10–16*, 83.

and strengthening the church with their Spirit-empowered proclamation of the gospel and instruction in it.

Recognizing the significant contribution of these ministries is not antithetical to Paul's argument throughout 1 Cor 12, and Paul's instruction to seek the greater gifts likely refers primarily to the apostles, prophets, and teachers (v. 31);[70] thus, "eagerly desire" (ζηλοῦτε; v. 31) should be translated as an imperative rather than an indicative verb (cf. 14:1, 39), and the sentence does not require the reader to find an elitist Corinthian slogan in the verse.[71] Paul does not argue that all the gifts make the same degree of contribution or are functionally equivalent. He affirms the divine source of all gifts, the sovereign will of God in distributing them, the importance of unity (12:25), the necessity of each gift (vv. 21–22), and the requirement for love and concern (vv. 25–26). He protests a narrow focus on a single gift (v. 19), but encourages a variety of functions within the body (vv. 14–17). Desiring to make a greater contribution to Christ's church is not incompatible with Paul's teaching: "The saying is trustworthy: If anyone aspires to the office of overseer, he desires a noble task" (1 Tim 3:1 ESV; cf. 5:17).[72]

Two tendencies among some scholars exert pressure on the interpretation of this passage and all of 1 Cor 12–14: excessive emphasis on the supposed elitist view of tongues at Corinth and a corresponding negative view of tongues that insists on a "last means least" perspective and a general desire to dismiss them. Fee has addressed these issues in depth, and he has made an important distinction between the superior attitude of some Corinthians and the assumption that the Corinthians held that

70. With Grudem, *Gift of Prophecy*, 56. However, Grudem's appeal to tongues in Acts 2:4 in order to refute the view that the enumeration in 1 Cor 12:28 is chronological is rightly challenged by Gardner. Grudem leaps contexts when he appeals to Acts 2 to establish the sequence of gifts in the church. Gardner, *1 Corinthians*, 548n51.

71. A minority of scholars have found Paul's imperative at odds with their appraisal of the Corinthian problem as one of an elitist view of tongues and have viewed 12:31 as a sarcastic Pauline rebuke, a Corinthian slogan opposed by Paul, or an interrogative intended to challenge the Corinthian position. The following scholars take the verb as an indicative: Bittlinger, *Gifts and Graces*, 73; Gardner, *1 Corinthians*, 553; Iber, "Zum Verständnis," 43–52; Talbert, *Reading Corinthians*, 108. For the Corinthian slogan position, see Martin, *Spirit and the Congregation*, 34. For viewing the verse as an interrogative, see Fitzmyer, *First Corinthians*, 484.

72. God's placement of apostles in the church in 12:28 is reminiscent of 1:1, where Paul is a "called apostle of Christ Jesus through the will of God." It is possible that Paul intended to remind the Corinthians that his own apostolic calling and service to the church was among the gifts and that they should view his ministry in this light. This would make sense if relations between him and the Corinthians were already eroding.

certain gifts were superior to others. Commenting on the personification of the body parts in 12:21, Fee remarks,

> It is common to see in this analogy a reference to those who speak in tongues as considering themselves superior to those in the community who do not. If so, then this is the only hint of such in the entire argument. Nothing in the concluding argument itself (chap. 14) suggests as much. That guess, therefore, as common as it is, is probably considerably off the mark in terms of Paul's own concerns. Since the implication of the analogy as Paul proceeds with it is that some *people* consider themselves superior to others, not that some *gifts* are superior, it seems more likely that one is to find the historical situation here addressed in a broader context within the church.[73]

Fee views the attitude expressed in this passage as a carryover from the discussion about the Lord's Table (11:17–34). He also sees this as a backdrop for Paul's comment on division in 12:25 and notes that chapter 14 "says nothing to indicate, or even to hint, that this gift was causing internal strife of any kind. Nor is there any suggestion that the Corinthians who spoke in tongues had an elitist view or considered themselves superior to others. That is read into the text on the basis of this analogy; for one then to read this analogy on the basis of that (surely incorrect) reading of chap. 14 is an altogether circular argument that in the end comes up wanting."[74] It is not hard to detect Fee's frustration with scholarship that takes a generally negative view of the gift of tongues.

There are reasons many scholars find Corinthian pride in the gift of tongues or elitism as the backdrop for Paul's discussion. The influence of a proud culture has been evident throughout the epistle, Paul directly contrasts boasting and arrogance with love (1 Cor 13:4), and his reference to "the tongues of men and of angels" could point to an unduly exalted view of tongues (v. 1). It is possible that some Corinthians did have an elitist view of the gift itself, but Fee is technically correct that there is a lack of clear evidence that the Corinthians viewed themselves as superior based on the superiority of tongues over other gifts. Paul focuses on the divine origin of the gifts, the need for diversification of gifts, the necessity of Christian love in the body, and especially the requirement of intelligibility for edification (ch. 14); he never overtly rebukes the Corinthians

73. Fee, *First Corinthians*, rev. ed., 678. Emphasis original.

74. Fee, *First Corinthians*, rev. ed., 680–81.

for having an elitist view of themselves because they exercise a superior spiritual gift (tongues).

Paul's general tone in discussing the gifts is very positive, as each gift has a divine origin. Consequently, not only the elitist claim but also the "last is least" claim has been overplayed.[75] Caution is in order when ranking tongues as last, as the list in 1 Cor 12:28 highlights the foundational ministries in the church but sets aside the enumeration thereafter, the order and content of the lists changes from list to list (cf. vv. 8–10), and even Paul's list of rhetorical questions (vv. 29–30) omits helps and leadership (v. 28) and adds interpretation. Paul apparently feels no need to repeat the entire list and desires to move more quickly to the issue at hand—tongues and interpretation. "The suggestion that this 'gift comes last again' because it has caused 'such problems in Corinth' is at the very least jumping the gun"[76] is not actually "jumping the gun" but is borne out by Paul's immediately placing tongues at the top of his next list in 13:1 and his consistent inclusion of "tongues" in his lists (12:10, 28, 30).[77]

Some scholars have expressed surprise at the absence of any clear mention of Christ in 1 Cor 13, but even though there is an inclusio marking off the chapter (12:31; 14:1), Paul's ethical emphasis on love is no mere disconnected afterthought. The image of the church as the body of Christ (12:12, 27) expressing care for one another (vv. 24–25) is simply elaborated on in chapter 13. Gardner grasps the connection well: "The behavior that entails being concerned for the building up and caring of other members will be summed up in 13:1 with the word 'love,' as it was in 8:1."[78] A discussion that has begun with the basic confession of the Lord Jesus (12:3) has now shifted in focus to the communal implications of that reality. The Corinthians must work out what it means to be the body of Christ, and the primary ethic guiding the practice of all the gifts, and tongues in particular, is the love of Christ.

75. Note the rather negative tone in Barrett's comment: "The Corinthians evidently valued too highly what Paul regarded as one of the lowest of gifts, that of speaking with tongues." Barrett, *First Corinthians*, 296.

76. Gardner, *1 Corinthians*, 549, quoting Ciampa and Rosner, *First Corinthians*, 614. While I might not phrase it the way Ciampa and Rosner do, the essential point that the misuse of tongues is the topic under discussion is correct.

77. It is also likely that the Corinthians knew where Paul was going in the discussion as soon as he engaged the topic in 12:1. This is especially so if his "Now concerning" reflects an issue that they brought to his attention.

78. Gardner, *1 Corinthians*, 547.

The Tongues of Men and of Angels

Paul sets out to show the Corinthians a superior way to function in the church and to express God's gifts—the way of love (1 Cor 12:31b; 13:1). That chapter 13 is a continuation of the previous argument is apparent by his mention of tongues at the outset: "If in the tongues of men and of angels I speak, but do not have love, I have become as a noisy gong or a clanging symbol" (v. 1).[79] The series of conditional clauses in verses 1–3 highlights the gifts of tongues, prophecy with accompanying knowledge, and faith; and prophecy, tongues, and knowledge are in view again in verse 8. Chapter 13, then, is not a foreign intrusion into the discussion but is essential to it. Paul continues to expound on what it means to be people of the Spirit (12:1). People of the Spirit confess Christ, are members of the body of Christ, and express the Spirit's gifts with the love of Christ.

Controversy surrounds the meaning of "tongues of men and of angels" (1 Cor 13:1) and the possible implications of this phrase for an understanding of the phenomenology of tongues; however, it must be stated at the outset that Paul shows little concern with satisfying curiosity over such questions. Just as Paul provides few definitions of the gifts he lists, he offers few clear comments on the phenomenology of tongues. J. G. Davies argues that Paul understands tongues to be known human languages based on Acts 2, his understanding of ἑρμηνεία and cognates to mean "translation," and Paul's reference to foreign languages in his quotation of Isa 28:11–12 (1 Cor 14:21).[80] However, it is difficult to apply an event from a Lukan context that is unique even to him (xenolalia) to a very different Pauline context. Davies' assertion that the ἑρμηνεία word group implies known languages in need of translation is problematic because most of his references come from the Septuagint or other places where the context is very dissimilar to that of 1 Cor 12–14. Speaking in tongues and interpretation of tongues are unique gifts that are not in view in passages where "translation" would be an appropriate word, and one might ask what word other than ἑρμηνεία Paul would use to describe a gift of interpretation of tongues?

79. There has been considerable discussion as to what noise-making devices Paul has in mind in this verse, but the auditory impact of the alliteration in "noisy gong or clanging symbol" (χαλκὸς ἠχῶν ἢ κύμβαλον ἀλαλάζον) may be nearly as important as the definition of the terms.

80. Davies, "Pentecost and Glossolalia," 228–31.

Robert Gundry builds on Davies' work, arguing that both "tongue" (γλῶσσα) and "interpretation" (διερμηνεύω) are words regularly used to describe human language and the translation of it. The problem is that what Paul describes are not normal, learned languages but miraculously inspired gifts of the Spirit.[81] Gundry also assumes tongues are foreign languages in Acts 10 and 19 and then transfers this perspective to Paul by virtue of association between Paul and Luke, but too much is assumed here, as the setting differs substantially between all the tongues passages.[82] In addition, Vern Poythress points out that public tongues at Corinth require "a special gift of the Spirit, not merely the natural ability to understand another language," implying that tongues are not generally normal, human languages (1 Cor 12:10, 30; 14:13, 28).[83] While Gundry is right to challenge some arguments for tongues as ecstatic utterances, his argument for tongues as human languages is not very convincing.[84] Nevertheless, Gundry's attention to the words used in connection with tongues does point to tongues as some sort of language and not random, broken, disconnected, fragmentary sounds.[85]

Others view tongues as an angelic language, emphasizing "angels" over "men" in 1 Cor 13:1, but as Forbes points out, both those who adhere to the human language view and the angelic language view find themselves in the unenviable position of having to explain away the other half of Paul's phrase.[86] Earle Ellis is among those who advocate a position

81. Gundry, "'Ecstatic Utterance,'" 299–300.

82. Gundry, "'Ecstatic Utterance,'" 300. Thiselton lists six reasons why he rejects the position that tongues are normal, human languages at Corinth. Thiselton, "'Interpretation' of Tongues," 28–31.

83. Poythress, "Corinthian Glossolalia," 132.

84. On the problem of defining ecstasy, see Forbes, *Prophecy*, 53–56. Poythress also notes one of the problems with the entire debate and with Gundry's article in particular: "Robert H. Gundry's article in J.T.S. confines us to two options: 'ecstatic utterance' or 'the miraculously given ability to speak a human language foreign to the speaker.' But the label 'ecstatic utterance' describes the psychological state of the speaker, whereas the description in terms of 'a human language foreign to the speaker' deals with the scientific classification of the utterance (the speech product). This is mixing apples and oranges." Poythress, "Corinthian Glossolalia," 130, citing Gundry, "'Ecstatic Utterance,'" 299.

85. Based on the terminology, Palma also sees tongues as languages. He follows John Ellicott in seeing two forms of tongues—human languages (Acts 2) and tongues as prayer or praise and requiring interpretation (1 Cor 14). Palma, "Tongues and Prophecy," 52–53. Ellicott, *First Corinthians*, 240.

86. Forbes, *Prophecy*, 58. Forbes takes the position that tongues are human languages and not angeloglossy. John Poirier challenges Forbes' position and advocates

of tongues as angeloglossy, but he builds his case on the rather unusual view that both the Holy Spirit and angelic spirits inspire the pneumatics at Corinth (1 Cor 14:12, 32).[87] Scholars generally find a reference to human spirits where Ellis sees angelic spirits.

A text sometimes cited as a potential backdrop for angelic tongues is the Testament of Job 48–52. In these chapters Job gives each of his daughters a cord with miraculous powers as an inheritance. The result was that his daughter, Hemera, "received another heart, no longer thinking the thoughts of the earth. She spoke [ἀπεφθέγξατο] in an angelic dialect, sending up a hymn to God, according [sic] the hymnody of the angels. And the hymns that she uttered [ἀπεφθέγξατο] she permitted The Spirit to be inscribed on her garment" (T. Job 48.2–3).[88] Likewise, Job's daughter, Kassia, received the "dialect of the rulers" (τὴν διάλεκτον τῶν ἀρχόντων; 49.2), and the third daughter "chanted verses in the dialect of those who dwell in heights" (ἀποφθεγγόμενον ἐν τῇ διαλέκτῳ τῶν ἐν ὕψει; 50.1) and "in the dialect of the cherubim [ἐν τῇ διαλέκτῳ τῶν Χερουβὶμ], praising the master of virtues" (50.2; cf. 52.7). The passage is noteworthy because of some language that overlaps with Acts 2 (ἀποφθέγγομαι; vv. 4, 14; διάλεκτος; vv. 6, 8), [89] the emphasis on praise and singing (Acts 2:11; 1 Cor 14:14–17), and the angelic language. It is difficult to assess the implications of the Testament of Job on the New Testament, as there is the possibility of Christian influence on the text.[90] There are also significant differences, as Job's daughters are not said to "speak in tongues," their dialect is angelic but not human languages as in Acts 2, and the biblical contexts are vastly different and devoid of the magical tenor present in the tale of Job. However, this passage points to the likelihood that first-century Christians had entertained the notion of angelic languages of praise.

The Apocalypse of Zephaniah 8 evinces a Jewish tradition of angelic languages. In this passage the seer observes myriads of angels engaged

an angeloglossic perspective. (I have borrowed the term "angeloglossy" from Poirier). Poirier, *Tongues of Angels*, 154–58.

87. Ellis, *Prophecy and Hermeneutic*, 31, 41.

88. Translation by Evans et al., *The Pseudepigrapha.*

89. Chapter 51.3 and 4 also describe the magnificence of their hymns with the term μεγαλεῖα, which is also used in Acts 2:11. Others have noticed the similarities in language with Acts 2. E.g., see Harrisville, "Speaking in Tongues," 49.

90. Spittler, "Testament of Job," 833. On the provenance and date, see Gurtner, *Introducing the Pseudepigrapha*, 178–79. See also the detailed discussion in Poirier, *Tongues of Angels*, 63–77.

in prayer and praise. After putting on an "angelic garment" (8.3–4), the seer claims, "I, myself, prayed together with them, I knew their language, which they spoke with me" (8.4–5).[91] The passage is noteworthy because the seer speaks in an angelic language and prays in this language (cf. 1 Cor 14:14). The Ascension of Isaiah was likely written after The Apocalypse of Zephaniah and was clearly authored by a Christian,[92] but it implies that Isaiah offered praise in an angelic language (Ascen. Isa. 8.16–20; cf. 9.21–23, 28). There are other texts that may point to the idea of angelic languages, but they are generally later texts and their meaning is sometimes obscure.[93] The significance of the texts mentioned above is that they provide evidence that the concept of angeloglossy was in the air around the time of the New Testament. It is possible that the Corinthians entertained the thought of angelic tongues, but conclusions beyond this are difficult to substantiate.[94]

"The tongues of men and of angels [τῶν ἀνθρώπων . . . καὶ τῶν ἀγγέλων]" (1 Cor 13:1) can best be described as a merism in which Paul envisions the extreme poles of exalted language. Paul uses a similar expression when he contrasts his suffering and shame with the arrogance of the Corinthians: "We became a spectacle to the universe, both to angels and to men [καὶ ἀγγέλοις καὶ ἀνθρώποις]" (4:9). Given the broad range of uses of the third-class conditional clauses used in 13:1–3,[95] the "If ['Εὰν] I speak" leaves open the question of what Paul himself actually thought about the phenomenology of tongues. The various mentions of angels in 1 Corinthians may suggest that the Corinthians had taken an interest in angels (6:3; 11:10), and some church members probably thought that their speaking in tongues involved the employment of angelic languages, but one can only ascertain so much from a literary device.

The "tongues of men" may refer to the Corinthian obsession with rhetoric and wisdom (1:17, 20).[96] Paul did not proclaim the gospel with "superiority of speech or wisdom" (2:1), as he did not want the Corinthians' faith to rest in "the wisdom of men [σοφίᾳ ἀνθρώπων]" (v. 5).

91. Wintermute, "Apocalypse of Zephaniah," 514.

92. Knibb, "Martyrdom and Ascension of Isaiah," 143.

93. E.g., see Apoc. Ab. 15.2–7; Gen. Rab. 74.7. See the analysis of several texts in Poirier, *Tongues of Angels*, 47–109.

94. Similarly, Forbes, *Prophecy*, 182–87. See his discussion of proposed Jewish parallels and backgrounds to angelic tongues.

95. Wallace, *Greek Grammar*, 696–98.

96. Martin, *Spirit and Congregation*, 43.

Paul stresses christocentric speech in contrast to human wisdom when he claims that "we speak [λαλοῦμεν] wisdom among the mature" (v. 6), that "we speak [λαλοῦμεν] the wisdom of God that has been hidden in mystery" (v. 7), and that "we speak [λαλοῦμεν] not in words taught by human [ἀνθρωπίνης] wisdom but taught by the Spirit" (v. 13). As 13:4–7 draws upon many issues discussed in the epistle, it is not unlikely that Paul includes not only heavenly languages in his tongues "of angels" but also the loftiest of human rhetoric in his "tongues of men" (13:1). Perhaps there is a bit of irony in this comment,[97] but it seems that the intent of Paul's merism is to encompass the widest imaginable range of exalted utterances—human and angelic—to highlight the utter vanity and emptiness of gifts of speech used without love. This passage gives us very little insight as to Paul's opinion of the phenomenology of tongues and does not satisfy the curiosity of the modern reader, but it does clarify what it truly means to be a person of the Spirit. The person of the Spirit not only utters what exalts Christ, but the person of the Spirit delivers inspired utterances with Christ's love.

Tongues and the Eschaton (1 Cor 13:8–13)

Paul continues his attempt to jar the Corinthians back to a balanced perspective on the gifts when he relativizes them by contrasting their temporal nature with the permanence of love (it never "falls"; πίπτει; 1 Cor 13:8). Paul has already primed the Corinthians for a discussion about the place of the gifts in light of the eschaton: "You do not lack in any gift [χαρίσματι] as you eagerly await the revelation [ἀποκάλυψιν] of our Lord Jesus Christ, who also will confirm you to the end [τέλους], blameless on the day of our Lord Jesus Christ" (1:7–8).[98] Paul portrays the gifts from his typical "already / not yet" eschatological perspective; that is, the gifts are graces already received through Christ Jesus, but they are not the ultimate goal—the full revelation of the person of Christ himself.[99] The charismatic, eschatological, and christological language in the

97. Fitzmyer finds hyperbole and irony here, but Schrage does not see irony in this passage. Fitzmyer, *First Corinthians*, 492. Schrage, *Korinther*, 284.

98. "In every word and all knowledge" (1:5b) supports the notion that Paul is anticipating the discussion of the gifts in chapters 12–14.

99. Contra Richard Gaffin, the gifts are eschatological in nature precisely because they are grace-gifts received in connection with union with Christ. All the blessings received in the present by virtue of this union not only point to the coming revelation

introduction prepares the reader for the eschatological language and the references to the parousia in 13:8–13. Although Christ is not personally named in the discussion, his coming is clearly in view (cf. 3:13; 4:5; 5:5; 6:14; 9:25; 11:26, 32; 15:1–58; 16:22).

Were it not for the claims of certain cessationist scholars who hold that tongues cease prior to the eschaton, one would scarcely need to comment on the eschatological orientation of 1 Cor 13:8–13, as the language is overwhelmingly eschatological. Five times Paul employs the future tense of his verbs,[100] and one of them is often associated with the eschaton in Pauline use (καταργέω, "to pass away, be abolished"; cf. 2:6; 6:13; 15:24, 26; 2 Thess 2:8; 2 Tim 1:10). Paul speaks of "when the complete [τέλειον] comes" (1 Cor 13:10a), and this adjective is associated with the eschaton in Col 1:28. So is its cognate noun τέλος ("end, goal") in 1 Cor 1:8, 10:11, and 15:24. Paul contrasts childhood with adulthood (13:11) to illustrate the differing ages and twice uses "now" (ἄρτι) and "then" (τότε) terminology (v. 12) to illustrate the difference between limitation in the present and fuller revelation at the parousia. He also speaks of partial (μέρους) knowledge in the present but looks to the full knowledge that comes only in the eschaton (v. 12). Finally, the mention of "hope" carries eschatological significance in Pauline use (v. 13). Richard Gaffin's apt comment on τέλειον ("perfect, complete") applies to the entire context: "To argue, as some cessationists do, that 'the perfect' has in view the completion of the New Testament canon or some other state of affairs prior to the Parousia is just not credible exegetically."[101] Consequently,

of Christ, but constitute a preliminary experiencing of the glory to come. Gaffin, "Cessationist View," 56–59.

100. The verbs are καταργέω (vv. 8 and 10), παύω (v. 8), and ἐπιγινώσκω (v. 12).

101. Gaffin, "Cessationist View," 55n81. Gaffin argues for the cessation of tongues by associating tongues with the revelatory gift of prophecy and arguing that such revelation was tied to the establishment of the church. Gaffin, *Perspectives on Pentecost*, 102. See his discussion on the "perfect" on pages 109–12. The Greek word τέλειον can be translated as either "perfect" or "complete." For a list of authors who view the "perfect" as a reference to the canon, see Ruthven, *On the Cessation*, 120n38, and Scott, "When Revelatory Gifts Cease," 281n56. Godet acknowledges that the coming of Christ is in view in 1 Cor 13:8–10 but then feels compelled to argue for cessationism by positing that the nature of the gifts change: "Prophecy may be transformed into animated preaching; speaking in tongues may appear in the form of religious poetry and music; knowledge continues to accomplish its task by the catechetical and theological teaching of Christian truth." Such claims are based on theological presuppositions rather than on the text at hand. Godet, *First Corinthians*, 250. Robert Gromacki grounds his cessationism in the end of the apostolic era, the death of those who spoke in tongues, and the completion of the New Testament. He posits, "Once the New Testament was

very few scholars continue to embrace the notion that Paul refers here to the canon of Scripture.[102]

Some cessationists draw attention to the use of the middle voice of παύω ("cease") in 1 Cor 13:8: "But as for prophecies, they will be brought to an end [καταργηθήσονται]; as for tongues, they will cease [παύσονται]; as for knowledge, it will be brought to an end [καταργηθήσεται]." Wallace suggests that παύσονται is probably an indirect middle and points to tongues ceasing "of their own accord" and "without an intervening agent."[103] This is in contrast to the surrounding passive verbs that imply the agency of God when the perfect comes. "The implication *may* be that tongues were to have 'died out' of their own *before* the perfect comes."[104] Wallace challenges the majority view that παύω is deponent in the future tense and "that the change in verbs is merely stylistic,"[105] yet he concludes, "But this is not to say that the middle voice in 1 Cor 13:8 *proves* that tongues already ceased! This verse does not specifically address when tongues would cease, although it is giving a *terminus ad quem*: when the perfect comes."[106] In the end, Wallace can only attempt to hold the door of possibility open for tongues to cease prior to the parousia, but if cessationism is the desired object, one is then left in the precarious position of admitting that the gifts of prophecy and knowledge do continue to the eschaton (they are not in the middle voice) and only tongues do not continue.

Wallace may be correct when he notes that "the real force of παύω in the middle is *intransitive*, while in the active it is transitive."[107] Mathewson and Emig agree with this assessment, but they argue that the use of the middle has no bearing on the question of when tongues will cease.

completed and circulated, the need and the purpose of these gifts were removed." Gromacki, *Modern Tongues Movement*, 118. See also pages 126–27.

102. But see Edgar for a cessationist view that points to the completion of the canon, although he ultimately decides that the "perfect" refers to the death of the believer. Edgar, *Miraculous Gifts*, 275, 340–44.

103. Wallace, *Greek Grammar*, 422. See also Gromacki, *Modern Tongues Movement*, 128–29.

104. Wallace, *Greek Grammar*, 422. Emphasis original. Robert Thomas suggests the gift will pass away "under its own power." Thomas, *Understanding Spiritual Gifts*, 78.

105. Wallace, *Greek Grammar*, 422.

106. Wallace, *Greek Grammar*, 423. Emphasis original. Wallace does not ascribe to the view that Paul has in mind the close of the canon when the perfect comes. See 423n44.

107. Wallace, Greek Grammar, 423. Emphasis original.

"The verb παύω in the active is transitive ('to stop something'), but in the middle (παύομαι) it becomes intransitive ('to cease'). Therefore, this verse cannot be used to argue for a distinction between what happens to tongues and what happens to prophecy and knowledge, as if tongues will cease in a different way—by themselves, or they will cease themselves, or they will die off. The middle here turns a transitive verb into an intransitive one and tells us that tongues will cease, with the point being the subject's heightened participation in the process, but it does not tell us how (or when) tongues will cease."[108] Mathewson and Emig have well summarized the grammatical function of the middle voice in 1 Cor 13:8.

Among those who see the change in verbs as merely stylistic, Fee comments, "The change of verbs is purely rhetorical; to make it otherwise is to elevate to significance something in which Paul shows no interest at all." For him, "The middle voice came along with the change of verbs."[109] Brookins and Longenecker see the shift in verbs as "an attempt to avoid monotonous repetition."[110] Carson discusses the cessationistic claims based on the middle voice of παύω and concludes, "Whatever the merits of this exegesis of 1 Corinthians 13:8–10 (and they are few), it is certainly wrong to rest so much on the middle verb παύσονται."[111] He summarizes some of the various uses of the middle voice and observes, "It never unambiguously bears the meaning 'to cease of itself.'"[112] Scholarship has increasingly broadened its definition of the middle voice to emphasize how the subject is affected by the verb's action.[113] This broad definition makes it difficult to identify the kind of ceasing of tongues that cessationists advocate, as the immediate context plays a determinative role in defining a particular use of the middle. The word "cease" is a fitting term to pair with "tongues" and is appropriate in the context of the termination of the gifts of prophecy and knowledge at the parousia.

B. J. Oropeza points out the ABA′ pattern in 1 Cor 13:8, where prophecy will be brought to an end (A), tongues will cease (B), and knowledge will be brought to an end (A′). He suggests that a change in the verb is warranted at the center of the chiasm and that the temporal

108. Mathewson and Emig, *Intermediate Greek Grammar*, 151.

109. Fee, *First Corinthians*, rev. ed., 713n375.

110. Brookins and Longenecker, *1 Corinthians 10–16*, 94.

111. Carson, *Exegetical Fallacies*, 78.

112. Carson, *Exegetical Fallacies*, 78–79. See also Carson, *Showing the Spirit*, 66–67.

113. See the list of resources on the middle voice in Mounce, *Basics of Biblical Greek*, 186n2.

nature of tongues is affirmed by placing this gift of particular interest at Corinth between two gifts that will also reach their expiration date at the parousia.[114] Indeed, the placement of tongues between the other two gifts affirms their similar end at the eschaton; it does not differentiate between times of their cessation.[115] The parallel construction of three "if" (εἴτε) statements, each containing a gift and a future verb expressing termination, points to one, unified thought.[116] If Paul had intended to advocate the cessation of tongues or any of the gifts prior to the parousia, he certainly had plenty of opportunities to do so, but throughout the entire discussion he assumes their continued use, promotes greater diversity of gifts (12:4–31), celebrates tongues as useful in private prayer (14:18), urges the use of the gift of prophecy, and charges the Corinthians not to forbid speaking in tongues (v. 39). In addition to all this, Paul's exhortation to use the gifts in an appropriate manner is framed with Christ (12:12, 27); thus, the gifts are grounded in Christ and have his endorsement to continue to function in edifying his body until the next phase of his kingdom when he returns in person and makes the partial obsolete (13:12). A christocentric perspective on tongues strengthens the continuationist position by locating the changes at the commencement of new phases of Christ's kingdom rather than at some ambiguous, indefinite time between the ages.

The three gifts of prophecy, tongues, and knowledge (1 Cor 13:8) are appropriately chosen as representative of all the gifts mentioned in the discussion. Tongues and prophecy will dominate the conversation in chapter 14, and the Corinthians have shown an obsession with knowledge throughout the letter.[117] The illustrations contrasting childhood

114. Oropeza, "Cessation of Speaking in Tongues," 492–93.

115. Although the verb καταργέω ("nullify, abolish") is used with prophecy and knowledge but not tongues in verse 8, the term is used in a general illustration of childhood versus maturity in verse 11. The illustration seems to encompass all the gifts, so that the term also applies to tongues. Consequently, caution is in order in putting too much emphasis on the change in verbs in verse 8.

116. Contra Thiselton, this construction and context combined with the expectation in 1 Cor 1:7 strongly implies that tongues continue to the eschaton. He comments, "All that is clear is that the gifts cease at the eschaton. It may be natural *to assume* that they continue *up to* the eschaton, since 'prophecy' and 'knowledge' belong together with 'tongues.'" Thiselton, *First Corinthians*, 1064. Emphasis original.

117. See the discussion in chapter 8 above. Because tongues are not directly mentioned again in 1 Cor 13:9, Robert Thomas has attempted to use this fact to buttress his argument for the early cessation of tongues on their own. "The nature of that third gift [tongues] did not require justification for its disappearance. Knowledge and prophecy

with adulthood (13:11) and indirect (αἰνίγματι)[118] sight with clear vision (v. 12a) reinforce Paul's instruction on the limitations of the gifts in the present era in contrast to the full realization of Christ's presence at the consummation. Paul draws from the description of Moses' unique prophetic revelation when he describes this future encounter as a "face to face" experience (v. 12b; Num 12:8; cf. Deut 34:10). In contrast to other prophets who have visions and dreams (Num 12:6), the Lord speaks to Moses "mouth to mouth" and not in "riddles" (αἰνιγμάτων; v. 8 LXX).[119] The allusion is particularly appropriate because the Corinthian and Numbers contexts share an appreciation for prophetic gifts (Num 11:29; 1 Cor 14:1) and contrast prophetic limitation with face-to-face experiences. In addition, the implications of Moses as a Spirit-filled leader from whom the Spirit is transferred to seventy elders (Num 11:16–30; cf. Acts 2), a great deliverer of his people, and one who typifies a greater prophet to come (Deut 18:15; cf. Acts 3:22), point to Christ as the ultimate fulfillment of the long-awaited, eschatological, face-to-face encounter with God.[120] Until then, eternal love must characterize the body of Christ (12:12, 27) as the church employs the temporal gifts (13:13; 14:1).

Summary

Paul establishes the lordship of Jesus in the discussion in 1 Cor 12:3 and then emphasizes the diversity of gifts within the unity of the Spirit, the Lord, and God (vv. 4–6). The multiple references to the Spirit reflect the Pauline presupposition that the eschatological age has been inaugurated and believers enjoy the benefits of the Spirit secured by the work of Christ. The lordship of Jesus is made explicit in 12:3 and 5, but his presence is felt

were different, however, because they were revelatory, and clarification was necessary to tell why these two channels of divine revelation would cease to exist at some time in the future." Thomas, *Understanding Spiritual Gifts*, 78. One finds a similar cessationistic perspective in Edgar, *Miraculous Gifts*, 337. It should be pointed out that in 13:9–13, prophecy is only directly mentioned once but knowledge occurs four times. The repetition of the cognates of knowledge in verse 12 fit well with Paul's illustration of the partial nature of gifts in the present age. That all the gifts are in view is evident from Paul's admonition to eagerly desire "spirituals" in 14:1, and the omission of the term "tongues" in 13:9–13 cannot be construed to imply that tongues cease on their own.

118. The term means an "indirect image." BDAG, 27.

119. See the discussion of Num 12:6–8 and the implications of it in Jewish history and on 1 Cor 13:12 in Ciampa and Rosner, *First Corinthians*, 658–60. See also Grudem, *Gift of Prophecy*, 145–47.

120. Lidbeck, *Resurrection and Spirit*, 45–47.

throughout the list of gifts (vv. 8–10). The word of wisdom and word of knowledge are intimately bound up with Christology, and these utterance gifts at the beginning of the list remind the Corinthians of the centrality of the gospel of Christ and suggest a christological orientation of the entire list. Kinds of tongues and interpretation of tongues are introduced last in the list, not because they should be devalued, but because they are the focus of attention in Paul's correction. The christological orientation of all the gifts prohibits negative judgments against any of God's good gifts. In addition, the combination of tongues and interpretation assumes that their corporate use is in view; consequently, Paul does not intend to place any limitations on the use of private tongues in his discussion in 1 Cor 12.

Christ is in clear view when Paul uses the metaphor of the body of Christ to frame his next block of material (1 Cor 12:12, 27). The confession that Jesus is Lord also has horizontal implications. All believers were baptized by one Spirit into the one body of Christ (v. 13), and this common initiation into Christ provides the basis for unity and love in the operation of the gifts. The preposition "by" could be a locative dative ("in"), an instrumental dative ("with" or "by"), or a dative of agency ("by"), but it probably expresses the agency of the Spirit, given the emphasis on agency in the immediate context, the flow of the sentence with this reading, and the syntax. However, one's view of the preposition is not determinative in regard to a Pentecostal baptism in the Spirit. The second half of the verse ("and all one Spirit were given to drink") implies an experiential aspect of the Christian life and points to continued participation in the gifts. The expression leaves the door open for continued experiences with the Spirit. The significance of 1 Cor 12:12–13 is that it establishes christocentric boundaries for the operation of the gifts as a prelude to Paul's correction of the misuse of tongues.

The body of Christ metaphor and the emphasis on the need for proper care for the community sets the tone for the discussion of the gifts and prepares the reader for the focus on love in chapter 13. Paul lists kinds of tongues and interpretation of tongues last in chapter 12 because they are the main topic under discussion, and not because they are defective gifts of the Spirit. Paul emphasizes the gifted persons of apostles, prophets, and teachers because of their key role in building and strengthening the church; Paul desires that believers seek such gifts that will edify the body. Some scholars have assumed a reconstruction of 1 Cor 12–14 in which Corinthian believers envisioned themselves as elitist and superior to other believers because of their speaking in tongues. Caution should be exercised in assuming this reconstruction, as this perspective may reflect more of one's current view on charismatic practices than Paul's actual intent. Regardless, Christ remains Paul's context and love his admonition at Corinth.

Paul gives precious little explanation of the phenomenology of tongues, but his discussion neither limits tongues to known human languages nor affirms an ecstatic view along the lines of the mystery religions. Paul seems content to recognize tongues as languages miraculously given by the Spirit. The expression "tongues of men and of angels" is best viewed as a literary device, a merism, which encompasses the most exalted forms of human rhetoric and heavenly language. Writings from near the time of the New Testament (such as the Testament of Job) make it likely that the Corinthians were aware of the concept of angelic languages and may even have conceived of tongues as angeloglossy, but Paul offers only a conditional "if I speak," and he does not certify any specific phenomenological perspective. He shows much more concern over the loving use of tongues than he does in articulating a definition of them.

Although the terms "Lord" and "Christ" do not occur in 1 Cor 13, Christ is obviously present. Eschatological language is ubiquitous in verses 8–13, and the parousia marks the termination of partial gifts and the full revelation that replaces them. Arguments for the cessation of tongues prior to the parousia on the basis of the middle voice of *παύω* ("cease"; v. 8) carry little weight. The immediate, eschatological context is determinative, and the middle voice makes the verb intransitive and is appropriate in the context. Christ also comes into view in Paul's "face to face" expression (v. 12b), which is likely drawn from the account of Moses' unique standing as a prophet (Num 12:8). As one who prefigures Christ, the reference is especially fitting in a discussion of the temporal nature of the gifts in light of Christ's parousia. The eternal nature of love and the return of Christ establish the proper framework for the use of tongues and all the gifts in the present age. Paul expounds on the practical implications of this in 1 Cor 14.

10

Tongues, Prophecy, and Groans

PAUL INTRODUCED HIS DISCUSSION of the gifts (1 Cor 12–14) by emphasizing what it means to be spiritual and what true knowledge involves. True knowledge is christocentric, and people of the Spirit confess that "Jesus is Lord" (12:1–3). All believers have been baptized by the Spirit into the one body of Christ (vv. 12–13), and the love of Christ must govern all relationships in the body (v. 25; ch. 13), especially since love is eternal while the gifts expire at the parousia (13:8–13). Paul has called attention to tongues several times (12:10, 28, 30; 13:1, 8) in preparation for a more detailed treatment of problems related to the gift, and in chapter 14 he narrows the discussion and applies the christological, pneumatic, and ethical principles to the functioning of tongues and prophesy in the local assembly.

The following discussion examines 1 Cor 14 in five sections marked by Paul's direct addresses to the Corinthian congregation: "Brothers" (ἀδελφοί; 14:6, 20, 26, 39). The first section (14:1–5) discusses Paul's concern for the edification of the body and his wish that all would speak in tongues. The second unit (vv. 6–19) highlights Paul's concern for intelligibility in the public use of tongues and addresses the thorny issues related to prayer "in my spirit," the content of tongues, spiritual hymnody (Col 3:16; Eph 5:18–21; 6:18), and Paul's claim to frequent prayer in tongues. The third segment (1 Cor 14:20–25) addresses Paul's implementation of Isa 28:11–12 in order to exhort the Corinthians to think in a mature manner, advocate intelligibility in the assembly, and avoid alienating unbelievers from the gospel. The fourth unit (1 Cor 14:26–36) reviews Paul's specific instructions on the orderly use of prophecy and tongues in the assembly and includes six observations about their use in light of Paul's emphasis on the body. The discussion over 1 Cor 14 concludes with an emphasis on the Lord's authority behind Paul's instructions (vv. 37–39) and the reappearance of the term "Lord" to frame chapters 12–14.

As 1 Cor 14 has been used by some scholars to support a glossolalic understanding of the "groans" of the Spirit in Rom 8:26–27, I address the debate over this issue. The christological elements of Romans are given due consideration in this discussion. A summary concludes the chapter.

Tongues and the Edification of the Body (1 Cor 14:1–5)

An inclusio frames chapter 13, with the same imperative verb beginning the phrase "and eagerly desire the greater grace-gifts [ζηλοῦτε δὲ τὰ χαρίσματα τὰ μείζονα]" (12:31) and the phrase "and eagerly desire the spiritual gifts [ζηλοῦτε δὲ τὰ πνευματικά]" (14:1). The subject of tongues precedes the first reference and follows the second, and the emphasis on love between them highlights the way believers must employ the gifts.[1] The final imperative before the close of the frame ("Pursue love"; 14:1) underscores the necessity of love. For Paul, it is not love or gifts but both, as the phrases "Pursue love" and "Eagerly desire the spiritual gifts" both begin with imperatives.[2] The incorporation of τὰ πνευματικά is noteworthy because the adjective has not appeared since 12:1, and its emergence at 14:1 reminds the reader that Paul has not departed from his original concerns. Although the adjective is neuter in 14:1 and more clearly refers to the gifts than does the more ambiguous πνευματικῶν (12:1),[3] the repetition of the term calls attention to the activity of the Spirit and Paul's fundamental principle that genuine people of the Spirit confess the lordship of Jesus. The term refers to the gifts but evokes thoughts of the christological pneumatology Paul has previously established.

1. Of course, tongues is also the topic in 1 Cor 13:1.

2. Nothing in the context clearly indicates that Paul is quoting the Corinthians and that Martin's translation of the verb as a present indicative is what Paul intends: "You are striving for *pneumatika*" (1 Cor 14:1; cf. 12:31a). Martin, *Spirit and the Congregation*, 66.

3. This term could be either masculine or neuter, and I have argued that it refers to people of the Spirit in 12:1. See the discussion in chapter 8. Li suggests that Paul speaks of the *pneumatika* in 1 Cor 14 in a "concrete manner" when she narrows the focus to tongues and prophecy. Li, *Paul's Teaching*, 340.

Paul follows his command to "eagerly desire the spiritual gifts" with "and especially [μᾶλλον] that you may prophesy" (1 Cor 14:1).[4] He then elucidates the benefits of prophesying over speaking in tongues in the assembly and concludes the initial comparison with another use of μᾶλλον to show his preference for prophecy, unless the tongues are interpreted (v. 5). The first reason Paul gives for this preference concerns the vertical orientation of tongues ("to God"; v. 2) compared to the horizontal orientation of prophecy ("to people"; v. 3). Paul explains that "no one understands" the tongues "but by the Spirit the person speaks mysteries" (v. 2). The two thoughts are parallel, suggesting that "mysteries" primarily refers to something unintelligible.[5] Forbes views the term as involving revelation and appeals to the revelatory nature of tongues in Acts 2, the association of tongues with other forms of inspired speech, and the benefit to the congregation when tongues are interpreted.[6] Paul usually speaks of "mystery" in reference to the gospel revealed in Christ, and although Gardner views the "mysteries" as something not understood, he adds, "This is not to say that the usual Pauline semantic content is altogether missing."[7] Gardner suggests the content is similar to the corporate praise to God for what he has done in Christ.[8] This is certainly consistent with the expression "mysteries," the emphasis on the lordship of Jesus (12:3), Paul's description of tongues as prayer and praise (1 Cor 14:14–17), and Acts 2. However, this understanding does not require that interpreted tongues be revelational in the sense of conveying a message of exhortation; an interpretation may simply enable the audience to participate in an utterance of praise.

According to Paul, the "mysteries" are spoken "by the Spirit [πνεύματι]" (1 Cor 14:2), and the context most naturally suggests that

4. Several translations include "especially" (e.g., CSB, ESV, NASB, NJB, NIV, NRSV), and this does seem to capture Paul's intention.

5. Barrett, *First Corinthians*, 315–26; Fee, *First Corinthians*, rev. ed., 727–28; Thiselton, *First Corinthians*, 1085–86; Witherington, *Conflict and Community*, 281. Hodge, however, views this definition as too limited in light of Pauline usage. *First Corinthians*, 280. Although Paul does speak of the mystery of the gospel in 1 Corinthians (2:1, 7; 4:1), he also uses the term in a more general sense in 13:2 and 15:51.

6. Forbes, *Prophecy*, 92–97.

7. Gardner, *1 Corinthians*, 592. See the following Pauline passages where the mystery is related to the gospel of Christ: Rom 16:25; 1 Cor 2:1, 7; 4:1; Eph 1:9; 3:3, 4, 9; 6:19; Col 1:26, 27; 2:2; 4:3; 1 Tim 3:9, 16. Paul also uses the term in a more general sense in 1 Cor 13:2.

8. Gardner, *1 Corinthians*, 592.

the divine Spirit is in view.[9] This is the second reference to the Spirit in this unit (14:1, 2), and the clear connection between the inspiration of the Spirit and tongues should quickly destroy any notion that Paul views tongues in a negative light. The real issue is made explicit in verse 3, where prophesy is connected with "edification [οἰκοδομὴν] and encouragement and comfort." This is the first of seven occurrences of the noun οἰκοδομὴν or its cognate verb in this segment of 1 Corinthians (14:3, 4 [2x], 5, 12, 17, 26), and, consistent with Paul's insistence on honoring the body of Christ, the term encapsulates Paul's central concern.[10] The concern is not even the intelligibility of tongues per se, but the edification of the body of Christ. Gardner sees a christocentric element in the "encouragement" and "comfort" in verse 3: "Since in 3:11 Paul has been explicit that the foundation is Jesus Christ and that any building must always be on that foundation, it is reasonable to assume that this 'encouragement' and 'consolation' is understood by Paul always to point in some way to Christ."[11] Once again, it is evident that the gifts do not function apart from the centrality of Christ in the New Testament.

Paul in no way intends to cast aspersions on tongues or the speaker when he acknowledges that "the one who speaks in tongues edifies himself," but he stresses how the one who prophesies "builds the church" (1 Cor 14:4).[12] Macchia rightly observes that even edification of self is not to be viewed in isolation from the body of Christ. Edification "must be seen in the light of Paul's emphasis elsewhere on being built up into the fullness of Christ with the help of all the saints (Eph. 4:12–13). It is not self-centered euphoria of good feelings but being conformed to the image of Christ so that we might move out as channels of God's grace to others."[13] Consequently, the use of tongues for self edification is not selfish or contrary to the work of the Spirit.

9. Thiselton rightly notes that "many commentators before the 1950s were unduly influenced by a view of human personhood dominated by idealist or Cartesian dualism, and πνεῦμα as human spirit plays a very minor role in Paul." Thiselton, *First Corinthians*, 1086. Contra Fitzmyer, *First Corinthians*, 511.

10. So also Fee, *First Corinthians*, rev. ed., 729.

11. Gardner, *1 Corinthians*, 593.

12. Contra Fitzmyer, who holds that Paul's remark about tongues building the individual is "derogatory." Fitzmyer, *First Corinthians*, 511. Similarly, House holds that "Paul merely conceded a point here for argument. He did not affirm the legitimacy of that believer's experience as from the Holy Spirit." House, "Tongues," 144.

13. Macchia, "Sighs Too Deep," 66–67.

Paul's wish in 1 Cor 14:5 ("And I want all of you [θέλω δὲ πάντας ὑμᾶς] to speak in tongues") confirms that Paul views both the gift and the idea of self edification positively, and he seems to have in mind the private use of the gift, as he does not wish that everyone would speak in tongues in the corporate assembly (vv. 18–19). Some scholars take a minimalist perspective on either the sincerity of Paul's wish or the potential of its realization. Fitzmyer views the wish as a concession,[14] Thiselton opts for a different translation ("I take pleasure in") because of his difficulty reconciling this wish with Paul's statements in 12:29–30,[15] and Carson compares the wish to Paul's wish for all to be celibate in 7:7 and rules out the possibility that Paul's "considered theological stance" is "that every Christian speak in tongues."[16] Recognizing the force of Paul's thanksgiving for his own use of tongues in 14:18, Turner rejects the latter argument but tempers too optimistic of an approach by arguing that Paul does not expect his wish to be realized, that his primary wish was for more prophecy, and that the wish for speaking in tongues may suggest that the gift "was *not* as widespread at Corinth as Paul might have liked."[17]

The most natural approach to 1 Cor 14:5 is to take Paul's statement at face value, translate θέλω with the common Pauline definition "I want," and take his "all" seriously and apply it to the whole church of Corinth. Examples where Paul truly wants something for all concerned are easy to find. He wants his audience to be informed (Rom 1:13; 11:25; 1 Cor 10:1; 11:3; 12:1), to be wise (Rom 16:19), to be without anxiety (1 Cor 7:32), and to avoid idolatrous participation with demons (10:21). Presumably, he does not want some of the congregation to share in a demonic sacrifice! Menzies is right that the particular nuance of the verb is determined by the context, and while the structure of the sentence in 7:7 (Paul's wish that others might be celibate like him) is similar to 14:5, the context is "strikingly different," and Paul's comments make it clear that he does not expect everyone to be celibate.[18] Garland does not attempt to restrict

14. Fitzmyer, *First Corinthians*, 512. House sees many of Paul's statements in this context as conciliatory. House, "Tongues," 143. Gardner sees a concession here but views Paul's intent more optimistically than Fitzmyer. Gardner also mentions that the "all" in 14:5 need not include every single person. *1 Corinthians*, 600.

15. He concludes, "Paul does not . . . *wish* that every member of the church at Corinth may speak with tongues." Thiselton, *First Corinthians*, 1097. Emphasis original.

16. Carson, *Showing the Spirit*, 102. See an explanation of this same argument in Turner, "Tongues: An Experience for all?" 244–45.

17. Turner, "Tongues: An Experience for All?" 245. Emphasis original.

18. Menzies, *Speaking in Tongues*, 99.

Paul's desire for "all" to speak in tongues but suggests the wish "basically democratizes the gift."[19] Neither does the context suggest that Paul's desire cannot or should not be realized.[20] The positive evaluation of tongues when used for prayer and praise in private (vv. 13–18) and for edification when interpreted in public (v. 5) is consistent with Paul's genuine desire that all speak in tongues.[21]

As for the suggestion that Paul's wish for more participation in glossolalia indicates a general lack of the gift, the context makes it more likely that a significant number of Corinthians spoke in tongues. The problem at Corinth was not a lack of speaking in tongues, but that the use of the gift was not couched in Christ. The Corinthians' public use of the gift neither magnified his lordship nor edified his body. That the gift was common is evinced by the need for Paul to write 1 Cor 12–14, to emphasize the need for diversity (ch. 12), and to place limitations on the number of public expressions (14:27). The ease with which he could speak of tongues and interpretation of tongues without giving clear definitions testifies to the familiarity with it. It is likely that the charismatic experience of Paul (Acts 9:17–19; 1 Cor 14:18) and the Ephesians (Acts 19:1–7; cf. Mark: 16:17; Acts 2:4; 10:44–47) typified the establishment of new churches and that the prevalence of tongues among immature believers naturally led to its misuse at Corinth.

Simon Kistemaker has also seen in Paul's wish a reference to Moses' wish: "Would that all the LORD'S people were prophets, that the LORD would put his Spirit on them!" (Num 11:29b ESV).[22] Fitzmyer calls this comparison "far-fetched" and claims "it has nothing to do with speaking in tongues—or with Paul's wish."[23] On the other hand, Thiselton believes that "Kistemaker has surely identified the source in the OT which lies behind Paul's formulation of argument and his use of θέλω." Thiselton builds on the identification and suggests that Paul has chosen this reference because of Moses' rejection of elitism when Eldad and Medad continue prophesying in the camp (vv. 26–30).[24] The

19. He views this democratization in light of elitist tendencies at Corinth. Garland, *1 Corinthians*, 634.

20. With Menzies, *Speaking in Tongues*, 99.

21. Fee, *First Corinthians*, rev. ed., 730, and Hovenden, *Speaking in Tongues*, 158, take a positive view of Paul's wish.

22. Kistemaker, *First Corinthians*, 481.

23. Fitzmyer, *First Corinthians*, 512.

24. Thiselton, *First Corinthians*, 1097. Ciampa and Rosner also see an echo of Num

possibility of an allusion to or echo of Numbers should not be quickly dismissed, as Paul has already made various references to exodus themes (e.g., 1 Cor 10:1–13 with 12:13; 11:25). Most importantly, Paul has just finished describing the eschaton in "face to face" terms (13:12), which is a reference to Moses' unique prophetic gifting found in Num 12:8. It is by no means "far-fetched" to think that Paul may be alluding to the same story again. Paul's primary desire in 1 Cor 14:5 is that church members prophesy in public for the edification of the body, although tongues with interpretation has a similar edifying effect (v. 5b). Paul's association of tongues (especially when interpreted) with prophecy and his references to Num 11–12 bring his theology nearer to Luke's than one might expect. One immediately thinks of Joel's prophecy (2:28–29) cited by Peter in reference to tongues (Acts 2:17–18). If this is the case, then both Luke and Paul have a pneumatology that includes the potential prophethood of all believers and that associates this inspiration with tongues.

Paul closes his inclusio in 1 Cor 14:5 with the identical phrase he used in verse 1: "and especially that you may prophesy" (μᾶλλον δὲ ἵνα προφητεύητε).[25] In so doing he emphasizes the benefits of prophesy for edification, and his next comment confirms that, for Paul, "greater gifts" (12:31) are those that most edify the body: "And greater is the one who prophesies than the one who speaks in tongues, unless [ἐκτὸς εἰ μὴ] he interprets, so that the church may receive edification" (14:5b). When glossolalia is interpreted, it edifies the church and is therefore of considerable value. The expression ἐκτὸς εἰ μὴ is pleonastic (cf. 15:2; 1 Tim 5:19)[26] and seems to emphasize the real possibility of edification taking place with interpretation of tongues. In this text, the interpreter is the same person as the one who speaks in tongues,[27] but based on 1 Cor 14:28, this need

11:29 in 1 Cor 14:5. *First Corinthians*, 675.

25. Several scholars have defined prophecy in the New Testament as essentially equal to preaching. E.g., Fitzmyer, *First Corinthians*, 510; Hill, *New Testament Prophecy*, 126–31; Robertson and Plummer, *First Corinthians*, 301; Thiselton, *First Corinthians*, 1061, 1076, 1084. Fee points to the "spontaneous" nature of the gift as supported by Paul's reference to a fresh "revelation" in the public assembly in 1 Cor 14:30. Fee, *First Corinthians*, rev. ed., 731. Those who limit prophecy to preaching seem to be attempting to desupernaturalize the gift and domesticate it. While prophecy does not have to be uttered spontaneously, this is one way it functions. Prophecy in the Bible does not typically arise out of intellectual forethought and study (although meditation on Scripture at times stirred the prophets) but from the direct impression of the Spirit upon the prophet.

26. BDF §376.

27. Thiselton, *First Corinthians*, 1098.

not always be the case. Dunn wonders why "this cumbersome two-stage gift" is necessary when prophecy or praise would potentially accomplish the goal of edification,[28] but although tongues with interpretation has a similar value to prophesy in regard to edification, "there is an interesting dynamic going on in the interplay and symbolism of tongues and interpretation that are [sic] not fully captured in a prophetic utterance alone."[29] The public expression of tongues may arrest the attention in a unique way, and the implementation of two gifts may add to the sense of wonder. If the interpreter is not also the one speaking in tongues, another dimension of communal cooperation becomes evident. Although Paul does not elaborate on any of this, it is also possible that the church had at least an elementary understanding of the symbolism of tongues as signifying the reign of Christ as Lord of the nations (Acts 2:36; 10:36). Thus, there are good reasons to reject the notion that tongues with interpretation is a superfluous manifestation.

The Necessity of Intelligibility (1 Cor 14:6–19)

Paul signals a transition into the next section of his argument with the vocative case in his opening: "But now, brothers [ἀδελφοί]" (1 Cor 14:6). This is followed by four rhetorical questions with each containing an ἐὰν ("if") clause (vv. 6, 7, 8, 9). All four clauses "have an identical grammatical structure and are presented in the form of third-class condition, formed with an aorist subjunctive in the protasis and a future in the interrogative apodosis."[30] The first "if" clause sets the course and focuses on the need for intelligibility in public worship. Paul asks what good it would do for him to come to the Corinthians speaking in tongues; he would need to speak "with a revelation, or knowledge, or prophecy, or teaching" to benefit them (v. 6). As Fee points out, the presence of prophecy as one among other intelligible utterances in the list demonstrates that Paul's primary concern "is not tongues and prophecy as such, but tongues and intelligibility, for which prophecy serves as the representative gift."[31] The following "if" clauses then provide analogies that reinforce Paul's point. The flute and harp must play distinct notes in order to have a recognizable

28. Dunn, *Jesus and the Spirit*, 248.

29. Macchia, "Groans Too Deep," Section 6.

30. Gardner, *1 Corinthians*, 602. Similarly, Fee, *First Corinthians*, rev. ed., 733n467.

31. Fee, *First Corinthians*, rev. ed., 734.

melody (v. 7), and a trumpet must give a clear signal so the troops can prepare for battle (v. 8). Paul completes the analogy in verse 9 by drawing a comparison to the tongue speaking an unintelligible word: "How will it be known [γνωσθήσεται] what is being spoken?" Perhaps there is a touch of irony in this argument, as the Corinthians have taken such pride in knowledge, but Paul must exhort them to value the right kind of knowledge (intelligibility) in the assembly.

Paul offers an additional analogy about using foreign languages in order to bring the various analogies to a climax. He points out the futility of speaking foreign languages to those who do not understand (1 Cor 14:10–11), emphasizing the alienation between the parties.[32] He concludes, "So also with you, since you are zealots for spirits, seek to excel in building up the church" (v. 12). Paul advocates prayer for the ability to interpret speaking in a tongue in the next verse (v. 13), and this combination of edification and interpretation closes out the analogies with the same content with which he concluded the previous unit at verse 5.

The phrase "you are zealots for spirits" (ζηλωταί ἐστε πνευμάτων; 1 Cor 14:12) has engendered considerable discussion, as the phrase is difficult. Most scholars take πνευμάτων as an objective genitive,[33] although Li views it as an attributive genitive in which "the genitive πνευμάτων indicates a quality, property, characteristic or feature (*Eigenschaft*) of the Corinthians."[34] In this case the genitive πνευμάτων acts as an attributive adjective, yielding "spiritual zealots."[35] Collins translates πνευμάτων more generally as "spiritual realities,"[36] and Thiselton suggests "powers of the Spirit" in order to bring out both the reference to the Spirit and the plural πνευμάτων.[37] Gardner shares Thiselton's emphasis on the Spirit in his translation "inspirations of the Spirit," pointing to Paul's reference

32. Fee is right to note that the analogy does not work well if tongues are actually human languages. In other words, xenolalia is not in view. Fee, *First Corinthians*, rev. ed., 736. Also Macchia, "Groans Too Deep," Section 3.

33. Lenski suggests that πνευμάτων "is objective because of the verbal idea contained in the noun zealots." Lenski, *Corinthians*, 589. Brookins and Longenecker follow the objective view and see "spirits" as metonymy for "manifestations of spirits." Brookins and Longenecker, *1 Corinthians 10–16*, 109. Conzelmann sees πνευμάτων as essentially the same as πνευματικῶν and representing "spiritual gifts." Conzelmann, *1 Corinthians*, 237.

34. Li, *Paul's Teaching*, 352.

35. Li, *Paul's Teaching*, 352.

36. Collins, *First Corinthians*, 499.

37. Thiselton, *First Corinthians*, 1107.

to "the spirits of the prophets" in verse 32 and drawing attention to the activity of the Spirit working through the Corinthians.[38] Similarly, Fee emphasizes the manifestation of the Spirit through the spirits of the Corinthians.[39]

The emphasis on language in 1 Cor 14:11 and on "speaking in a tongue" in verse 13 adds credence to Fee's assertion that the "spirits" in verse 12 refers specifically to speaking in tongues and not to the gifts in general (contra most Bible translations).[40] The Corinthians, then, are especially zealous for tongues, and perhaps the plural "spirits" is appropriate for spiritual language described with the plural "tongues." More importantly, those scholars who perceive an emphasis on the Spirit in the expression rightly relate the term to Paul's many references to the Spirit and the similar pneumatic terms in 12:1 and 14:1, 2. In this way, Paul once again draws attention to his initial claims of what it means to be people of the Spirit: people of the Spirit confess that Jesus is Lord (12:1–3). In addition, the Corinthians have been baptized by the one Spirit into the one body (v. 13), and they must therefore seek to edify the body with their "spirits." The horizontal implications of their union with Christ continue to guide Paul throughout his argument.

The discussion in 1 Cor 14:13–19 is closely connected to Paul's emphasis on edification expressed in verse 12, as indicated by his use of the inferential conjunction "therefore" (Διὸ) at the beginning of verse 13: "Therefore let the one who speaks in a tongue pray that he may interpret." Intelligibility in the assembly remains in view. Paul employs the first person in verses 14–15 and uses himself to illustrate the inadequacy of uninterpreted tongues used in private prayer for the public assembly: "For if I pray in a tongue, my spirit prays, but my mind is unfruitful" (ἐὰν γὰρ προσεύχωμαι γλώσσῃ, τὸ πνεῦμά μου προσεύχεται, ὁ δὲ νοῦς μου ἄκαρπός ἐστιν; v. 14). This description of tongues as prayer is consistent with the speaking "to God" in verse 2. It is remarkable that Paul so easily assumes a mutual understanding between him and the Corinthians that speaking in tongues is fundamentally a form of prayer. He argues

38. Gardner, *1 Corinthians*, 605.

39. Fee, *First Corinthians*, rev. ed., 738. Lenski also thinks along these lines and finds support for this perspective in 1 Cor 12:7, suggesting that "the manifestation of the Spirit" is "given to each one as though the Spirit individualizes himself in each person." He also refers to 14:32; 1 John 4:1, 2; and Rev 1:4; 5:5, 6. Lenski concludes, "This term 'spirits' designates the different manifestations of the one Holy Spirit in the individual Christians." Lenski, *Corinthians*, 589–90.

40. Fee, *First Corinthians*, rev. ed., 738.

from this presupposition and not for it. As such, it makes tongues unique among the gifts, as all the gifts that Paul lists in his epistles are intended for corporate edification, but tongues has an additional private application for personal edification (14:4). It is this private prayer element of speaking in tongues that lends credence to the notion that this aspect of the manifestation of the Spirit may be available for all believers. It seems counterintuitive to think that a form of personal prayer would be restricted to only select believers in the body.

The possessive "my spirit" in 1 Cor 14:14 has met with considerable discussion among scholars.[41] To account for the Spirit's inspiration of tongues as evinced in 1 Cor 12:7–11; 14:2; and 14:16, Fee suggests, "The most viable solution to this ambiguity is that by the language 'my spirit prays' Paul means his own spirit is praying as the Holy Spirit gives the utterance. Hence, 'my S/spirit prays.'"[42] Ciampa and Rosner see the phrase as an unambiguous reference to Paul's own spirit and object to Fee's rendering of the passage.[43] In turn, Fee responds in his revised commentary that Ciampa and Rosner have failed to offer a clear explanation of what "my spirit prays" means and how one would otherwise explain such "prayer that bypasses the cortex of the brain."[44] Thiselton also rejects Fee's understanding and lists two reasons. "First, Pauline specialists generally agree that Platonic or Idealist notions of the human spirit as a point of 'divine contact' are alien to Paul and plainly alien to the explicit thrust of 1 Cor 2:10–12. Second, to read this into 14:15 is to fall into the very trap to which the Corinthians and many today fall prey, namely, of associating the operation of the Holy Spirit more closely with noncognitive

41. Schweizer views the reference to "my spirit" in 1 Cor 14:14 as an anthropological use of πνεῦμα. Schweizer, "πνεῦμα, πνευματικός, κτλ.," 435. But he concludes "that Paul thinks wholly in terms of the work of the Spirit of God and perceives that the whole existence of the believer is determined thereby." He continues, "For this reason the πνεῦμα, though always God's Spirit and never evaporating into the πνεῦμα given individually to man, is also the innermost ego of the one who no longer lives by his own being but by God's being for him." Schweizer, "πνεῦμα, πνευματικός, κτλ.," 436.

42. Fee, *First Corinthians*, 1st ed., 670. In Fee's review of how various translations have handled the difficulties associated with Paul's use of πνεῦμα, he bemoans how "the English tradition has let the troublesome '*my* spirit' in v. 14 control their rendering of πνεῦμα in the whole passage. The NEB resolved this exegetical/translational issue rather nicely by rendering 'the Spirit in me prays,' since the context seems to demand that that is precisely what Paul means." Fee, "Translational Tendenz," 355.

43. Ciampa and Rosner, *First Corinthians*, 689n97. Fitzmyer objects to Fee's interpretation on the grounds that the phrase would imply ownership of the Spirit. *First Corinthians*, 515.

44. Fee, *First Corinthians*, rev. ed., 742n527.

'spontaneous' phenomena than with a self-critical reflection upon the word of God as that which addresses the understanding and thereby transforms the heart (cf. 14:23–25)."[45] Several scholars have expressed a concern to avoid associating Paul's comment with Platonic or Hellenistic thought,[46] but with this concern often comes an interpretation of verses 14–15 that essentially eliminates the practice of unintelligible, private prayer in tongues in favor of combining the spirit and mind to pray only in an intelligible manner.[47] Regarding Thiselton's second concern, one can agree in principle that "noncognitive 'spontaneous' phenomenon" should not replace study of the Scriptures, but one can also reject any excessively rationalistic presuppositions that may be fueling this argument.[48]

A few scholars have suggested that Paul's "my spirit" is a reference to a person's spiritual gift, but there is a difficulty in making a gift the subject of "prays."[49] In fairness to Fee, although his "S/spirit" may be "inelegant"[50] and the idea of the possessive pronoun with Spirit may be unthinkable for some, the essential point that "Paul means his own spirit is praying as the Holy Spirit gives the utterance" is quite in keeping with the context and with Acts 2:4.[51] Paul's "unfruitful" mind simply points to the problem of the incomprehensibility of tongues, which, if exercised in public, would not benefit the community. Paul is not depreciating his claim that his spirit prays, as if this private practice were not edifying and beneficial for the individual (1 Cor 14:2, 4, 5). Nor is he capitulating to Hellenistic dualism when he suggests that prayer can have a supra-rational dimension.[52] His Hebrew tradition allows for various experiences that do not fit comfortably with modernist standards of intellect-based communication with God. Prophetic visions (Gen 15), dreams (Gen 40–41; Joel 2:28), an angel in a burning bush (Exod 3:1–3), music as prophetic inspiration (1

45. Thiselton, *First Corinthians*, 1112–13.

46. E.g., Ciampa and Rosner, *First Corinthians*, 689; Collins, *First Corinthians*, 501; Garland, *1 Corinthians*, 638–39; Gardner, *1 Corinthians*, 606.

47. E.g., Kistemaker, *First Corinthians*, 491–92.

48. His advocating the complete abolition of speaking in tongues in a public service points in this direction. Thiselton, *First Corinthians*, 1118.

49. Hodge, *First Corinthians*, 287. See the discussion in Barrett, *First Corinthians*, 320.

50. Fee, *God's Empowering Presence*, 613.

51. Fee, *First Corinthians*, rev. ed., 742. Were it not for Fee's "S/spirit" designation, a number of scholars would likely relax their objections.

52. Giving the human spirit its due in Paul's statement avoids the problem of intimating that prayer with the mind is any less "of the Spirit" than prayer in the spirit.

Sam 10:5–7; 16:14–23), pneumatic transport (1 Kings 18:12; Acts 8:39), trances (Acts 10:10), and visionary raptures (2 Cor 12:1–6; Rev 4:1) illustrate the diverse kinds of encounters that contributed to the worldview of the biblical characters. From this prophetic tradition comes the notion of prayer with the human spirit that operates by the inspiration of the divine Spirit; it does not come from Hellenism.

The answer to Paul's question, "What should I do about this?" (1 Cor 14:15), is "I will pray in the spirit, and I will pray with the mind; I will sing in the spirit, and I will sing with the mind."[53] This is not a singular, simultaneous event of prayer or event of song as Kistemaker suggests: "As the spirit and the mind work together in praying, so they ought to be in tandem when singing,"[54] but two distinct ways of praying: private, unintelligible tongues, and ordinary, public prayer. The same applies to the singing. Kistemaker's interpretation loses sight of the contrasting unintelligible/private πνεῦμα ("spirit") and intelligible/public νοῦς ("mind") expressions of worship and practically disregards the unintelligible element (v. 14).[55] Paul is not implying that prayer with the understanding is not prompted by the Spirit, but he is using a shorthand way of contrasting two forms of prayer.[56] The repetition of "I will pray" and "I will sing" (v. 15) lends to the notion of distinct forms of prayer (and of singing), as Paul could have used one of his common constructions for indicating "both," that is, a singular spirit and mind event.[57] Paul uses the future tense in a volitive sense when he affirms, "I will pray [προσεύξομαι]" and "I will sing [ψαλῶ]" (v. 15),[58] but he also accentuates prayer and singing

53. I have translated πνεῦμα here as lower case "spirit" for consistency with verse 14, but this sentence likely carries the same idea of the anthropological spirit inspired by the divine Spirit.

54. Kistemaker, *First Corinthians*, 492.

55. This fits with Kistemaker's generally negative view of tongues, referring to tongues as the "least" of the gifts and even suggesting that there is no record in the New Testament of Paul or Peter speaking in tongues outside 1 Cor 14:18. This is a remarkable oversight of Peter's participation at Pentecost (Acts 2). Kistemaker, *First Corinthians*, 495–96. Behm defines the νοῦς as the "understanding" in this context. Behm, "νοέω, νοῦς, κτλ.," 959.

56. Barrett attributes the difficulty with the language to Paul's compressing multiple ideas into few words. Barrett, *First Corinthians*, 320.

57. Paul often uses a combination of τέ and καί (Rom 1:12, 14 [2x]; 3:9; 1 Cor 1:24; Phil 1:7), or καί twice (Rom 14:9; 1 Cor 6:13; Phil 2:13; 1 Thess 2:15; 1 Tim 4:16; Titus 1:15; Phlm 16), or ἀμφότεροι (Eph 2:14, 16, 18) to indicate "both." See also Eph 6:9 for another construction.

58. Lenski, *Corinthians*, 592.

with the understanding by adding "but also [δὲ καὶ]" before "the mind." In this manner, Paul expresses that he will decidedly practice both forms of praying and singing, but he emphasizes intelligible prayer and singing in public for the edification of others.

It is striking how Paul introduces singing "in the spirit [τῷ πνεύματι]" (i.e., in tongues) without fanfare (1 Cor 14:15); one gets the impression that the Corinthians were well versed in such charismatic practices.[59] At the same time, Paul is resolute about the necessity of intelligibility in public: "Otherwise, if you bless with the spirit [εὐλογῇς ἐν πνεύματι], how will the one who fills the place of the outsider [ἰδιώτου] say the 'Amen' to your thanksgiving [εὐχαριστίᾳ], since the person does not know what you are saying?" (v. 16).[60] Paul concludes the thought: "For you are giving thanks [εὐχαριστεῖς] well enough, but the other person is not edified [οἰκοδομεῖται]" (v. 17).[61] Speaking in tongues is consistently described as some form of prayer or praise directed toward God in verses 13–17. In Paul's encouragement to pray for interpretation (v. 13), he uses the verb προσεύχομαι ("to pray"), which obviously involves petition in this case. He uses the term four more times in reference to tongues in verses 14–15, but he identifies no specific kind of praying at this point. However, after he mentions the singing in the spirit, Paul switches to the second person and describes tongues as blessing and then thanksgiving. Conzelmann is right that the two word groups "are used in practically a synonymous sense,"[62] although Lenski also notes that the term "blessing" connotes the form of the speaking and "thanksgiving" focuses more on the content.[63] The terms Paul uses, then, are prayer, singing, blessing, and thanksgiving.

59. The problem of how to translate the pneumatic terms continues in verses 15–16. It is precisely this difficulty that makes it likely that the reader is supposed to understand that the divine Spirit is functioning through the human spirit.

60. Paul's meaning of ἰδιώτης (translated "outsider" above) has long been debated, but Schlier rightly points to the immediate context in which Paul argues that this person does not know what the gifted person is saying and cannot say "Amen" to it. Schlier, "ἰδιώτης," 217. Consequently, "the one who fills the place of the outsider" could be any member of the congregation who does not understand the charismatic utterance. Unfortunately, Schlier ends up interpreting this passage in light of 1 Cor 14:23, which emphasizes the perspective of the unbeliever, as Gardner points out. Gardner, *1 Corinthians*, 609n39.

61. The NASB also translates the verse this way. I agree with it and the NIV that the statement should not be translated as a subjunctive ("may be") as in the CSB, ESV, NJB, and NRSV.

62. Conzelmann, *1 Corinthians*, 238.

63. Lenski, *Corinthians*, 593.

Prayer is too general a term to know for certain what Paul has in mind, though it could include petition or intercession, but singing and blessing convey more the idea of praise, and thanksgiving clearly identifies an element of the content.[64]

Although Paul clearly distinguishes between the private and public use of tongues in 1 Cor 14:13–19, he does not distinguish the content of tongues in private from the content in public. In other words, he offers no reason to think that the vertical orientation of tongues as praise and thanksgiving varies between public and private manifestations of tongues. If tongues were interpreted in either setting, one would expect that the content might have generous portions of praise and thanksgiving. This vertical orientation and emphasis on praise comes as no surprise, as "this doxological function of tongues is anticipated in 1 Cor. 12.2–3."[65] Menzies rightly observes the continuity in Paul's discussion: "While the idols are mute, the true God inspires praise to Jesus through the Holy Spirit (1 Cor. 12.3)."[66] Paul's christological lens from the confession in 12:3 continues to exert an influence on his argument, just as emphasis on baptism into the one body of Christ impresses itself on the argument for intelligibility in the public use of tongues.

This christological perspective is also evident in two related texts concerning spiritual song (Col 3:16; Eph 5:19). Paul exhorts the Colossians to "Let the word of Christ dwell in you richly, teaching and admonishing one another in all wisdom with psalms [ψαλμοῖς], hymns [ὕμνοις], and spiritual songs [ᾠδαῖς πνευματικαῖς], singing with thanksgiving in your hearts to God" (3:16). In addition, everything should be done "in the name of the Lord Jesus, giving thanks [εὐχαριστοῦντες] to God the Father through him" (v. 17b). This passage has a strong christological context and also shares with 1 Cor 14 an emphasis on thanksgiving (vv. 16 and 17), instruction (v. 26), singing psalms (vv. 15 and 26), and pneumatic singing (v. 15). The similarities to 1 Cor 14 and the inclusion of "spiritual songs" have led some scholars to suggest that Paul may have singing in tongues in mind in Col 3:16,[67] although Fee doubts whether

64. It is uncertain whether the terminology of praise clarifies what Paul means by prayer or simply broadens the range of what could be expressed in glossolalia, but the argument leans more heavily toward praise than petition or intercession as it progresses.

65. Menzies, *Speaking in Tongues*, 133.

66. Menzies, *Speaking in Tongues*, 131.

67. As reflected in multiple translations, the feminine πνευματικαῖς fits naturally with ωἰδαῖς ("spiritual songs") but does not seem to modify "psalms" and "hymns" in this passage. For a differing opinion, see Lincoln, *Ephesians*, 546. Menzies views the

the emphasis on "teaching and admonishing one another" fits with Paul's emphasis on intelligibility in 1 Cor 14.[68]

The parallel passage in Eph 5:18–20 lacks Paul's reference to the indwelling gospel message of Christ ("word of Christ") in relation to "teaching and admonishing" (Col 3:16) and presents less difficulties for the possibility that tongues are in view, yet it also emphasizes the centrality of Christ in various ways. The immediate context includes what may be an early Christian hymn: "Awake, sleeper, and rise from the dead, and Christ will shine on you" (Eph 5:14).[69] William Hendrickson suggests it was a Christian hymn rooted in Isa 60:1 (cf. 26:19) and that it anticipates the discussion of hymns in Eph 5:19.[70] This may be correct, and the content is likely intended to be a call to conversion and a reminder to the saints to live in an awakened manner. [71] The hymn is thoroughly christocentric with its promise of Christ's light. Paul advocates wise rather than unwise living (v. 15) and wants the Ephesians to "understand what the will of the Lord is" (v. 17b). Paul then contrasts a negative imperative regarding drunkenness with the positive imperative "but be filled in Spirit [ἀλλὰ πληροῦσθε ἐν πνεύματι]" (v. 18) and follows this with five participles describing how one lives the Spirit-filled life.[72] His instruction includes, "speaking to one another in psalms [ψαλμοῖς] and hymns [ὕμνοις] and spiritual songs [ᾠδαῖς πνευματικαῖς], singing and making

"spiritual songs" as a reference to singing in tongues. *Speaking in Tongues*, 138–39. Dunn and Patzia are open to the possibility that glossolalia is included. Dunn, *Jesus and the Spirit*, 238–39; and Dunn, *Epistles to the Colossians and to Philemon*, 239; Patzia, *Ephesians, Colossians, Philemon*, 81. Various scholars view the "spiritual songs" more broadly as charismatic singing. E.g., Fee, *God's Empowering Presence*, 653; McKnight, *Colossians*, 332–33; Witherington, *Philemon, Colossians, Ephesians*, 181.

68. Fee, *God's Empowering Presence*, 654n71. Fee's caution is in order, although it does not absolutely prohibit the possibility that tongues might fall under the umbrella of "spiritual song."

69. Bruce sees it as "a primitive baptismal hymn." Bruce, *Colossians, Philemon, Ephesians*, 376. So also Lincoln, *Ephesians*, 331.

70. Hendrickson, *Galatians, Ephesians*, 235–36.

71. Thielman does not see any reference to the Old Testament in Eph 5:14 but emphasizes the call to conversion. Thielman, *Ephesians*, 348–51. O'Brien argues for a heavy reliance on the Old Testament but also emphasizes the call to conversion. O'Brien, *Ephesians*, 374–77.

72. Arnold also sees the participles as expressing means. Arnold, *Ephesians*, 351. However, it is likely that the participles both describe the character of the Spirit-filled and demonstrate the means of life in the Spirit. Paul likely sees the Spirit as both the source of the activities and the activities as a means of continually accessing the Spirit's fullness.

music in your heart to the Lord, giving thanks always for everything in the name of our Lord Jesus Christ to God and the Father, submitting to one another in reverence for Christ" (vv. 19–21). The emphasis on Christology is obvious, and the singing is done directly "to the Lord" (v. 19) instead of "to God" as in Col 3:16.[73] The praise given to God is also done in light of what he has accomplished in Christ, so that the praise is remarkably "trinitarian" (cf. 1 Cor 12:4–6).

There are several parallels to 1 Cor 14 in Eph 5. First, there is once again the difficulty of handling Paul's reference to the Spirit. Clearly the divine Spirit is in view, but the language of "filled in spirit" (πληροῦσθε ἐν πνεύματι; Eph 5:18) suggests that the human spirit is the vehicle of the divine Spirit. Second, the passages share an emphasis on praise to God or Christ with music. Both employ the term "psalm" (ψαλμός) as a noun (Eph 5:19; 1 Cor 14:26) and as a verb (Eph 5:19; 1 Cor 14:15). Third, thanksgiving takes a prominent place; it features as the fourth participle in the sequence (Eph 5:20) under the command to be filled (v. 18), and Paul describes tongues as thanksgiving in 1 Cor 14:16. Fourth, as Paul piles on the musical terms in Eph 5:19, he includes "spiritual songs" (ᾠδαῖς πνευματικαῖς); this does not seem far removed from Paul's determination to sing in the Spirit (ψαλῶ τῷ πνεύματι; 1 Cor 14:15). Given these similarities, Paul's charismatic worldview, and Luke's account of tongues accompanying Paul's ministry at Ephesus (Acts 19:6), it is not at all unreasonable to infer that singing in tongues is likely included in the "spiritual songs" of Eph 5:19.[74]

The christocentric hymn of Eph 5:14 anticipates Paul's encouragement to christocentric praise in verses 18–20, and Pauline hymnody in general evinces a celebration of Christ. Philippians 2:6–11 may be an early hymn adapted by Paul; it celebrates the exaltation of Christ.[75] Colossians 1:15–20 emphasizes Christ's preeminence over all things. Philip Towner describes the "Christ hymn" of 1 Tim 3:16 as the "rhetorical and

73. Delling, "ὕμνος, ὑμνέω, κτλ.," 498.

74. O'Brien's elimination of glossolalia as possibly represented in this passage is too restrictive. He points to the believers "speaking to one another" as evidence for this. However, as I have mentioned, the language has softened from the Col 3:16 passage, and the second part of Eph 5:19 emphasizes singing and making music "in your heart." In other words, the application is not limited to intelligible exhortation between believers. O'Brien, *Ephesians*, 395.

75. For an overview of the long debate over the genre, origin, and authorship of Phil 2:6–11, see Fee, *Philippians*, 191–97. Although he doubts that this passage is a hymn, he suggests that Rom 11:33–36 is hymnic. *Philippians*, 194.

christological high point of the letter."[76] This christocentric hymnody along with Paul's encouragement to share in "spiritual songs" predisposes the interpreter to think that both the intelligible and unintelligible singing in tongues in 1 Cor 14:15 is also christocentric in nature.

When Paul instructs the Ephesians how to "be strong in the Lord [Jesus]" (6:10), he encourages them to engage in various kinds of prayers and to "pray [προσευχόμενοι] at all times in the Spirit [ἐν πνεύματι]" (v. 18b). The language is similar to 1 Cor 14:15: "I will pray in the Spirit [προσεύξομαι τῷ πνεύματι]." The similarities between the Ephesians passages and 1 Cor 14 make it harder to imagine that speaking in tongues is not included under the umbrella of song and prayer in the Spirit than that it is included.

Despite the difficulties in pinpointing Paul's precise meaning of his various grammatical constructions related to the Spirit, it is important to remember that Paul portrays the Spirit as "the Spirit of Christ" (Rom 8:9), or "the Spirit of his Son" (Gal 4:6), or "the Spirit of Jesus Christ" (Phil 1:19). While Paul's templing language is that of the Spirit indwelling believers (Rom 8:9; 1 Cor 3:16; 6:19), it is also "Christ in you" (Rom 8:10), and it is through the Spirit that believers are united with Christ and other believers (1 Cor 12:12–13). Ulrich Luz is right to point to the presence of the Spirit as "the experiential basis of Pauline Christ-mysticism."[77] While it is important to avoid a complete identification of the Spirit with Christ and lose sight of the trinitarian distinctions, it is also important to bear in mind that the experience of speaking in tongues, singing in tongues, and of any gift is also inherently an experiencing of Christ. In this way, too, speaking in tongues and singing in tongues are christocentric.

Were speaking in tongues not in some way an experiencing of Christ by the Spirit, Paul's personal reference to the use of this charism would be inexplicable. He twice describes the charismatic activity as "thanksgiving" (1 Cor 14:16–17) and then uses the cognate verb to launch into an argument for intelligibility based on his own experience: "I give thanks to God that I speak in tongues more than all of you; but in church I would rather speak five words with my mind, in order that I may

76. Towner, *Timothy and Titus*, 276.

77. Luz, "Paul as Mystic," 137. Luz rightly maintains that "it is not the many 'particular' charismatic experiences of Paul—such as speaking in tongues, prophecy, ecstasy, and miracles—that could be described as central to what counts as 'mysticism' in Paul," but he too narrowly restricts his view of mysticism by focusing only on a perceived "ambivalence" by Paul of the charismatic experiences rather than celebrating them as experiences of Christ. Luz, "Paul as Mystic," 137–38.

instruct others also, than ten thousand words in a tongue" (vv. 18–19). This appeal to Paul's own experience reveals that Paul's use of the first person in the verbs for prayer and singing in verses 14–15 is not merely hypothetical.[78] It also points to the possibility of doubts about Paul's charismatic credentials among some of the Corinthians,[79] although it is not unlikely that the Corinthians were introduced to the Spirit's manifestations by Paul himself. This was the case with some disciples at Ephesus (Acts 19:6), but perhaps the Corinthians needed reminding about who fathered them in the faith (1 Cor 4:14–15) and introduced them to the power of the Holy Spirit (2:4–5). Although Paul does not comment on when his private practice of glossolalia began, his filling with the Spirit under the ministry of Ananias (Acts 9:17) best explains his charismatic ministry at Ephesus (19:6) and Corinth.

Some commentators have attempted to avoid the force of Paul's claim to frequent, private prayer in tongues (1 Cor 14:18). Fitzmyer dismisses the claim entirely as just ironic, Pauline rhetoric and chides a long list of scholars for taking Paul "seriously."[80] Others, usually without contextual justification, limit the frequency of Paul's speaking in tongues by interpreting his "more than" (μᾶλλον) as qualitative rather than quantitative,[81] but this notion is flatly contradicted by the second half of Paul's statement when he gives the numbers five and ten thousand to illustrate the irrelevance of quantity without intelligibility. Paul's reference to his frequent use of tongues has effectively invalidated any argument against his authority to speak to this issue.[82]

78. Similarly, Fee, *First Corinthians*, rev. ed., 748.

79. Signs of the opposition to Paul that reaches a crisis stage in 2 Corinthians already appear at the time of 1 Corinthians. E.g., see 1 Cor 4:1–21; 9:3; 14:37; and possibly 7:40.

80. Fitzmyer, *First Corinthians*, 518. The evidence offered above from Acts, Paul's various life experiences, and the argument of 1 Cor 12–14 tell against his view.

81. Kistemaker, *First Corinthians*, 496, following Grosheide, *De Erste Brief van den Apostel Paulus aan de Kerk te Korinthe*, 466. Grosheide actually takes the position that the comparison is quantitative in his later commentary. Grosheide, *First Epistle to the Corinthians*, 327n14. Others who see the comparison as qualitative or likely so include Garland, *1 Corinthians*, 642; Oropeza, *1 Corinthians*, 180; and Thiselton, *First Corinthians*, 1117.

82. Robertson and Plummer correctly infer from this passage that Paul's private use of "a tongue" implies that known, foreign languages are not in view. *First Corinthians*, 314. Contra Hodge, who claims that Paul speaks in foreign languages. *First Corinthians*, 292.

An Exhortation to Mature Thinking (1 Cor 14:20–25)

The direct address, "Brothers," (1 Cor 14:20) signals a new argument in Paul's lengthy admonition to speak intelligible words in the gathered assembly. Although this passage is fraught with exegetical difficulties, what is clear is that Paul advocates mature thinking (v. 20), which means consideration for the potential presence of unbelievers in the assembly and how uninterpreted glossolalia and prophecy might affect them. The latter is clearly preferred, as it could result in their conversion and recognition "that God is truly among you" (v. 25c; Isa 45:14).

The difficulties begin when Paul employs a rough quotation of Isa 28:11–12: "In the law it is written, 'With other tongues and by the lips of foreigners I will speak to this people, and even then they will not listen to me,' says the Lord" (1 Cor 14:21). The quotation follows neither the Hebrew text nor the Septuagint very closely, although it favors the Hebrew text a bit over the other.[83] Paul's quotation omits Isaiah's mention of rest (Isa 28:12), adds an emphatic "says the Lord" (1 Cor 14:21), reverses the order of "tongues" and "lips" (Isa 28:11),[84] and intensifies both the Hebrew text and the Septuagint in altering "they would not hear" (ἀκούειν; v. 12 LXX) to "they will not obey me" (εἰσακούσονταί μου).[85] The differences may be accounted for by Paul's application of the text to suit his own agenda, but this does not solve the additional problem of determining to what extent Paul intends the reader to consider the original context of the quotation. Does Paul completely ignore the original context, draw a principle or two from it, or expect the reader to know and apply the details of Isaiah's text?

The exegetical difficulties mount when the interpreter inquires as to what Paul means when he says that "tongues are a sign not for those who believe, but for unbelievers, but prophecy is not for unbelievers but

83. Origen has commented that the quotation in 1 Cor 14:21 "is in effect what I found in Aquila's interpretation." Origen, *Philocalia*, 9.2. The Septuagint has the foreigners speaking to the people ("they will speak"), but Paul agrees with the Hebrew text (MT and 1QIsa) that the Lord is the one who speaks through the strange lips, although Paul uses the first person ("I will speak to this people") instead of the third person. See Ciampa and Rosner, "1 Corinthians," 741.

84. Fee suggests Paul makes this change to prioritize his interest in other tongues. Fee, *First Corinthians*, rev. ed., 754.

85. See Garland's list for additional differences. *1 Corinthians*, 646–47. Also Thiselton, *First Corinthians*, 1120, 1122.

for those who believe" (1 Cor 14:22). Should "sign" be taken positively or negatively? An even more vexing problem concerns how prophecy can then be a sign for believers but not unbelievers (v. 22) when Paul illustrates how an unbeliever could respond to prophecy with conversion resulting (v. 25). In other words, prophecy seems like a sign for unbelievers.

Attempts to address the apparent conflicts in the text abound.[86] Conzelmann simply dismisses part of the problem when he asserts, "The wording of v 22 is overdone for the sake of rhetoric (parallelism between the statements on speaking with tongues and on prophecy)."[87] Stendahl dispenses with the problem of prophesy serving as a sign by observing the omission of "sign" in the second half of 1 Cor 14:22; however, the parallelism implies that "sign" is intended in the ellipsis.[88] Some scholars have understood verse 22 as either a Corinthian slogan that Paul rejects[89] or a rhetorical question inspired by the claims of the glossolalists.[90] The latter view, espoused by Bruce Johanson, has gained some traction with a few scholars,[91] but it suffers from the same problem as the previous view in that there are no clear textual indicators of a quotation or the use of a rhetorical question.[92] Johanson's view also assumes that tongues are a positive sign—a perspective that others have also adopted. Stephen Chester suggests, "Uninterpreted tongues are a positive sign to the outsider of divine activity among the Corinthian believers, but are inadequate from Paul's perspective as they fail to communicate the gospel."[93] Chester's position depends on a positive view of the verb *μαίνομαι* ("be mad, be out of

86. For an overview of various positions, see Carson, *Showing the Spirit*, 108–17, and Thiselton, *First Corinthians*, 1122–26.

87. Conzelmann, *1 Corinthians*, 242.

88. Stendahl, *Paul among Jews*, 116n9.

89. Sweet, "A Sign," 141.

90. In this scenario Paul imagines the glossolalists to ask the question this way: "Are tongues, then, meant as a sign not for believers but for unbelievers, while prophecy is meant as a sign not for unbelievers but for believers?" Johanson, "Tongues, a Sign for Unbelievers?" 193.

91. E.g., Macchia, "Sighs Too Deep," 63; Menzies, *Speaking in Tongues*, 112–13.

92. See the criticism of Johanson's proposal in Carson, *Showing the Spirit*, 111–12; Chester, "Divine Madness?" 418n1; and Forbes, *Prophecy*, 177n58.

93. Chester, "Divine Madness?" 417. David Robinson builds on Chester's thesis but emphasizes the allusion to Isa 45:14 in 1 Cor 14:25. Robinson, "'By the Lips of Foreigners,'" 313–18. Robinson contends that "the larger context of Isaiah 45:14 therefore shows Israel in deep need of a clear, external word of confirmation that God is among them." The Corinthians also need such a confirmation of God's presence in their midst. Robinson, "'By the Lips of Foreigners,'" 317.

one's mind")[94] in verse 23, but the negative tone in Paul's quotation of Isa 28:11–12 makes it unlikely that Paul intends the term to have a positive connotation in any cultural setting. When Paul argues that unbelievers will view the Corinthians as mad on account of their corporate participation in uninterpreted tongues, he is not suggesting that outsiders would approve of such practices because of their association with the mystery religions.[95]

Numerous scholars have adopted some version of the position that Isa 28:11–12 depicts judgment on Israel and illustrates the sense of alienation and divine disfavor that uninterpreted tongues communicates to the unbeliever.[96] Paul's familiarity with the Isaian context and his ability to apply it to new settings has already been demonstrated in 1 Cor 1:19, where he quotes and applies Isa 29:14 to the Corinthian obsession with wisdom. In Isa 28 Israel's leaders, characterized by drunkenness (vv. 7–8), mock Isaiah for his simple message, as if he were trying to "teach knowledge" to children (v. 9). The repetitive language of verses 10 and 13 could be infantile speech or a reference to the slow instruction of children (probably the latter): "For it is precept upon precept, precept upon precept, line upon line, line upon line, here a little, there a little [כִּ֣י צַ֤ו לָצָו֙ צַ֣ו לָצָ֔ו קַ֥ו לָקָ֖ו קַ֣ו לָקָ֑ו זְעֵ֥יר שָׁ֖ם זְעֵ֥יר שָֽׁם]" (v. 10 ESV). The mockery of God's simple and clear message would result in them hearing God's voice through foreign invaders who speak with "strange lips" and "a foreign tongue" (v. 11 ESV).[97] As J. Alec Motyer summarizes, "When the simple intelligibility of the word of God is refused, divine judgment falls in the shape of the unintelligible (*cf.* 1 Cor 14:20ff.)."[98] Even in the midst of such a pronunciation of judgment, the Lord extends an invitation to faith and to respond to the one who lays a precious cornerstone in Zion (Isa 28:16). Consequently, there are a variety of points of contact with the Corinthian situation, including tongues (unintelligible languages), childish behavior, alienation from God, worldly knowledge, and an invitation to faith.[99] Given these points of contact and Paul's prior use of the Old

94. BDAG, 610.

95. See Thiselton's study of this term. *First Corinthians*, 1126.

96. Carson lists several scholars in agreement with this position. *Showing the Spirit*, 113n16.

97. While the reference is likely to the Assyrian armies, it should be noted that the warning also goes out to the scoffers in Jerusalem (v. 14).

98. Motyer, *The Prophecy of Isaiah*, 232.

99. Gardner also considers this broader relationship between the Corinthian

Testament in 1 Corinthians, it seems likely that he took Isaiah's context into consideration and expected the Corinthians to do so as well.

In this reading of the text, Paul cautions the Corinthians against the unintelligible use of tongues in corporate gatherings because such activity would signal alienation and judgment to unbelievers rather than invitation. In Isaiah's context, the foreign languages were a sign of judgment to those hardened in rebellion, but such a sign is inappropriate during the age of salvation in Christ. Paul can also say that prophecy is a sign for believers because intelligible language not only edifies, encourages, and comforts (1 Cor 14:3) but evinces God's gracious favor toward his people and his presence among them. That σημεῖόν ("sign"; v. 22) has both a positive and negative application in this passage is not problematic, as Grudem has demonstrated that the term is often "an indication of God's attitude" that varies depending on a response of faith or unbelief.[100]

Several scholars have pointed to the conversion of the unbeliever in 1 Cor 14:25 and the declaration that "God is truly among you" to explain how prophecy is a sign to believers.[101] Paul cites Isa 45:14, where the prophet depicts Israel's return from exile, the blessings of restoration, and the response of nations recognizing the presence of God in Israel's midst.[102] It is this acknowledgement of God's presence that serves as the sign to Israel of its restoration. Likewise, the unbeliever's declaration affirms God's presence with the Corinthian church and confirms the arrival of the eschatological period of God's favor. It is also the time of invitation for the unbeliever to abandon the "mute idols" and confess that "Jesus is Lord" (1 Cor 12:2–3). The international invitation to salvation in Isa 45

context and Isaiah's text. *1 Corinthians*, 612.

100. Grudem, *Gift of Prophecy*, 194. See also Chrysostom, *Homilies on the Epistle of Paul to the Corinthians*, 36.2 (*NPNF*[1] 12:216).

101. E.g., Fee, *First Corinthians*, rev. ed., 757, 761; Forbes, *Prophecy*, 179; Gardner, *1 Corinthians*, 615; Garland, *1 Corinthians*, 653; Grudem, *Gift of Prophecy*, 197–98; Robinson, "'By the Lips of Foreigners,'" 315. Paul seems comfortable describing his hypothetical visit of the unbeliever to the assembly with the believers "all" speaking in tongues (1 Cor 14:23) or "all" prophesying (v. 24). The unbeliever is also "convicted by all" and "called to account by all" (v. 24). Thiselton suggests this is "impressionist rather than numerical." Thiselton, *First Corinthians*, 1127. Even if one allows for some literary exaggeration, it is not unlikely that a number of Corinthians spoke in tongues all at once (v. 27), and Paul's comfort with entertaining the possibility that all might prophesy points to the real possibility that the Corinthian church could potentially function in such a way.

102. Robinson discusses the context of Isa 45:14 and its significance for the Corinthian church in detail. "'By the Lips of Foreigners,'" 315–18.

is instructive: "Assemble yourselves and come; draw near together, you survivors of the nations! They have no knowledge who carry about their wooden idols, and keep on praying to a god that cannot save" (v. 20 ESV). Again, the Lord invites, "Turn to me and be saved, all the ends of the earth! For I am God, and there is no other" (v. 22 ESV).

Paul's argument makes sense when understood in light of the different time periods represented by Isa 28:11–12 and 45:14 and the latter text's anticipation of an eschatological time of restoration in Jesus Christ.[103] A sign of alienation and judgment (uninterpreted tongues) on prospective converts is out of place at a time when God is extending an invitation to the nations. But prophecy is an appropriate sign for the church, as it confirms God's gracious presence in this era through its effect on unbelievers. Prophecy not only serves as a sign to believers, but it has the practical benefit of intelligibility for bringing conviction to the unbeliever. This view, then, depends on an eschatological reading of the text grounded in Isaiah's prophecies and the recognition of the inauguration of a new era in Christ. Just as the *charismata* have temporal limitations to this present period of redemptive history (1 Cor 13:8–13), so also the gifts have specific guidelines for their use that are shaped by God's mission in Christ during this time.

J. P. M. Sweet has seized on this passage in Paul as an opportunity to refute Pentecostal teaching about tongues as a sign of reception of the Spirit.[104] However, Paul's discussion of tongues as a negative sign to unbelievers in the specific context of the gathered assembly ("the whole church")[105] need not be applied universally to every possible setting where tongues may occur. Speaking in tongues serves as an evidential sign of reception of the Spirit in Acts 10:46: "For they were hearing them speaking in tongues and magnifying God," and this is likened to Pentecost in 11:15. It is a mistake to read Luke's very different agenda through the lens of Paul's very specific context and make universal claims about the sign value of tongues on that basis. Although the two authors complement each other, they are not addressing the same issues or answering the same questions. Paul's main concern is that believers learn to think in

103. Ciampa and Rosner, "1 Corinthians," 742.

104. Sweet, "A Sign," 240–41, 256. See also Gardner's cautions against Pentecostal teaching. *1 Corinthians*, 618.

105. Fee provides evidence arguing for a corporate meeting of believers from the various house churches. *First Corinthians*, rev. ed., 757.

a mature manner and realize that the time of salvation in Christ is not a time to misuse a good gift and signal alienation to an unbeliever.

"When You Come Together" (1 Cor 14:26–36)

Paul indicates a transition into the next segment of his argument with his rhetorical question, "What then, brothers?" (1 Cor 14:26). The vocative case ἀδελφοί ("brothers") is the third of four in chapter 14 (vv. 6, 20, 39), and the question indicates Paul is drawing conclusions based on his previous argument. Edification (v. 26) and order (vv. 33, 40) are the primary concerns as Paul gives his final instructions on the use of tongues (vv. 26–28) and prophecy (vv. 29–33) in the assembly before his concluding admonitions (vv. 37–40).

That Paul is still discussing the corporate gathering (perhaps of multiple house churches?) is evident from his prefacing his instructions with "when you come together" (1 Cor 14:26). In this setting, "each one [ἕκαστος] has [ἔχει] a psalm, has a teaching, has a revelation, has a tongue, has an interpretation" (v. 26). The antistrophe (the repetition of ἔχει at the end of each line) emphasizes the diversity of expressions and the broad participation assumed of church members.[106] As in 12:7–11, the list is probably representative and not exhaustive and implies the generosity of God in distributing the means of edification to the body. Paul's recurring concern comes at the end of 14:26 when he exhorts, "Let everything be done for edification [οἰκοδομὴν]."

Tongues and interpretation are listed together at the end of the list (1 Cor 14:26; cf. 12:10), not because Paul attempts to diminish them in some way but because instruction for proper use of them immediately follows. Paul offers three main guidelines for the corporate use of tongues: only two, or at the most three, should speak; participants must take turns; and one person should interpret (v. 27).[107] There is some difference of opinion as to whether Paul means that the maximum is three utterances in tongues before interpretation or three per service, but the variety of participants assumed in verse 26 probably suggests that he is

106. Brookins and Longenecker point out the antistrophe but attribute it to Paul's dissatisfaction with excess interruptions of the service. *1 Corinthians 10–16*, 122.

107. Keener suggests that the principles of edification and order are universal but the specific instructions here are *ad hoc* and not "universal for all Paul's churches." Keener, *1–2 Corinthians*, 116. If this is so, then one would assume that the numerical restrictions imposed at Corinth could be lighter in churches typified by order.

limiting the number to allow for the contribution of others with different gifts in the service.[108] His requirement that speakers proceed one at a time is essential for order and implies that a potential visitor's estimation of a Corinthian service as madness (v. 23) is partially due to the chaos of multiple people speaking in tongues simultaneously. There is also disagreement over whether the "one" (εἷς) who interprets is the same person as the one who speaks in tongues,[109] but the emphasis on a variety of gifts in verse 26 as well as in 12:7–10 and 28–30 points in the direction of an independent interpreter. In any event, Paul probably intends the "one" to limit the chaos that could ensue if multiple interpreters joined the fray.[110] Paul's instruction to remain silent if no interpreter is present implies that the church recognizes members of the assembly who are reputed to practice the gift. Without such a gifted person present, one who speaks in tongues should "speak to himself and to God" (14:28).

Paul gives similar instructions to the church in regard to prophesying (1 Cor 14:29–33) and concludes this segment by underscoring God's character as peaceable—he is not a God of "disorder" (ἀκαταστασίας; v. 33).[111] Paul could easily draw this principle from the Genesis creation account (1:1–2), where the Spirit of God brings order and beauty out of emptiness and chaos. The guidelines Paul establishes imply a few other noteworthy points. First, both tongues and prophecy are welcomed and have beneficial effects when used properly.[112] Second, some scholars are uncomfortable with the notion that some gifts are spontaneously given during a church service,[113] but it is difficult to explain how tongues and

108. Fee points to Paul's use of "most" as a reason for cautiously landing on the position that Paul is limiting the number of utterances in a particular service. Fee, *First Corinthians*, rev. ed., 766. Schrage also understands Paul to refer to two or three in total. Schrage, *Korinther*, 447.

109. E.g., these scholars see the speaker and interpreter as the same person: Collins, *First Corinthians*, 518; Gardner, *1 Corinthians*, 625. These view the two as potentially or actually distinct: Brookins and Longenecker, *1 Corinthians 10–16*, 123; Fee, *First Corinthians*, rev. ed., 767; Fitzmyer, *First Corinthians*, 525; Montague, *First Corinthians*, 250. Schrage, *Korinther*, 448.

110. Brookins and Longenecker, *1 Corinthians 10–16*, 27.

111. The term ἀκαταστασία is defined as "opposition to established authority, *disorder, unruliness*." BDAG, 35.

112. Contra Fitzmyer, who posits that "what is said in vv. 27–28 reveals that Paul would gladly do away with speaking in tongues, but he knows he cannot (see v. 39)." Fitzmyer, *First Corinthians*, 526.

113. E.g., Ciampa and Rosner, *First Corinthians*, 709–10; Gardner, *1 Corinthians*, 624.

interpretation would operate in a service without some spontaneity if the interpreter is other than the one who speaks in tongues. Regarding prophecy, it appears that the evaluation of the utterance happens during the assembly (v. 29). Spontaneity is especially implied if the gift of the discerning of spirits is employed in the evaluation (12:10).[114] In addition, Paul entertains the possibility that one of the seated members may receive a "revelation," in which case the first speaker should be quiet and make room for the other member to share (14:30).[115]

Third, the concern that the church properly functions as Christ's body continues to guide the discussion. Paul emphasizes the whole body with the repetition of "all": "For you are all able to prophesy in turn [δύνασθε γὰρ καθ' ἕνα πάντες προφητεύειν] so that all [πάντες] may learn and all [πάντες] may be encouraged" (14:31; cf. vv. 23–24). The language is reminiscent of the "all" who were "baptized into one body" and the "all" who were "given one Spirit to drink" (12:13). Christ's body is still front and center in the discussion.

Fourth, Paul sees the potential for all the Corinthian believers to prophesy. Brookins and Longenecker highlight the emphasis on "all" in 14:31: "The anaphora of πάντες (3x in this verse) underscores the fact that the instructions have implications for the whole community. This first instance is right-dislocated at a significant distance from the verb for more surprising impact ('You are able, one-by-one—I mean, *all* of you—to prophesy')."[116] There is the potential for any member of the community to participate in prophesying (even if the member does not bear the title "prophet") and for any member to receive instruction and encouragement. Given that not all members are prophets in the formal sense of the word (12:29) but may function as prophets, it should not be too difficult to see how the related utterance gift of speaking in tongues could also have a broader application in private prayer even if the practitioner never exercises the gift of tongues in public for the edification of the assembly.[117] This perspective is consistent with Paul's wish that all would speak in tongues (14:5).

Fifth, Paul depicts those who speak in tongues or prophesy as in control of their faculties and not as those overcome by pagan ecstasy.

114. In 1 Cor 12:10 the noun διάκρισις ("distinguish") is used, and in 14:29 the cognate verb διακρίνω ("weigh, evaluate") is employed.

115. Oropeza, *1 Corinthians*, 187.

116. Brookins and Longenecker, *1 Corinthians 10–16*, 125.

117. Menzies makes this argument. *Speaking in Tongues*, 94.

Those who speak in tongues have the ability to choose silence when no interpreter is present and can pray quietly (14:28). Similarly, prophets can cease giving an utterance and yield the floor to another prophet (v. 30). Paul insists, "The spirits of prophets are subject to prophets" (v. 32), and then grounds his claim in the peaceful and orderly character of God (v. 33a).

Finally, Paul appeals to the common standards for worship in the other churches: "as in all the churches of the saints" (14:33b). Scholars debate whether this passage belongs with the preceding argument about peace and order or with the following directives on women's silence in the church (vv. 34–35). If the latter passage is an interpolation as some think,[118] then the phrase certainly concludes the preceding discussion. Regardless of where one lands on that issue, there are good reasons to favor including verse 33b with the previous argument.[119] Robertson and Plummer note that the phrase "in the churches" in verse 34 seems unnecessarily redundant, occurring soon after "all the churches" in verse 33b. They also observe how "nor the churches of God" concludes the discussion in 11:16 in a manner very similar to that in 14:33b.[120] Paul has referred to the broader church on several occasions in the epistle, even locating the Corinthian church among "all those who call on the name of our Lord Jesus Christ in every place" at the outset of the letter (1:2; cf. 16:19). He reminds the Corinthians that his instructions are common to all the churches (4:17; 7:17; 16:1) and that he and the other apostles preach the same message (15:11). He holds up the common practices in the churches as a standard to emulate (11:16) and cautions the Corinthians to consider the effects of their behavior on the church (10:32). In 14:36 he alludes to the broader church again when he asks, "Or did the word of God originate from you? Or did it reach only you?" The combination of "all the churches" in verse 33b, Paul's rhetorical questions in verse 36, and his requirement that the true prophet or person of the Spirit recognize his writing as the Lord's command (v. 37 vis-á-vis 4:17; 7:17; 16:1) suggests that the principles of order and peace must be

118. E.g., Fee, *First Corinthians*, rev. ed., 780–86; Hays, *First Corinthians*, 248.

119. With Fitzmyer, *First Corinthians*, 527; Keener, *1–2 Corinthians*, 116; Oropeza, *1 Corinthians*, 187.

120. Robertson and Plummer, *1 Corinthians*, 324. See also Brookins and Longenecker, *1 Corinthians* 10–16, 126–27. Fee expands on this basic idea and includes 1 Cor 4:17 and 7:17 to buttress his case. He also offers additional reasons for taking 14:33b with what precedes. Fee, *First Corinthians*, rev. ed., 773.

applied not only to the prophets (14:32, 37) but also to the employment of all the gifts (v. 40). Paul establishes a framework for his corrections that includes both the lordship of Jesus Christ and the common teachings and practices of Christ's body. In addition, if "as in all the churches of the saints" (v. 33b) continues Paul's thought about God as a God of order and peace, as I have argued, then Paul may also be implying the charismatic nature of other churches.[121]

The Lord's Authority (1 Cor 14:37–40)

The final verses of 1 Cor 14 (vv. 37–40) gather up several words from verses 1–2 that conclude the chapter's discussion, including the terms ζηλόω ("to eagerly desire"), πνευματικός ("spiritual gift/person"), προφητεύω ("to prophesy"), and γλῶσσα ("tongue"). The addition of the "Lord" and three references to knowledge in verses 37–38 also indicate that Paul is rounding out his entire discussion that began in 12:1–3. There he started this unit with the topic of "spirituals" (πνευματικῶν), incorporated three knowledge terms, contrasted types of speech, and emphasized that "Jesus is Lord." The combination of key terms in 14:37–38 is instructive: "If anyone thinks he is a prophet or spiritual [πνευματικός], let him acknowlege [ἐπιγινωσκέτω] that what I write to you is a command of the Lord [κυρίου ἐστὶν ἐντολή]. And if anyone ignores [ἀγνοεῖ] this, then he will be ignored [ἀγνοεῖται]." The play on words with the knowledge terms reinforces Paul's repeated rejection of human pride and its misplaced association with the Corinthian definition of spirituality.[122] A true person of the Spirit will "acknowledge" the Lord Jesus as the source of Paul's letter, and failure to do so will result in judgment.[123] Carson also notes how submission to the apostolic writings is submission to the Lord's command and is "therefore tied irrevocably to the believer's confession, 'Jesus is Lord!' (12:1–3)."[124] The placement of the "Lord" at the beginning of the

121. This reading does not view Paul as insisting on the silence of women in all the churches but rather on order in all the churches.

122. Hays, building on the work of Fee, points out how the occurrences of "if anyone" in 1 Cor 3:18, 8:2, and 14:37 "target precisely the terms that characterize the self-understanding of the 'strong' Corinthians: wisdom, knowledge, and spirituality." Hays, *First Corinthians*, 245. See also Fee, *First Corinthians*, rev. ed., 777.

123. Paul almost always has Jesus in view when he employs the term κύριος ("Lord"). As Fitzmyer notes, references to the Septuagint are an exception. *First Corinthians*, 537.

124. Carson, *Showing the Spirit*, 133.

clause in verse 37c makes it emphatic, so that one cannot help but recall the christological confession in 12:3 and conclude that the lordship of Jesus has been the primary standard for measuring Corinthian attitudes and behavior throughout the discussion.[125]

Paul signifies the close of the discussion with "So then, my brothers," (Ὥστε, ἀδελφοί μου)[126] and wraps up the unit with three final imperatives: "Be zealous to prophesy, and do not forbid to speak in tongues; but let everything be done properly and in an orderly manner" (1 Cor 14:39–40).[127] Paul's strong endorsement of prophecy in the assembly is felt one last time, but his requirement for intelligibility in the corporate meetings should not be construed as a prohibition of tongues. This passage is reminiscent of Paul's caution not to "quench the Spirit" or "despise prophesies" but rather to "test everything" (1 Thess 5:19–21a). His response to the misuse of prophecy at Thessalonica was not a ban on the gift, but an exhortation to proper weighing within the context of right attitudes "in Christ Jesus" (v. 18) and sanctification from "the God of peace" at "the coming of our Lord Jesus Christ" (v. 23). The word order of "do not forbid to speak in tongues" (τὸ λαλεῖν μὴ κωλύετε γλώσσαις; 1 Cor 14:39b) does not indicate a mere concession under compulsion, but a strong prohibition. Brookins and Longenecker point out the emphasis on "seek" or "be zealous" (ζηλοῦτε) as the first word in the first clause, but "in the parallel clause, however, the infinitive advances to first position so as to frame the action and thus to make the shift in topic more prominent. In effect: '*Seek* the gift of prophecy, but as for speaking in tongues—*do not prohibit* it.'"[128] The final instruction, "but let everything be done properly and in an orderly manner," (v. 40) moves the imperative to the end of the sentence and accentuates the need for propriety and order by starting the clause with a broad application of the principle: "but everything" (πάντα δὲ). Paul's command for order is "from the Lord" (v. 37b), and the inclusio of Jesus' lordship (12:3) provides the authority to insist that all the gifts—and particularly tongues—must function according to

125. Carson rightly observes, "It is hard to resist seeing an inclusio (a figure of speech in which everything in these three chapters, sandwiched between two strong references to the lordship of Jesus, must be read in the light of that lordship)." Carson, *Showing the Spirit*, 132.

126. The vocative ἀδελφοί is the final of four in this chapter (1 Cor 14:6, 20, 26), but this time Paul adds the possessive "my" (μου) to it (assuming it is original).

127. Smit views 1 Cor 14:37–40 as the *peroratio* that concludes the speech begun in 12:1–3. Smit, "Argument and Genre," 214–16. See also Garland, *1 Corinthians*, 673–74.

128. Brookins and Longenecker, *1 Corinthians 10–16*, 133. Emphasis original.

the principle of decency and order. According to this principle, utterance gifts will operate in a manner consistent with the confession that "Jesus is Lord" and will edify the body of Christ.

"Groans without Words" (Rom 8:26)

A study of glossolalia would not be complete without entering into the fray revolving around Rom 8:26–27: "And likewise also the Spirit helps in our weakness, for we do not know what we should pray as is necessary, but the Spirit himself intercedes for us with wordless groans. And the one who searches the hearts knows what is the mind of the Spirit, because he intercedes according to God on behalf of the saints." The majority of scholars reject the notion that Paul has tongues in mind in this passage, but the opposite opinion also has a long history and is represented by various scholars.[129] A considerable number of Pentecostal or charismatic scholars find a reference to tongues in this passage, but even they are divided on the issue.[130] In this section I will analyze the arguments for and against a reference to tongues, offer a suggestion based on exegetical considerations, and point out the christological emphasis in the immediate context.

Ernst Käsemann has drawn considerable attention for his emphatic endorsement of tongues in Rom 8:26. In his view the στεναγμοῖς ἀλαλήτοις ("groanings too deep for words"; ESV) occur in the assembly gathered for worship and are a noticeable phenomenon, just as the cry "Abba, Father" (v. 15) is an exclamation that occurs during worship.[131] According to Käsemann, the groans are not "wordless" but "unspeakable," akin to what Paul heard in his visionary experience in 2 Cor 12:4. Consequently, the groans are not silent but audible expressions.[132] Käsemann sees a clear parallel with Paul's discussion of tongues in 1 Cor 14

129. E.g., Delling, "αντιλαμβάνομαι, ἀντίλημψις, συναντιλαμβάνομαι," 375–76; Fee, *God's Empowering Presence*, 580–85; Godet, *Romans*, Rom 8:26; Gunkel, *Influence of the Holy Spirit*, 80–81; Käsemann, *Perspectives*, 131; Origen, *Epistle to the Romans*, 7.6; Stendahl, *Paul among Jews*, 111.

130. Those favorably disposed to tongues in Rom 8:26–27 include: Fee, *God's Empowering Presence*, 580–85; Hovenden, *Speaking in Tongues*, 135–41; Macchia, "Sighs Too Deep," 47–73; and Menzies, *Speaking in Tongues*, 139–45. Some who do not see a clear reference to tongues include: Horton, *What the Bible Says*, 189; Keener, *Romans*, 107n37; Lim, *Spiritual Gifts*, 140n3; and Warrington, *Pentecostal Theology*, 65–66.

131. Käsemann, *Perspectives*, 129–30.

132. Käsemann, *Perspectives*, 130.

and even asserts that the Romans require the same kind of correction that the Corinthians needed. In both cases they have a somewhat triumphalistic view of tongues, according to Käsemann, but he suggests tongues are actually a form of intercession by the Spirit that identifies the believer with weakness and creation's "cry for liberty."[133] Käsemann's argument has received considerable criticism, and he has not found a wide following among scholars.[134] His insistence that Rom 8 depicts corporate worship lacks significant exegetical support, his definition of ἀλάλητος ("unspeakable" or "unspoken"?) is debatable, and his "assumption of indulgent 'enthusiasm' of the Corinthian kind in Rome"[135] is not defensible.

Fee has presented a much stronger case that Paul envisioned glossolalia when he wrote Rom 8:26, even though he has arrived at his conclusions "with far less passion than one might expect."[136] The first of eight reasons why he believes tongues are in view is that prayer in the first century was audible, implying that the groans could not be silent prayer.[137] His second and third reasons are related and are based on perceived parallels between Rom 8:26 and 1 Cor 14. In both passages the Spirit prays within the believer and the content is not understood. Paul can speak of the Spirit's activity through the human spirit but change his emphasis at times from the Spirit to human participation, but the same S/spirit prayer is in view in both texts. His fourth reason engages the debate about the definition of ἀλάλητος, which he asserts does not have to mean "unspoken" or "inexpressible" but probably something more like "inarticulate." He questions why Paul did not simply say "silent" or use the term ἀνεκλάλητος ("inexpressible") if that is what he meant. Fee's fifth reason addresses the problem of Paul's use of "groans" rather than directly mentioning tongues. He sees this as "a typically Pauline adaptation to context," as Paul had already used the term "groan" twice (8:22,

133. Käsemann, *Perspectives*, 122, 131–37. This view of tongues as intercession in weakness has been taken up by Macchia, "Groans Too Deep," Section 4; and Stendahl, *Paul among Jews*, 111. Fee also addresses the issue of weakness, though from a different perspective than Käsemann. Fee, "Toward a Pauline Theology," 35–36.

134. E.g., see Cranfield, *Romans*, 422–23; Mounce, *Romans*, 187; O'Brien, "Romans 8.26–27," 70–71; and Wedderburn, "Romans 8:26," 369–77.

135. Fee, *God's Empowering Presence*, 580n323.

136. Fee, *God's Empowering Presence*, 577n311.

137. See the eight reasons in Fee, *God's Empowering Presence*, 581–85. Paul's admonition to the glossolalist to "pray to himself and to God" in 14:28 could be taken as instruction to pray privately, but it could also be understood to mean "quietly" or "silently" in the assembly instead of out loud (1 Cor 14:28).

23).[138] His sixth reason points out that God's knowledge of the Spirit's prayer would be superfluous in the passage if nothing more than normal prayer offered with the aid of the Spirit were in view. In this case the believer knows the content. In his seventh argument, Fee emphasizes that Paul appears to be "speaking about a common, every-day *experience* of prayer for himself and others."[139] Fee's eighth reason builds on this, and he argues that scholars fail to provide a phenomenological explanation for Rom 8:26 and that only 1 Cor 14 provides anything similar to this passage.

Scholars commonly argue against a reference to tongues by contrasting the gift of tongues ostensibly for a select few in 1 Corinthians (especially 12:30) with the application of the Spirit's intercession to all believers in Rom 8:26.[140] Peter O'Brien suggests that the "weakness" in verse 26 cannot apply only to people with the gift of tongues and that the Spirit helps all believers. To him, this argument is "decisive" against tongues in this passage.[141] Thomas Schreiner also appeals to this argument when he addresses Fee's comparison of 8:26 with tongues at Corinth. Schreiner comments, "It is mystifying to me how he thinks that this solves the problem."[142] The two opposing positions highlight a fundamentally different perspective on the extent of the gifts in general and tongues in particular in the primitive church. Fee views the common experience of tongues at Corinth as typical of believers at that time.[143] If the gift of tongues used in the assembly is not for all (1 Cor 12:30) but the use of tongues in prayer is potentially available for all (14:5, 18–19), then it is possible that tongues were also a common expression of prayer in Rome.[144] The limitation versus abundance difference in perspective often lies at the center of the debates on these issues. If tongues were ubiquitous in the early church, the force of the argument against tongues

138. Fee, *God's Empowering Presence*, 583.

139. Fee, *God's Empowering Presence*, 583. Emphasis his.

140. E.g., Moo, *Romans*, 525; Osborne, *Romans*, 216n8:26; Schlatter, *Gottes Gerechtigkeit*, 280.

141. O'Brien, "Romans 8.26–27," 70–71.

142. Schreiner, *Romans*, 445.

143. Fee, *God's Empowering Presence*, 584n333. Although Moo takes a different position on glossolalia, he notes the use of the gifts in Rome (Rom 12:3–8). Paul's "assumption that these gifts are operative in the Roman church, which Paul has neither founded nor visited, shows that the operation of gifts was widespread, if not universal, in the early church." Moo, *Romans*, 764.

144. Menzies argues along these lines. *Speaking in Tongues*, 141.

in Rom 8:26 is severely diminished, as the Roman Christians could have related to Paul's argument. However, it may not completely nullify the argument made by Schreiner and others.

Another common criticism of the glossolalic perspective on Rom 8:26 is that the groans connected with intercession seem quite distinct from Paul's description of tongues in 1 Cor 14 as praise, worship, and thanksgiving.[145] Menzies views this line of argumentation as "a classic example of over exegesis." He suggests that "Paul here is not speaking as a linguist; rather, he speaks as one who shares this dramatic, powerful experience with the Christians at Rome. The similarities between speaking in tongues and 'groans' were for Paul and his readers . . . so vivid and clear that they do not require explanation."[146] Paul does use the verb προσεύχομαι ("to pray") in both passages (Rom 8:26; 1 Cor 14:14–15), and Menzies' caution regarding an excessively narrow interpretation of prayer is duly noted. Nevertheless, both the "groans" and the element of intercession would broaden the description of tongues offered in Mark, Acts, and 1 Corinthians. In short, this argument opposed to tongues has some merit but is not nearly as airtight as some may think.

The definition of the adjective ἀλάλητος ("unspeakable" or "unspoken"?) is a perpetual sticking point in the debate. The lexicons define it as "unspeakable, unutterable,"[147] or "unspoken,"[148] or "unexpressed, wordless."[149] In the context of Rom 8:26, Bauer famously defines στεναγμοῖς ἀλαλήτοις as "sighs too deep for words"[150] (cf. NRSV). It is also similarly translated, "groanings too deep for words" (ESV, NASB). The difficulty in definition is due to the rarity of the term, as it is a hapax legomenon in the Greek Bible. Moo opines that ἀλάλητος "probably means 'unspoken' rather than 'ineffable'; and this makes it almost impossible to identify the 'groans' with glossolalia; for tongues, of course, are verbalized if not understandable." A concomitant understanding is that the "groans" are metaphorical, along with those in verses 22 and 23.[151]

145. Cranfield, *Romans*, 423; Longenecker, *Romans*, 734; Schlatter, *Gottes Gerechtigkeit*, 280; Sweet, "A Sign," 248.

146. Menzies, *Speaking in Tongues*, 144.

147. LSJ, 60.

148. Balz and Schneider, "ἀλάλητος," 56.

149. BDAG, 41.

150. BDAG, 41.

151. Moo, *Romans*, 525–26. See also Osborne, *Romans*, 216n8:26; and Shreiner, *Romans*, 445.

A decision on this matter is difficult, but the context seems to favor a rendering of ἀλάλητος that emphasizes the wordless aspect of the term. There are at least three reasons why this is preferred. First, Paul's two phrases, "for we do not know what we should pray as is necessary" and "the Spirit himself intercedes for us with wordless groans" is separated by the strong contrasting conjunction ἀλλ' ("but"; 8:26b). Presumably, human prayer with known content is sometimes inadequate, so divine intercession with groans assists believers. The contrast suggests more than a different kind of prayer offered by the believer; it suggests a different person praying.[152] Second, the emphatic αὐτὸ τὸ πνεῦμα ("Spirit himself"), the intensifying effect of the double compound verb συναντιλαμβάνεται ("helps"),[153] and the compound verb ὑπερεντυγχάνει ("intercedes on our behalf")[154] all accentuate the Spirit's initiative without any mention of human participation. Third, the most natural way to understand the negated term (ἀ-λάλητος) in this contrast is to take it as "wordless."[155] Although I am sympathetic to Fee's concern that the phenomenological aspect of the Spirit's work be recognized in the New Testament (see above), much of the comfort in this passage is found in what the Spirit does rather than anything the believer must do.[156]

Some scholars have also pointed out the lack of any mention of tongues elsewhere in Romans—especially in the list of gifts in 12:6–8. Such an occurrence would certainly have strengthened the argument for

152. Some argue that the Spirit's intercession occurs apart from or "external" to the believer. In this view, the groans are strictly the Spirit's without reference to his indwelling the believer. Hultgren, *Romans*, 325. See also Johannes Schneider, "στενάζω, στεναγμός, συστενάζω," 602; Warrington, *Pentecostal Theology*, 65. While the emphasis rightly belongs on the intercession of the Spirit, the Spirit's abiding presence in the believer has also been emphasized throughout Rom 8, and the addition of "the one who searches the hearts" in verse 27 may also point to this reality. In other words, the Spirit does the interceding but from the position of his templing presence in the believer.

153. Schreiner suggests it is "probably intensive, indicating not merely that the Spirit joins in helping but also that the Spirit himself and alone renders the assistance believers need." Schreiner, *Romans*, 442.

154. The term lacks the attached preposition in verse 27 and verse 34, but the preposition occurs immediately after the term in both cases. The compound suits Paul's purposes well in verse 26 because it emphasizes the Spirit's role in providing assistance and it avoids creating a more complex sentence.

155. Also Schreiner, *Romans*, 445.

156. Käsemann is right to protest against the idea that all normal prayer is entirely inadequate. The intention of Paul is not to disparage the regular prayers of believers but to encourage them that the Spirit exceeds human limitations in praying exactly what is required. *Perspectives*, 28.

tongues in 8:26, but lack of its mention proves very little. And if one accepts an early date of the Markan longer ending, then perhaps there is some evidence of the knowledge of tongues among the Romans (see chapter 6 above). But if one must resort to arguments from silence, the absence of the typical expressions for tongues in our text is more compelling. There is nothing like the various versions of the technical phrase "speaking in tongues" (Mark 16:17; Acts 2:4, 10:46; 19:6; 1 Cor 12:30; 13:1; 14:2, 4, 5 [2x], 6, 13, 18, 19, 23, 27, 39) in Rom 8. That the technical phrase occurs so commonly gives one serious pause before assuming that the "groans" of the Spirit are the identical charism. In addition, tongues are consistently depicted as language (of whatever sort) in every text where they clearly occur. The "groans" would be considered a departure from this typical description. Consequently, it seems unwise to build a biblical theology of tongues on such an uncertain passage.

Nonetheless, the great joy and encouragement of this passage must not be missed. The "glory" frame at Rom 8:18 and 30 points to the eschatological goal of the believer's salvation.[157] Believers already have the "Spirit of life" (v. 2) but look forward to life from the dead via the indwelling Spirit (v. 11). They have already received the Spirit of adoption and cry, "Abba, Father," yet the same children groan as they eagerly await their adoption, the redemption of their bodies (v. 23). The "now time" (v. 18) is characterized by suffering (vv. 17–18) and weakness (v. 26) but also by expectation and hope (vv. 24–25). Thus, the weakness of believers is not primarily their sinfulness, but rather their limitations (v. 26) and hardships in pre-resurrection bodies and a fallen world. How will God's children make it from suffering to resurrection, from weakness to glory? They can be confident that God will get them there (v. 28, 30), because the "Spirit himself" intercedes for them (v. 26) and the risen one, Christ Jesus, who is at God's right hand, also intercedes (v. 34). Paul is not concerned to identify or explain any particular charism, but to encourage believers that they will safely make it to glory with the help of Christ and the Spirit.[158]

Regardless of whether or not one finds a reference to tongues in Rom 8:26, it is clear that Romans is thoroughly christocentric throughout the epistle. The term "Christ" (Χριστός) occurs sixty-five times and "Lord" (κύριος) occurs in reference to Jesus about thirty-four times. In

157. For a discussion of glory in this text, see Berry, "Groaning for Glory," 281–96.

158. Similarly, Warrington, *Pentecostal Theology*, 66.

Rom 8 Jesus is called "Christ" nine times, God's "Son" three times (vv. 3, 29, 32), and "the one who loved us" one time (v. 37). Paul refers to his risen status in relation to his exaltation at the "right hand of God" (v. 34) and as the basis for the believer's resurrection (v. 11; cf. vv. 23, 29). The groans of the Spirit help move believers to their eschatological and christological goal. Paul repeats the term "know" to advance his argument, as "we do not know [οἴδαμεν]" what to pray (v. 26), but God "knows [οἶδεν]" the Spirit's mind (v. 27), and so "we know [Οἴδαμεν]" that God is working everything out for our (eschatological) good (v. 28), "because those whom he foreknew [προέγνω] he also predestined to be conformed to the image of his Son" (v. 29). The believer rests not in his or her own, limited knowledge, but in the assurance of God's omniscience. Thus, the Spirit's groans will escort believers to the christological goal of conformity "to the image of his Son."[159]

Paul also employs the triple designation "Lord Jesus Christ" (and variations) at advantageous places in Romans, especially in the introduction (1:4, 7), near the end (15:6, 30), as a frame around a major unit (5:1; 8:39), and at key junctures within that unit (5:11, 21; 6:23; 7:25).[160] The phrase "through Jesus Christ our Lord" caps off the discussion of Adam and Christ at 5:21 and serves as a transition into what is our sixth chapter. Similarly, "in Christ Jesus our Lord" functions as a climax and transition at 6:23. Paul escapes the frustration of life under the law and the accompanying death sentence with this climactic thanksgiving: "But thanks be to God through Jesus Christ our Lord" (7:25). This rejoicing leads into Rom 8, which reaches the pinnacle of the argument begun in 5:1: "Neither height nor depth nor any other created thing will be able to separate us from the love of God in Christ Jesus our Lord" (8:39). God's initiative, the Spirit's intercession (v. 26), and Christ's intercession (v. 34) all contribute to the eschatological realization of resurrection life and enjoyment of God's love "in Christ Jesus our Lord." Whatever form of prayer is going on in 8:26, it is clearly christologically oriented.

It is not surprising that a number of Pentecostal and charismatic scholars have found a reference to tongues in Rom 8:26, as the description

159. With Moo, I understand this goal as achieved at the eschaton. Moo, *Romans*, 535.

160. The only other occurrence of the eleven uses of the triple designation in Romans is at 13:14. Paul also incorporates the christological confession "Jesus is Lord" (10:9), the "Lord Jesus" (14:14), "our Lord Christ" (16:18), "our Lord Jesus" (16:2), and a book-closing "Lord" (16:22).

there does not seem too distant from their own experiences. Even some who entertain the possibility that a broader kind of prayer may be in view here think tongues should at least be included.[161] Some have even posited a specific kind of groaning prayer that is a form of intercession akin to tongues but also distinct from tongues.[162] Nonetheless, the negative term ἀλάλητος, the likelihood of its translation as "wordless," the presence of "groans" and corresponding absence of tongues as language, and the emphasis on the Spirit's activity as opposed to the believer's efforts leads me to conclude that tongues are not in view. In either case, the goal of Rom 8 is conformity to the image of Christ, and the prayer of the Spirit is offered in the context of the Lord Jesus Christ.

Summary

In 1 Cor 14 Paul continues the discussion of true spirituality begun in 12:1–3. The confession of Jesus as Lord (v. 3) and the emphasis on Christ's body (vv. 12–13) continue to exert an influence on his instruction. The edification of Christ's body is a central concern in public worship, motivating Paul to prefer prophecy over tongues in that context, unless the tongues are accompanied by interpretation. Paul sincerely wishes that all would speak in tongues (14:5), thereby holding out the potential for all believers to pray in tongues in private. He by no means denigrates glossolalia, but he takes issue with any use of the charism that is not couched in Christ—that is, any use in public that fails to honor Christ as Lord by failing to edify his body.

In 1 Cor 14:6–19 Paul exhorts the Corinthians to value intelligibility in corporate worship and reserve uninterpreted tongues for private prayer. Such prayer is inspired by the Spirit but occurs through the human spirit. Glossolalia is unique in that it functions both as a gift for corporate edification and as a means of private prayer; it is also unique in that its public use requires a second gift of interpretation to operate in tandem with it. Paul also mentions a form of glossolalic singing and associates tongues with praise and thanksgiving. This description is reminiscent of other Pauline passages that likely include charismatic singing (Eph 5:18–19) or praying (6:18). The heavy christological emphasis in Pauline hymnic passages is also consistent with the vertical orientation

161. E.g., Hovenden, *Speaking in Tongues*, 138.

162. See the examples offered by Stone, "Inward Groans," 90–91.

of prayer and song in tongues and the christological confession of 1 Cor 12:3. What is remarkable in Paul's discussion in 1 Cor 14 is how much he assumes his readers can relate to the experiences of praying, singing, and praising in tongues. How easily he incorporates his own experience in the discussion, even claiming he speaks in tongues more than the Corinthians do (v. 18)!

Paul continues encouraging intelligibility in the gathered assembly (1 Cor 14:20–26) and challenges the Corinthians to think in a mature manner about this. He quotes Isa 28:11–12 in order to demonstrate that tongues signal alienation to an unbeliever. Prophecy is to be preferred in the assembly because it signifies the presence of God in their midst (Isa 45:14) and has the potential to bring the unbeliever to salvation. The use of Isaiah implies an eschatological perspective and indicates that unintelligible tongues are an inappropriate sign to the unbeliever in the era of salvation in Christ Jesus. As usual, the glory of Christ and the edification of his body (this time through concern for its numerical growth) are foundational to Paul's exhortations.

The next segment of Paul's discussion (1 Cor 14:26–36) outlines specific instructions for the orderly functioning of tongues and prophecy in the assembly in order to ensure the edification of all. Paul welcomes both gifts as beneficial for the body and assumes a certain amount of spontaneity in their use. His inclusive approach to the use of the gifts implies a concern for Christ's body, and the potential for all to prophesy assumes God's generosity and an abundance of his gifts rather than a lack of manifestations of utterance. That believers are in full control of their faculties when exercising prophetic gifts demonstrates that pagan ecstasy is not in view. Paul's appeal for order based on the common practices of all the churches cautions against isolationism, provides some standards based on the apostolic practices instituted in the churches, and implies the charismatic nature of all the churches.

In the closing of 1 Cor 14 (vv. 37–40), Paul repeats several terms from the beginning of the chapter and from the introduction to the entire discussion in 12:1–3. He makes it clear that he is still concerned with the true definition of "spiritual," and that truly spiritual people will acknowledge that Paul's writing "is the command of the Lord" (v. 37). He exhorts them to desire to prophesy and gives a strong prohibition against forbidding to speak in tongues. This final prohibition is no mere conciliation, but a firm warning not to take an extreme view of his corrections by excluding one of God's good gifts. The final mention of the "Lord" forms an inclusio around chapters 12–14, refers back to the christological confession ("Jesus is Lord"; 12:3), and reinforces the truth that the utterance gifts (and all gifts) must align with this confession and must function under the umbrella of Jesus' lordship.

An examination of the "groans" in Rom 8:26 leads me to conclude that Paul does not have tongues in view in this passage. The preferred definition of the negative term ἀλάλητος as "wordless," the absence of the usual terms for speaking in tongues, the typical depiction of tongues as language and not "groans," and the emphatic activity of the Spirit points away from a reference to tongues. Nevertheless, the believer can take encouragement in knowing that the Spirit intercedes to help believers make it through the difficulties of this life to the safety of resurrection life in the Lord Jesus Christ.

Conclusion

Glossolalia has been analyzed from numerous perspectives and has been the subject of much debate, but the full significance and beauty of this gift and sign cannot be appreciated apart from an understanding of its roots in the Old Testament and its clear association with Christology in the New Testament. Despite the various contexts in which tongues occur, the manifestation appears to be essentially the same phenomenon, but the real common denominator in the various passages is the exaltation of Christ as Lord.

Luke's kingdom context, focus on the eschatological fulfillment of a Davidic Messiah, and employment of the threefold designation of Jesus as Lord and Christ in key passages such as Acts 2 and 10 prime the reader to interpret tongues in a christocentric manner. The climactic declaration of Jesus' identity as "Lord and Christ" at Pentecost (Acts 2:36) in response to the question, "What does this mean?" (v. 12), necessitates the incorporation of Christology into the explanation of glossolalia. The eschatological, missiological, pneumatological, and christological atmosphere of the event provides insight into the significance and meaning of speaking in tongues. Tongues are, at their core, a response to the enthronement of Jesus as Lord and Christ. This response is inspired by the Spirit and is therefore prophetic in nature. The content of tongues consists of praise that is oriented toward God and Christ and is directly connected with what God has done in Jesus' resurrection, ascension, session, and investiture with the Spirit. Tongues exhibit a missiological/christological significance in that they symbolize nations—they are a fitting indicator that God has empowered his servants to declare the lordship of Christ over all nations and to all nations. In short, tongues are a celebration of Christ's lordship over the nations.

Luke's intentional construction of the Pentecostal narrative as a type-scene built on Old Testament themes related to the giving of the Spirit informs the reader that the episode functions as a lens through which the rest of Acts should be understood. The constellation of various themes recurring together suggests that Luke sees important themes as integrally tied together and expects his readers to also draw that conclusion. Tongues travel with Luke's emphases on the spread of the gospel and lordship of Jesus over the nations. This speaks to two important concerns raised about tongues—their continuation and their potential for regular use among believers. Luke's employment of the type-scene suggests that this gift will continue to recur so long as Christ is expanding his reign over the nations through the proclamation of the gospel. Luke places no expiration date on this charismatic manifestation in the gospel era, and the type-scene also gives credence to the notion that Christ's missionaries can continue to receive the empowerment of the Spirit with the accompanying sign of tongues. Christ's messengers may expect to continue to respond to Christ's enthronement with a celebration of charismatic praise.

Christology is accentuated again in the account of the Spirit's outpouring at Cornelius's household, where "Jesus Christ" is "Lord of all" (Acts 10:36), references to his divine identity frame the outpouring (vv. 36 and 42), and the triple designation "Lord Jesus Christ" provides a conclusion to Peter's explanation of the event (11:17). This "gentile Pentecost" mirrors Acts 2 in numerous ways, and the speaking in tongues is once again directly connected with praise. The added miracle of xenolalia is evidently not in view, and no foreign audience is present, but the symbolism of tongues has already been established at Pentecost, and the speaking in tongues is an appropriate indicator of the cross-cultural nature of the gospel. The Jewish believers refer to the speaking in tongues as providing evidence of the outpouring of the Spirit, as they recognize that tongues are integral to the experience. The central point is that the outpouring of the Spirit testifies to the enthronement of the divine Lord (v. 36) and Judge (v. 42) and his acceptance of the gentiles as participants in the gospel; tongues are an appropriate sign of this because of their international significance. In other words, tongues (as Spirit-inspired, prophetic languages) are uniquely suited to signify a baptism in the Spirit for missional proclamation. Other signs that accompanied the Pentecostal outpouring and the later progress of the gospel lack the same international symbolism that is so integral to the filling of the Spirit in

Acts. Thus, although the experience of the Spirit is important, the Spirit's testimony to the identity of Jesus as the exalted and divine Lord, Christ, and Judge—who reigns over all—is central. The response of tongues points to this greater reality of Jesus' identity.

The centrality of Jesus as Lord is also in view when Paul brings the gospel message to Ephesus. Luke employs a literary chiasm (Acts 19:1–7) that centers on Jesus (v. 4), and he highlights the necessity of submission to Jesus by recording the baptism of about twelve Ephesian men "into the name of the Lord Jesus" (v. 5). At this point in the story, it becomes clear that these men belong to Christ. Paul's laying on of hands results in their reception of the Spirit and speaking in tongues. Tongues at Ephesus are associated with the lordship of Christ, the advancement of the gospel to a new region, and the empowerment of about twelve new leaders of the church in that region.

Jesus' prediction that believers "will speak in new tongues" (Mark 16:17) has largely been ignored because of the textual problem casting doubt on verses 9–20. My primary contention that tongues are christologically oriented remains intact despite one's perspective on the longer ending (LE). Nevertheless, a fresh look at the controverted ending has led to some surprising evidence in favor of its Markan authorship and originality. External evidence points to a first-century origin of the LE, and the manuscript evidence appears to isolate the textual problem to the Alexandrian tradition. Regarding internal evidence, the LE forms an appropriate frame around the book, contains themes consistent with the rest of the book (e.g., faith, deliverance, the gospel, and Christology), brings the new exodus theme to an appropriate conclusion, and gives a satisfactory glimpse of the expected baptism in the Spirit (1:8). The "signs" of 16:17–18 appear to reflect the exodus story (Exod 4–7), and Mark's "new tongues" (16:17) are likely a play on words from Moses' complaint of having a "slow tongue" (Exod 4:10). Mark's "new tongues" are consistent with the Spirit's inspiration of prophetic speech in the body of Mark's Gospel (12:36; 13:11), and they are also associated with Christ's missionaries and mission (16:20). These emphases are also found in Luke's passages on tongues,[1] and the linguistic, conceptual, and thematic elements of tongues in Mark and Acts are compatible. The primary differences lie in the brevity of Mark's description, the more direct tie of tongues to the exodus story in Mark, and Mark's mention of tongues as

1. E.g., the new exodus theme is often found in Luke-Acts but, particularly, in Acts 10:38.

a prediction from Jesus himself. Although Mark's account is brief, he is very much in alignment with Luke in presenting tongues in a context where the sign of tongues occurs because Christ is Lord, in response to his enthronement as Lord, and as an indicator that he is the resurrected Lord. The christological associations of tongues in Mark and Luke provide an underlying theological unity between the different writers.

The introduction of 1 Corinthians (1:1–9) quickly informs the reader that the Lord Jesus Christ will be the center of Paul's letter addressing a variety of issues in the church. Thus, it should come as little surprise to the reader when Paul frames his discussion (chs. 12–14) of *pneumatikōn* ("spirituals"; 12:1) with the lordship of Jesus (12:3; 14:37). The christological confession, "Jesus is Lord" (12:3), not only serves to define the beginning of a new unit, but also functions to identify the Christian and provide the context in which all Christian behavior and speech, in particular, must occur. For Paul, the Spirit inspires the christological confession, therefore spiritual people will exercise the grace-gifts (*charismatōn*; v. 4) in a Christ-exalting manner. The confession that "Jesus is Lord" anticipates Paul's discussion of the utterance gifts of prophecy and tongues. Paul's discussion soon focuses on the Corinthian's misuse of tongues, but the primary corrective has been in place from the outset. Tongues must function within the boundaries of Christ's lordship and bring honor to him. It is precisely this point that is often missed in discussions about tongues.

The "word of wisdom" and "word of knowledge" head Paul's list of gifts in 1 Cor 12:8–10, and the close association of this terminology with Christology in the early chapters of the epistle suggest a christological orientation of the entire list. The Spirit does not distribute any defective gifts, and tongues and interpretation of tongues are not listed last because they are least but because they are the topic under discussion (cf. 12:28–30; cf. 13:1–3). The metaphor of the body of Christ (12:12, 27) frames a significant portion of the discussion and draws attention to the horizontal implications of the lordship of Christ; in other words, the metaphor establishes christocentric boundaries for the use of the gifts, especially tongues. All believers share in a baptism "by one Spirit" into the body of Christ and were also given to drink of that same Spirit (v. 13); consequently, there is no room for division but only for mutual care (v. 25). The preposition "by" is likely a dative of agency, based on the Spirit's agency in the immediate context, and the drinking of the Spirit implies an experiential aspect to the Spirit's work that includes but likely extends beyond salvation. Paul appears to use the baptismal metaphor as a description of the Spirit's agency in salvation while Luke uses the metaphor for an empowering work where Christ is the baptizer in the Spirit. Still, Paul's main concern is to bring the behavior of believers who exercise the Spirit's good gifts into alignment with the model, Christ Jesus.

Love summarizes the example of Jesus, so it is fitting that Paul pens his beautiful words about love in this context of Christ. Some have taken the opening words of chapter 13 as a teaching on the phenomenology of tongues, but "the tongues of men and of angels" is likely a merism encompassing the opposite poles of exalted human rhetoric and angelic languages. Paul does not satisfy our curiosity on this matter; rather, he exhorts believers to exercise the gift of tongues in a loving manner. While tongues will cease at the parousia, love (as the essence of Christ's work for us and the very nature of God) has no expiration date. Arguments for a cessation of tongues prior to the eschaton on the basis of verse 8 are very weak, and the "face to face" terminology (v. 12b) is appropriate for a reference to the parousia and has its source in Moses' unique relationship with God (Num 12:8). Paul's wish that all would speak in tongues (14:5) may also have its roots in Moses' wish in Num 11:29, which would indicate that Luke, Mark, and Paul all identified the roots of speaking in tongues in the stories of Moses' prophetic calling and ministry.

Paul insists on intelligibility in the gathered assembly (1 Cor 14), as the edification of believers is consistent with the christocentric principles he has already established. He wishes that all would speak in tongues (v. 5), holding out the potential for all believers to pray in tongues privately. Paul's teaching on the subject reveals that tongues are unique in having both a private application in prayer and a public role when interpreted. Glossolalia is also unique in that it has a required, companion gift of interpretation for public use. Consistent with Luke's accounts of an initial experience of tongues at Pentecost and Cornelius's house, Paul elaborates on the vertical orientation of tongues. They are a form of prayer that entails praise and thanksgiving; they can even incorporate singing. The commonality of such experiences at Corinth is evidenced by the ease with which Paul discusses these functions of the gift. Other passages in Paul may also testify to this kind of charismatic activity (Eph 5:18–19; 6:18), and Paul even claims to speak in tongues more than the Corinthians do (1 Cor 14:18). While some people may be uncomfortable with such charismatic expressions of worship among contemporary believers, members of the ancient church appear to have readily accepted them.

The recurring emphasis in 1 Cor 14 is the proper expression of the gifts in the corporate gathering, and Paul cites Isa 28:11–12 to promote mature thinking in the assembly (1 Cor 14:21). Tongues without interpretation signals alienation and judgment to the unbeliever, and this is an inappropriate sign for them in the era of salvation in Christ. Prophecy is preferred in such circumstances. Paul gives details about the orderly use of tongues and prophecy in the congregation and appeals to the apostolic practices established in other churches to encourage the Corinthians to conform to standards that assure the edification of all (vv. 26–36). Some of his admonitions imply a degree of spontaneity in the employment of the gifts, so prophecy is not the same as a prepared sermon. Paul envisions a charismatic church that has an abundance of God's gifts in operation but that also maintains order for the edification of all under the lordship of Christ.

That Paul has been concerned with the right definition of "spiritual" throughout his entire argument is evident by his use of the term (*pneumatikos*; 1 Cor 14:37) in the closing frame (vv. 37–40) of the unit. Those who are truly "spiritual" will recognize that the Lord (Jesus) is the source of Paul's instruction (v. 37). The term "Lord" recalls the christological confession in 12:3 and reinforces Paul's insistence that the gifts must function in a Christ-exalting manner. His strong prohibition against forbidding the use of tongues serves as a guard against the notion that correction of a misuse of a gift is a rejection of the gift itself or of its proper use in private or public.

Regarding the "groans" of Rom 8:26, I have concluded that the terminology is not typical of tongues and that the emphasis in verses 26–27 is on the Spirit's activity rather than on anything the believer does. Consequently, tongues are probably not in view in this passage. If this is correct, then both Luke and Paul focus on tongues as a form of praise and do not directly address the topic of tongues as a form of intercessory prayer. Because Paul does describe glossolalia with the general term for prayer (1 Cor 14:13, 14, 15), the door is left open for intercession as a form of glossolalic prayer. However, this is not Paul's primary topic and not where his emphasis lies.

A biblical theology of tongues finds that tongues are prophetic in nature, a phenomenon of languages from the Spirit, symbolic of nations, and vertical in orientation. Regarding their prophetic nature, Mark, Luke, and Paul all associate tongues with the prophetic call or vocation of Moses. In addition, tongues are associated with the prophetic response to the Spirit's coming in power—as so often exhibited in Old Testament scenes. In regard to phenomenology, tongues are essentially the same among the biblical authors in that they are languages inspired by the Spirit. Only at Pentecost is there also the additional miracle of known human languages understood by observers. On the whole, the New Testament authors show little concern with phenomenological definitions. Even Paul's "tongues of men and of angels" is a hypothetical statement and a literary device (a merism) that leads to his main point about loving others in the body of Christ.

The symbolic aspect of tongues is most clearly seen in Luke's missiological context. Tongues (languages) symbolize nations. They are directly connected to Jesus as the long-expected Messiah and Lord of all nations. The symbol is appropriate for people who are filled with the Holy Spirit in order to proclaim Christ as Lord of the nations to the nations.

Finally, tongues are vertical in orientation. That is, they are praise to God for the work he has accomplished in Christ. They are a response to the enthronement of Jesus as Lord and Christ; they are a form of prayer, a charismatic kind of singing, and an expression of thanksgiving. They are a celebration of our Lord and Christ.

Christology is the common bond that ties together the various accounts of tongues in Mark, Luke, and Paul, and this understanding has practical implications for the use of the gift today. Because all gifts must glorify Christ and build his body, practitioners of the gift must demonstrate sensitivity to their context. The exercise of the gift must bring edification to the hearers in a context of corporate worship. Sensitivity to the presence of unbelievers must always be practiced in such meetings in order to avoid alienating people whom Christ is working to draw to himself during this era of redemptive history. Practitioners must employ the wisdom God gave Paul in distinguishing between the time to employ tongues in private prayer and the time to exercise the gift in public with the accompanying, Christ-exalting interpretation.

In terms of the content of a manifestation of tongues, the christological thread among the biblical authors' discussions and the repeated references to tongues as praise suggest that some people in the contemporary church may have an imbalanced perspective on the content of tongues. In many circles prayer in tongues or an interpretation in tongues is assumed to be primarily intercession or a message from God to a person or congregation. Although biblical writers seldom give clear definitions of the gifts, and it is inadvisable to place too many restrictions on how the

Spirit might function in a particular moment, it is also problematic when the church ignores the consistent association of tongues with praise and with Jesus' lordship. In other words, the biblical precedent creates an expectation that prayer in tongues and an interpretation of tongues would have a healthy element of christocentric praise. Church leaders could potentially remove barriers to the expression of this gift by informing their congregations of this biblical pattern.

Knowledge of the christocentric nature of tongues also assists believers in assuaging fears. Speaking in tongues is not a frightening experience to be dreaded, but a wonderful avenue of praise to God and Christ. The child of God who humbly submits to the lordship of Jesus Christ does not give ground to the adversary but offers Spirit-inspired adoration to the Lord of all. The congregation of God's people need not fear the operation of this gift in public; rather, the body of Christ should weigh the interpretation and test the manifestation for Christ-honoring content and the witness of the Spirit (1 Thess 5:19–22). To forbid the use of tongues is to deny the people of God the blessing that the orderly function of the gift brings.

For those who desire to pray in other tongues, Paul holds out the potential for all believers to pray in tongues privately (1 Cor 14:5). The Spirit's basic posture toward the body of Christ is one of generosity. Mark lists tongues as a sign that typically follows believers engaged in delivering the gospel (16:17). Luke appeals to the goodness of the Father when he encourages the disciples to pray for the gift of the Spirit (Luke 11:13) in anticipation of Pentecost (Acts 2). He also promises that those who seek find (Luke 11:9) and that the empowering gift of the Spirit as experienced by the 120 disciples at Pentecost is available for all (Acts 2:38–39). The sign of tongues that is integral to the experience of Pentecost accompanies this empowering of the Spirit and enables believers to participate in an alternative form of christocentric prayer and to renew their dependence on the Spirit's power on a regular basis. Knowledge of the christocentric nature of tongues can assist the believer in placing the manifestation in its proper context, avoiding an undue obsession with the manifestation itself, and removing barriers to the experience.

Although differences of opinion may remain on some of the finer points on this topic, I sincerely hope that believers from all backgrounds will see the christological nature of speaking in tongues and have a more profound appreciation for the glory of Christ and his kindness in bestowing such a gift. A biblical theology of tongues views the charism as a celebration of our Lord and Christ, and it anticipates the day when a great crowd "from all nations and tribes and peoples and tongues" stands before the throne and the Lamb and worships God and Christ (Rev 7:9–10).

Appendix

Themes in Filling Passages in Acts

THEME/TERM	*ACTS 2*	*ACTS 4*	*ACTS 8*	*ACTS 9*	*ACTS 10*	*ACTS 19*
HOLY SPIRIT COMES/ MANIFESTA-TIONS						
*Holy Spirit arrival	v. 4	v. 31	vv. 15–20	v. 17 implied	v. 44 (vv. 45, 47)	v. 6 (cf. v. 2)
"Filled with the Holy Spirit"	v. 4	v. 31		v. 17 "be filled with the Holy Spirit"		
Theophany/ Manifestation	vv. 2–3	v. 31 place shakes		Christ appears; scales v. 18		
Agency/Hands laid			v. 17	v. 17		v. 6
Signs and Wonders	vv. 19, 22	v. 30	v. 6, 13		v. 38 (Jesus healing)	
*In response to Prayer	1:14	vv. 24–31	vv. 15, 22, 24	vv. 9, 11, 17	vv. 2, 3, 4, 9, 30, 31	v. 6 (hands)

Unity	v. 1	vv. 24, 32	v. 6		v. 33 (not *homothymodon*)	
CHRISTOLOGY						
Ascension/ Exaltation	1:9–11; 2:33					
*"Christ"	vv. 36, 38	vv. 26	vv. 5, 12	v. 22	vv. 36, 48; 11:17	18:28
Christological title		vv. 27, 30		v. 20		
David	vv. 25, 29, 34	v. 25				
*"Lord"	vv. 20, 21, 36	v. 33	vv. 16, 22, 24, 25	vv. 1, 5, 10, 13, 15, 17	vv. 33?, 36; 11:16, 17	18:25; 19:5, 10, 13, 17, 20
*"Name" of Jesus	vv. 21, 38	v. 30	vv. 12, 16	vv. 14, 15, 16, 21	vv. 43, 48	vv. 5, 13, 17
Resurrection	vv. 24, 27, 28, 31, 32, 36	v. 33		vv. 5, 10 (Jesus appears)	vv. 40, 41	
Kingdom/ Throne	vv. 30, 33, 34		v. 12			v. 8
EMPOWERMENT/ RECOGNITION OF GOD'S CHOSEN PEOPLE						
Power	Luke 24:49; Acts 1:8	vv. 29, 31, 33	ἐπιπίπτω v. 16; v. 19 (implied)	v. 22 implied	ἐπιπίπτω v. 44; 11:15	v. 7 implied, "twelve"
Acceptance of God's people	v. 18	v. 29	v. 17	vv. 15–17	vv. 34–35	v. 6
FULFILLMENT						

Divine will/ purpose	vv. 23, 31	v. 28			v. 41	
Eschatology	vv. 1, 17ff.				v. 42	
Fulfillment term	v. 1					
Use of Scripture	vv. 17–21, 25–28, 31, 34–35	vv. 25–26; Ps 2:12			v. 43 (all the prophets)	(Basis of Apollos's ministry, 18:28)
INSPIRED SPEECH						
Prophecy	vv. 4, 17, 18, 30					v. 6
Speech	vv. 14–36	United prayer vv. 23–30	Peter's rebuke vv. 20–23		Peter's speech, vv. 34–43	
Tongues	v. 4		Implied? v. 18	1 Cor 14	v. 46	v. 6
Inspired/bold speech	v. 14	vv. 31, 33				
MISSIONS/ GOSPEL						
*Nations	vv. 5–12, 17	vv. 25, 27 egatively	Samaria	v. 15	v. 35, gentiles	Ephesus, followers of John
Forgiveness of sins	v. 38				v. 43	
Save/salvation	vv. 21, 40, 47				11:14	v. 5 (concept)
Witness	vv. 32, 40	v. 33	v. 25	v. 14 (bear the name)	vv. 39, 41, 42, 43	
The Word	v. 41	vv. 29, 31	vv. 4, 14, 21, 25		vv. 36, 44; 11:1	vv. 10, 20
Gospel term			vv. 4, 12, 25		v. 36	

Faith/Belief	v. 44	v. 32	vv. 12, 13		v. 43; 11:17	18:27; 19:2, 4 18
Water baptism	vv. 38, 41		v. 16	v. 18	v. 48	v. 5
Numerical growth	vv. 41, 47		v. 25	v. 31 (later summary)	11:14, 18 Cornelius's family	v. 7 (12); v. 20 summary
SOCIAL INTEREST						
Emotional reaction	vv. 6, 7, 12		vv. 9, 11, 13	v. 21	v. 45	
Laos/people		v. 25			vv. 2, 42	v. 4
Women	1:14; 2:17–18		v. 12	v. 3	Implied in 11:14	

Notes:

*Indicates that it occurs in all six passages.

Bibliography

Ackland, Randal H. *Toward a Pentecostal Theology of Glossolalia*. Cleveland, TN: CPT Press, 2020.

Aker, Ben. "New Directions in Lucan Theology: Reflections on Luke 3:21–22 and Some Implications." In *Faces of Renewal: Studies in Honor of Stanley M. Horton*, ed. Paul Elbert, 108–127. Peabody, MA: Hendrickson, 1988.

Aland, Barbara, et al., eds. *The Greek New Testament*. 5th rev. ed. Accordance electronic ed. Stuttgart: Deutsche Bibelgesellschaft, 2014.

Aland, Kurt, and Barbara Aland. *The Text of the New Testament: An Introduction to the Critical Editions and to the Theory and Practice of Modern Textual Criticism*. 2nd ed. Translated by Erroll F. Rhodes. Grand Rapids: Eerdmans, 1989.

Alter, Robert. *The Art of Biblical Narrative*. Rev. ed. New York: Basic Books, 2011.

Anderson, Kevin L. *"But God Raised Him from the Dead": The Theology of Jesus's Resurrection in Luke-Acts*. Eugene, OR: Wipf & Stock, 2006.

Arnold, Clinton E. *Ephesians*. ZECNT. Grand Rapids: Zondervan, 2010.

Arrington, French L. *The Acts of the Apostles: An Introduction and Commentary*. Peabody, MA: Hendrickson, 1988.

Atkinson, William P. *Baptism in the Spirit: Luke-Acts and the Dunn Debate*. Eugene, OR: Pickwick, 2011.

Aune, David E. *Prophecy in Early Christianity and the Ancient Mediterranean World*. Grand Rapids: Eerdmans, 1983.

Baker, Daniel J. "'Two-Stage' Spirit Reception in the Writings of Paul." *Pneuma* 44 (2022) 41–59.

Balz, Horst, and Gerhard Schneider. "ἀλάλητος." In *EDNT* 1:56.

———. "ἀποφθέγγομαι." In *EDNT* 1:147.

Barker, Kenneth L. and Waylon Baily. *Micah, Nahum, Habakkuk, Zephaniah*. NAC 20. Nashville, TN: Broadman & Holman, 1998.

Barrett, C. K. *A Commentary on the First Epistle to the Corinthians*. 1968. Reprint, Peabody, MA: Hendrickson, 1987.

———. *A Critical and Exegetical Commentary on the Acts of the Apostles*. Vol. 1, *Acts 1–14*. ICC. New York: T&T Clark, 1994.

———. *A Critical and Exegetical Commentary on the Acts of the Apostles*. Vol. 2, *Acts 15–28*. ICC. New York: T&T Clark International, 1998.

Bassler, Jouette M. "1 Cor 12:3—Curse and Confession in Context." *JBL* 101, no. 3 (1982) 415–21.

Bauckham, Richard. *Jesus and the Eyewitnesses: The Gospels as Eyewitness Testimony*. Grand Rapids: Eerdmans, 2006.

Beare, Frank W. "Speaking with Tongues: A Critical Survey of the New Testament Evidence." In *Speaking in Tongues: A Guide to Research on Glossolalia*. Edited by Watson E. Mills, 107–126. Grand Rapids: Eerdmans, 1986.

Behm, Johannes. "ἀνατίθημι, προσανατίθημι, ἀνάθεμα, κτλ." In *TDNT* 1:353–56.

———. "ἀποφθέγγομαι." In *TDNT* 1:447.

———. "νοέω, νοῦς, κτλ." In *TDNT* 4:951–60.

Berkhof, Louis. *Systematic Theology*. New edition containing the full text of *Systematic Theology* and the original *Introductory Volume to Systematic Theology*. Grand Rapids: Eerdmans, 1996.

Berry, Donnie. "Groaning for Glory: Another Look at the Spirit's Intercession in Romans 8:26–27." *JETS* 63, no. 2 (2020) 281–96.

Bittlinger, Arnold. *Gift and Graces: A Commentary on 1 Corinthians 12–14*. Grand Rapids: Eerdmans, 1967.

Bock, Darrell L. *Acts*. BECNT. Grand Rapids: Baker Academic, 2007.

———. *Luke*. Vol. 1, *1:1—9:50*. BECNT. Grand Rapids: Baker Academic, 1994.

———. *Luke*. Vol. 2, *9:51—24:53*. BECNT. Grand Rapids: Baker Academic, 1996.

———. *Mark*. NCBC. New York: Cambridge University Press, 2015.

———. *A Theology of Luke and Acts: God's Promised Program, Realized for All Nations*. BTNT. Edited by Andreas J. Köstenberger. Grand Rapids: Zondervan, 2012.

Brannan, Rick, et al., eds. *The Lexham English Septuagint*. Bellingham, WA: Lexham Press, 2012.

Broadus, John A. "Exegetical Studies." *BQ* (July 1869) 355–62.

Brookins, Timothy A. and Bruce W. Longenecker. *1 Corinthians 10–16: A Handbook on the Greek Text*. Waco, TX: Baylor University, 2016.

Brown, Raymond E. *The Birth of the Messiah: A Commentary on the Infancy Narratives in Matthew and Luke*. New York: Doubleday, 1977.

Bruce, F. F. *The Acts of the Apostles: The Greek Text with Introduction and Commentary*. 1951. Reprint, Grand Rapids: Eerdmans, 1984.

———. *The Book of the Acts*. Rev. ed. NICNT. Grand Rapids: Eerdmans, 1988.

———. *The Epistles to the Colossians, to Philemon, and to the Ephesians*. NICNT. Grand Rapids: Eerdmans, 1984.

———. *1 and 2 Corinthians*. NCBC. Grand Rapids: Eerdmans, 1971.

Brueggemann, Walter. "From Dust to Kingship." *ZAW* 84 (1972) 1–18.

Brumback, Carl. *"What Meaneth This?": A Pentecostal Answer to a Pentecostal Question*. Springfield, MO: Gospel Publishing House, 1947.

Bruner, Frederick Dale. *A Theology of the Holy Spirit: The Pentecostal Experience and the New Testament Witness*. Grand Rapids: Eerdmans, 1970.

Buckwalter, H. Douglas. *The Character and Purpose of Luke's Christology*. Cambridge Univeristy Press, 1996.

Bühner, Jan-Adolf. "κάθημαι." In *EDNT* 2:222–24.

Bultmann, Rudolf. "γινώσκω, γνῶσις, κτλ." In *TDNT* 1:689–719.

Burchard, Christoph. "A Note on 'PHMA' in JosAs 17:1 f.; Luke 2:15, 17; Acts 10:37." *NovT* 27, no. 4 (1985) 281–95.

Burgess, Stanley M., ed. *Christian Peoples of the Spirit: A Documentary History of Pentecostal Spirituality from the Early Church to the Present*. New York University, 2011.

Burgon, John W. *The Last Twelve Verses of the Gospel According to S. Mark*. Ann Arbor, MI: Cushing-Malloy, 1959.

Burkett, Delbert. *Rethinking the Gospel Sources: From Proto-Mark to* Mark. New York: T&T Clark, 2004.

Calvin, John. *Commentary on the Epistles of Paul the Apostle to the Corinthians*. Translated by John Pringle. Vol. 1. Grand Rapids: Eerdmans, 1948.

Capper, Brian. "Reciprocity and the Ethic of Acts." In *Witness to the Gospel: The Theology of Acts*, edited by I. Howard Marshall and David Peterson, 499–518. Grand Rapids: Eerdmans, 1998.

Carson, D. A. *Exegetical Fallacies*. Grand Rapids: Baker Book House, 1984.

———. *Showing the Spirit: A Theological Exposition of 1 Corinthians 12–14*. Grand Rapids: Baker Academic, 1983.

Casey, Robert Pierce. *The Excerpta ex Theodoto of Clement of Alexandria*. Studies and Documents 1. London: Christophers, 1934.

Chan, Simon. *Pentecostal Theology and the Christian Spiritual Tradition*. Eugene, OR: Wipf & Stock, 2000.

Charette, Blaine. "'Tongues as of Fire': Judgment as a Function of Glossolalia in Luke's Thought." *JPT* 13, no. 2 (2005) 173–86.

Chase, F. H. *The Credibility of the Acts of the Apostles*. London: Macmillan, 1902.

Chester, Stephen J. "Divine Madness? Speaking in Tongues in 1 Corinthians 14.23." *JSNT* 27, no. 4 (2005) 417–46.

Cho, Youngmo. *Spirit and Kingdom in the Writings of Luke and Paul: An Attempt to Reconcile These Concepts*. PBM. Eugene, OR: Wipf & Stock, 2005.

Chrysostom, John. *Homilies on the Epistle of Paul to the Corinthians*. In *NPNF1* 12:215–222.

Chuen, Lim Yeu. "Acts 10: A Gentile Model for Pentecostal Experience." *AJPS* 1, no. 1 (1998). https://www.aptspress.org/wp-content/uploads/2018/06/00-1-lim-yeu-chuen.pdf.

Ciampa, Roy E. and Brian S. Rosner. "1 Corinthians." In *Commentary on the New Testament Use of the Old Testament*, edited by G. K. Beale and D. A. Carson, 695–752. Grand Rapids: Baker Academic, 2007.

———. *The First Letter to the Corinthians*. PNTC. Grand Rapids: Eerdmans, 2010.

Cole, R. Alan. *The Gospel According to Mark: An Introduction and Commentary*. Leicester: Inter-Varsity, 2000.

Collins, John J. "The Kingdom of God in the Old Testament." In *The Kingdom of God in 20th-Century Interpretation*, edited by Wendell Willis, 81–95. Peabody, MA: Hendrickson, 1987.

Collins, Raymond F. *First Corinthians*. SP, vol. 7. Collegeville, MN: The Liturgical Press, 1999.

Colwell, Ernest C. "Mark 16:9–20 in the Armenian Version." *JBL* 55 (1937) 369–86.

Comfort, Philip W. *Encountering the Manuscripts: An Introduction to New Testament Paleography and Textual Criticism*. Nashville, TN: B&H, 2005.

———. *New Testament Text and Translation Commentary*. Accordance electronic ed. Wheaton, IL: Tyndale House, 2008.

Conzelmann, Hans. *Acts of the Apostles*. Hermeneia. Philadelphia, PA: Fortress, 1987.

———. *1 Corinthians: A Commentary on the First Epistle to the Corinthians*. Translated by James W. Leitch. Edited by George W. MacRae. Hermeneia. Minneapolis, MN: Fortress, 1975.

———. *The Theology of St. Luke*. Translated by Geoffrey Buswell. London: Faber and Faber, 1960.

Cotton, Roger D. "The Pentecostal Significance of Numbers 11." *JPT* 10, no. 1 (2001) 3–10.

Cottrell, Jack. *The Faith Once for All: Bible Doctrine for Today*. N.p.: College Press, 2002.

Cox, Steven Lynn. *A History and Critique of Scholarship Concerning the Markan Endings*. Lewiston NY: Mellen Biblical Press, 1993.

Cranfield, C. E. B. *A Critical and Exegetical Commentary on the Epistle to the Romans*. ICC. *Vol 1: Introduction and Commentary on Romans I–VIII*. London/New York: T&T Clark, 1975.

———. *The Gospel according to Saint Mark*. Cambridge University Press, 1959.

Croy, N. Clayton. *The Mutilation of Mark's Gospel*. Nashville, TN: Abingdon, 2003.

Danker, Frederick W. *Benefactor: Epigraphic Study of a Graeco-Roman and New Testament Semantic Field*. St. Louis, MO: Clayton Publishing House, 1982.

———. *Jesus and the New Age: A Commentary on St. Luke's Gospel*. Rev. ed. Philadelphia, PA: Fortress, 1988.

Davies, J. G. "Pentecost and Glossolalia." *JTS* 3, no. 2 (October 1952) 228–31.

Decker, Rodney J. *Mark 9–16: A Handbook on the Greek Text*. BHGNT. Waco, TX: Baylor University Press, 2014.

Del Colle, Ralph. "Postmodernism and the Pentecostal-Charismatic Experience." *JPT* 17 (2000) 97–116.

Delling, Gerhard. "αντιλαμβάνομαι, ἀντίλημψις, συναντιλαμβάνομαι." In *TDNT* 1:375–76.

———. "ὕμνος, ὑμνέω, κτλ." In *TDNT* 8:489–503.

Dempster, Murray W. "The Church's Moral Witness: A Study of Glossolalia in Luke's Theology of Acts." *Paraclete* 23, no. 1 (1989) 1–7.

Dibelius, Martin. *Studies in the Acts of the Apostles*. Edited by Henreich Greeven. Miflintown, PA: Sigler Press, 1999.

Dodd, C. H. *The Apostolic Preaching and its Developments*. New York: Harper & Row, 1964.

———. "The Framework of the Gospel Narrative." In *New Testament Studies*, edited by C. H. Dodd, 1–11. 1953. Reprint, Manchester University Press, 1967.

Donahue, John R., and Daniel J. Harrington. *The Gospel of Mark*. SP 2. Collegeville, MN: The Liturgical Press, 2002.

Dunn, James D. G. *The Acts of the Apostles*. Grand Rapids: Eerdmans, 1996.

———. *Baptism in the Holy Spirit: A Re-examination of the New Testament Teaching on the Gift of the Spirit in Relation to Pentecostalism Today*. Philadelphia, PA: Westminster Press, 1970.

———. *The Epistles to the Colossians and to Philemon*. NIGTC. Grand Rapids: Eerdmans, 1996.

———. *Jesus and the Spirit: A Study of the Religious and Charismatic Experience of Jesus and the First Christians as Reflected in the New Testament*. NTL. London: SCM Press, 1975.

Edgar, Thomas R. *Miraculous Gifts: Are They for Today?* Neptune, NJ: Loizeaux Brothers, 1983.

Edwards, James. "Initial Evidence of Holy Spirit Baptism and Pentecostal Type-Scenes in Acts." A paper presented at the annual meeting of the Society for Pentecostal Studies. South Hamilton, MA, 1984.

Edwards, James R. *The Gospel According to Mark.* Grand Rapids: Eerdmans, 2002.

Ellicott, Charles J. *A Critical and Grammatical Commentary on St. Paul's First Epistle to the Corinthians.* Andover: W. F. Draper, 1889.

Elliott, James K. "The Last Twelve Verses of Mark: Original or Not?" In *Perspectives on the Ending of Mark: 4 Views*, edited by David Alan Black, 80–102. Nashville, TN: B&H Academic, 2008.

———. "The Text and Language of the Endings to Mark's Gospel." *TZ* 27 (1971) 255–56.

Ellis, Earle E. *Prophecy and Hermeneutic in Early Christianity.* Grand Rapids: Eerdmans, 1978.

Epstein, Isidore, ed. *The Babylonian Talmud.* London: The Soncino Press, 1938.

Erickson, Millard J. *Christian Theology.* 2nd ed. Grand Rapids: Baker Academic, 1998.

Ervin, Howard M. *Conversion-Initiation and the Baptism in the Holy Spirit: A Critique of James D. G. Dunn, "Baptism in the Holy Spirit".* Peabody, MA: Hendrickson, 1984.

———. *Spirit-Baptism: A Biblical Investigation.* Peabody, MA: Hendrickson, 1987.

Esler, Philip F. "Glossolalia and the Admission of Gentiles into the Early Christian Community." *BTB* 22, no. 3 (August 1992) 136–42.

Eusebius. *Eusebius of Caesarea, Gospel Problems and Solutions.* Edited by Roger Pearce. Translated by David J. D. Miller, Adam C. McCollum, Carol Downer, et al. Ipswich: Chieftain Publishing, 2010.

Evans, Craig A. *Mark 8:27—16:20.* WBC 34B. Nashville, TN: Thomas Nelson, 2001.

Evans, Craig A., Danny Zacharias, Matt Walsh, Scott Kohler, and Daniel Christiansen, trans. *The Pseudepigrapha.* Acadia Divinity College, Wolfville, Nova Scotia, CAN. Copyright © 2009 by OakTree Software, Inc. Version 3.2.

Everts, Jenny. "Tongues or Languages? Contextual Consistency in the Translation of Acts 2." *JPT* 4 (1994) 71–80.

Farmer, William R. *The Last Twelve Verses of Mark.* London: Cambridge University Press, 1974.

Fee, Gordon D. *The First Epistle to the Corinthians.* NICNT. Grand Rapids: Eerdmans, 1987.

———. *The First Epistle to the Corinthians.* NICNT. Rev. ed. Grand Rapids: Eerdmans, 2014.

———. *God's Empowering Presence: The Holy Spirit in the Letters of Paul.* Peabody, MA: Hendrickson, 1994.

———. *Gospel and Spirit: Issues in New Testament Hermeneutics.* Peabody, MA: Hendrickson, 1991.

———. *Listening to the Spirit in the Text.* Grand Rapids: Eerdmans, 2000.

———. *Pauline Christology: An Exegetical-Theological Study.* Peabody, MA: Hendrickson, 2007.

———. *Paul's Letter to the Philippians.* NICNT. Grand Rapids: Eerdmans, 1995.

———. "Toward a Pauline Theology of Glossolalia." In *Pentecostalism in Context: Essays in Honor of William W. Menzies*, edited by Wonsuk Ma, 25–37. Eugene, OR: Wipf & Stock, 2008.

———. "Translational Tendenz: English Versions and Πνεῦμα in Paul." In *The Holy Spirit and Christian Origins: Essays in Honor of James D. G. Dunn*, edited by Graham N. Stanton, Bruce W. Longenecker, and Stephen C. Barton, 349–59. Grand Rapids: Eerdmans, 2004.

Fitzmyer, Joseph A. *The Acts of the Apostles: A New Translation with Introduction and Commentary*. AB. New York: Doubleday, 1998.

———. *First Corinthians: A New Translation with Introduction and Commentary*. AYB 32. New Haven: Yale University, 2008.

———. *The Gospel According to Luke (I–IX): Introduction, Translation, and Notes*. AB 28. Garden City, NY: Doubleday, 1981.

———. *The Gospel According to Luke (X–XXIV): A New Translation with Introduction and Commentary*. AB 28A. New York: Doubleday, 1985.

Foerster, Werner. "κύριος, κυρία, κτλ." In *TDNT* 3:1039–98.

Forbes, Christopher. *Prophecy and Inspired Speech: In Early Christianity and its Hellenistic Environment*. Peabody, MA: Hendrickson, 1997.

France, R. T. *The Gospel of Mark: A Commentary on the Greek Text*. Grand Rapids: Eerdmans, 2002.

Freedman, H. and Maurice Simon, eds. *Midrash Rabbah*. 3rd ed. Vol. 2, *Genesis*. Translated by H. Freedman. New York: Soncino Press, 1983.

———. *Midrash Rabbah*. 3rd ed. Vol. 3, *Exodus*. Translated by S. M. Lehrman. New York: Soncino, 1983.

Gaffin, Richard B., Jr. "A Cessationist View." In *Are Miraculous Gifts for Today? 4 Views*, edited by Stanley N. Gundry and Wayne A. Grudem, 25–64. Grand Rapids: Zondervan, 1996.

———. *Perspectives on Pentecost: Studies in New Testament Teaching on the Gifts of the Holy Spirit*. Phillipsburg, NJ: Presbyterian and Reformed, 1979.

———. "Systematic Theology and Biblical Theology." *WTJ* 38 (1976) 281–99.

Gardner, Paul. *1 Corinthians*. ZECNT. Grand Rapids: Zondervan, 2018.

Garland, David E. *1 Corinthians*. BECNT. Grand Rapids: Baker Academic, 2003.

Gilbert, Gary. "The List of Nations in Acts 2: Roman Propaganda and the Lukan Response." *JBL* 121, no. 3 (2002) 497–529.

Godet, Frederic. *Commentary on St. Paul's First Epistle to the Corinthians*. Translated by A. Cusin. CFTL 30. Edinburgh: T&T Clark, 1887.

———. *The Epistle of St. Paul to the Romans*. Godet's Commentaries on Luke, John, Romans, and 1 Corinthians. Translated by Talbot W. Chambers. Accordance electronic edition, version 1.6. Altamonte Springs: OakTree Software, 2006.

Gregory of Nazianzen. "Oration XLI: On Pentecost." In *NPNF2* 7:378–85.

Gromacki, Robert Glenn. *The Modern Tongues Movement*. Philadelphia, PA: Presbyterian and Reformed, 1967.

Grosheide, F. W. *Commentary on the First Epistle to the Corinthians: The English Text with Introduction, Exposition and Notes*. NICNT. Grand Rapids: Eerdmans, 1953.

———. *De Erste Brief van den Apostel Paulus aan de Kerk te Korinthe*. Kommentaar op het Nieuwe Testament series. Amsterdam: Van Bottenburg, 1932.

Grudem, Wayne A. *The Gift of Prophecy in 1 Corinthians*. Washington, D. C.: University Press of America, 1982.

———. *Systematic Theology: An Introduction to Biblical Doctrine*. Grand Rapids: Zondervan, 1994.

Grundmann, W. "μέγας, μεγαλεῖον, κτλ." In *TDNT* 4:529–44.

Gundry, Robert H. "'Ecstatic Utterance' (N.E.B.)?" *JTS* 17, no. 2 (October 1966) 299–307.

Gunkel, Hermann. *The Influence of the Holy Spirit: The Popular View of the Apostolic Age and the Teaching of the Apostle Paul.* Translated by Roy A. Harrisville and Philip A. Quanbeck II. Minneapolis, MN: Fortress, 2008.

Gurtner, Daniel M. *Introducing the Pseudepigrapha of Second Temple Judaism: Message, Context, and Significance.* Grand Rapids: Baker Academic, 2020.

Guthrie, Donald. *New Testament Introduction.* 3rd ed. Downers Grove, IL: InterVarsity, 1970.

Haenchen, Ernst. *The Acts of the Apostles: A Commentary.* Philadelphia, PA: Westminster, 1971.

Hamilton, Victor P. *The Book of Genesis: Chapters 1–17.* NICOT. Grand Rapids: Eerdmans, 1990.

Harrison, Everett Falconer. *Acts: The Expanding Church.* Chicago, IL: Moody Bible Institute, 1975.

Harrisville, Roy A. "Speaking in Tongues: A Lexicographical Study." In *Speaking in Tongues: A Guide to Research on Glossolalia*, edited by Watson E. Mills, 35–51. Grand Rapids: Eerdmans, 1986.

Haya-Prats, Gonzalo. *Empowered Believers: The Holy Spirit in the Book of Acts.* Edited by Paul Elbert. Translated by Scott A. Ellington. Eugene, OR: Cascade Books, 2011.

Hays, Richard B. *First Corinthians.* IBC. Louisville, KY: John Knox, 1997.

Hendrickson, William. *Exposition of the Gospel According to Mark.* NTC. Grand Rapids: Baker Books, 1975.

———. *Galatians, Ephesians, Philippians, Colossians, and Philemon.* NTC. Grand Rapids: Baker Books, 1995.

Henrichs-Tarasenkova, Nina. *Luke's Christology of Divine Identity.* Edited by Chris Keith. LNTS 542. New York: T&T Clark, 2016.

Hildebrandt, Wilf. *An Old Testament Theology of the Spirit of God.* Peabody, MA: Hendrickson, 1995.

Hill, David. *New Testament Prophecy.* NFTL. Atlanta, GA: John Knox, 1979.

Hodge, Charles. *Commentary on the First Epistle to the Corinthians.* Reprint. Grand Rapids: Eerdmans, 1980.

Holladay, Carl R. *Acts: A Commentary.* NTL. Louisville, KY: Westminster John Knox Press, 2016.

Holmes, Michael W. *The Apostolic Fathers: Greek Texts and English Translations.* Rev. ed. Grand Rapids: Baker Books, 1999.

Hooker, Morna D. *The Gospel According to Saint Mark.* BNTC. Grand Rapids: Baker Academic, 1991.

Horstmann, Axel. "οἶδα." In *EDNT* 2:494.

Horton, Stanley M. *The Book of Acts.* Springfield, MO: Gospel Publishing House, 1981.

———. *What the Bible Says about the Holy Spirit.* Rev. ed. Springfield, MO: Gospel Publishing House, 2005.

House, H. Wayne. "Tongues and the Mystery Religions of Corinth." *Bibliotheca Sacra* 140 (April-June 1983) 134–50.

Hovenden, Gerald. *Speaking in Tongues: The New Testament Evidence in Context.* JPTSup 22. London: Sheffield Academic Press, 2002.

Hultgren, Arland J. *Paul's Letter to the Romans: A Commentary.* Grand Rapids: Eerdmans, 2011.

Hur, Ju. *A Dynamic Reading of the Holy Spirit in Luke-Acts*. JSNTSup 211. Sheffield Academic Press, 2001.

Hurtado, Larry W. *Lord Jesus Christ: Devotion to Jesus in Earliest Christianity*. Grand Rapids: Eerdmans, 2003.

———. "Normal, but Not a Norm: 'Initial Evidence' and the New Testament." In *Initial Evidence: Historical and Biblical Perspectives on the Pentecostal Doctrine of Spirit Baptism*, edited by Gary B. McGee, 189–201. Peabody, MA: Hendrickson, 1991.

Iber, Gerhard. "Zum Verständnis von 1. Korinther 12, 31." *ZNW* 54 (1963) 43–52.

Irenaeus. *Against Heresies*. In *ANF* 1:309–567.

Iverson, Kelly R. "A Further Word on Final Γάρ (Mark 16:8)." *CBQ* 68 (2006) 79–94.

Jerome. *Dialogue against the Pelagians*. In *NPNF2* 6:466–71.

———. *Epistle 120, To Hedibia*. Translated by James Snapp. 2009. https://tertullian.org/fathers/jerome_hedibia_2_trans.htm.

Johanson, Bruce C. "Tongues, a Sign for Unbelievers?: A Structural and Exegetical Study of 1 Corinthians XIV. 20–25." *NTS* 25 (1979) 180–203.

Johns, Donald A. "Some New Directions in the Hermeneutics of Classical Pentecostalism's Doctrine of Initial Evidence." In *Initial Evidence: Historical and Biblical Perspectives on the Pentecostal Doctrine of Spirit Baptism*, edited by Gary B. McGee, 145–67. Peabody, MA: Hendrickson, 1991.

Johnson, Luke Timothy. *The Acts of the Apostles*. SP 5. Collegeville, MN: The Liturgical Press, 1992.

———. *Prophetic Jesus, Prophetic Church: The Challenge of Luke-Acts to Contemporary Christians*. Grand Rapids: Eerdmans, 2011.

———. *Religious Experience in Earliest Christianity: A Missing Dimension in New Testament Studies*. Minneapolis, MN: Fortress, 1998.

Käsemann, Ernst. *Perspectives on Paul*. Philadelphia, PA: Fortress, 1971.

Keener, Craig S. *Acts*. NCBC. Cambridge University Press, 2020.

———. *Acts: An Exegetical Commentary*. 3 vols. Grand Rapids: Baker Academic, 2012–14.

———. *1–2 Corinthians*. NCBC. New York: Cambridge University Press, 2005.

———. *For All Peoples: A Biblical Theology of Missions in the Gospels and Acts*. The APTS Press Occasional Papers Series. Baguio City, Philippines: Asia Pacific Theological Seminary, 2020.

———. *Romans: A New Covenant Commentary*. Cambridge: The Lutterworth Press, 2009.

———. *The Spirit in the Gospels and Acts: Divine Purity and Power*. Grand Rapids: Baker Academic, 1997.

———. "Why Does Luke Use Tongues as a Sign of the Spirit's Empowerment?" *JPT* 15, no. 2 (2007) 177–84.

Kelhoffer, James A. *Miracle and Mission: The Authentication of Missionaries and Their Message in the Longer Ending of Mark*. Tübingen: Mohr Siebeck, 2000.

———. "The Witness of Eusebius' *ad Marinum* and Other Christian Writings to Text-Critical Debates Concerning the Original Conclusion to Mark's Gospel." *ZNW* 92 (2001) 78–112.

Kelsey, Morton T. *Tongue Speaking: An Experiment in Spiritual Experience*. Garden City, NY: Doubleday, 1964.

Kistemaker, Simon J. *Exposition of the First Epistle to the Corinthians*. NTC. Grand Rapids: Baker Books, 1993.

Knibb, M. A. “Martyrdom and Ascension of Isaiah: A New Translation and Introduction.” In *OTP* 2:143–55.

Kuhn, Karl Allen. *The Kingdom according to Luke and Acts: A Social, Literary, and Theological Introduction*. Grand Rapids: Baker Academic, 2015.

Kurz, William S. *Acts of the Apostles*. CCSS. Grand Rapids: Baker Academic, 2013.

———. *Reading Luke-Acts: Dynamics of Biblical Narrative*. Louisville, KY: Westminster/John Knox, 1993.

Lane, William L. *The Gospel of Mark*. Grand Rapids: Eerdmans, 1974.

Larkin, William J. *Acts*. IVPNTC. Downers Grove, IL: InterVarsity Press, 1995.

Leaney, A. R. C. *A Commentary on the Gospel According to St. Luke*. Peabody, MA: Hendrickson, 1988.

Lehrman, S. M., trans. *Midrash Rabbah: Exodus*. 3rd ed. New York: Soncino Press, 1983.

Lenski, R. C. H. *The Interpretation of the Acts of the Apostles*. Columbus, OH: The Wartburg Press, 1944.

———. *The Interpretation of St. Mark's Gospel*. Commentary on the New Testament. Peabody, MA: Hendrickson, 2001.

———. *The Interpretation of St. Paul's First and Second Epistles to the Corinthians*. Commentary on the New Testament. Peabody, MA: Hendrickson, 2001.

Levison, John R. *Filled with the Spirit*. Grand Rapids: Eerdmans, 2009.

Li, Soeng Yu. *Paul's Teaching on the Pneumatika in 1 Corinthians 12–14: Prophecy as the Paradigm of ta Charismata ta Meizona for the Future-Oriented Ekklēsia*. WUNT 2. Reihe. Tübingen, Germany: Mohr Siebeck, 2017.

Lidbeck, Brian W. *Resurrection and Spirit: From the Pentateuch to Luke-Acts*. Eugene, OR: Wipf & Stock, 2020.

Lim, David. *Spiritual Gifts: A Fresh Look*. Springfield, MO: Gospel Publishing House, 1991.

Lincoln, Andrew T. *Ephesians*. WBC 42. Grand Rapids: Zondervan, 1990.

Longenecker, Richard N. “The Acts of the Apostles.” In *The Expositor's Bible Commentary*, vol. 9, edited by Frank E. Gaebelein, 205–573. Grand Rapids: Zondervan, 1981.

———. *The Epistle to the Romans: A Commentary on the Greek Text*. NIGTC. Grand Rapids: Eerdmans, 2016.

Lunn, Nicholas P. *The Original Ending of Mark: A New Case for the Authenticity of Mark 16:9–20*. Eugene, OR: Pickwick, 2014.

Luz, Ulrich. “Paul as Mystic.” In *The Holy Spirit and Christian Origins: Essays in Honor of James D. G. Dunn*, edited by Graham N. Stanton, Bruce W. Longenecker, and Stephen C. Barton, 131–43. Grand Rapids: Eerdmans, 2004.

Macchia, Frank D. “Babel and the Tongues of Pentecost: Reversal or Fulfilment?: A Theological Perspective.” In *Speaking in Tongues: Multi-Disciplinary Perspectives*, edited by Mark J. Cartledge, 34–51. Eugene, OR: Wipf and Stock, 2006.

———. *Baptized in the Spirit: A Global Pentecostal Theology*. Grand Rapids: Zondervan, 2006.

———. “Baptized in the Spirit: Towards a Global Theology of Spirit Baptism.” In *The Spirit in the World: Emerging Pentecostal Theologies in Global Contexts*, edited by Veli-Matti Kärkkäinen, 3–20. Grand Rapids: Eerdmans, 2009.

———. “Groans Too Deep for Words: Towards a Theology of Tongues as Initial Evidence.” *AJPS* 1, no. 2 (July 1998) 149–73. https://www.aptspress.org/wp-content/uploads/2018/06/98-2-macchia.pdf.

———. "Sighs Too Deep for Words: Towards a Theology of Glossolalia." *JPT* 1 (October 1992) 47–73.

———. "Tongues as a Sign: Towards a Sacramental Understanding of Pentecostal Experience." *Pneuma* 15, no. 1 (Spring, 1993) 61–76.

MacDonald, William G. "Glossolalia in the New Testament." In *Speaking in Tongues: A Guide to Research on Glossolalia*, edited by Watson E. Mills, 127–40. Grand Rapids: Eerdmans, 1986.

Maly, Karl, "1 Kor 12,1–3, eine Regel zur Unterscheidung der Geister?" *BZ* 10 (1966) 82–95.

Mann, C. S. *Mark: A New Translation with Introduction and Commentary*. AB 27. Garden City, NY: Doubleday, 1986.

Marshall, I. Howard. *The Acts of the Apostles: An Introduction and Commentary*. TNTC. Grand Rapids: Eerdmans, 1980.

———. *The Gospel of Luke*. NIGTC. Grand Rapids: Eerdmans, 1978.

———. *Luke: Historian and Theologian*. Grand Rapids: Zondervan, 1970.

Martin, Ralph P. *The Spirit and the Congregation: Studies in 1 Corinthians 12–15*. Grand Rapids: Eerdmans, 1984.

Mathews, Kenneth A. *Genesis 1—11:26*. NAC 1A. Nashville, TN: Broadman & Holman, 1996.

Mathewson, David L. and Elodie Ballantine Emig. *Intermediate Greek Grammar: Syntax for Students of the New Testament*. Grand Rapids: Baker Academic, 2016.

McKnight, Scot. *The Letter to the Colossians*. NICNT. Grand Rapids: Eerdmans, 2018.

Menzies, Glen. "Pre-Lucan Occurrences of the Phrase 'Tongue(s) of Fire.'" *Pneuma* 22, no. 1 (Spring 2000) 27–60.

Menzies, Robert P. *Empowered for Witness: The Spirit in Luke-Acts*. New York: T&T Clark, 2004.

———. *Pentecost: This Story is Our Story*. Springfield, MO: Gospel Publishing House, 2013.

———. *Speaking in Tongues: Jesus and the Apostolic Church as Models for the Church Today*. Cleveland, TN: CPT Press, 2016.

Menzies, William. "The Methodology of Pentecostal Theology: An Essay on Hermeneutics." In *Essays on Apostolic Themes: Studies in Honor of Howard M. Ervin*, edited by Paul Elbert, 1–14. Peabody, MA: Hendrickson, 1985.

Menzies, William W. and Robert P. Menzies. *Spirit and Power: Foundations of Pentecostal Experience*. Grand Rapids: Zondervan, 2000.

Metzger, Bruce M. "Ancient Astrological Geography and Acts 2:9–11." In *Apostolic History and the Gospel*, edited by W. Ward Gasque and Ralph P. Martin, 123–33. Grand Rapids: Eerdmans, 1970.

———. A *Textual Commentary on the Greek New Testament*. United Bible Societies, 1971.

———. A *Textual Commentary on the Greek New Testament*. 2nd ed. New York: United Bible Societies, 1994.

Metzger, Bruce M. and Bart D. Ehrman. *The Text of the New Testament: It's Transmission, Corruption, and Restoration*. 4th ed. Oxford University Press, 2005.

Michaelis, Wilhelm. "ὁράω, εἶδον, κτλ." In *TDNT* 5:315–82.

Mills, Watson E. *Glossolalia: A Bibliography*. New York: Edwin Mellen Press, 1985.

———. *Speaking in Tongues: A Guide to Research on Glossolalia*. Grand Rapids: Eerdmans, 1986.

———. *A Theological/Exegetical Approach to Glossolalia*. Lanham, MD: University Press of America, 1985.

Mittelstadt, Martin William. *Reading Luke-Acts in the Pentecostal Tradition*. Cleveland, TN: CPT Press, 2010.

———. "Spirit and Peace in Luke-Acts: Possibilities for Pentecostal/Anabaptist Dialogue." Paper presented at the annual meeting of the Society for Pentecostal Studies, Eugene, OR, March 26–28, 2009.

Moessner, David P. "*Two* Lords 'at the Right Hand'? The Psalms and an Intertextual Reading of Peter's Pentecost Speech (Acts 2:14–36)." In *Literary Studies in Luke-Acts: Essays in Honor of Joseph B. Tyson*, edited by Richard P. Thompson and Thomas E. Phillips, 215–32. Macon, GA: Mercer University Press, 1998.

Moloney, Francis J. *The Gospel of Mark: A Commentary*. Grand Rapids: Baker Academic, 2002.

Montague, George T. *First Corinthians*. CCSS. Grand Rapids: Baker Academic, 2011.

———. *The Holy Spirit: The Growth of a Biblical Tradition*. Eugene, OR: Wipf and Stock, 1976.

Moo, Douglas J. *The Epistle to the Romans*. Grand Rapids: Eerdmans, 1996.

———. *Galatians*. BECNT. Grand Rapids: Baker Academic, 2013.

———. *A Theology of Paul and His Letters: The Gift of the New Realm in Christ*. BTNT. Grand Rapids: Zondervan Academic, 2021.

Motyer, J. Alec. *The Prophecy of Isaiah: An Introduction and Commentary*. Downers Grove, IL: InterVarsity Press, 1993.

Moulton, James Hope. *Prolegomena*. Vol. 1 of *A Grammar of New Testament Greek*, edited by James Hope Moulton. 3rd ed. Edinburgh: T. & T. Clark, 1985.

Mounce, Robert H. *The Book of Revelation*. Rev. ed. NICNT. Grand Rapids: Eerdmans, 1998.

———. *Romans*. NAC 27. Nashville, TN: Broadman & Holman, 1995.

Mounce, William D. *Basics of Biblical Greek Grammar*. 4th ed. Grand Rapids: Zondervan, 2019.

Neirynck, Frans. "Acts 10,36a τὸν λόγον ὃν." *ETL* 60 (1984) 118–23.

Neyrey, Jerome H. "Ceremonies in Luke-Acts: The Case of Meals and Table Fellowship." In *The Social World of Luke-Acts*, edited by Jerome H. Neyrey, 361–87. Peabody, MA: Hendrickson, 1991.

Nineham, D. E. "The Order of Events in St. Mark's Gospel—an Examination of Dr. Dodd's Hypothesis." In *Studies in the Gospels: Essays in Memory of R. H. Lightfoot*, edited by D. E. Nineham, 223–39. Oxford: Basil Blackwell, 1967.

Nunnally, Wave. *The Book of Acts: An Independent-Study Textbook*. Springfield, MO: Global University, 2007.

O'Brien, Peter T. *The Letter to the Ephesians*. PNTC. Grand Rapids: Eerdmans, 1999.

———. "Romans 8.26–27. A Revolutionary Approach to Prayer?" *RTR* 46, no. 3 (September-December, 1987) 65–73.

Origen. *Commentary on the Epistle to the Romans: Books 6–10*. Vol. 104 of *The Fathers of the Church: A New Translation*. Translated by Thomas P. Scheck. Washington, D. C.: The Catholic University of America Press, 2002.

———. *Contra Celsum*. Translated by Henry Chadwick. New York: Cambridge University Press, 1965.

———. *The Philocalia*. Translated by Joseph Armitage Robinson. Edinburgh: T. and T. Clark, 1911.

Oropeza, B. J. *1 Corinthians*. NCCS. Eugene, OR: Cascade Books, 2017.

———. "When Will the Cessation of Speaking in Tongues and Revelatory Gifts Take Place?: A Reply to Updated Interpretations of 1 Corinthians 13:8–10." *Pneuma* 40 (2018) 489–97.

Osborne, Grant R. *Romans*. IVPNTC. Downers Grove, IL: IVP Academic, 2004.

Oss, Douglas A. "A Pentecostal/Charismatic View." In *Are Miraculous Gifts for Today? 4 Views*, edited by Stanley N. Gundry and Wayne A. Grudem, 237–83. Grand Rapids: Zondervan, 1996.

O'Toole, Robert F. "Acts 2:30 and the Davidic Covenant of Pentecost." *JBL* 102, no. 2 (1983) 245–58.

———. "The Kingdom of God in Luke-Acts." In *The Kingdom of God in 20th-Century Interpretation*, edited by Wendell Willis, 147–62. Peabody, MA: Hendrickson, 1987.

Paige, Terence. "1 Corinthians 12:2: A Pagan *Pompe*?" *JSNT* 44 (1991) 57–65.

Palma, Anthony D. *The Holy Spirit: A Pentecostal Perspective*. Springfield, MO: Logion Press, 2001.

———. "Tongues and Prophecy—A Comparative Study in Charismata." Master of Sacred Theology Thesis, Concordia Seminary, St. Louis, 1966. https://scholar.csl.edu/stm/357.

Pao, David W. *Acts and the Isaianic New Exodus*. Grand Rapids: Baker Academic, 2002.

Parsons, Mikeal C. *Acts*. PCNT. Grand Rapids: Baker Academic, 2008.

Patrick, Dale. "The Kingdom of God in the Old Testament." In *The Kingdom of God in 20th-Century Interpretation*, edited by Wendell Willis, 67–79. Peabody, MA: Hendrickson, 1987.

Patzia, Arthur G. *Ephesians, Colossians, Philemon*. NIBCNT 10. Peabody, MA: Hendrickson, 1995.

Peterson, David G. *The Acts of the Apostles*. PNTC. Grand Rapids: Eerdmans, 2009.

Philo of Alexandria. *The Works of Philo: Complete and Unabridged*. New Updated ed. Translated by C. D. Yonge. Peabody, MA: Hendrickson, 1993.

Poirier, John C. *The Tongues of Angels: The Concept of Angelic Languages in Classical Jewish and Christian Texts*. WUNT 2. Tübingen: Mohr Siebeck, 2010.

Polhill, John B. *Acts*. NAC 26. Nashville, TN: B&H, 1992.

Powers, Janet Evert. "Missionary Tongues?" *JPT* 17 (2000) 39–55.

Poythress, Vern S. "The Nature of Corinthian Glossolalia: Possible Options." *WTJ* 40 (1977) 130–35.

Ridderbos, Herman. *The Coming of the Kingdom*. Translated by H. de Jongste. Edited by Raymond O. Zorn. Philadelphia, PA: Presbyterian and Reformed, 1962.

Riesenfeld, Harald. "The Text of Acts x.36." In *Text and Interpretation: Studies in the New Testament Presented to Matthew Black*, edited by Ernest Best and R. McL. Wilson, 191–94. Cambridge University Press, 1979.

Robertson, Archibald Thomas. *Word Pictures in the New Testament*. Vol. 3, *The Acts of the Apostles*. 1930. Reprint, Grand Rapids: Baker Book House, n.d.

———. *Word Pictures in the New Testament*. Vol. 4, *The Epistles of Paul*. 1931. Reprint, Grand Rapids: Baker, n.d.

Robertson, Archibald, and Alfred Plummer. *A Critical and Exegetical Commentary on the First Epistle of St Paul to the Corinthians*. 2nd ed. ICC. Edinburgh: T. & T. Clark, 1914.

Robertson, O. Palmer. *The Books of Nahum, Habakkuk, and Zephaniah*. NICOT. Grand Rapids: Eerdmans, 1990.

Robinson, David S. "'By the Lips of Foreigners': Disclosing the Church in 1 Corinthians 14:20–25." *Ecclesiology* 14 (2018) 306–21.

Robinson, Maurice A. "The Long Ending of Mark as Canonical Verity." In *Perspectives on the Ending of Mark: 4 Views*, edited by David Alan Black, 40–79. Nashville, TN: B&H Academic, 2008.

Rosner, Brian S. "The Progress of the Word." In *Witness to the Gospel: The Theology of Acts*, edited by I. Howard Marshall and David Peterson, 215–33. Grand Rapids: Eerdmans, 1998.

Ruthven, Jon Mark. *On the Cessation of the Charismata: The Protestant Polemic on Post-Biblical Miracles*. Rev. ed. Tulsa, OK: Word and Spirit, 2011.

Sailhamer, John H. "Genesis." In *The Expositor's Bible Commentary*, edited by Frank E. Gaebelein, 1–284. Vol. 2. *Genesis-Numbers*. Grand Rapids: Zondervan, 1990.

Schatzmann, Siegried S. *A Pauline Theology of Charismata*. Peabody, MA: Hendrickson, 1987.

Schlatter, Adolf. *Gottes Gerechtigkeit: Ein Kommentar Zum Römerbrief*. Stuttgart: Calwer Verlag, 1952.

Schlier, Heinrich. "ἰδιώτης." In *TDNT* 3:215–17.

Schmithals, Walter. *Gnosticism in Corinth: An Investigation of the Letters to the Corinthians*. Translated by John E. Steely. Nashville, TN: Abingdon, 1971.

Schnabel, Eckhard J. *Acts*. ZECNT. Grand Rapids: Zondervan, 2012.

Schneider, Gerhard. *Die Apostelgeschichte II. Teil: Kommentar zu Kap. 9, 1–28, 31*. HThKNT. Freiburg: Herder, 1982.

———. "ἐπιπίπτω." In *EDNT* 2:32.

Schneider, Johannes. "στενάζω, στεναγμός, συστενάζω." In *TDNT* 7:600–603.

Schrage, Wolfgang. *Der erste Brief an die Korinther*. Band VII/3. EKKNT. Germany: Patmos Verlag, 1999.

Schreiner, Thomas R. *Romans*. BECNT. Grand Rapids: Baker Academic, 1998.

Schweizer, Eduard. "πνεῦμα, πνευματικός, κτλ." In *TDNT* 6:332–455.

Scott, James M. "Luke's Geographical Horizon." In *The Book of Acts in Its Graeco-Roman Setting*, edited by David W. J. Gill and Conrad Gempf, 483–544. Vol. 2 of *The Book of Acts in Its First Century Setting*. Edited by Bruce W. Winter. Grand Rapids: Eerdmans, 1994.

———. *Paul and the Nations: The Old Testament and Jewish Background of Paul's Mission to the Nations with Special Reference to the Destination of Galatians*. WUNT 84. Tübingen: J. C. B. Mohr, 1995.

Scott, James W. "The Time When Revelatory Gifts Cease (1 Cor 13:8–12)." *WTJ* 72 (2010) 267–89.

Severian of Gabala. "Severian of Gabala." In *1 Corinthians Interpreted by Early Christian Commentators*, translated and edited by Judith L. Kovacs, 14. The Church's Bible. Grand Rapids: Eerdmans, 2005.

Shauf, Scott. *Theology as History, History as Theology: Paul in Ephesus in Acts 19*. New York: Walter de Gruyter, 2005.

Shelton, James B. *Mighty in Word and Deed: The Role of the Holy Spirit in Luke-Acts*. Eugene, OR: Wipf & Stock, 2000.

Smalley, Stephen S. "The Christology of Acts Again." In *Christ and Spirit in the New Testament: Studies in Honour of C. F. D. Moule*, edited by Barnabas Lindars and Stephen S. Smalley, 79–93. Cambridge University Press, 1973.

Smit, Joop. "Argument and Genre of 1 Corinthians 12–14." In *Rhetoric and the New Testament: Essays from the 1992 Heidelberg Conference*, edited by Stanley E. Porter and Thomas H. Olbricht, 211–30. JSNTSup 90. Sheffield Academic, 1993.

Smith, James K. A. *Thinking in Tongues: Pentecostal Contributions to Christian Philosophy*. Grand Rapids: Eerdmans, 2010.

Snapp, James Jr. *Authentic: The Case for Mark 16:9–20: 2016 Edition*. 2016. Kindle edition.

Soards, Marion L. *1 Corinthians*. UBC. Grand Rapids: Baker Books, 1999.

———. *The Speeches in Acts: Their Content, Context, and Concerns*. Louisville, KY: Westminster/John Knox, 1994.

Spencer, F. Scott. *Journeying through Acts: A Literary-Cultural Reading*. Grand Rapids: Baker Academic, 2004.

Spittler, Russel P. "Testament of Job: A New Translation and Introduction." In *OTP* 1:829–38.

Stagg, Frank, "Glossolalia in the New Testament." In *Glossolalia: Tongue Speaking in Biblical, Historical, and Psychological Perspective*, by Frank Stagg, E. Glenn Hinson, and Wayne E. Oates, 20–44. Nashville, TN: Abingdon, 1967.

Stanton, G. N. *Jesus of Nazareth in New Testament Preaching*. Cambridge University Press, 1974.

Stein, Robert H. "The Ending of Mark." *BBR* 18, no. 1 (2008) 79–98.

———. *Mark*. BECNT. Grand Rapids: Baker Academic, 2008.

Stendahl, Krister. *Paul among Jews and Gentiles and Other Essays*. Philadelphia, PA: Fortress, 1976.

Stone, Jesse D. "Inward Groans and Unknown Tongues: Interpretation of Romans 8.26 in Early Pentecostal Literature." *JPT* 30 (2021) 83–102.

Strack, H. L. and Günter Stemberger. *Introduction to the Talmud and Midrash*. 2nd ed. Translated and edited by Markus Bockmuehl. Minneapolis, MN: Fortress Press, 1996.

Stronstad, Roger. *The Charismatic Theology of St. Luke: Trajectories from the Old Testament to Luke-Acts*. 2nd ed. Grand Rapids: Baker Academic, 2012.

———. *The Prophethood of All Believers: A Study in Luke's Charismatic Theology*. Cleveland, TN: CPT Press, 2010.

———. *Spirit, Scripture and Theology: A Pentecostal Perspective*. Baguio City, Philippines: Asia Pacific Theological Seminary, 1995.

Stuart, Douglas K. *Exodus*. NAC 2. Nashville, TN: B&H, 2006.

Studebaker, Steven M. "Pentecostal Soteriology and Pneumatology." *JPT* 11, no. 2 (2003) 248–70.

Sweet, J. P. M. "A Sign for Unbelievers: Paul's Attitude to Glossolalia." *NTS* 13 (April 1967) 240–57.

Talbert, Charles H. *Reading Acts: A Literary and Theological Commentary on the Acts of the Apostles*. Rev. ed. Macon, GA: Smyth and Helwys, 2005.

———. *Reading Corinthians: A Literary and Theological Commentary*. Rev. ed. Macon, GA: Smyth & Helwys, 2002.

Tannehill, Robert C. *The Narrative Unity of Luke-Acts: A Literary Interpretation*. Vol. 1, *The Gospel according to Luke*. Philadelphia, PA: Fortress, 1986.

———. *The Narrative Unity of Luke-Acts: A Literary Interpretation*. Vol. 2, *The Acts of the Apostles*. Minneapolis, MN: Fortress, 1994.

Tarr, Del. *The Foolishness of God: A Linguist Looks at the Mystery of Tongues*. Springfield, MO: The Access Group, 2010.

Taylor, Charles. "Some Early Evidence for the Twelve Verses St. Mark XVI. 9–20." In *The Expositor*, vol. 8, edited by Robertson Nicholl, 71–80. London: Hodder & Stoughton, 1893.

———. *The Witness of Hermas to the Four Gospels*. London: Clay, 1892.

Terry, Bruce. "The Style of the Long Ending of Mark." https://www.bterry.com/articles/mkendsty.htm.

Thielman, Frank. *Ephesians*. BECNT. Grand Rapids: Baker Academic, 2010.

Thiselton, Anthony C. *The First Epistle to the Corinthians*. NIGTC. Grand Rapids: Eerdmans, 2000.

———. *The Holy Spirit—In Biblical Teaching, through the Centuries, and Today*. Grand Rapids: Eerdmans, 2013.

———. "The 'Interpretation' of Tongues: A New Suggestion in the Light of Greek Usage in Philo and Josephus." *JTS* 30, no. 1 (April 1979) 15–36.

———. "Realized Eschatology at Corinth," *NTS* 24, no. 4 (July 1978) 510–26.

Thomas, John Christopher, and Kimberly Ervin Alexander. "'And the Signs are Following': Mark 16.9–20—A Journey into Pentecostal Hermeneutics." *JPT* 11, no. 2 (2003) 147–70.

Thomas, Robert L. *Understanding Spiritual Gifts: A Verse-by-Verse Study of 1 Corinthians 12–14*. Rev. ed. Grand Rapids: Kregel, 1999.

Thompson, Alan J. *The Acts of the Risen Lord Jesus: Luke's Account of God's Unfolding Plan*. NSBT 27. Downers Grove, IL: InterVarsity, 2011.

Thompson, Richard P. *Acts: A Commentary in the Wesleyan Tradition*. Kansas City, KS: Beacon Hill, 2015.

Torrey, Charles Cutler. *The Composition and Date of Acts*. HTS 1. Harvard University Press, 1916. Reprint, New York: Kraus, 1969.

Towner, Philip H. *The Letters to Timothy and Titus*. NICNT. Grand Rapids: Eerdmans, 2006.

Tregelles, Samuel Prideaux. *An Account of the Printed Text of the Greek New Testament: With Remarks on its Revision upon Critical Principles*. New York: Cambridge University Press, 2013. First published 1854 by Samuel Bagster and Sons.

Trenchard, Warren C. *Complete Vocabulary Guide to the Greek New Testament*. Rev. ed. Grand Rapids: Zondervan, 1992.

Turner, Max. "Early Christian Experience and Theology of 'Tongues'—A New Testament Perspective." In *Speaking in Tongues: Multi-Disciplinary Perspectives*, edited by Mark J. Cartledge, 1–33. SPCI. Paternoster, 2006.

———. *The Holy Spirit and Spiritual Gifts*. Rev. ed. Peabody, MA: Hendrickson, 2005.

———. *Power from on High: The Spirit in Israel's Restoration and Witness in Luke-Acts*. Sheffield Academic Press, 2000.

———. "Tongues: An Experience for All in the Pauline Churches?" *AJPS* 1 (1998) 231–53.

Turner, Nigel. *Syntax*. Vol. 3 of *A Grammar of New Testament Greek*, edited by James Hope Moulton. Edinburgh: T. & T. Clark, 1963.

Van Henten, Jan Willem. "The Hasmonean Period." In *Redemption and Resistance: The Messianic Hopes of Jews and Christians in Antiquity*, edited by Markus Bockmuehl and James Carleton Paget, 15–28. London: T&T Clark, 2007.

Van Unnik, W. C. "Jesus: Anathema or Kyrios (1 Cor 12:3)." In *Christ and Spirit in the New Testament*, edited by Barnabus Lindars and Stephen S. Smalley, 113–26. Cambridge: Cambridge University Press, 1973.

Vermes, Geza. *The Complete Dead Sea Scrolls in English*. Rev. ed. New York: Penguin Books, 2011.

Viviano, B. T. "The Kingdom of God in the Qumran Literature." In *The Kingdom of God in 20th-Century Interpretation*, edited by Wendell Willis, 97–107. Peabody, MA: Hendrickson, 1987.

Vos, Geerhardus. *Biblical Theology: Old and New Testaments*. Grand Rapids: Eerdmans, 1948.

Wallace, Daniel B. *Greek Grammar Beyond the Basics: An Exegetical Syntax of the New Testament*. Grand Rapids: Zondervan, 1996.

———. "Mark 16:8 as the Conclusion to the Second Gospel." In *Perspectives on the Ending of Mark: 4 Views*, edited by David Alan Black, 1–39. Nashville, TN: B&H Academic, 2008.

Warfield, Benjamin B. *Counterfeit Miracles*. 1918. Reprint, Edinburgh: The Banner of Truth Trust, 1976.

Warrington, Keith. *Pentecostal Theology: A Theology of Encounter*. London; New York: T & T Clark, 2008.

———. "The Synoptic Gospels." In *A Biblical Theology of the Holy Spirit*, edited by Trevor J. Burke and Keith Warrington, 84–103. Eugene, OR: Cascade Books, 2014.

Watts, Rikki E. *Isaiah's New Exodus in Mark*. Grand Rapids: Baker Academic, 1997.

Wedderburn, A. J. M. "Romans 8:26—Towards a Theology of Glossolalia?" *SJT* 28 (1975) 369–77.

Wenham, Gordon J. *Genesis 1–15*. WBC 1. Waco, TX: Word Books, 1987.

Wenham, John. *Easter Enigma: Are the Resurrection Accounts in Conflict?* 1992. Reprint, Eugene, OR: Wipf & Stock, 2005.

Wenk, Matthias. *Community-Forming Power: The Socio-Ethical Role of the Spirit in Luke-Acts*. London: T&T Clark, 2000.

Wessel, Walter W. "Mark." In *The Expositor's Bible Commentary*, vol. 8, edited by Frank E. Gaebelein, 601–793. Grand Rapids: Zondervan, 1984.

Westcott, Brooke Foss and Fenton John Anthony Hort. *The New Testament in the Original Greek*. 1882. Reprint, Forgotten Books, 2012.

Wiley, H. Orton. *Christian Theology*. 3 vols. Kansas City, MO: Beacon Hill, 1952.

Williams, C. S. C. *A Commentary on the Acts of the Apostles*. Harper's New Testament Commentaries. Peabody, MA: Hendrickson, 1988.

Williams, J. Rodman. *Renewal Theology: Systematic Theology from a Charismatic Perspective*. 3 vols. in 1. Grand Rapids: Zondervan, 1996.

Wilson, Steven G. *The Gentiles and the Gentile Mission in Luke-Acts*. Cambridge University Press, 1973.

Winter, Bruce W. *After Paul Left Corinth: The Influence of Secular Ethics and Social Change*. Grand Rapids: Eerdmans, 2001.

Wintermute, O. S. "Apocalypse of Zephaniah: A New Translation and Introduction." In *OTP* 1:497–515.

Witherington, Ben III. *The Acts of the Apostles: A Socio-Rhetorical Commentary*. Grand Rapids: Eerdmans, 1998.

———. *Conflict and Community in Corinth: A Socio-Rhetorical Commentary on 1 and 2 Corinthians*. Grand Rapids: Eerdmans, 1995.

———. *The Gospel of Mark: A Socio-Rhetorical Commentary*. Grand Rapids: Eerdmans, 2001.

———. *The Letters to Philemon, the Colossians, and the Ephesians: A Socio-Rhetorical Commentary on the Captivity Epistles*. Grand Rapids: Eerdmans, 2007.

Woyke, Johannes, *Götter, 'Götzen', Götterbilder, Aspekte einer paulinischen 'Theologie der Religionen'*. BZNW. Berlin: Walter de Gruyter, 2005.

Wright, N. T. *The Resurrection of the Son of God*. COQG 3. Minneapolis, MN: Fortress Press, 2003.

Wright, R. B. "Psalms of Solomon: A New Translation and Introduction." In *OTP* 2:639–70.

Wyckoff, John W. "The Baptism in the Holy Spirit." In *Systematic Theology*, rev. ed, edited by Stanley M. Horton, 423–55. Springfield, MO: Logion Press, 1998.

Yong, Amos. *The Spirit Poured Out on All Flesh: Pentecostalism and the Possibility of Global Theology*. Grand Rapids: Baker Academic, 2005.

Ancient Document Index

Old Testament/Hebrew Bible

Genesis

Leviticus

Numbers

Deuteronomy

Joshua

Judges

1 Samuel

2 Samuel

1 Kings

2 Kings

1 Chronicles

Mark

Luke

John

Acts

Romans

1 Corinthians

2 Corinthians

Galatians

Ephesians

Philippians

Colossians

1 Thessalonians

2 Thessalonians

1 Timothy

Rabbinic Writings

Greco-Roman Writings

Early Christian Writings

www.ingramcontent.com/pod-product-compliance
Lightning Source LLC
LaVergne TN
LVHW020521100826
845148LV00010B/1301

* 9 7 9 8 3 8 5 2 6 7 0 6 4 *